Demons of Change

Demons of Change

Antagonism and Apotheosis in Jewish and Christian Apocalypticism

Andrei A. Orlov

Cover: "Saint Anthony Tormented by Demons" engraving by Martin Schongauer, courtesy of the Metropolitan Museum of Art, New York.

Published by State University of New York Press, Albany

For information, contact State University of New York Press, Albany, NY
www.sunypress.edu

Library of Congress Cataloging-in-Publication Data

Names: Orlov, Andrei A., 1960– author.
Title: Demons of change : antagonism and apotheosis in Jewish and Christian apocalypticism / Andrei A. Orlov.
Description: Albany : State University of New York Press, [2020] | Includes bibliographical references.
Identifiers: LCCN 2020023193 (print) | LCCN 2020023194 (ebook) | ISBN 9781438480893 (hardcover : alk. paper) | ISBN 9781438480886 (pbk. : alk. paper) | ISBN 9781438480909 (ebook)
Subjects: LCSH: Theomachy in the Bible. | Apocalyptic literature—History and criticism. | Apocryphal books (Old Testament—Criticism, interpretation, etc.) | Apocalypse of Abraham—Criticism, interpretation, etc. | Bible. Revelation—Criticism, interpretation, etc.
Classification: LCC BS1199.T447 O75 2020 (print) | LCC BS1199.T447 (ebook) | DDC 220/.046—dc23
LC record available at https://lccn.loc.gov/2020023193
LC ebook record available at https://lccn.loc.gov/2020023194

10 9 8 7 6 5 4 3 2 1

If there were no accuser, the righteous would not inherit the supernal treasures that they are to possess in the world to come. Happy are they who have met the accuser, and happy are they who have not met him.

—*Zohar* II.162b–163b

Contents

Preface

An earlier version of the chapter "Glorification through Fear in *2 Enoch*" was previously published in the *Journal for the Study of the Pseudepigrapha* 25.3 (2016), 171–188. I am thankful to Sage Publishing for permission to reuse the material. The format and style of the essay have been changed to comply with the standards of this book.

I am grateful to my research assistants, Patrick Bowman, Joshua Miller, Hans Moscicke, and Daniel Mueller, who worked very hard through different versions of the manuscript to help improve the text in both style and substance.

I am thankful to the Metropolitan Museum of Art, New York for permission to use a digital reproduction of Martin Schongauer's engraving "Saint Anthony Tormented by Demons" as the cover image.

Last, though not least, I offer my sincere thanks to Rafael Chaiken, Ryan Morris, and the editorial team of SUNY Press for their diligent support and patient professionalism during the preparation of this book for publication.

—Andrei A. Orlov
Milwaukee
The Feast of the Exaltation of the Holy Cross, 2019

Abbreviations

AB	Anchor Bible
AGAJU	Arbeiten zur Geschichte des antiken Judentums und des Urchristentums
AJEC	Ancient Judaism and Early Christianity
AOAT	Alter Orient und Altes Testament: Veröffentlichungen zur Kultur und Geschichte des Alten Orients und des Alten Testaments
ArBib	Aramaic Bible
ASE	*Annali di storia dell' exegesi*
AUSS	*Andrews University Seminary Studies*
AYB	Anchor Yale Bible
BAR	*Biblical Archaeology Review*
BJRL	*Bulletin of the John Rylands Library*
BJSUC	Biblical and Judaic Studies of the University of California
BR	*Bible Review*
BRLJ	Brill Reference Library of Judaism
BS	Biblical Seminar
BZAW	Beihefte zur Zeitschrift für die alttestamentliche Wissenschaft
CBQ	*Catholic Biblical Quarterly*
CBQMS	Catholic Biblical Quarterly Monograph Series
CBR	*Currents in Biblical Research*
CEJL	Commentaries on Early Jewish Literature
CRINT	Compendia Rerum Iudaicarum ad Novum Testamentum
CSCO	Corpus Scriptorum Christianorum Orientalium
EB	Eichstätter Beiträge
EE	*Estudios eclesiásticos*
EJL	Early Judaism and Its Literature
EKKNT	Evangelisch-Katholischer Kommentar zum Neuen Testament
ErJb	*Eranos Jahrbuch*

EstBib	*Estudios biblicos*
FAT	Forschungen zum Alten Testament
FRLANT	Forschungen zur Religion und Literatur des Alten und Neuen Testaments
FS	*Frühmittelalterliche Studien*
GCS	Die Griechischen Christlichen Schriftsteller der ersten drei Jahrhunderte
GUS	Gorgias Ugaritic Studies
HDR	Harvard Dissertations in Religion
HNT	Handbuch zum Neuen Testament
HR	*History of Religions*
HSM	Harvard Semitic Monographs
HTR	*Harvard Theological Review*
HUCA	*Hebrew Union College Annual*
ICC	International Critical Commentary on the Holy Scriptures of the Old and New Testaments
IHC	Islamic History and Civilization
JAJS	Journal of Ancient Judaism Supplements
JANES	*Journal of the Ancient Near Eastern Society of Columbia University*
JAOS	*Journal of the American Oriental Society*
JBL	*Journal of Biblical Literature*
JCTCRS	Jewish and Christian Texts in Contexts and Related Studies
JJS	*Journal of Jewish Studies*
JQR	*Jewish Quarterly Review*
JR	*Journal of Religion*
JSHRZ	Jüdische Schriften aus hellenistisch-römischer Zeit
JSJ	*Journal for the Study of Judaism in the Persian, Hellenistic and Roman Period*
JSJSS	Journal for the Study of Judaism in the Persian, Hellenistic and Roman Period: Supplement Series
JSNT	*Journal for the Study of the New Testament*
JSNTSS	Journal for the Study of the New Testament. Supplement Series
JSOTSS	Journal for the Study of the Old Testament. Supplement Series
JSPSS	Journal for the Study of the Pseudepigrapha. Supplement Series
JTI	*Journal of Theological Interpretation*
JTS	*Journal of Theological Studies*
JZWL	*Jüdische Zeitschrift für Wissenschaft und Leben*
LCJP	Library of Contemporary Jewish Philosophers
LCL	Loeb Classical Library
LNTS	Library of New Testament Studies

LSTS	Library of Second Temple Studies
NHS	Nag Hammadi Studies
NIVAC	NIV Application Commentary
NovTSup	Supplements to Novum Testamentum
NSBT	New Studies in Biblical Theology
NTOA	Novum Testamentum et Orbis Antiquus
NTS	*New Testament Studies*
NTTS	New Testament Tools and Studies
OBO	Orbis biblicus et orientalis
OP	Oriental Publications
OTF	Oriental Translation Fund
OTL	Old Testament Library
PVTG	Pseudepigrapha Veteris Testamenti Graece
RB	*Revue biblique*
ResQ	*Restoration Quarterly*
RevQ	*Revue de Qumrân*
RSR	*Recherches de sience religieuse*
SBL	Studies in Biblical Literature
SBLDS	Society of Biblical Literature Dissertation Series
SBLSP	Society of Biblical Literature Seminar Papers
SC	Sources chrétiennes
SGTK	Studien zur Geschichte der Theologie und der Kirche
SHR	Studies in the History of Religions
SJ	Studia Judaica
SJJTP	Supplements to the Journal of Jewish Thought and Philosophy
SJLA	Studies in Judaism in Late Antiquity
SJS	Studia Judaeoslavica
SOTBT	Studies in Old Testament Biblical Theology
SPB	Studia Post Biblica
SSEJC	Studies in Scripture in Early Judaism and Christianity
STDJ	Studies on the Texts of the Desert of Judah
SVC	Supplements to Vigiliae Christianae
SVTP	Studia in Veteris Testamenti Pseudepigrapha
TBN	Themes in Biblical Narrative
TCS	Text-Critical Studies
TED	Translations of Early Documents
ThZ	*Theologische Zeitschrift*
TSAJ	Texte und Studien zum antiken Judentum
UNT	Untersuchungen zum Neuen Testament
VC	*Vigiliae Christianae*
VetTSup	Vetus Testamentum Supplements

VT	*Vetus Testamentum*
WBC	Word Biblical Commentary
WMANT	Wissenschaftliche Monographien zum Alten und Neuen Testaments
WUNT	Wissenschaftliche Untersuchungen zum Neuen Testament
WZKM	*Wiener Zeitschrift fur die Kunde des Morgenlandes*
YJS	Yale Judaica Series
ZAW	*Zeitschrift für die alttestamentliche Wissenschaft*
ŹM	Źródła i monografie
ZNW	Zeitschrift für die neutestamentliche Wissenschaft und die Kunde der älteren Kirche

Introduction

Scholars of Second Temple Judaism and early Christianity have long identified the presence of antagonistic imagery in early Jewish and Christian apocalypses. One of the traditional avenues for the exploration of such symbolism has been research on the so-called *Chaoskampf* motif, which stems from the groundbreaking study of Hermann Gunkel's *Schöpfung und Chaos in Urzeit und Endzeit.*[1] Although some of Gunkel's positions later came under criticism,[2] his intuitions about antagonistic imagery in ancient Near Eastern and Jewish materials have proven their lasting methodological value. Reflecting on Gunkel's legacy, John Collins notes that "since the discoveries at Ugarit, Gunkel's theory of Babylonian influence has been seen to be exaggerated, but his insight into the importance of the conflict motif has been vindicated."[3] Indeed, with Peter Machinist we must say that scholarly recognition of its importance is "due to the impetus and commanding analysis offered by Gunkel's volume."[4]

Gunkel's research into patterns of primordial conflict was later appropriated and developed in a large number of further contributions to the field, all of which helped to elucidate various aspects of such imagery. In the North American academic environment, one of the most influential adaptations of Gunkel's methodology for the study of early Jewish and Christian apocalypses is the concept of "combat myth," advanced by Adela Yarbro Collins in her seminal study *The Combat Myth in the Book of Revelation.*[5] Analyzing the antagonistic patterns found in Revelation, Yarbro Collins argued that "much of its imagery has strong affinities with a mythic pattern of combat which was widespread in the ancient Near East and the classical world."[6] This pattern is characterized by "a struggle between two divine beings and their allies for universal kingship. One of the combatants is usually a monster, very often a dragon. This monster represents chaos and sterility, while his opponent is associated with order and fertility. Thus, their conflict is a cosmic battle whose outcome will constitute or abolish order in society and fertility in nature."[7] According to Yarbro Collins, "in the first century CE, this basic pattern was current in a variety of forms; nearly every major ethnic tradition had one or more versions of its own."[8]

Experts such as Frank Moore Cross have drawn attention to the fact that in the ancient Near Eastern *Chaoskampf* traditions, the motif of the Divine Warrior's battle against chaos often coincides with his theophany, when he "returns to take up kingship among the gods, and is enthroned on his mountain."[9] In these instances, the primordial battle itself conveys the theophany, often hinted through the epiphanic nature of the Divine Warrior's weapons.[10] In this antagonistic pattern, even the theophanic splendor of the Divine Warrior becomes "not just an attendant circumstance to the battle against chaos, but rather a weapon within that warfare."[11] This connection between cosmic conflict and the Divine Warrior's apotheosis was perpetuated in a variety of biblical accounts,[12] including Daniel 7. John Collins points out that "the old Canaanite type myth of the conflict with the forces of chaos emerges clearly in Daniel 7. . . . The adversaries in Daniel 7 are four beasts who rise from the sea. The analogy with the sea monster of Canaanite myth is obvious. . . . The beasts are symbols of chaos and the chaos is reduced to order by the elevation to the kingship of one like a son of man."[13] In this scene the theophany of two divine figures, in the forms of the Ancient of Days and the Son of Man, is juxtaposed with both the epiphany and demotion of the four-fold antagonistic figure.[14] Furthermore, already in Daniel 7 the antagonist strives to imitate the anthropomorphic features of the protagonist by assuming a human posture, which in the Danielic account is envisioned as a divine attribute.[15] This mirroring of attributes between heroes and antiheroes, discernable already in *Chaoskampf* traditions, will eventually become one of the chief conceptual features in Jewish and Christian visionary accounts.

Although the link between patterns of primordial conflict and divine theophanies found in Jewish lore has been acknowledged and explored in previous studies,[16] the significance of such symbolic constellations for another type of epiphany, the adept's apotheosis, has not received proper attention. Yet in Jewish and Christian visionary accounts, the ancient role of the Divine Warrior[17] who fights against the demonic forces was often taken by a human adept. As a result of his encounter with the otherworldly antagonists, this human hero would be exalted and glorified.[18] In early Jewish and Christian mediatorial lore, therefore, the Divine Warrior motif enters its novel afterlife, now refashioned through the stories of biblical exemplars. Like in ancient Near Eastern traditions, the hero's conflict with the antagonist became a prerequisite for his final apotheosis. Moreover, like the monsters of ancient Near Eastern accounts who undergo their own metamorphoses during battles against the divine warriors, the antagonists of the apocalyptic stories also change from their original forms and conditions. The antagonistic tension, present in the apocalyptic stories, plays a crucial part both in the exaltation of the protagonist and in the demotion of his opponent.

The aim of this volume is to explore the significance of such antagonistic interactions for the transformations of the hero and antihero in early Jewish and Christian apocalyptic accounts. Our study will pay special attention to the meaning of the conflict in the adept's ascent and transformation, as well as to the formative value of such interplay between antagonism and apotheosis for Jewish and Christian martyrological accounts.

Ancient Near Eastern *Chaoskampf* traditions closely connect protology with eschatology. Similarly, Jewish and Christian apocalyptic accounts often tell of heroes who undergo an eschatological reversal that returns them to the glory lost by the protoplasts in the Garden of Eden. As in their ancient Near Eastern counterparts, such transitions are dominated by various antagonistic situations in which personified adversaries attempt to interfere with the protagonist's progress. This attempted interference inadvertently serves to assist and facilitate the seer's transformation. This is a curious reversal of the protological conflict wherein the antagonist who initially participated in the corruption of humankind is also present in the final battle.

Like in the initial protological settings where the enemies of humankind, represented by the fallen angels, Satan, or the Serpent, play a crucial part in the fall of humankind, here, in the final moment, such a conflict is reiterated and finally resolved for humankind's benefit. In some ways the re-play can be seen as a cosmic psychodrama, the whole purpose of which is to heal and restore humanity to its original prelapsarian condition in the last days. Indeed, various antagonistic figures are predestined to play a decisive role at the adept's final metamorphosis. Some of them, such as Satan of the *Primary Adam Books* and Azazel in the *Apocalypse of Abraham*, are portrayed as the deity's former favorites, whose glorious status and luminous garments are inherited by the deity's new, human, favorites. Indeed, in Jewish and Christian apocalyptic accounts, exalted adepts often paradoxically emulate some emblematic features of their formerly exalted antagonists, thus signaling their final defeat, demotion, and the transference of their lofty attributes to the new favorites of the deity. This volume will explore these eschatological transfers. Not only the particular features, but the entire way of life and former habitats of antiheroes are radically refashioned and deconstructed at the seer's apotheosis as his progression towards the heavenly realm inversely mirrors the antagonist's exile.

These trajectories of the hero's elevation and the antihero's demotion frequently cross. In this peculiar antagonistic framework, which envisions the seer's ascent and apotheosis as a result of the ultimate test of the adept's loyalty and endurance in faith, adversaries are predestined to play a very special role in the hero's metamorphosis. They are responsible for bringing a crucial, inimical element to the story of the seer or martyr through their nefarious plots. These plots are attempts to intimidate and discourage the hero and impede his progress to immortality. Such early Jewish patterns of the antagonistic interaction, which impede, yet also ironically assist, the adept's progress to his final apotheosis, will play a crucial role in Jewish and Christian martyrological accounts in which human and otherworldly figures, in the form of kings, monsters, and spectators, are envisioned as the protagonist's adversaries.

Furthermore, paralleling the adept's exaltation, the adversary's demotion is also understood as a crisis and a transformation. This tendency is present already in the ancient Near Eastern *Chaoskampf* traditions. In these traditions, the primordial monsters undergo the change of their original form as the result of battles with the divine warriors. Such a metamorphosis of the antagonists can be seen as a negative reaffirmation of the adept's apotheosis. During their own trials, each fallen angel and monster will ultimately encounter their own nemesis, often in the form of an archangel, whose mission will be to fulfill God's judgment toward these agents of chaos and destruction. In these gory routines, the figure of the punishing angel usually appears. One can see this element in the so-called apocalyptic scapegoat traditions, where the angelic handlers will strip garments of light from the former favorites of the deity before forwarding them into their subterranean prisons.

Another important feature pertains to the adept's inner condition, which itself is sometimes portrayed as the seat of the primordial conflict. In such traditions, various otherworldly antagonists, like Satan, Mastema, Belial, and Azazel, are able to act directly through the inclinations of the human heart, the locus of the eschatological battle.

~

The first chapter of this volume, "Between God and Satan: Inauguration into the Divine Image in Early Jewish and Christian Accounts," explores the antagonistic context of the protagonist's metamorphosis by concentrating on the ritual of Adam's induction into the office of the *Imago Dei*. According to a story found in several versions of the *Primary Adam Books*, immediately after Adam's creation, the archangel Michael presented the new human to the angels and asked them to bow down before Adam. Some angels acquiesced to this proposal, yet others, including Satan, rejected it. In consequence of his refusal, Satan was demoted from his exalted status.

Some peculiar features of this protological initiation were later adopted in various Jewish and Christian materials. In these stories many biblical exemplars, such as Enoch, Jacob, and Moses, were predestined to regain the image of God in the eschatological time. As in the *Primary Adam Books,* where Satan plays a pivotal role during the adept's inauguration, antagonistic figures are also frequently present in these eschatological accounts. And like in the Adamic traditions where Satan's rebellion constitutes an important element of the ritual, in the later versions of the story, the adepts' metamorphoses unfold in the midst of conflicts with various antagonistic figures who are often represented by hostile angels, who play an important role at the adept's inauguration.

This chapter explores the tradition of the so-called angelic opposition, which became a crucial element in several versions of the *Imago Dei* ritual attested in the *Exagoge* of Ezekiel the Tragedian, *2 Enoch,* and the *Ladder of Jacob.* In the polemical framework of the inauguration ritual, exaltation and demotion are closely intertwined as the antagonist's demotion became the prerequisite for the hero's exaltation. This chapter explores these peculiar details of Adam's inauguration ritual and their impact on later Jewish and Christian accounts in which Enoch, Jacob, Moses, the Son of Man, and Jesus became inducted into the office of the image of God.

The second chapter of the volume, "Furnace that Kills and Furnace that Gives Life: Fiery Trials and Martyrdom in the *Apocalypse of Abraham,*" continues the exploration of the antagonist's role at the adept's apotheosis by turning to the tradition of Abraham's fiery trials. This tradition received unprecedented attention in Jewish lore at various stages of its development. In different sources, Abraham is depicted as one who fights against idolatry and one whose faith is repeatedly tested in flames induced by opponents ranging from earthly rulers to otherworldly villains. This chapter pays special attention to the developments found in the *Apocalypse of Abraham,* where the fallen angel Azazel is portrayed as an antagonistic force at the adept's ascent to heaven. An important feature of this account is that the antagonist's demotion becomes the prerequisite for the hero's metamorphosis, as the text clearly states, that the fallen angel's garment will be given to the patriarch, while Abraham's iniquities will be bestowed on Azazel.

This study demonstrates that the tradition of the fiery trial, rooted in the story of Hananiah, Azariah, and Mishael in the Book of Daniel, had a rich and multifaceted afterlife in both Jewish and Christian martyrological accounts. In the course of such fiery tests, the adepts often experienced ascent and theophany. The study argues that Abraham's fiery trials in the *Apocalypse of Abraham*—trials that coincide with his ascent and theophany—might also reveal a similar martyrological dimension. Furthermore, these early Abrahamic accounts influenced the formation of early Christian martyrologia insofar as antagonists in the form of earthly or otherworldly characters are present during the trials of Christian martyrs.

The third chapter of the volume, “Leviathan’s Knot: The High Priest’s Sash as a Cosmological Symbol,” continues the investigation of the antagonist’s role in the transformation of the hero who is envisioned as the high priest. In Jewish sacerdotal traditions, the high priest was often understood as a paradigm of eschatological transformation. This cultic figure was envisioned as the new Adam entering the primordial Garden on Yom Kippur, symbolized by the Holy of Holies of the Jerusalem Temple. In the earliest descriptions of this pivotal cultic event, the procession of the high priest was juxtaposed with the inverse movement of the antagonist, represented by the infamous goat for Azazel. In such inverse parallel settings, two sacerdotal agents were envisioned as sacerdotal mirrors of each other. This reflects some ancient Near Eastern traditions where the *Chaoskampf* motif was placed in sacerdotal settings. Two figures, who reflect each other, also share similar attributes, especially discernable in their cultic features. This study attempts to explore this parallelism between the attributes of the high priest and the antagonist by focusing on the high priest’s sash, which is portrayed in Josephus’s *Jewish Antiquities* 3.154–156 with serpentine symbolism. In light of the sash’s associations with a serpent’s skin, some scholars have suggested that this sacerdotal item might symbolize the defeated Leviathan. In order to better understand the meaning of the priestly sash, this study examines its precise function in the broader context of Josephus’s description of the high priest’s accoutrement found in the third book of his *Jewish Antiquities*. It suggests that in Josephus’s account the temple was represented by the high priest and his sacerdotal garments. In such a cultic reinterpretation, the serpentine sash was understood as the courtyard of the microcosmic sanctuary, cosmologically corresponding to the primordial sea and its ruler—Leviathan.

Our study helps to elucidate two important aspects: first, connections between the Second Temple Jewish patterns of primordial conflict and their ancient Mesopotamian mythological roots; second, connections between Josephus’s account and other pseudepigraphical testimonies about the Leviathan found in *1 Enoch*, *2 Baruch*, *4 Ezra*, the *Apocalypse of Abraham* and the *Ladder of Jacob*. Despite the hints in some biblical texts of an early victory of God over the sea monster, these pseudepigraphical accounts also reveal a current or upcoming conflict between Leviathan and a second character who was usually exalted as a result of this battle.[19] Thus, according to Debra Scoggins Ballentine, “*2 Baruch*, *1 Enoch*, and *4 Ezra* also utilize the conflict motif within an eschatological framework to promote a secondary figure. This secondary figure is said to be endorsed by the primary deity, and he is awarded power by the primary deity. . . . The figures promoted in *2 Baruch*, *1 Enoch*, and *4 Ezra* are the ‘Messiah’; ‘Son of Man’ and ‘Elect One’; and ‘my son’ respectively.”[20] For our purpose it is important that some of these pseudepigraphical texts, similar to Josephus’s account, envision their heroes as priestly figures.

The fourth chapter, "Apocalyptic Scapegoat Traditions in the Book of Revelation," continues the exploration of sacerdotal dimensions of the antagonistic conflict by drawing attention to the imagery of the eschatological scapegoat in the Book of Revelation represented by the dragon. Scholars are in agreement that the antagonistic proclivities of apocalyptic literature reached a symbolic high point in this early Christian text. The conflict reaches its crescendo in the antagonist's story unfolded in Rev 12 and 13. As Norman Cohn rightly observes, "Chapters 12 and 13 of Revelation offer a Christian—and most impressive—version of the ancient combat myth."[21] As in other previously mentioned accounts, in these chapters one can detect a cultic parallelism between the protagonists and antagonists of the story. Similar to the Yom Kippur rituals attested in biblical and extrabiblical accounts, where the high priest and the scapegoat display strikingly similar attributes, here too the features of the eschatological scapegoat, embodied by the dragon, imitate traits of the heavenly high priest, represented by Christ.

Our study suggests that the portrayal of the dragon in the Book of Revelation reiterates the main features of the final moments of the scapegoat ritual, as reflected in apocalyptic, mishnaic, and patristic testimonies. These features include the following elements: the motif of the scapegoat's removal; the motif of the handler who binds and pushes the scapegoat off the cliff; the motif of the scapegoat's binding; the motif of sealing the abyss of the scapegoat; the motif of the temporary healing of the earth; the motif of the scapegoat's temporary unbinding before its final demise; and, finally, the motif of the scarlet band of the scapegoat.

As in other apocalyptic reinterpretations of the scapegoat imagery found in the *Book of the Watchers* and the *Apocalypse of Abraham*, the processions of the apocalyptic scapegoat, represented by the dragon in the Book of Revelation, encompass a two-stage development. He is first banished to the earth in chapter 12, and then to the underground realm, which is represented by the abyss in chapter 20. The two-stage progression of the antagonist's exile resembles the two stages of the earthly scapegoat's movements, found in later rabbinic and patristic sources: first, the scapegoat's banishment to the wilderness, and then its descent into the abyss when the animal was pushed off the cliff.

The fifth chapter, "Azazel's Will: Internalization of Evil in the *Apocalypse of Abraham*," investigates the internalization of the antagonistic conflict in early Jewish accounts. In these materials, antagonistic forces were embodied not only by personified adversaries in the form of Satan, Belial, and Azazel, but also by the inner conditions of human beings—their inclinations, thoughts, and emotions. Indeed, in some early Jewish accounts, the evil deeds of the famous adversaries found in Jewish lore became closely linked to the inclination of the human heart, thus connecting the outside power of evil with the inside force. Some personified antagonists of the old demonological paradigms, like Satan or Azazel, were able to execute their evil deeds directly through the internal faculties of a person. In such a framework, the human inclination or *yetzer* becomes envisioned as an entity that is able to bridge anthropological and demonological dimensions by connecting external personalized demonic forces with human will, thoughts, and emotions. Scholars sometimes label such symbiosis as a "psychodemonic" entity. This study explores the roots and the initial development of this entity in early Enochic accounts, the *Book of Jubilees,* and the Dead Sea Scrolls.

Our study also demonstrates how these early Jewish materials incorporated the external (angelic) antagonists into the framework of various psychodemonic anthropologies by assigning them the role of a decisive controlling force over inner human inclinations, both good and evil. Christian traditions further perpetuate this demonological paradigm in which the external antagonists were linked with the internal human inclinations.

Of particular interest is the concept of the malevolent spirits developed in early Enochic writings. The *Book of the Watchers* advances a certain type of demonology in which the adversaries of humankind are presented as disembodied spirits who are able to function inside a human body and soul. In the *Book of the Watchers,* this conceptual move is closely connected with the Giants' story whose hybrid anthropology, mingling the angelic and the human, opened the door for a novel psychodemonic synthesis. The importance of the evil spirits of the Giants is that they are able to bridge conventional anthropological boundaries through their ability to afflict the human body.

This chapter concludes with an analysis of the demonological developments found in the *Apocalypse of Abraham*, where the main antagonist of the story, the fallen angel Azazel, receives from God a mysterious "will" enabling him to control human inclinations. It argues that such bridging of the demonological and anthropological boundaries through the category of "will" establishes a new paradigm of the internalized demonology.

Finally, the sixth chapter, "Glorification through Fear in *2 Enoch,*" deals with the role of fear in the adept's transformation. The reference to this human reaction often precedes the adept's apotheosis in various Jewish and Christian accounts. This chapter argues that the adept's fear is connected with the primordial trauma, experienced by the first humans during their transgression in the Garden of Eden. In the course of the adept's transformation, this protological crisis is reiterated through the emotion of fear as he returned in his metamorphosis to the original glorious condition of the prelapsarian Adam. Some scholars argue that Jewish and Christian apocalyptic accounts represent reactions to "the experience of trauma, both individual and collective, personal and communal."[22] Yarbro Collins suggests that apocalyptic accounts allow the emotions of the audience to be purged in such a way that "their feelings of fear and pity are intensified and given objective expressions. The feelings are thus brought to consciousness and become less threatening."[23] In light of this, we might say that the fear of the protagonist and the audience's fear are indeed connected. This connection provides a unique opportunity for the audience's experiential appropriation of the visionary account.

This study also proposes that in some apocalyptic accounts the antagonistic context was created not only by the external antagonistic forces embodied by the personified villains and their allies, but also by inner conditions of human beings, their inclinations, thoughts, and emotions, including feelings of fear that facilitate the adepts' metamorphoses.

Chapter One

Between God and Satan

Inauguration into the Divine Image in Early Jewish and Christian Accounts

> Then Michael came; he summoned all the troops of angels and told them, "Bow down before the likeness and the image of the divinity." . . . And I [Satan] told him, "Go away from me, for I shall not bow down to him who is younger than me; indeed, I am master prior to him and it is proper for him to bow down to me." The six classes of other angels heard that and my speech pleased them and they did not bow down to you. Then God became angry with us and commanded us, them and me, to be cast down from our dwellings to the earth.
>
> —The Georgian version of the Primary Adam Books 14.1–16.1

Introduction

The Armenian, Georgian, and Latin versions of the *Primary Adam Books* each contain an etiological tale that deals with events occurring immediately after Adam's creation. According to the story, told retrospectively by Satan, the newly created protoplast was presented by the archangel Michael to angels whom he asked to bow down before Adam. Some angels agreed to venerate the first human being, while others, including Satan, rejected this proposal. As a result of his refusal, Satan was demoted from his exalted place. This scene exhibits several features of an inauguration ceremony during which the protagonist becomes inducted into the exalted role of the deity's representative, understood by some interpreters as the office of the image or the icon of God. In the *Primary Adam*

Books, Adam's role as God's icon did not last long insofar as he was promptly removed from his exalted position after his fall. Some peculiar features of this protological initiation, however, are reiterated and adopted later in various Jewish and Christian materials in which the heroes were predestined to become new "Adams" by regaining the image of God in the eschatological age. As in the *Primary Adam Books,* where Satan plays a pivotal role during the hero's inauguration, some other accounts include the presence of antagonistic figures. Our study will explore these peculiar details of Adam's inauguration ritual and their impact on later Jewish and Christian accounts in which Enoch, Jacob, Moses, the Son of Man, and Jesus are inducted into the office of the image of God.

I. Induction into the Divine Image in Early Jewish Materials

Primary Adam Books: The Protoplast's Inauguration

In order to better understand the complete pattern of conceptual developments pertaining to the ritual of induction into the divine image, we must carefully explore the description of it found in the *Primary Adam Books.* Although the macroforms of these books represent products of later Christian milieus, these Christian compositions can be seen as important compilations of early Jewish Adamic traditions.[1]

Although many details of the induction ceremony can be found in other early Jewish accounts—including the Book of Daniel, the *Exagoge* of Ezekiel the Tragedian, *2 Enoch*, the *Prayer of Joseph*, the *Ladder of Jacob*—in the Armenian, Georgian, and Latin versions[2] of the *Primary Adam Books,* one can find almost all of the crucial elements of this ritual in its full conceptual complexity. From these versions of the *Primary Adam Books,* we learn that immediately after the protoplast's creation, the archangel Michael brought Adam into the divine presence and forced him to bow down before God. This initial veneration of the deity will become a crucial component of other Jewish and Christian descriptions of the ritual. Adam's veneration of the deity implicitly indicates that God may also be present in the account. Several other references suggest the deity's presence, such as God's address to Adam after the ritual obeisance. In this address, as it appears in the Latin *Vita,* the deity tells Adam that his body was created in the likeness of the divine form: "Behold, Adam, I have made you in our image and likeness."[3] In the Georgian version God's address is directed not to the protoplast but instead to the archangel Michael: "And God told Michael, 'I have created Adam according to (my) image and my divinity.' "[4]

We learn further from the *Primary Adam Books* that all the angels were ordered to bow down to this human "icon."[5] A significant feature of the story is that Michael, who summons the celestial citizens for the act of veneration, does not ask them to venerate *Adam*, but instead commands them to bow down before *the image and the likeness of God*. So Adam, who previously was described as created *after the image of God*, here becomes suddenly identified as the image of God. Crispin Fletcher-Louis is right to posit that "the identification of Adam as God's image is by no means an incidental detail of the Worship of Adam Story."[6]

In the Georgian version, Michael's command takes the following form: "Bow down before the likeness and the image of the divinity."[7] The Latin version also speaks of the divine image: "Worship the image of the Lord God, just as the Lord God has commanded."[8] Likewise in the Armenian version, although Adam's name is not mentioned, he seems to be understood now as the divine representative: "Then Michael summoned all the angels, and God said to them, 'Come, bow down to the god whom I made.' "[9]

The results of Michael's order to venerate the "icon" of the divinity are mixed. Some angels agreed to bow down before it, while others, including Satan, refuse to do obeisance. In the Latin version the tradition of the image of God is reiterated when Michael personally invites Satan to "worship the image of God Jehovah."[10] In comparison with Michael's command that does not invoke Adam's name, but rather refers to him as the "image of God," Satan's refusal to worship now specifically mentions Adam's name, seeing him not as an "icon" but instead as a creature which is "younger," or "posterior," to the antagonist.[11] In Satan's refusal to venerate Adam, one can also find the theme of "opposition" to the divine image. Yet, in the complimentary framework of the *Primary Adam Books*, such an opposition motif is not intended to deconstruct the exalted protagonist who is envisioned as God's image. Instead, it functions within the narrative as a device to reaffirm the protagonist's unique position.

Both motifs—angelic veneration and angelic opposition[12]—play an equally significant role in the construction of Adam's unique heavenly identity,[13] which climaxes in his exaltation.[14] Angelic veneration as well as angelic opposition lead the human protagonist into his new supra-angelic ontology when he becomes an "image" or "face" of the deity. Yet, it is important that the accounts contain not only angelic responses but also Adam's own veneration of the deity.[15] Adam's own obeisance further establishes his intermediate position between God and the angels in his role as an "icon" of the deity. Fletcher-Louis rightly points out that, "because the angels are commanded to respond to Adam as the image and likeness of God, the 'worship' of Adam (if that is what it is) does not necessarily mean that God's singular, unique identity is now threatened by the worship of another figure."[16] Adam is presented "not as the ultimate object of veneration but rather as a representation or an icon of the deity through whom the angels are able to worship God."[17] The identity of the protagonist, therefore, is constructed through the concept of the divine image. We will see similar developments in the Enochic, Mosaic, and Jacobite traditions where the exaltation of these biblical characters is executed through the concept of the divine image. The same initiatory device will manifest itself in early Christological currents where Jesus is envisioned as the image of the invisible God.

In the beginning of the Georgian and Latin versions of the aforementioned story in the *Primary Adam Books*, one finds some important additions to the version contained in Genesis regarding the motif of Adam's face. These additions, attested in the Georgian and Latin versions, are of paramount significance for our study. The Georgian version recounts that God breathed a spirit onto the face of Adam.[18] The same detail is also found in the Greek version of Gen 2:7. Though the Hebrew text does not mention Adam's *panim*, in the Septuagint's rendering of the passage, the deity breaths the breath of life into Adam's *face*.[19] In the Latin *Vita* 13:2 the face motif appears again. This time it seems to convey a novel tradition by declaring that the protoplast's countenance was made in God's image: "when God blew into you the breath of life and your countenance (*vultus*) and likeness were made in the image of God. . . ."[20] Some scholars see the "face" as the cognate of "image" in this passage. Thus, Steenburg argues that "the use of 'face' in this passage is an irregular departure from the standard idiom of 'image,' a departure occasioned by the concern to relate God's image in Adam directly to his physical shape or visible appearance."[21] Fletcher-Louis follows Steenburg's suggestion, postulating that when the Latin version of the *Primary Adam Books* 13:3 says Adam's countenance is made in the image of God, it "accentuates the focus on Adam's role as God's visible and physical presence."[22] The Latin version, therefore, seems to entertain a conceptual link between the protoplast's *panim* and the *tselem*, a link that will reappear in various other Jewish accounts of the "inauguration."

To conclude our analysis of the inauguration ceremony in the *Primary Adam Books*, we must outline several important elements of this ritual:

1. Postulation of resemblance between the deity's form and the protagonist's form (Adam is first described as being created *in* the image of God and then later becomes understood as an icon of the deity—the image of God);
2. Understanding the protagonist's *panim* as his *tselem*;
3. The motif of the angelic veneration as an important element of the inauguration ceremony;

4. The motif of the angelic opposition/rejection as an important element of the inauguration ceremony;
5. The motif of the demotion of the exalted antagonist as an important element of the inauguration ceremony.

As this study will show, all of these elements can be found, in one form or another, in other early Jewish and Christian descriptions of the inauguration ritual where the motifs of angelic veneration and angelic rejection of the newly inducted divine image often coincide with the already familiar terminology of "face."

Inauguration of the Seventh Antediluvian Hero: 2 Enoch and 3 Enoch

2 ENOCH

Although in the *Primary Adam Books* the inauguration ceremony takes place within the story of Adam, in some other Jewish accounts the ritual is extended to other biblical characters. In *2 Enoch*, for example, one again encounters the constellation of familiar traditions reminiscent of the Adamic ritual. Here, however, the protological setting is replaced by an eschatological one in which a new hero, the patriarch Enoch, supplants the protoplast in becoming a new embodiment of the divine image. The storyline of this text, which was probably written in the first century CE before the destruction of the Second Jerusalem Temple,[23] deals with Enoch's heavenly journey to the throne of God. There, in the deity's abode, the seventh antediluvian hero undergoes a luminous transformation into a celestial being, one predestined to become a new icon of the divinity. An important nexus of conceptual developments relevant to our study occurs in chapters 21–22 of the text in which Enoch's transformation is depicted. In this cryptic portrayal there are several familiar motifs reminiscent of Adam's initiation in the Armenian, Georgian, and Latin versions of the *Primary Adam Books*. The story portrays angels bringing Enoch to the edge of the seventh heaven. By God's command, the archangel Gabriel invites the seer to stand in front of the deity forever. Enoch agrees, and Gabriel takes him to the deity's Face, where the patriarch does obeisance to God. God then personally repeats the invitation to Enoch to stand before Him forever. Following this invitation, the archangel Michael brings the patriarch before God's face. The deity then summons his angels with a resounding call: "Let Enoch join in and stand in front of my face forever!" In response to this address, the Lord's glorious ones do obeisance to Enoch saying, "Let Enoch yield in accordance with your word, O Lord!"[24]

Michael Stone has suggested that the story found in *2 Enoch* 21–22 recalls the account of Adam's elevation and veneration by angels found in the Armenian, Georgian, and Latin versions of the *Primary Adam Books.*[25] As Stone indicates, along with Adam's elevation and veneration by angels, the author of *2 Enoch* also appears to be aware of the motif of angelic disobedience and refusal to venerate the first human. Stone draws the reader's attention to the phrase "sounding them out," found in *2 Enoch* 22:6, which another translator of the Slavonic text rendered as "making a trial of them."[26] Stone suggests that the expression "sounding them out" or "making a trial of them" implies that it is the angels' obedience that is being tested.[27]

Comparing the similarities between Adamic and Enochic accounts, Stone proposes that the order of events in *2 Enoch* follows the exact order found in the *Primary Adam Books,* since both sources are familiar with the three steps of Adam's initiation:[28]

I. *Primary Adam Books:* Adam is created and placed in heaven.
2 Enoch: Enoch is brought to heaven.

II. *Primary Adam Books*: The archangel Michael brings Adam before God's face. Adam does obeisance to God.
2 Enoch: The archangel Michael brings Enoch before the Lord's face. Enoch does obeisance to the Lord.

III. *Primary Adam Books*: God commands the angels to bow down. Some of the angels do obeisance. Satan and his angels disobey.
2 Enoch: "The rebellion . . . is assumed. God tests whether this time the angels will obey. The angels are said to bow down and accept God's command."[29]

Stone concludes that the author of *2 Enoch* 21–22 was cognizant of the traditions resembling those found in the Armenian, Georgian, and Latin versions of the *Primary Adam Books.*[30] He is confident that these traditions did not enter *2 Enoch* from the Slavonic *Life of Adam and Eve* because the specific elements outlined above did not occur in the Slavonic recension of the *Primary Adam Books.*[31]

Other scholars have followed Stone's lead in this interpretation of the *2 Enoch* traditions. Gary Anderson suggests that *2 Enoch* "does contain a story that appears quite close to our narrative from the *Vita,*" since "the manner in which this glorification of Enoch proceeds is strikingly similar to the elevation of Adam the *Vita.*"[32] Like Stone, Anderson also argues that both sources (*2 Enoch* and the *Primary Adam Books*) develop the inauguration ceremony in a tripartite manner:

I. Adam is created and situated in heaven; Enoch is brought to heaven.

II. An angel escorts Adam to God so as to render obeisance to God, and so for Enoch;

III. The angels are exhorted to respond in kind to Adam, and so for Enoch.[33]

Anderson rightly sees the story found in *2 Enoch* as an *eschatological* version of the inauguration ceremony where the last Adam, represented by Enoch, is newly inducted into the office that the protoplast lost after his fall. The seventh human being here replaces the first one. According to Anderson, "the *Vita* presents the opening scene of a tradition whose final act, at least according to one level of its development, takes place during the era of Enoch."[34] The eschatological ritual is fashioned as an abbreviated version of the first (full) ceremony which nevertheless still preserves the memory of its crucial steps. In relation to these changes Anderson notes that

> In the *Vita* the angels are commanded to venerate Adam but Satan and his host refuse. In *2 Enoch*, the situation is slightly different. The striking motif here is God's intention to test the angels by parading Enoch before them. The test appears to be that of examining what the angel's reaction to this heavenly figure in the divine court will be. When the angels accord him the obeisance he is due, Enoch is then formally clothed with the garments of glory, anointed with the oil of joy and thereby fully transformed into any angel. By according Enoch the veneration that was his due, the angels passed their test. But is this not more than slightly odd? No command was given to venerate Enoch; the angels seem to know that this is what is implied by the action of God. How would they know this? The easiest solution would be to presume that the angels (or a portion of them) failed such a test the first time and did not show honor toward the first man. With Enoch, the angels relent and accord the human figure the honor that he is due.[35]

Anderson concludes that "one cannot imagine that the tradition in the Enoch materials was created independently from the tradition found in the *Vita*."[36]

For our purpose in this study, it is significant that the climax of the inauguration ceremony as it appears in *2 Enoch* is overlaid with a panoply of distinctive Adamic motifs reminiscent of the traditions found in the *Primary Adam Books*. Immediately after God tested the angels, Enoch receives the form and the luminous garments which the First Adam lost after his transgression. The longer recension of *2 Enoch* 22:7–10 describes this endowment in the following way:

> And the Lord's glorious ones did obeisance and said, "Let Enoch yield in accordance with your word, O Lord!" And the Lord said to Michael, "Go, and extract Enoch from his earthly clothing. And anoint him with my delightful oil, and put him into the clothes of my glory." And so Michael did, just as the Lord had said to him. He anointed me and he clothed me. And the appearance of that oil is greater than the greatest light, and its ointment is like sweet dew, and its fragrance myrrh; and it is like the rays of the glittering sun. And I looked at myself, and I had become like one of his glorious ones, and there was no observable difference.[37]

2 Enoch 22:9 portrays the archangel Michael extracting Enoch from his clothes and anointing him with delightful oil. The anointing with oil initiates the patriarch's transition from the garments of skin to the luminous garment of an immortal angelic being—one of the glorious ones. It appears that that the oil used in Enoch's anointing comes from the Tree of Life, which in *2 Enoch* 8:3–4 is depicted with similar symbolism. *2 Enoch* 8:3–4 reports that "the tree [of life] is indescribable for pleasantness and fine fragrance, and more beautiful than any (other) created thing that exists. And from every direction it has an appearance which is gold-looking and crimson, and with the form of fire."[38] The shorter recension also refers to a second tree near the first one "flowing with oil continually."[39]

Enoch's anointing with oil in *2 Enoch* is a unique motif in the Enochic tradition. Enoch's approach to the throne in the *Book of the Watchers* and his transformation into the Son of Man in the *Book of the Similitudes* do not involve anointing with, or any usage of, oil. Later Enochic traditions are also silent about oil. For example, it does not appear in the account of Metatron's transformation in *3 Enoch*.

Yet, though mostly unknown in the Enochic literature, the motif of anointing with oil from the Tree of Life looms large in the Adamic tradition. The *Primary Adam Books* contain a story of Adam's sickness. The patriarch finds himself in great distress and pain. Trying to find a cure, Adam sends Eve and Seth to paradise in order to fetch the oil of the Tree of Life that will relieve his illness. Their mission, however, is unsuccessful. The archangel Michael refuses to give the oil to Eve and Seth, telling them that the oil will be used "when the years of the end are filled completely" for those who will "be worthy of entering the Garden."[40]

Several corresponding characteristics can be detected between the *Primary Adam Books* and *2 Enoch*:

1. The purpose of the anointing is similar in both traditions. Its function is the "resurrection of Adam's body," that is, the reversal of the fallen human condition into the incorruptible luminous state of the protoplast.[41] It is not coincidental that in *2 Enoch* 22 anointing with oil transforms Enoch into a luminous angelic being. It parallels the description of the protoplast in *2 Enoch* 30:11 as a glorious angelic being.
2. The subject of the anointing is also identical. In *2 Enoch* and in the *Primary Adam Books*, the oil is used (or will be used) for transforming the righteous ones into angels in the celestial realm. In the *Primary Adam Books*, the oil is prepared for those who will "be worthy of entering the Garden."[42] Michael Stone observes that *2 Enoch* also "knows an anointing with the heavenly perfumed oil that brings about a transformation of the righteous."[43] The same situation is attested in *3 Baruch*, where the reward of the righteous is oil. This theme in *3 Baruch* has a connection with the Adamic tradition. In the words of Harry Gaylord, by his disobedience Adam lost "the glory of God" (4:16[G]), which may have been comparable to that of angels (cf. 13:4[S]). The reward of the righteous is oil, possibly the sign of the glory of God, which the angel-guide promises to show Baruch several times in this text (6:12; 7:2; 11:2; 16:3[S]). It is hardly accidental that there are traditions that Adam sought to receive the "oil of mercy" at the point of death, and that Enoch was transformed by the "oil of his glory."[44]
3. In *2 Enoch* and in the *Primary Adam Books*, the one in charge of the oil is the archangel Michael.[45] In *2 Enoch* 22, he anoints Enoch with shining oil, causing his luminous metamorphosis. In *3 Baruch* 15:1, Michael brings oil to the righteous.[46] In the *Primary Adam Books*, he also seems to be in charge of the oil, since it is he who refuses to give it to Seth.
4. Both *2 Enoch* and the *Primary Adam Books* refer to the flowing of the oil. Thus, the Georgian version of the *Primary Adam Books* 36(9):4 relates that God "will send his angel to the Garden where the Tree of Life is, from which the oil flows out, so that he may give you a little of that oil."[47] *2 Enoch* 8:5 highlights this same detail: "and another tree is near it, an olive, flowing with oil

> continually." Michael Stone notes that "it is striking that *2 Enoch* highlights the flowing of the oil, just like the Adam books."[48]

These similarities demonstrate that the motif of oil from the Tree of Life in *2 Enoch* might have Adamic provenance. It is unlikely that this tradition represents a later interpolation. Attested in both recensions, it plays a pivotal role in the scene of Enoch's metamorphosis.

One can see another tendency in *2 Enoch* which was previously detected in the *Primary Adam Books,* namely, the juxtaposition of the image and face symbolism. Thus, *2 Enoch* 39:3–6 has the patriarch, upon his brief return to earth, revealing to his children his earlier dramatic encounter with the divine Face. The shorter recension of *2 Enoch* contains the following address:

> You, my children, you see my face, a human being created just like yourselves; I am one who has seen the face of the Lord, like iron made burning hot by a fire, emitting sparks. For you gaze into my eyes, a human being created just like yourselves; but I have gazed into the eyes of the Lord, like the rays of the shining sun and terrifying the eyes of a human being. You, my children, you see my right hand beckoning you, a human being created identical to yourselves; but I have seen the right hand of the Lord, beckoning me, who fills heaven. You see the extent of my body, the same as your own; but I have seen the extent of the Lord, without measure and without analogy, who has no end.[49]

This passage portrays the deity's form as an incomprehensible entity—"without measure and without analogy." Yet, while the text argues that God's form transcends any analogy, the account of Enoch's vision itself represents a set of analogies in which the descriptions of the patriarch's face and the parts of his body are compared with the descriptions of the divine Face and the parts of the deity's body. These analogies appear to underline once again Enoch's role as the image of God.

Furthermore, in *2 Enoch* the translated human has become a visible representation, or icon, of the deity, and is now able to able to glorify its beholders, like the divine *Kavod.* In the later chapters of the apocalypse, the elders of the earth will approach the transformed Enoch in order to be glorified before the patriarch's "face."[50]

This brings us to another important conceptual trajectory found in *2 Enoch* 39: the motifs concerning the divine Face and the face of the visionary. These corresponding terms are closely related to the concept of the divine image. As I have already argued elsewhere, in *2 Enoch*, "the symbolism of the divine image, or, more precisely, its conceptual correlative in the form of the deity's *panim*, becomes a pivotal conduit in the creation of the patriarch's upper identity."[51] Scholars have argued that the divine Face symbolism in *2 Enoch* is closely linked to the notion of the divine image.[52] Unlike the *Primary Adam Books*, however, *2 Enoch* does not explicitly mention the divine image in his description of the creation of Enoch's heavenly identity. Instead, it often refers to another pivotal celestial entity—the divine Face. The divine Face features prominently in the process of the seer's initiation into the role of the deity's icon. Indeed, the angelic veneration of the hero takes place in immediate proximity to the divine Face, the reality upon which the patriarch's metamorphosis is patterned.

In light of these connections, it is likely that in *2 Enoch*, as in some other Jewish accounts,[53] the divine *Panim* performs the role of the divine *tselem*. The divine Face represents the cause and prototype after which Enoch's new celestial identity is formed. New creation modeled after the divine Face signifies a return to the prelapsarian condition of Adam, who, according to *2 Enoch*, was also molded in conformity with the face of God. Support for this view can be found in *2 Enoch* 44:1, where we learn that the first human was also made after the *Panim* of God. The text says that "the Lord with his own two hands created humankind; in a facsimile of his own face, both small and great, the Lord created them."[54] *2 Enoch* departs from the conventional reading attested in Gen 1:26–27, where Adam was created not after the face of God, but after His image (*tselem*).[55] Francis Andersen observes that *2 Enoch*'s "idea is remarkable from any point of view. . . . This is not the original meaning of *tselem*. . . . The text uses *podobie lica* [in the likeness of the face], not *obrazu* or *videnije*, the usual terms for 'image.' "[56] However, it is clear that this reading did not arise in the Slavonic environment, but rather belonged to the original argument of *2 Enoch* in which the creation of the luminous first human after the deity's Face corresponds to a similar angelic creation of the seventh antediluvian patriarch.

3 ENOCH

The Adamic makeup of Enoch's inauguration receives its new afterlife in later Jewish mystical lore. We encounter it in the initial chapters of *3 Enoch*, a Hekhalot macroform[57] also known to scholars as *Sefer Hekhalot*, where Enoch's transformation into the supreme angel Metatron is accompanied by the familiar motifs of angelic opposition[58] and angelic veneration. *3 Enoch* 4 portrays Enoch's exaltation in the heavenly realm, where the hero encounters the hostile reaction of the ministering angels:

> And the Holy One, blessed be he, appointed me (Enoch) in the height as a prince and a ruler among the ministering angels. Then three of ministering angels, ᶜUzzah, ᶜAzzah, and ᶜAzaʾel, came and laid charges against me in the heavenly height. They said before the Holy One, blessed be he, "Lord of the Universe, did not the primeval ones give you good advice when they said, do not create man!" The Holy One, blessed be he, replied, "I have made and I will sustain him; I will carry and I will deliver him." When they saw me they said before him, "Lord of the Universe, what right has this one to ascend to the height of heights? Is he not descended from those who perished in the waters of the Flood? What right has he to be in heaven?" Again the Holy One, blessed be he, replied and said to them, "What right have you to interrupt me? I have chosen this one in preference to all of you, to be a prince and a ruler over you in the heavenly heights." At once they all arose and went to meet me and prostrated themselves before me, saying, "Happy are you, and happy your parents, because your Creator has favored you." Because I am young in their company and a mere youth among them in days and months and years—therefore they call me "Youth."[59]

Some have noted that this account, where the Adamic motifs of the angelic veneration and the angelic opposition were applied to Enoch-Metatron, is reminiscent of *2 Enoch* 22.[60] Like in the previously explored accounts, the angelic hostility here is provoked by the human origin of the protagonist who attempts to enter the celestial realm, violating the boundaries separating the human and angelic regions. Yet the angels who initially opposed Enoch are eventually persuaded by God and obliged to give obeisance to the human.

This reminiscence of the Adamic tradition in *3 Enoch* 4 is evidence of the Adamic provenance of the Hekhalot story and its connection with the protoplast's inauguration ritual. Commenting on this passage, Gary Anderson suggests that if "we remove those layers of the tradition that are clearly secondary . . . we are left with a story that is almost identical to the analog we have traced in the Adam and Eve literature and *2 Enoch*."[61] According to Anderson, the acclamation of Enoch as the "Youth" in *Sefer Hekhalot* serves as another link to Adam's inauguration, since the reason *3 Enoch* supplies for this title is deceptively simple and straightforward: "Because I am young in their company and a mere youth among them in days and months and years—therefore they call me 'Youth.'" Such an explanation for the epithet "Youth" recalls the reason for the angelic refusal to worship Adam in the *Vita* on the basis of his inferiority to them by way of his age.[62]

Unlike in the *Primary Adam Books*, in *2* and *3 Enoch* the event of angelic opposition comes before the event of angelic veneration. This underlines the difference between the initial induction of the protoplast and its later eschatological counterparts, in which the angels are already cognizant of the first inauguration. In *2 Enoch* such prior knowledge is hinted by through God's testing of the angelic hosts. In *3 Enoch* this detail becomes even more transparent, since the ministering angels mention the event of the initial angelic opposition to humanity: "They said before the Holy One, blessed be he, 'Lord of the Universe, did not the primeval ones give you good advice when they said, do not create man!' "[63] Dealing with this passage, Anderson notes that "the angels remind God of their prior opinion about Adam."[64]

Book of Daniel and the Book of the Similitudes: The Son of Man Induction

DANIEL 7

Already in the first chapter of Genesis the divine corporeality was envisioned as a prototype of human form. In light of this, Elliot Wolfson helpfully suggests that "a critical factor in determining the biblical (and, by extension, subsequent Jewish) attitude toward the visualization of God concerns the question of the morphological resemblance between the human body and the divine."[65] The priestly ideology postulates that the deity created humanity in his own image (Gen 1:27) and is therefore frequently described as possessing a humanlike form.[66] This correspondence between the deity's form and the human body through the notion of the divine image becomes a crucial stratagem in the construction of several "eschatological Adams" in various early Jewish and Christian materials.

Such anthropomorphic symbolism plays a special role in Daniel 7, where protagonists appear in human form while antagonists are fashioned in their distinctive theriomorphic shapes. In the symbolic code of the Danielic account, such anthropomorphism, associated both with the Ancient of Days and the Son of Man, signals authority[67] and dominion.[68] This understanding is rooted in Gen 1, where the anthropomorphic shape of the prelapsarian Adam endows him with authority over the animals, as well as in Ezek 1, where the "animals" of the upper realm—the Living Creatures, or the *Hayyot*—are envisioned as servants who hold the foundation of the anthropomorphic glory of God. It has been proposed that these traditions constitute the background of Daniel 7, where the deity and its envoy in the form of the Son of Man appear together.[69] According to Amy Merrill Willis, Dan 7 is "closely connected to Gen 1:26–28, in which the human form resembles the divine and is also connected to ruling power."[70] Willis further notes that the aforementioned traditions "situate divine anthropomorphic features in a hierarchy of bodily forms in which the human form resides at the pinnacle and signals dominion over the beasts of air, land, and sea."[71] In this context the anthropomorphism of the Son of Man itself can be seen as a divine attribute bestowed on the embodied image of God. Willis perceptively argues that the Son of Man "is visually aligned with divine righteous rule through his shape. . . . Unlike the first beast, who must be made humanlike in a process that is never completed,[72] this figure possesses the divine image from the beginning."[73] The postulation of a resemblance of form between the deity and the Son of Man recalls the protological induction of Adam in the *Primary Adam Books,* where the protoplast's resemblance to the deity commands obedience and respect from the heavenly citizens. Furthermore, the imagery of the first beast who tries to imitate the divine anthropomorphic attribute brings to mind Satan and his role in the *Primary Adam Books* and in the temptation narrative of the synoptic gospels.

Another important detail that connects Dan 7 with the inauguration scene found in the *Primary Adam Books* is the motif of "service" to the Son of Man. This feature appears to signal an important connection with the angelic veneration motif. The passage tells that "all peoples, nations, and languages should serve him." It remains unclear if the Aramaic text speaks here about worship of the Son of Man. Fletcher-Louis suggests that "the Aramaic at Dan 7:14 might itself intend a worship of the man figure since the verb usually translated 'serve' (*pelakh*) is used repeatedly in the previous chapters of Aramaic Daniel for full-blown cultic worship (Dan 3:12, 14, 17–18; 6:17, 21, cf. 7:27)."[74] The Old Greek version of Dan 7:14 further supports understanding "service" as "worship" by using the Greek verb *latreuō,* which "in its eight previous occurrences in Daniel always refers either to a legitimate worship given to God or to an illegitimate worship of the pagan gods and their idols (see Dan 3:12, 14, 18; 4:37; 6:17, 21, 27)."[75]

Finally, an additional important aspect of Dan 7 is the resemblance between the first Adam, the protoplast, and the last Adam, the Son of Man, who appears to be envisioned as an eschatological version of the prelapsarian human. In relation to this, Fletcher-Louis comments that Dan 7 suggests that the "one like a son of man" who appears with clouds in verse13 is an Adamic figure. Furthermore, as a symbol of future hope, the Son of Man cannot simply be Adam, but rather represents an eschatological character who takes up the identity and calling of the original Adam.[76]

THE BOOK OF THE SIMILITUDES

In the *Book of the Similitudes,* the Son of Man's appearances once again evoke the memory of the inauguration pattern. *1 Enoch* 46:1–2[77] presents the Danielic theophany in this manner:

> And there I saw one who had a head of days, and his head (was) white like wool; and with him (there was) another, whose face had the appearance of a man, and his face (was) full of grace, like one of the holy angels. And I asked one of the holy angels who went with me, and showed me all the secrets, about that Son of Man, who he was, and whence he was, (and) why he went with the Head of Days.[78]

One of the intriguing features of this account is the *panim* symbolism. It portrays the Son of Man as the one "whose *face* had the appearance of a man," a "*face* (which was) full of grace."[79] This repeated attention to the "face" (Eth. *gaṣṣ*) of the heavenly protagonist does not appear to be coincidental. As in some other inauguration accounts, "face" here functions as a cognate for the divine *tselem*. Concerning the Son of Man's *panim*, George Nickelsburg and James VanderKam point out that this text "expands the description of the figure's face, likening it to that of one of the holy angels (v. 1d). That is, the deity is accompanied by another divine figure. The expression 'full of grace' is not used here theologically but denotes a physical characteristic."[80]

Like the Book of Daniel, the *Similitudes* surrounds the Son of Man with a panoply of Adamic allusions. Fletcher-Louis draws attention to some of these Adamic details, pointing out that in Jewish lore, Adam is sometimes depicted as being enthroned and wearing glorious garments. If this is true, it is easy to see how the person of Adam is brought to mind by "the Son of Man's position on God's throne of divine Glory which somehow leads to the righteous receiving 'glory and honor' (*1 Enoch* 50:1) and 'garments of incorruptible glory' (62:15–16)."[81]

It is also worth noting that in the *Similitudes*, the Son of Man "appears to receive worship."[82] Several scholars have connected this feature with the motif of angelic veneration to Adam in the *Primary Adam Books*. According to them, "in the *Similitudes of Enoch* the Son of Man (/Elect One/Messiah) appears to receive worship in two passages (48:5 and 62:6–9).[83] In several others the propriety of worshipping the Son of Man seems to be assumed (46:5; 52:4)."[84] In light of these parallels, Fletcher-Louis suggests that the angelic adoration of Adam in the *Primary Adam Books* could be used to provide theological justification for the worship of the Son of Man in the *Similitudes*.[85]

Moses's Induction: The Exagoge of Ezekiel the Tragedian

Exagoge 67–90 of Ezekiel the Tragedian represents another early Jewish account that contains some traces of the inauguration ritual. Given its quotation by Alexander Polyhistor (ca. 80–40 BCE), the *Exagoge*'s account can be taken as a witness to traditions of the second century BCE.[86] Preserved in fragmentary form by several ancient sources,[87] *Exagoge* 67–90 reads:

> Moses: I had a vision of a great throne on the top of Mount Sinai and it reached till the folds of heaven. A noble man was sitting on it, with a crown and a large scepter in his left hand. He beckoned to me with his right hand, so I approached and stood before the throne. He gave me the scepter and instructed me to sit on the great throne. Then he gave me a royal crown and got up from the throne. I beheld the whole earth all around and saw beneath the earth and above the heavens. A multitude of stars fell (ἔπιπτ') before my knees and I counted them all. They paraded past me like a battalion of men. Then I awoke from my sleep in fear.
>
> Raguel: My friend, this is a good sign from God. May I live to see the day when these things are fulfilled. You will establish a great throne, become a judge and leader of men. As for your vision of the whole earth, the world below and that above the heavens—this signifies that you will see what is, what has been, and what shall be.[88]

The *Exagoge*'s description brings to mind several details of the protoplast's induction in the *Primary Adam Books*. Moses seems to take on the role of the prelapsarian Adam by supplanting him as the eschatological image of God. Silviu Bunta convincingly advanced this argument in his unpublished dissertation, "Moses, Adam, and the Glory of the Lord in Ezekiel the Tragedian." Considering the unnamed enthroned figure in the *Exagoge*, Bunta sees in him Adamic features echoing the protoplast's association with the *Kavod* in the Jewish pseudepigrapha and Qumran materials.[89] Bunta also identifies an Adamic allusion in the fact that the *Exagoge* defines the enthroned figure as φῶς, arguing that "Adam is particularly associated in late Second Temple Judaism with the ambivalent term φως."[90]

It is noteworthy that Moses's exaltation in the *Exagoge* entails two major developments. First, Moses replaces the "noble man" on the throne while being endowed with the exalted status. Second, a multitude of stars react to him by falling before his knees and by parading before the prophet "like a battalion of men." These two parts are reminiscent of the two pivotal stages of Adam's inauguration into his role as the divine image in the *Primary Adam Books*. As we recall, the protagonist in that account is first created in the image of God and becomes God's icon, and then he is subsequently venerated by the angelic hosts. It is possible that in the *Exagoge*, like in the previously explored accounts of the protoplast's elevation from the *Primary Adam Books*, the reader encounters the initiatory ritual of endowment into the office of the divine image,[91] which in the Adamic story coincides with angelic veneration. Such angelic adoration is likely also present in the *Exagoge*.[92] This account portrays a "multitude of stars" falling down before Moses.[93] This prostration is rendered through the Greek verb πίπτω, a term that will be used later in some Christian inauguration accounts. Considering the Enochic influences on the *Exagoge*, where the stars often designate angelic beings,[94] the multitude of stars kneeling before the seer seems to be a reference to angelic veneration. Some scholars previously entertained the possibility that the kneeling stars in fact represent angelic hosts. Thus, reflecting on the obeisance of the stars, Larry Hurtado supports this contention, suggesting that the obeisance of the stars "may represent the acceptance by the heavenly hosts of Moses' appointed place as God's chief agent. Stars are a familiar symbol for angelic beings in Jewish tradition (e.g., Job 38:7) and are linked with divine beings in other religious traditions as well."[95] Fletcher-Louis goes even further, comparing the astral prostration in the *Exagoge* with the angelic veneration found in the *Primary Adam Books*.[96]

In the *Exagoge* the stars are not only falling down before the protagonist but are also parading before Moses. This detail brings to mind a version of Adam's inauguration ritual reflected in the *Cave of Treasures,* where all creation paraded before Adam during his inauguration into the office of God's image. *Cave of Treasures* 2:10–24 transmits the following rendering of the familiar ceremony:

> God formed Adam with His holy hands, in His own image and Likeness, and when the angels saw Adam's glorious appearance they were greatly moved by the beauty thereof. For they saw the *image of his face* burning with glorious splendor like the orb of the sun, and the light of his eyes was like the light of the sun, and the image of his body was like unto the sparkling of crystal. And when he rose at full length and stood upright in the center of the earth, he planted his two feet on that spot whereon was set up the Cross of our Redeemer; for Adam was created in Jerusalem. There he was arrayed in the apparel of sovereignty, and there was the crown of glory set upon his head, there was he made king, and priest, and prophet, there did God make him to sit upon his honorable throne, and there did God give him dominion over all creatures and things. And all the wild beasts, and all the cattle, and the feathered fowl were gathered together, and *they passed before Adam* and he assigned names to them; and they bowed their heads before him; and everything in nature worshipped him, and submitted themselves unto him. And the angels and the hosts of heaven heard the Voice of God saying unto him, "Adam, behold: I have made thee king, and priest, and prophet, and lord,

> and head, and governor of everything which hath been made and created; and they shall be in subjection unto thee, and they shall be thine, and I have given unto thee power over everything which I have created." And when the angels heard this speech they all bowed the knee and worshipped Him. And when the prince of the lower order of angels saw what great majesty had been given unto Adam, he was jealous of him from that day, and he did not wish to worship him. And he said unto his hosts, "Ye shall not worship him, and ye shall not praise him with the angels. It is meet that ye should worship me, because I am fire and spirit; and not that I should worship a thing of dust, which hath been fashioned of fine dust."[97]

Reflecting on this version of the inauguration, Gary Anderson notes that "the *Cave of Treasures* shows a slight divergence from the *Vita* as to the moment in time when Adam was to be venerated by all of creation. In the *Cave*, the prostration scene does not occur at the moment of Adam's animation (Gen 2:7), but at that time when the animals are paraded before him to receive their names (Gen 2:19–20)[98]. . . In other words, the moment of name-giving becomes the occasion for Adam's elevation as king over all creation."[99] It is possible that the author of the *Exagoge* was cognizant of this version of the inauguration story, so that the stars parading before the protagonist "like a battalion of men" can be seen as another important element of the eschatological induction.

If the *Exagoge* indeed contains the veneration motif, it is possible that here, as in other accounts where the angelic veneration take place, Moses is implicitly envisioned as the personification of the divine image.[100] If so, it is not coincidental that in later targumic accounts Moses's shining face is often interpreted as his *iqonin*.

Inauguration into the Image in the Prayer of Joseph

Another source that attests to a pattern within accounts of induction into the divine icon is the *Prayer of Joseph,* where the patriarch Jacob takes on the role of the eschatological image of God.[101] Only three fragments of the *Prayer* are currently extant.[102] The original composition most likely represents "a midrash on the Jacob narrative in Genesis."[103] The pseudepigraphon is usually dated to the first century CE.[104] The surviving materials contain the following fragments:

> Fragment A
>
> I, Jacob, who is speaking to you, am also Israel, an angel of God[105] and a ruling spirit.[106] Abraham and Isaac were created before any

> work. But, I, Jacob, who men call Jacob but whose name is Israel, am he who God called Israel, which means a man seeing God because I am the firstborn of every living thing to whom God gives life.[107] And when I was coming up from Syrian Mesopotamia, Uriel, the angel of God, came forth and said that "I (Jacob-Israel) had descended to earth and I had tabernacled among men and that I had been called by the name of Jacob." He envied me and fought with me and wrestled with me, saying that his name and the name that is before every angel was to be above mine. I told him his name and what rank he held among the sons of God. "Are you not Uriel, the eighth after me? And I, Israel, the archangel of the power of the Lord and the chief captain among the sons of God? Am I not Israel, the first minister before the face of God? And I called upon my God by the inextinguishable name."
>
> Fragment B
>
> For I have read in the tablets of heaven all that shall befall you and your sons.
>
> Fragment C
>
> [Origen writes] Jacob was greater than man, he who supplanted his brother and who declared in the same book from which we quoted "I read in the tablets of heaven" that he was a chief captain of the power of the Lord and had, from of old, the name of Israel; something which he recognizes while doing service in the body, being reminded of it by the archangel Uriel.[108]

Pertinent to our study is the presence of the concept of the image or *tselem* of God—a prominent motif of later Jacob legends. In these fragments, Jacob mentions his unique place in God's creation by uttering the following statement: "I, Jacob, who is speaking to you, am also Israel, an angel of God and a ruling spirit. Abraham and Isaac[109] were created before any work (προεκτίσθησαν).[110] But . . . I am the firstborn (πρωτόγονος) of every living thing to whom God gives life."[111]

The designation of Jacob as πρωτόγονος[112] may point to his role as the image of God, the office that Adam occupies in Jewish inauguration accounts. According to Howard Schwartz, such an expression "suggests that Jacob was a kind of proto-human, an Adam-like figure."[113] Jarl Fossum points to another key parallel, previously noticed by other experts as well,[114] namely, a possible connection with Col 1:15, where Christ's role as "the image of the invisible God" (εἰκὼν τοῦ Θεοῦ τοῦ ἀοράτου) is tied to his designation as πρωτότοκος πάσης κτίσεως ("the firstborn of all creation"). According to Fossum, "the closest parallel to the phrase in Col 1:15b is found in a fragment of the *Prayer of Joseph* preserved by Origen."[115]

Another crucial detail suggestive of the *tselem* concept in the *Prayer of Joseph* is the motif of angelic opposition which, as we already saw, often plays a pivotal part in inauguration rituals attested in Adamic and Enochic lore. Thus, in the *Prayer,* Jacob mentions that the angel Uriel envied him, wrestled with him, and argued that his own name was above Jacob's.[116] Although the *Prayer of Joseph* is obviously drawing on the biblical story of Jacob's struggle with a supernatural opponent at the river Jabbok, angelic jealousy and the angel's arguments about his superior status are entirely new developments here, in comparison with the biblical account. In relation to these novel additions, Richard Hayward notes that "the Bible gives no motive for the supernatural attack on Jacob [at Jabbok]. . . . The *Prayer*, however, attributes the attack to jealousy, and adds something entirely foreign to both the Bible and Philo: what is at issue between the two combatants is their relative status as angels, and their exact positions within the celestial hierarchy."[117] Uriel's jealousy and peculiar arguments about his superiority to the patriarch bring to mind the angelic opposition to Adam as the image of God in the inauguration story of the *Primary Adam Books.* There, as we recall, its chief antagonist Satan also expressed similar feelings of jealousy,[118] justifying his refusal to worship Adam on the basis of the first human's inferior celestial status in comparison with his own, more exalted, position.[119] The appearance of angelic jealousy and resistance thus implicitly affirms the presence of the inauguration pattern. In view of these connections, it is possible that in the *Prayer of Joseph,* Jacob's heavenly identity is envisioned as the eschatological image of God.

Jacob's Inauguration in the Ladder of Jacob

JACOB'S IQONIN

Another early witness to the induction ceremony is the *Ladder of Jacob,* where the upper identity of the patriarch Jacob is again portrayed as the divine image. Like in some other Jewish accounts, the inauguration receives soteriological significance and can be seen as an eschatological version of Adam's protological endowment. Like in the *Prayer of Joseph*, Jacob's initiation here takes the form of his unification with his upper identity, which is envisioned as the image of God. While the *Prayer of Joseph* only vaguely hints at the whole process, here it unfolds in great detail before the reader's eyes. *Lad. Jac.* 1:3–10 offers the following description of this process:

> And behold, a ladder was fixed on the earth, whose top reaches to heaven. And the top of the ladder was the face as of a man, carved out of fire.[120] There were twelve steps leading to the top of the ladder, and on each step to the top there were two human faces, on the right and on the left, twenty-four faces (or busts) including their chests. And the face in the middle was higher than all that I saw, the one of fire, including the shoulders and arms, exceedingly terrifying, more than those twenty-four faces. And while I was still looking at it, behold, angels of God ascended and descended on it. And God was standing above its highest face, and he called to me from there, saying, "Jacob, Jacob!" And I said, "Here I am, Lord!" And he said to me, "The land on which you are sleeping, to you will I give it, and to your seed after you. And I will multiply your seed. . . ."[121]

As in some previously explored accounts, one encounters the presence of the *panim* imagery, which serves as the conceptual cognate for the "image." The story relates that Jacob sees twenty-four human faces with their chests on a ladder, two of them on each step of the ladder. At the top of the ladder, the seer also beholds another human visage "carved out of fire"[122] with its shoulders and arms.[123] In comparison with the previous countenances, this highest fiery face is described as "exceedingly terrifying." The imagery of this highest face on the ladder deserves close attention.

Experts have suggested that in the *Ladder of Jacob* the blazing face not only exemplifies God's Glory,[124] but also represents the heavenly counterpart of Jacob in the form of the divine image.[125] Thus, while dealing with the terminological peculiarities found in the first chapter of the text, James Kugel argues that the authors of the text were familiar with Jewish traditions about Jacob's image or *iqonin* (איקונין) installed in heaven.[126] Responding to Horace Lunt, who suggested that "no other Slavonic text has *lice*, 'face,' used to mean 'statue' or 'bust' (1:5 etc.), and there is no Semitic parallel,"[127] Kugel argues that such a Semitic parallel can indeed be found, embodied in the Greek loan word into Mishnaic Hebrew—*iqonin*, which in some rabbinic texts did in fact come to mean "face."[128] Indeed, the basic meaning of *iqonin* as "portrait" or "bust"[129] is preserved in a number of rabbinic usages.[130] In light of these connections, Kugel concludes the following: "There is little doubt that our pseudepigraphon, in seeking to 'translate' the biblical phrase 'his/its head reached to Heaven,' reworded it in Mishnaic Hebrew as 'his [Jacob's] *iqonin* reached Heaven,' and this in turn gave rise to the presence of a heavenly bust or portrait of Jacob on the divine throne."[131] Some other scholars also affirm[132] the presence of the *iqonin* tradition in the *Ladder*, arguing that "in the fiery bust of the terrifying man we are probably correct to see the heavenly 'image' of Jacob."[133]

THEME OF THE ANGELIC OPPOSITION

Another important feature of the *Ladder of Jacob* connected with the inauguration ceremony is the presence of the motif of angelic opposition—the theme often found in many early Jewish versions of this ritual.

In later rabbinic accounts, it often appears in the context of the stories about Jacob's heavenly image engraved or installed on the Throne of Glory. One specimen of this tradition is reflected in *Gen. Rab.* 68:12, a passage which tells both about the angelic exaltation of the heavenly Jacob and about the angelic opposition to such exaltation:

> R. Hiyya the Elder and R. Jannai disagreed. One maintained: They were ascending and descending the ladder; while the other said: They were ascending and descending on Jacob. The statement that they were ascending and descending the ladder presents no difficulty. The statement that they were ascending and descending on Jacob we must take to mean that some were exalting him and others degrading him, dancing, leaping, and maligning him.[134]

One can easily detect in this account the distant memory of Adamic and Enochic currents, in which newly appointed "icons" of the deity have faced not only obeisance of the angelic hosts, but also their fierce opposition. Thus, a salient feature of the text is the postulation that some angelic servants seem to oppose Jacob's heavenly image by "degrading . . . and maligning him," thus exemplifying the motif of angelic resentment. Angelic hostility is already reflected in some talmudic materials that constitute the background of *Gen. Rab.* 68:12. For example, *b. Hul.* 91b contains the following tradition:

> A Tanna taught: They ascended to look at the image above and descended to look at the image below. They wished to hurt him, when Behold, the Lord stood beside him (Gen 28:13). R. Simeon b. Lakish said: Were it not expressly stated in the Scripture, we would not dare to say it. [God is made to appear] like a man who is fanning his son.[135]

We find that in these rabbinic accounts, the motif of the patriarch's heavenly image "is placed in the context of another well-known motif regarding the enmity or envy of the angels toward human beings. That is, according to the statements in *Genesis Rabbah* and *Bavli Hullin* the angels, who beheld Jacob's image above, were jealous and sought to harm Jacob below."[136]

Angelic opposition also appears in chapter 5 of the *Ladder of Jacob,* which offers an interpretation of the protagonist's vision. The interpreting angel explains to the earthly Jacob the following meaning of the ladder:

> Thus he [*angelus interpres*] said to me [Jacob]: "You have seen a ladder with twelve steps, each step having two human faces which kept changing their appearance. The ladder is this age, and the twelve steps are the periods of this age. But the twenty-four faces are the kings of the ungodly nations of this age. Under these kings the children of your children and the generations of your sons will be interrogated. These will rise up against the iniquity of your grandsons. And this place will be made desolate by the four ascents . . . through the sins of your grandsons. And around the property of your forefathers a palace will be built, a temple in the name of your God and of (the God) of your fathers, and in the provocations of your children it will become deserted by the four ascents of this age. For you saw the first four busts which were striking against the steps . . . angels ascending and descending, and the busts amid the steps. The Most High will raise up kings from the grandsons of your brother Esau, and they will receive all the nobles of the tribes of the earth who will have maltreated your seed."[137]

In this description the twelve steps of the ladder represent the twelve periods of "this age," while the twenty-four "minor" faces denote the twenty-four kings of the ungodly nations. Ascending and descending angels on the ladder are envisioned as the guardian angels belonging to the nations hostile to Jacob and his descendants. The angelic locomotions, or "ascents," appear to be construed in the passage as sets of arrogations against Israel. The historic framework of this revelation is influenced by the fourfold scheme of the antagonistic empires reflected in the Book of Daniel through the reference to the "four ascents" and also through the familiar features of the Danielic empires (specifically, the last of the four kingdoms, Rome, represented by Esau).[138]

The description found in the *Ladder* has been obscured by the text's long journey in various ideological milieus, but a clearer presentation of the same constellation of peculiar details is extant in several rabbinic accounts.[139] Thus, for example, *Lev. Rab.* 29:2 provides the following description:

> R. Nahman opened his discourse with the text, Therefore fear thou not, O Jacob My servant (Jer 30:10). This speaks of Jacob himself, of whom it is written, And he dreamed, and behold, a ladder set

> up on the earth . . . and behold the angels of God ascending and descending on it (Gen 28:12). These angels, explained R. Samuel b. Nahman, were the guardian Princes of the nations of the world. For R. Samuel b. Nahman said: This verse teaches us that the Holy One, blessed be He, showed our father Jacob the Prince of Babylon ascending seventy rungs of the ladder, the Prince of Media fifty-two rungs, the Prince of Greece one hundred and eighty, while the Prince of Edom ascended till Jacob did not know how many rungs. Thereupon our father Jacob was afraid. He thought: Is it possible that this one will never be brought down? Said the Holy One, blessed be He, to him: Fear thou not, O Jacob My servant. Even if he ascend and sit down by Me, I will bring him down from there! Hence it is written, Though thou make thy nest as high as the eagle, and though thou set it among the stars, I will bring thee down from thence. R. Berekiah and R. Helbo, and R. Simeon b. Yohai in the name of R. Meir said: It teaches that the Holy One, blessed be He, showed Jacob the Prince of Babylon ascending and descending, of Media ascending and descending, of Greece ascending and descending, and of Edom ascending and descending.[140]

A similar understanding of the descending and ascending angels as political entities that are hostile to Israel can be found in *Midrash on Psalms* 78:6:

> R. Berechiah, R. Levi, and R. Simeon ben Jose taught in the name of R. Meir that the Holy One, blessed be He, let Jacob see a ladder upon which Babylon climbed up seventy rungs and came down, Media climbed up fifty-two rungs and came down, Greece climbed up a hundred and eighty rungs and came down. But when Edom climbed higher than these, Jacob saw and was afraid. The Holy One, blessed be He, said to him, Therefore fear thou not, O Jacob My servant (Jer 30:10). Even as the former fell, so will the latter fall.[141]

The similarities with the Danielic account are even more apparent in these rabbinic passages than in the *Ladder*, since the familiar fourfold structure is now represented by Babylon, Media, Greece, and Edom, the empires which are often associated in the history of interpretation with the four beasts of Daniel 7.[142] Kugel notes that in these materials, like in the *Ladder of Jacob*, "the four beasts [of Daniel's vision] are transformed into 'angels of God' said to go up and down Jacob's ladder."[143]

This peculiar theme of the hostile angels on the heavenly ladder, who arrogate against Jacob and his progeny by their ascents and descents, provides additional evidence that the authors of the *Ladder* were cognizant of the motif of angelic opposition that plays such a pivotal role in the inauguration ritual.

II. Induction into the Divine Image in Early Christian Materials

Enlightened by the legacy of Jewish traditions, we can now proceed to a close analysis of traces of the inauguration ritual in the earliest Christian materials. Indeed, some Christian writers appear to be cognizant of the story of Adam's induction. Crispin Fletcher-Louis argues that "there are passages in the New Testament that may know the story. Chief among these is Heb 1:6, which says when God brought the firstborn into the world, he said 'Let all the angels of God worship (*proskynēsatōsan*) him.' "[144] He further suggests that

> given the ways in which Jesus undoes the disobedience of Adam in the Gospel temptation story, it is also possible that the reference to the angels serving him in Mark 1:13 and Matt 4:11 is an allusion to the story of the angelic worship of Adam that is meant to alert the reader to the fact that the angels already recognize his true identity as the one who inaugurates a new humanity, and in rendering him worshipful service they anticipate the future worship of him by his human followers.[145]

Fletcher-Louis's suggestions are valuable contributions. Keeping his insights in mind, we will turn to developments found in the synoptic gospels.

Adoration of the Magi

The second chapter of the first gospel speaks about mysterious visitors from the East who came to pay homage to the newborn king of the Jews. Some details of the Matthean version suggest that it unfolds not simply as a story of veneration by foreign guests, but possibly as an account of angelic obeisance to the newly inaugurated image of God. Some scholars have identified important angelological details within the narrative. For example, the mysterious star that assists the magi on their journey to the messiah may, in fact, be an angel—specifically, a guiding angel whose function is to lead the foreign visitors to Jesus.[146] This role is reminiscent of the archangel Michael's actions during Adam's inauguration in the *Primary Adam Books*, where he directs the angelic hosts for the purpose of venerating the protoplast. Other features of the story also betray the presence of familiar details of Adam's inauguration. In both stories, the protagonists just come into existence. Furthermore, like in other eschatological reinterpretations of the inauguration ceremony, the baby Jesus is envisioned as an eschatological counterpart of the first human. Just as in the protoplast's creation, which is marked by angelic veneration in the *Primary Adam Books*, the entrance of the last Adam into the world ought to be celebrated by a similar ritual of angelic obeisance.

Other features of the magi story also reveal possible Adamic roots. The origin of the magi from the East (ἀπὸ ἀνατολῶν) hints at a possible connection with Eden, a garden which, according to biblical testimonies, was planted in the East.[147] Gifts of the magi, including frankincense and myrrh, were traditionally used in antiquity as ingredients of incense.[148] These bring to mind Adam's sacrifices, which, according to Jewish extrabiblical lore, the protoplast was offering in the Garden of Eden in fulfillment of his sacerdotal duties. Such sacrifices are mentioned in *Jub.* 3:27, a passage depicting Adam as the protological high priest[149] who once burned incense sacrifices in Paradise.[150] In view of these possible cultic features of the magi story, Jesus might be understood there not simply as the last Adam, but as a priestly eschatological Adam in a fashion reminiscent of the *Book of Jubilees*. In light of these traditions, the magi could be understood as visitors, possibly even angelic visitors, from the Garden of Eden, once planted in the East, who bring to a new protoplast the sacerdotal tools used in the distant past by Adam.[151] This exegetical connection is not implausible given that some later Christian materials, including *Cave of Treasures*, associate the gifts of the magi with Adam's sacrifices.[152]

Other details of the magi narrative, such as the peculiar juxtaposition of its antagonistic figure with the theme of worship, again bring to mind the protoplast story reflected in various versions of the *Primary Adam Books* with its motifs of angelic veneration and Satan's refusal to worship the first human. Matthew even connects the main antagonist of the magi story, Herod, with the theme of veneration by telling how the evil king promised to worship the messianic child,[153] but, in reality, was planning to kill him for fear that he would take his royal place. Here, the tension between the former and new claimant to the exalted position is reminiscent of Satan's demotion and Adam's exaltation in the *Primary Adam Books*.

The magi narrative initiates the peculiar pattern of veneration that will continue to dominate the first gospel. The significance of the veneration motif for Matthew will be further illustrated in our analysis below of the inauguration patterns found in the temptation story and the transfiguration account.[154] All three narratives (the magi, the temptation, and the transfiguration) share identical terminology of veneration through their usage of the Greek verb πίπτω.[155] The same Greek verb was also used by the author of the *Exagoge*—the only account among Jewish witnesses to the inauguration ceremony that survived in Greek. At the end of Jesus's transfiguration on the mountain in Matthew's gospel, the familiar veneration motif will appear again, when the disciples, overwhelmed with their vision, throw themselves down with their faces to the ground.[156] This depiction of the disciples' prostration at Jesus's transfiguration is absent in both Mark and Luke. Yet in Matthew, this motif seems to fit nicely in the chain of previous veneration occurrences, thus evoking the memory of both the falling down of the magi and Satan's quest for prostration—traditions, likewise, absent from other synoptic accounts.[157]

Temptation Account

In previous studies, I have suggested that Jesus's identity as the *Imago Dei* may be present in the Matthean version of Jesus's temptation in the wilderness, where one can find traces of the inauguration ritual.[158] Two of the most notable features are the motifs of angelic opposition and angelic veneration, which we have seen in the *Primary Adam Books*, *2 Enoch*, the *Prayer of Joseph*, the *Ladder of Jacob*, and, possibly, the *Exagoge*.[159] In each case these motifs are crucial narrative markers connected with the protagonist's role as the image of God.[160]

Even a cursory look at the temptation story as found in Matthew's gospel reveals a striking panoply of allusions to Adam's inauguration. Like the *Primary Adam Books*, which portray Satan as a celestial power endowed with attributes of the deity, the temptation story associates its enigmatic antagonist with a plethora of exalted attributes, placing him on the high mountain of his theophany, reminiscent of the summit of the divine Glory as it is depicted in some biblical and pseudepigraphical accounts. The choice of the mountain for the antagonist's apotheosis is not happenstance, since in the Enochic and Mosaic traditions such a place is often envisioned as the seat of the divine Glory. If the Gospel of Matthew has in mind the mountain of the *Kavod*, in Satan's ability to show Jesus all the kingdoms of the world and their splendor, we may have a possible reference to the celestial curtain, *Pargod*, the sacred veil of the divine presence, which in *3 Enoch* 45 is described as an entity that literally depicts all generations and all kingdoms simultaneously at the same time.[161]

These associations of the antagonist with this familiar symbolism that is usually tied in Jewish apocalyptic and mystical accounts to the *Kavod* imagery are noteworthy. Furthermore, in the temptation story, Satan fulfills the roles of Jesus's psychopomp and the *angelus interpres*. Here we find another allusion to Satan's role as a celestial power. Scholars have noted terminological similarities between the temptation narrative and Deut 34:1–4,[162] in which God serves as an *angelus interpres* for Moses, showing him the promised land during the prophet's vision on Mount Nebo.[163]

In the *Primary Adam Books*, Satan serves as a negative "mirror" of Adam and, in this respect, a negative icon of the deity, often revealing and reaffirming the protagonist's exalted status by comparing the new appointee's glory with his own previous exalted state. In the *Primary Adam Books*, therefore, a bulk of information about the exalted attributes of the protoplast is conveyed through Satan's laments. These laments also narrate a conflict between two favorites of the deity, when the former holder of this exalted office retaliates for his lost status by attempting to seduce and to corrupt the new darling of the deity. To this end, the antagonist assumes various celestial forms in an attempt to mislead the first human and his consort. This tradition about the antagonist, who serves as an inverse mirror and contender with the protagonist, can also be found in the longer versions of the temptation story reflected in Matthew and Luke.

Furthermore, one finds a curious reversal in the temptation story—Satan, who fell because he once refused to venerate the First Adam, now takes revenge by asking the Last Adam to bow down before him.[164]

Such Adamic typology is often recognized as a conceptual backbone of the temptation story. Some studies suggest that the chain of pivotal Adamic themes known from biblical and extra-biblical accounts is already present in the terse narration of Jesus's temptation in the Gospel of Mark.[165] For example, Joachim Jeremias argued that the description found in Mark 1:12 telling that Jesus "was with the wild beasts" (ἦν μετὰ τῶν θηρίων) is reminiscent of Adam living among the wild animals in paradise, according to Gen 2:19. Jeremias suggests that Jesus is identified in Mark as an eschatological Adam who restores peace between humans and animals.[166] Mark's account sets forth the belief that "paradise is restored, the time of salvation is dawning; that is what ἦν μετὰ τῶν θηρίων means. Because the temptation has been overcome and Satan has been vanquished, the gate to paradise is again opened."[167] Jeremias's insights are important for our study as they point to the possibility that already in the Markan version of Jesus's temptation, Jesus is understood as the image of God. In this respect, it is noteworthy that the *Primary Adam Books* construe the possession/absence of the image of God in humanity through motifs of obedience or hostility of the wild beast.

Jeremias also discerns Adamic typology in the saying that the angels gave Jesus "table service" (διηκόνουν αὐτῷ). In his view, "this feature, too, is part of the idea of paradise and can only be understood in that light. Just as, according to the Midrash, Adam lived on angels' food in paradise, so the angels give Jesus nourishment. The table-service of angels is a symbol of the restored communion between man and God."[168] Richard Bauckham also sees a cluster of Adamic motifs in Mark's version of the temptation story and argues that it envisions Jesus "as the eschatological Adam who, having resisted Satan, instead of succumbing to temptation as Adam did, then restores paradise: he is at peace with the animals and the angels serve him."[169] From this perspective, Jesus's temptation by Satan plays a pivotal role in the unfolding of the Adamic typological appropriations.[170] Dale Allison draws attention to yet another possible connection with the protoplast story by wondering whether Mark's "forty days" is also part of his Adamic typology. According to *Jub.* 3:9, Adam was placed in Eden forty days after he was created, and, in the *Primary Adam Books,* Adam does penance for forty days.[171]

In Matthew and Luke, the Adamic typology hinted at in Mark receives further development, being closely tied now to already familiar features of the inauguration ritual. Thus, in Matthew's gospel the tempter asks Jesus to prostrate himself, suggesting literally that he "fall down" (πεσών) before Satan. The same verb πίπτω was used in the description of the stars' obeisance in the *Exagoge* and later in Matthew's version of the transfiguration account, where the disciples fall on their faces in fear. In this case Matthew seems to stick more closely to the Adamic blueprint than Luke, since in Luke πεσών is missing.

The theme of veneration is introduced in the temptation story by Satan himself. Here the old motif of obeisance is reformulated in the novel Christian framework. Instead of giving obeisance to the new, eschatological image of God, who has just been inaugurated in his office at the Jordan theophany, the antagonist seeks to reverse this process by asking Jesus to venerate him. It again demonstrates the essential nature of angelic obeisance in the formation of the identity and authority of the personified divine image. Such veneration usually comes at the final stage of the inauguration, signifying the acceptance of the adept into his new role as the deity's icon. Yet here it may also be compared to the first veneration that Adam rendered to God. Satan, endowed with striking divine attributes, might paradoxically take the deity's role.

The motif of the rejection of veneration, explicitly narrated in the *Primary Adam Books* and then reiterated in many other Jewish accounts, plays its own unique role in the construction of a new Adam within the temptation story. By refusing to venerate Satan, Jesus provides an eschatological revenge for Satan's protological refusal.

Jesus's installation into the office of the image of God, which takes place especially in the baptism and temptation narratives, does not result in mockery but in actual angelic veneration.[172] Mark and Matthew both record that the angels ministered to him (διηκόνουν αὐτῷ). As in *2 Enoch* and in some other eschatological reinterpretations of the inauguration ceremony, where the motif of angelic opposition precedes the motif of angelic veneration, here, too, in the temptation story, Jesus's opposition to the veneration of Satan is narrated prior to the angelic obeisance at the end of the story. The temptation story, like some other versions of the induction ritual, deconstructs the protological scenario of the protoplast's inauguration ceremony found in the *Primary Adam Books* by refashioning it into a new eschatological ordeal that still preserves memories of the old encounter. In this respect, it is not coincidental that Satan, the old antagonist, is again present during the inauguration of Jesus into the office of the image of God, just as he was during Adam's inauguration.

The Transfiguration Account

JESUS'S IQONIN

Our study has demonstrated that in some early Jewish versions of the inauguration ritual, "face" served as a cognate for "image." Such symbolic interplay may also be found in the accounts of the transfiguration story, by Matthew and Luke,[173] in which one can find references to Jesus's transformed face.[174]

In previous studies, Jesus's visage was almost exclusively interpreted through the spectacles of the biblical traditions of Moses's *panim*. Yet, these studies ignored another important conceptual stream in which the *panim* became a terminological correlative for different concept prominent in many early Jewish accounts: namely, the image of God, or His *iqonin*. We have discerned such a correlation in early Enoch and Jacob traditions, where *tselem* was often used interchangeably with *panim*. If in Matthew and Luke's transfiguration account Jesus's face was indeed understood as his *iqonin*, it provides an important connection with other early Jewish accounts where the protagonist's role as the image of God is closely linked with the symbolism of his *panim*. It is especially noticeable in the *Ladder of Jacob*. There, the conceptual bridge between the notions of image and face is solidified through the concept of Jacob's *iqonin*.[175]

It is important that some later reinterpretations of the synoptic transfiguration accounts contain references to Jacob's face. This can be seen, for example, in the *Apocalypse of Peter* 17:2–6, which reworks the transfiguration scene into an account of Jesus's ascension. Jacques van Ruiten previously noted that "the description of the ascension is connected with the transfiguration scene in the Gospel of Matthew" where "Matt 17:5b is quoted literally."[176] In the conclusion of this reworking, *Apoc. Pet.* 17:4 evokes the motif of God's face and connects it with the name of Jacob: "And the word of scripture was fulfilled: 'This generation seeks him and seeks the face of the God of Jacob.' "[177] This expression "the face of the God of Jacob" explicitly links the Matthean version of transfiguration story—with its imagery of Jesus's face that is referenced by the author(s) of the *Apocalypse of Peter*—to the Jewish theophanic tradition about Jacob's *iqonin* engraved on the face of God.[178]

If an idea of the *iqonin* is indeed present in the symbolism of Jesus's luminous face in the synoptic transfiguration accounts, it is possible that such imagery was not borrowed directly from the Jacob tradition, but instead came from the Mosaic currents that exercised an unmatched formative influence on this Christian theophany. In the extra-biblical Jewish lore, Moses's luminous face is often reinterpreted as his *iqonin*.

For instance, in rendering the account of Moses's shining visage from Exod 34:29, *Targum Pseudo-Jonathan* adds to it the *iqonin* terminology: "At the time that Moses came down from Mount Sinai, with the two tables of the testimony in [his] hand as he came down from the mountain, Moses did not know that the splendor of the *iqonin* of his face shone because of the splendor of the Glory of the Shekinah of the Lord at the time that he spoke with him."[179] The next verse (34:30) of the same targumic account also uses the *iqonin* formulae: "Aaron and all the children of Israel saw Moses, and behold, the *iqonin* of his face shone; and they were afraid to go near him."[180] Finally, verses 33–35 speak about Moses's veil, again demonstrating the appropriation of the *iqonin* symbolism:

> When Moses ceased speaking with them, he put a veil on the *iqonin* of his face. Whenever Moses went in before the Lord to speak with him, he would remove the veil that was on the *iqonin* of his face until he came out. And he would come out and tell the children of Israel what he had been commanded. The children of Israel would see Moses' *iqonin* that the splendor of the *iqonin* of Moses' face shone. Then Moses would put the veil back on his face until he went in to speak with him.[181]

In these targumic renderings of the biblical passages about Moses's shining face, one can see the creative interplay between the *panim* and *tselem* symbolism. The application of the "image" terminology to Moses's story here has profound anthropological significance insofar as Moses's luminosity eventually was envisioned as a restoration of Adam's original *tselem*, which, according to some traditions, was itself a luminous reality. The Adamic connection is often articulated in various non-biblical accounts that describe Moses's luminous face. Thus, the Samaritan *Memar Marqah* makes a connection between the shining face of Moses and the luminosity of Adam's image. Linda Belleville notes that several passages of this Samaritan collection link Moses's light with the primordial light with which Adam was first invested, but later lost.[182]

Such an understanding of Moses's shining face as a restoration of the original luminous *tselem* is also indicated in later rabbinic midrashim where the protoplast's glorious image conspicuously parallels the radiant *panim* of the great prophet.[183] We find this parallel in *Deut. Rab.* 11:3:

> Adam said to Moses: 'I am greater than you because I have been created in the image of God.' Whence this? For it is said, And God

created man in His own image (Gen 1:27). Moses replied to him: "I am far superior to you, for the honor which was given to you has been taken away from you, as it is said, But man (Adam) abideth not in honor (Ps 49:13); but as for me, the radiant countenance which God gave me still remains with me."[184]

Another specimen of this tradition is found in *Midrash Tadshe* 4, where the creation of Adam in God's image is compared with the bestowal of luminosity on Moses's face: "In the beginning: 'and God created man in his image,' and in the desert: 'and Moses knew not that the skin of his face shone.'"[185] Later rabbinic materials often speak of the luminosity of Adam's face,[186] the feature that most likely points to the Adam-Moses connection. For example, in *Lev. Rab.* 20:2, the following correlation can be found:

> Resh Lakish, in the name of R. Simeon the son of Menasya, said: The apple of Adam's heel outshone the globe of the sun; how much more so the *brightness of his face*! Nor need you wonder. In the ordinary way if a person makes salvers, one for himself and one for his household, whose will he make more beautiful? Not his own? Similarly, Adam was created for the service of the Holy One, blessed be He, and the globe of the sun for the service of mankind.[187]

In a similar tradition, *Genesis Rabbah* 11 does not focus on Adam's luminous garments, but rather on his glorious face:

> Adam's glory did not abide the night with him. What is the proof? But Adam passeth not the night in glory (Ps 49:13). The Rabbis maintain: His glory abode with him, but at the termination of the Sabbath He deprived him of his splendor and expelled him from the Garden of Eden, as it is written, Thou changest *his countenance*, and sendest him away (Job 14:20).[188]

The initial roots of the preceding rabbinic trajectories can be traced to the documents of the Second Temple period. For example, the theme of the superiority of Moses over Adam can already be detected in Philo. Wayne Meeks draws attention to a similar tradition from the *Quaestiones et Solutiones in Exodum* 2.46, which identifies the ascendant Moses with the heavenly man[189] created in God's image on the seventh day:[190]

> But the calling above of the prophet is a second birth better than the first. . . . For he is called on the seventh day, in this (respect)

> differing from the earth-born first molded man, for the latter came into being from the earth and with body, while the former (came) from the ether and without body. Wherefore the most appropriate number, six, was assigned to the earth-born man, while to the one differently born (was assigned) the higher nature of the hebdomad.[191]

It is possible that such an interpretation of Moses's shining visage, not merely as the luminous face but also functioning as the luminous image, could stand behind the symbolism of Jesus's luminous face within the synoptic versions of the transfiguration account. In the peculiar theophanic context of the transfiguration account, with its postulation of God's invisibility, the famous Pauline dictum about Christ as the image of the invisible God can be seen in an entirely new light.

PROSTRATION MOTIF

Among the synoptic gospels, only Matthew relates the tradition in which the disciples, upon hearing the divine utterance, fall on their faces (ἔπεσαν ἐπὶ πρόσωπον αὐτῶν), overwhelmed by fear. Jesus then raises them up, encouraging them not to be afraid. Scholars often see these additions as the most important Matthean contributions. Ulrich Luz, for example, argues that "the most important Matthean change in the transfiguration story is the addition of vv. 6–7, telling of the disciples' fear and how Jesus raises them up."[192]

Scholars often see the disciples' reactions of fear and obeisance in Matthew as related solely to the aural manifestation of God, namely, His Voice.[193] Yet Jesus's peculiar affirmations to "get up" and "don't be afraid," often found in the Jewish and Christian visionary accounts, lead us to a different interpretation. Very similar exhortations to get up or not to fear are usually given to visionaries in Jewish theophanic accounts by the very objects of such visions: angelic or divine figures, whose sudden appearance provokes feelings of fear and reverence.[194] For example, Dan 10:9–12 has a similar constellation of distinctive features when a celestial visitor touches a prostrated seer filled with fear and tells him not to be afraid:

> then I heard the sound of his words; and when I heard the sound of his words, I fell into a trance, face to the ground. But then a hand touched me and roused me to my hands and knees. He said to me, "Daniel, greatly beloved, pay attention to the words that I am going to speak to you. Stand on your feet, for I have now been sent to you." So while he was speaking this word to me, I stood up trembling. He said to me, "Do not fear, Daniel, for from the first day that you

set your mind to gain understanding and to humble yourself before your God, your words have been heard, and I have come because of your words."

In Dan 10:18–19, nearly the same pattern emerges: "Again one in human form touched me and strengthened me. He said, 'Do not fear, greatly beloved, you are safe. Be strong and courageous!' When he spoke to me, I was strengthened and said, 'Let my lord speak, for you have strengthened me.'"

This pattern is also found in the Jewish pseudepigrapha.[195] The shorter and longer recensions of *2 Enoch* 1:6–8 portray angels appearing before Enoch. The text recounts that, being overwhelmed with fear, the patriarch prostrates himself before them. The angels then tell the seer not to be afraid: "Then I awoke from my sleep, and saw those men, standing in front of me, in actuality. Then I bowed down to them; and I was terrified; and the appearance of my face was changed because of fear. Then those men said to me, 'Be brave, Enoch! In truth, do not fear!'"[196]

In *2 Enoch* 22 we find a similar scene during the patriarch's encounter with the deity's glorious form, labeled there as God's "face": "I saw the view of the face of the Lord, like iron made burning hot in a fire and brought out, and it emits sparks and is incandescent. . . . And I fell down flat and did obeisance to the Lord. And the Lord, with his own mouth, said to me, 'Be brave, Enoch! Don't be frightened! Stand up, and stand in front of my face forever.'"[197] Here again the phrase "do not fear" (or "be brave") coincides with the action of bringing the adept into a standing position ("stand up").

In the Gospel of Matthew, the disciples' obeisance occurs immediately after the divine affirmation regarding Jesus's exalted status. Therefore, it is possible that the content of the utterance, and not the voice itself, is in fact what provokes the disciples' sudden reaction. William Davies and Dale Allison perceptively notice a certain correspondence between the disciples' bowed faces and the face of the transfigured Jesus: "the motif of falling on one's face in fear is a standard part of any heavenly ascent or revelation story. But here there is more, for there is a contrast between Jesus's face, which is shining, and the faces of the disciples, which are hidden."[198]

It is also important that, unlike Mark, Matthew applies the symbolism of luminous *panim*/face to Jesus, which here, as in other Jewish accounts, may signify the divine image. If so, the disciples' obeisance provides additional evidence that Jesus's face may be envisioned as the *iqonin* in some synoptic versions of the transfiguration story. This conceptually links the transfiguration account to previously explored Jewish narratives with their understanding of the protagonist as the image of God, the office that requires angelic veneration. In addition, the disciples' obeisance in Matthew is rendered through the Greek verb πίπτω. This same verb was used in the *Exagoge* in the depiction of the stars' obeisance to Moses, in the magi story, and in the temptation narrative, when Satan asks Jesus to bow down before him.

Another important similarity with Jewish apocalyptic accounts is how the disciples' prostration occurs after the deity's affirmation about the protagonist's status. The early specimens of this tradition can already be found in *2 Enoch*[199] and the *Primary Adam Books*,[200] where angelic obeisance coincides with affirmations of the protagonist's unique status.

To conclude our analysis of the disciples' obeisance, we can see that in Matthew, such a motif—found only in this gospel—fits very nicely in the chain of previous veneration occurrences, evoking both the memory of the falling down of the magi and that of Satan's quest for prostration.

Conclusion

Previous scholars who searched for remnants of Adam's induction in early Jewish and Christian materials often concentrated on the worship motif, even arguing that the account in the *Primary Adam Books* should be called the "Worship of Adam Story."[201] These studies, however, often ignored other significant features of the inauguration ceremony that provide important indicators which are helpful in the search for other specimens of such rituals. One crucial marker in this respect is the motif of angelic hostility to the newly created protoplast—a motif which maintains an extensive afterlife in various Jewish and Christian materials, including the *Exagoge*, 2 *Enoch*, the *Prayer of Joseph*, the *Ladder of Jacob*, and the synoptic renderings of Jesus's temptation in the wilderness.

Another important marker is the link between notions of "image" and "face," which in later Jewish materials was expressed through the concept of *iqonin*. Attention to this peculiar terminological correspondence, manifested already in early Jewish pseudepigraphical materials such as the *Book of the Similitudes*, *2 Enoch*, and the *Ladder of Jacob*, helps us to discern the traces of the inauguration story in some early Christian materials, including the transfiguration account. The imagery of Jesus's countenance found in these early Christian materials has puzzled generations of scholars who were often quick to default to the biblical tradition of Moses's face in order to explain such symbolism. Yet the story of Adam's inauguration and its perdurance in Enochic, Jacobite, and Mosaic traditions, together with its peculiar juxtaposition of the notions of "face" and "image," provides a new insight into the motif of Jesus's transformed visage in the synoptic gospels.

Close attention to the aforementioned features of the inauguration story may help scholars to locate other early remnants of this conceptual trajectory in which the original Adamic motif received a novel eschatological reinterpretation. Indeed, Adam's induction into the divine image provided a formative blueprint for many eschatological encounters in which various biblical patriarchs and prophets were initiated into the office of the eschatological image of God, thus restoring the crucial protological condition lost by the first human after his transgression in the Garden of Eden.

Chapter Two

Furnace that Kills and Furnace that Gives Life

Fiery Trials and Martyrdom in the *Apocalypse of Abraham*

> And the impure bird spoke to me and said, "What are you doing, Abraham, on the holy heights, where no one eats or drinks, nor is there upon them food of men? But these will all be consumed by fire and they will burn you up. Leave the man who is with you and flee! Since if you ascend to the height, they will destroy you."
>
> —Apocalypse of Abraham 13:4–5

Introduction

Chapters 15–18 of the *Apocalypse of Abraham* discuss the patriarch's journey from the earthly realm to the divine abode, where the seer is predestined to encounter God's presence. Abraham's ascent, however, is marked by grave obstacles in the form of fiery tests that pose danger to his life. The atmosphere of the patriarch's imminent demise looms large in light of earlier events of the story, when Abraham's father, Terah, and his brother, Nahor, died in fire sent by God. Furthermore, immediately before the patriarch's ascension, the main antagonist of the story, the fallen angel Azazel, warns the seer that he will also perish in heavenly fire. Yet despite Azazel's predictions, Abraham safely traverses the fiery thresholds with the help of his angelic guide, Yahoel.

The conceptual background of Abraham's fiery tests has puzzled students of the *Apocalypse*. It has been noticed that Abraham's fiery ordeals echo the tests of Shadrach, Meshach, and Abednego, who were rescued from a fiery furnace by an otherworldly helper. The Danielic story also became an important blueprint for Jewish and Christian martyrdoms in which martyrs, like the protagonist of the *Apocalypse of Abraham*, also endure ascent and theophany by passing through flames. Despite these parallels, the *Apocalypse of Abraham* has rarely been studied in light of Jewish and Christian martyrological traditions. This study attempts to fill this lacuna by closely exploring Abraham's fiery trials and their possible ties to the ordeals of Jewish and Christian martyrs.

I. Fiery Trials in Jewish Lore

Daniel 3

Daniel 3 sets the pattern for future fiery tests of Jewish and Christian martyrs and, accordingly, serves as an important conceptual background for the fiery trials in the *Apocalypse of Abraham*. Several important motifs in the Danielic story became influential precedents not only for the tribulations of Abraham's family in various Jewish accounts, but also for Jewish and Christian martyrdoms in which exemplars of faith are tested by their evil executors. In light of this, it is not coincidental that some see Daniel 3 as a story of martyrdom.[1] A question, however, remains: Can accounts in which protagonists survive their persecution be considered martyrdom? Norman Porteous entertains such a possibility. Comparing Jewish martyrdoms with Daniel 3, Porteous argues:

> The martyr story takes two forms. Either the martyr is faithful unto death and the reward is reserved for another world or a miracle takes place and the martyr's faith is visibly justified. To the former type belongs the story of the martyrdom of the seven heroic brothers and their mother who are all put to a most painful death and are supported in their agony by the hope of a blessed resurrection (2 Macc 7). To the latter type belongs the present story in which faith is justified by manifest miracle. It is quite likely that there is no essential difference in ultimate meaning between these two types of story. They may merely represent two different ways of saying that God will honour the loyalty of his servants. Indeed the link between the two types of story seems to be provided by the magnificent "but if not" of v. 18. The martyr must stand firm whether a miracle takes place or not.[2]

Notably, the story of the three Israelite youths reveals several structural elements that reappear in Jewish and Christian martyrological accounts. These accounts mimic the main narrative steps of the Danielic story: its initial accusations, ultimatums, attempts to persuade, counterarguments, temporary delays and reprieves, final refusals, descents into the furnace, theophanies during the fiery test, miraculous escapes, help of an otherworldly being, and the fiery demise of antagonists or collaborators. All these elements will later secure the role of Daniel 3 as a crucial blueprint for subsequent Jewish and Christian martyrdoms in which the suffering of the righteous was understood as an opportunity for God's vision.[3]

In this respect the Danielic account manifests an important link that connects martyrdom with theophany, attesting to a succession of the adept's demise and exaltation—an element which is at times pivotal in various Jewish and Christian martyrological accounts.[4] Echoes of Daniel 3 are already discernable in the earliest Jewish accounts of martyrological literature devoted to the Antiochian crisis. Although an optimistic story of the three rescued Israelites "did not materialize for those under the reign of Antiochus who chose to follow the youths' example, deliverance for them was simply postponed to an eschatological future time."[5] According to Paul Middleton, "The theology of the second and fourth books of Maccabees, as well as much intertestamental literature, anticipates future vindication of those who die for the Law."[6] While providing an archetype for Jewish martyrs, Daniel 3 was also influential for Christian martyrologies. We can detect, for example, formative influences of the Danielic story already on early Christian accounts, including the *Martyrdom of Polycarp*. It also shaped the ideology of Christian martyrological literature in general. Indeed, Dennis Tucker notes that Daniel 3, and the book as a whole, was formative in shaping a Christian theology of martyrdom, with the three youths in Daniel 3 functioning as a "pattern" (ὑπόδειγμα) for the faithful.[7]

Another influential feature of the Danielic account was its cultic dimension. The fiery trials of Shadrach, Meshach, and Abednego unfold in the midst of sacerdotal debates about proper and improper sacrifices, false and genuine piety, and idolatrous and true manifestations of the deity. Often in such debates the sacerdotal practices and rituals of one religious tradition were tested and deconstructed by other systems of belief and religious practices. Such tension was important to authors of Jewish and Christian martyrological accounts, precisely because resistance to the foreign sacerdotal and sacrificial system constituted the very heart of the conflict. In Daniel 3, for instance, the protagonists of the story make an important choice by refusing to succumb to false piety by declining to worship the king's golden statue. The story of the fiery test therefore is strategically told (as it will be later in the *Apocalypse of Abraham* and many other accounts) in the midst of debates about true and false representations of the deity.

Another important conceptual marker linking Daniel 3 to the *Apocalypse of Abraham* is the presence of a heavenly figure who protects the faithful during their fiery trials. Recall how in Daniel 3 Shadrach, Meshach, and Abednego were rescued by an otherworldly being who miraculously appeared in the midst of fire.[8] Commentators have noted that the Aramaic text preserves the mystique of the otherworldly visitor by not revealing his exact identity. On the other hand, Greek translators of Daniel 3 specify that it is the Angel of the Lord who rescues the three faithful Jews.[9] The fact that the Israelite youths and their otherworldly rescuer are unharmed by the fiery test is polemically juxtaposed with the idolatrous statue of the king; they appear to be understood as forms superior to the idol created by Nebuchadnezzar. In this respect the imagery of the blazing crematory in Daniel 3 represents an important theophanic locus where tested and transformed human beings are able to encounter the divine manifestation in the fire. This portentous opportunity—both for the metamorphosis and vision in the midst of deadly flames—is repeated in Jewish and Christian martyrological accounts, where suffering is understood as a chance for transformation, ascent, and theophany. With respect to the use of Daniel 3 and other Jewish accounts of fiery trials in the martyrdom literature, some note that the story "became a widely used narrative and ideological foundation in the literature of martyrdom. The narrative genre of martyrology resonates in other parts of the story: the saint puts an end to the worship of false gods in his family. He is brought before the regime, and a public debate or investigation of his heresy ensues. He is sentenced to death but is unharmed by the fire or the lions. This is one of the most prevalent patterns in the stories of the tortured Christian saints."[10]

Other studies emphasize the theophanic and transformational proclivities of the Danielic story. Choon Leong Seow, for example, rightly observes that the three Israelite youths "do not only survive the ordeal, they even encounter divine presence in the fire ordeal."[11] He goes on to write:

> The narrator does not say that the four individuals are walking in the furnace, but that they are walking amid the fire . . . the story is that they are with a divine being in the midst of the fire. They encounter divine presence in the middle of the fire. Here, as often in the Old Testament, fire is associated with the presence of God. On Mount Sinai, the presence of God was accompanied by, perhaps even made manifest by, the appearance of fire (Exod 19:16, 19; 20:18, 21) and in Israel's hymnody fire is often associated with the manifestation of God (e.g., Ps 18:8–16; 77:17–20).[12]

The furnace of perdition and death is thus miraculously transformed into the theophanic furnace. Again and again one encounters this inexplicable metamorphosis in Jewish and Christian martyrdoms. By linking the fatal fiery ordeal with the memory of biblical and extra-biblical theophanies, Daniel 3 executes an important paradigm shift in a long-lasting theophanic development within Jewish traditions, thus creating a novel revelatory framework which some scholars designate as "traumatic mysteries."[13] Of course, even classic biblical and pseudepigraphical encounters with divine and angelic beings are laden with profound crises for the human adepts who dare to approach the otherworldly subjects. Yet what is different in the martyrdom theophanies, and often missing in early theophanic patterns, is the presence of an otherworldly antagonist, represented by Satan, Azazel, and other demonic characters, who acts through the physical bodies of the martyrs' persecutors—rulers, priests, soldiers, governors, and judges. Such an antagonist, already present in Daniel 3 in the form of the evil king, is also found in later Jewish and Christian martyrological accounts.

Abraham's Fiery Trials

The theme of the adept's fiery test received further development in Jewish legends about the patriarch Abraham, especially in rabbinic lore.[14] In these sources Abraham is often depicted as a fighter against idolatry whose faith is repeatedly tested in flames by various unjust rulers.

The origins of the "patriarch's fiery ordeal" motif is shrouded in mystery.[15] An early hint regarding Abraham's fiery test may be present in Jud 8:25–27:

> In spite of everything let us give thanks to the Lord our God, who is putting us to the test as he did our ancestors. Remember what he did with Abraham, and how he tested Isaac, and what happened to Jacob in Syrian Mesopotamia, while he was tending the sheep of Laban, his mother's brother. For *he has not tried us with fire, as he did them*, to search their hearts, nor has he taken vengeance on us; but the Lord scourges those who are close to him in order to admonish them.

Though some scholars see here a reference to Abraham's trials in the furnace,[16] this cannot be established with certainty, since it also could refer to the wood/fire of the Akedah, or to the fiery sacrifices of the patriarch in Gen 15, or even to the fire of Sodom and Gomorrah.

Another early witness that might attest to the early existence of a tradition of Abraham's fiery trials is a testimony preserved in Eusebius's *Praeparatio Evangelica* 9.20.1 and attributed to Philo the Epic Poet, an author who flourished in the second century BCE. Eusebius cites the following fragment of Philo: "For this one [Abraham] who left the splendid enclosure of the awesome race, the praiseworthy One [God] with a thundering sound prevented (Abraham from carrying out) the immolation."[17] According to James Kugel, scholars traditionally interpret the immolation motif in this passage "as a reference to God's stopping of the sacrifice of Isaac, or the destruction of Sodom and Gomorrah."[18] Despite these common interpretations, however, Kugel suggests that "it may well be that the 'immolation' in question was the burning of Abraham in a fiery furnace. If so, then this motif would arguably go back to the second century BCE."[19]

The earliest surviving account in which the theme of Abraham's fiery trial appears with certainty, and already in full-blown narrative complexity, is a lengthy passage found in Pseudo-Philo's *Biblical Antiquities (Liber Antiquitatum Biblicarum)*.[20] *LAB* 6:1–18 runs as follows:

> Then all those who had been separated while inhabiting the earth afterwards gathered and dwelled together. Setting out from the east, they found a plain in the land of Babylon. They dwelled there and said to each other, "Behold, it will come about that we will be scattered from each other and in later times we will be fighting each other. Therefore, come now, let us build for ourselves a tower whose top will reach the heavens, and we will make for ourselves a name and a glory upon the earth." They said to each other, "Let us take bricks and let each of us write our names on the bricks and burn them with fire; and what will be burned will serve as mortar and brick." They each took their own bricks, aside from twelve men who refused to take them. These are their names: Abram, Nahor, Lot, Ruge, Tenute, Zaba, Armodat, Jobab, Esar, Abimahel, Saba, Aufin. The people of that land seized them and brought them to their chiefs. . . . Joktan, who was the chief of the leaders, answered, ". . . a period of seven days will be given them, and if they repent their evil plans and are willing to contribute bricks with you, they may live. If not, let it be done, let them be burned then in accord with your judgment."
>
> When seven days had passed, the people assembled and spoke to their leader, "Deliver to us the men who refused to join in our plan, and we will burn them in the fire." The leaders sent men to bring them, but they found no one except Abram alone. . . . They took Abram and brought him to their leaders. . . . They took him and built a furnace and lit it with fire. They threw the bricks into the furnace to be fired. Then the leader Joktan, dismayed, took Abram and threw him with the bricks into the fiery furnace. But God stirred up a great earthquake, and burning fire leaped forth out of the furnace into flames and sparks of flame, and it burned up all those standing around in front of the furnace. All those who were consumed in that day were 83,500. But there was not even the

> slightest injury to Abram from the burning of the fire. Abram arose out of the furnace, and the fiery furnace collapsed. And Abram was saved and went off to the eleven men who had been hiding in the mountains, and he told them everything that had happened to him. They went down with him from the mountains, rejoicing in the name of the Lord. No one who met them frightened them that day. They named that place after the name of Abram and in the language of the Chaldeans "Deli," which means "God."[21]

Pseudo-Philo's account demonstrates conceptual and structural complexities indicating that the theme of fiery trials for Abraham and his household was already quite popular in early Jewish lore prior to *LAB*. Indeed, students of this account often point to another important earlier witness to the fiery trials of Abraham's family found in *Jubilees* 12, where one finds the following description of the fiery ordeal of Abraham's brother, Haran:

> In the sixtieth year of Abram's life (which was the fourth week in its fourth year), Abram got up at night and burned the temple of the idols. He burned everything in the temple but no one knew (about it). They got up at night and wanted to save their gods from the fire. Haran dashed in to save them, but the fire raged over him. He was burned in the fire and died in Ur of the Chaldeans before his father Terah. They buried him in Ur of the Chaldeans.[22]

Already in *Jubilees* one notices a number of important details that are later present in Abraham's story in Pseudo-Philo, the *Apocalypse of Abraham,* and rabbinic materials. Yet, in comparison with *Jubilees*' witness, which tells about Haran's death, Pseudo-Philo's passage reveals an important paradigm shift by extending the fiery ordeal to Abraham himself, presenting him with a crucial challenge that tests both Abraham's faith and the power of his God.

From *Jubilees* 12, we learn that Haran "was burned in the fire and died in Ur of the Chaldeans." Already here "fire" and "Ur" are conspicuously connected. Such a link will reappear in the later accounts. As a result, some suggest that "the legend of Abraham in a furnace is based on the interpretation of the place-name Ur (Gen 15:7) as 'fire.' "[23] Geza Vermes claims that "by interpreting אור as 'fire,' ancient commentators of Genesis 15:7 ('I am the Lord who brought you out of אור of the Chaldeans') created a legend out of a pun."[24] Still, Vermes rightly notes that the haggadah of Abraham in the fiery furnace does not originate merely from a verbal pun, but from the reinterpretation of one scriptural account by another.[25] This scriptural passage is, of course, the story about the three Israelite youths in Daniel 3.

Several scholars have noticed that Pseudo-Philo's testimony was profoundly shaped by the tradition of the fiery trials found in the third chapter of the Book of Daniel. Vermes argues that the exegetical association with Daniel 3 is further substantiated by *Genesis Rabbah* and other rabbinic accounts. In this respect, the Danielic allusions help to establish the chronological boundaries for the origins of the Abrahamic tradition. In view of Daniel 3 as a possible source of the fiery trials tradition, Vermes stresses that "from the point of view of dating, the *terminus a quo* for the legend of the fiery furnace is the Book of Daniel, and the *terminus ad quem*, Pseudo-Philo, i.e., roughly the period between 150 BC and 50 AD."[26] John Collins has also discerned the conceptual ties between Abraham's trials in Pseudo-Philo and the story of Shadrach, Meshach, and Abednego,[27] noting that "the tradition that Abraham was saved out of a fiery furnace (which involves a Hebrew wordplay on Ur, his place of origin in the Bible) is later than Daniel and may be influenced by it."[28]

LAB 6 as a Martyrological Account

It is important for our study that the first extant narrative attesting to the story of Abraham's fiery tests exhibits the features of a martyrological account.[29] This association has been noted by many. Thus, Howard Jacobson draws attention to the motif of the time extension that the antagonist of the story gives to Abraham. He notes that "the theme of an 'extension of time' which the tyrant grants the Jew (or Christian) to enable him to decide whether or not he will rebel against God in some fashion or other is regular in martyrologies."[30] Jacobson suggests that *LAB*'s account falls into the martyr-tale pattern in a number of other features, including attempts to persuade, counterarguments, temporary delay and reprieve, and final refusal.[31] Recall that these elements are especially prominent in Daniel 3. In this respect, Pseudo-Philo's passage further develops martyrological proclivities of the Danielic story, shepherding its martyrological features into the framework of Abrahamic lore. James Kugel has also pointed out the distinct martyrological thrust in the motif of Abraham's fiery trials, even suggesting that the roots of such martyrological tradition are traceable to the time of Roman persecution. The fact "that Abraham in this new motif became a martyr willing to surrender his very life for his beliefs may also suggest a post-*Jubilees* dating: the theme of Jewish martyrdom became particularly characteristic of midrashic creation from the period of the Roman persecution."[32]

The Theme of Idolatry

Similar to Daniel 3, where the fiery trial unfolds in the midst of polemics involving idolatry, Pseudo-Philo envisions Abraham's ordeals as a distinct stand against idols. Noting this theme, scholars have entertained the possibility that the infamous biblical tower in Pseudo-Philo's passage might be representative of an idol.[33] If so, it is no coincidence that our account juxtaposes the story about the builders of the idolatrous structure with Abraham's spiritual career, thereby listing this paradigmatic biblical opponent of idolatry among those who refused to participate in the infamous international project.

Another important feature of the account is the presence of an unjust leader who conducts fiery tests against the patriarch; this is similar to the royal opponent in Daniel. Although in Pseudo-Philo the antagonist's role is played by the mysterious Joktan, in later rabbinic accounts this treacherous task is attributed to Nimrod.[34] One can discern in the imagery of the unjust rulers who put Abraham in the fiery oven a subtle allusion to Daniel's depiction[35] of Nebuchadnezzar.[36] Despite the fact that earlier accounts obscure the parallel between Nimrod and Nebuchadnezzar, later rabbinic versions make the connection more lucid and explicit.

The story of Abraham's fiery test was not forgotten by early Christian exegetes. The tradition was often invoked in an attempt to reconcile the chronology of Abraham's life. Thus, Augustine in *De civitate Dei* XVI.15 seems to have knowledge of this motif when he writes: "the seventy-five years of Abraham when he departed out of Haran are reckoned from the year in which he was delivered from the fire of the Chaldeans."[37] Jerome, in his *Hebrew Questions on Genesis* 11–12 (ca. 392 CE), provides even more details concerning the patriarch's test in flames:

> And Aran died before his father in the land in which he was born in the territory of the Chaldeans. In place of what we read as in the territory of the Chaldeans, in the Hebrew it has in *ur Chesdim*, that is, "in the fire of the Chaldeans." Moreover the Hebrews, taking the opportunity afforded by this verse, hand on a story of this sort to the effect that Abraham was put into the fire because he refused to worship fire, which the Chaldeans honour; and that he escaped through God's help, and fled from the fire of idolatry. What is written [in the Septuagint] in the following verses, that Thara with his offspring "went out from the territory of the Chaldeans" stands in place of what is contained in the Hebrew, from the fire of the Chaldeans. And they maintain that this refers to what is said in this verse: Aran died before the face of Thara his father in the land of his birth in the fire of the Chaldeans; that is, because, he refused to worship fire he was consumed by fire. Then afterwards the Lord spoke to Abraham: I am the One Who led you out of the fire of the Chaldeans . . . and Thara with his sons went out from the fire of Chaldeans, and that

> Abram, when surrounded by the Babylonian fire because he refused to worship it, was set free by God's help.[38]

One can see that, like their Jewish counterparts, Christian exegetes are also familiar with the connection between "fire" and "Ur."

Some Samaritan materials that are based on early traditions also demonstrate familiarity with the story of the patriarch's martyrdom in the hands of the evil king. For example, *Asatir* 5:25–28 reads:

> And Nimrod commanded that each man should return to his place. And after that Abraham was born with mighty glory. And Nimrod took him and threw him into the fire because he has said "The world has a God." And when Haran was wroth with Abraham and said he was a wizard the fire came out and consumed him "and Haran died in the presence of his father Terah in Ur Kasdim." After seven years he (Nimrod) died.[39]

The theme of Abraham's fiery trials then receives wide circulation in various rabbinic corpora. For our study it is important that in these later accounts, the martyrological dimension of the fiery exams often comes to the fore.[40] Thus, the authors of various Palestinian targums are cognizant of the patriarch's fiery ordeal. *Targum Pseudo-Jonathan* to Gen 11:28 reads:

> It came to pass, when Nimrod cast Abram into the furnace of fire because he would not worship his idol, the fire had no power to burn him. Then Haran was undecided, and he said: "If Nimrod triumphs, I will be on his side; but if Abram triumphs, I will be on his side." And when all the people who were there saw that the fire had no power over Abram, they said to themselves: "Is not Haran the brother of Abram full of divination and sorcery? It is he who uttered charms over the fire so that it would not burn his brother." Immediately fire fell from the heavens on high and consumed him; and Haran died in the sight of Terah his father, being burned in the land of his birth in the furnace of fire which the Chaldeans had made for Abram his brother.[41]

This passage attempts to advance a controversial profile of Haran, linking him to practices of divination and sorcery. Such a tendency is reminiscent of some details found in the first, haggadic portion of the *Apocalypse of Abraham*, where members of Terah's household are involved in various divinatory routines.

Targum Pseudo-Jonathan to Gen 14:1 continues the theme of the patriarch's fiery test by underlying Nimrod's role as the chief antagonist: "in the day of Amraphel—he is Nimrod who ordered Abram to be thrown into the fire. . . ."[42] Further references to the fiery ordeals can also be found in *Targum Pseudo-Jonathan* to Gen 15:7[43] and Gen 16:5.[44]

Another Palestinian targumic composition, *Targum Neofiti,* is cognizant of Haran's demise and Abraham's survival of the Chaldean fire. From *Targum Neofiti* to Gen 11:28–31 we learn that "Haran died during the lifetime of Terah his father in the land of his birth, in the furnace of fire of the Chaldeans. . . . And Terah took Abram his son and Lot, his grandson, and Sarai his daughter-in-law, his son Abram's wife, and went forth with them from the furnace of the fire of the Chaldeans, to go to the land of Canaan; and they arrived at Haran and dwelt there."[45] *Targum Neofiti* to Gen 15:7 further continues the theme of fiery tribulations by telling that the deity rescued Abraham out of the Chaldean furnace.[46]

Some other targumic compositions are also cognizant of the fiery trials story. For example, *Targum Rishon of Esther* 5:14 mentions that "Into the fire you cannot cast him [Mordecai], for his ancestor Abraham was saved from it."[47] *Targum of Second Chronicles* 28:3, furthermore, provides an interesting list of various biblical characters who endured the test of flames:

> It was he who offered up incense in the valley of Bar Hinnom and made his sons pass through the fire. Of them, however, the Memra of the Lord rescued Hezekiah, because it had been revealed before the Lord, that from him three righteous men were destined to come forth, Hananiah, Mishael, and Azariah, who were determined to hand over their bodies to be thrown into the midst of the furnace of burning fire for the sake of the great and glorious Name, and they were rescued from the fire. First of all, Abraham was rescued from the burning of the furnace of fire of the Chaldeans, into which Nimrod had cast him because he would not serve his idols. Secondly, Tamar was rescued from the burning of the fire of Judah's tribunal when he had said: "Take her out and let her be burned!" Thirdly, Hezekiah, the son of Jotham, was rescued from the burning of the fire when his father threw him into the valley of Bar Hinnom, on the altars of Topheth. Fourthly, Hananiah, Mishael, and Azariah were rescued from the furnace of burning fire of Nebuchadnezzar, the king of Babylon. Fifthly, Joshua, the son of Jehozadak, the chief priest, was rescued when the wicked Nebuchadnezzar threw him into the furnace of burning fire along with Ahab, the son of Kolaiah and Zedekiah, the son of Measeiah, the prophets of falsehood: they

> were burned in the fire, but Joshua, the son of Jehozadak, was rescued because of his merits.[48]

Abraham's test is mentioned here alongside the fiery ordeal of Hananiah, Mishael, and Azariah, and the repeated affirmation of the Danielic motifs leaves the impression that the composers of the passage interpreted it as a formative blueprint.

We also encounter Abraham's fiery trials in the Talmudic corpora. A passage from *b. Eruvin* 53a, while explaining Nimrod's name as Amraphel, posits that the evil ruler is called by this name because "he ordered our father Abraham to be cast into a burning furnace."[49] Another passage from *b. Pesahim* 118a inserts into the familiar story a new otherworldly protagonist, the archangel Gabriel, who volunteers to go down and cool Abraham's fiery furnace:

> [For] when the wicked Nimrod cast our father Abraham into the fiery furnace, Gabriel said to the Holy One, blessed be He: "Sovereign of the Universe! Let me go down, cool [it], and deliver that righteous man from the fiery furnace." Said the Holy One, blessed be He, to him: "I am unique in My world, and he is unique in his world: it is fitting for Him who is unique to deliver him who is unique. But because the Holy One, blessed be He, does not withhold the [merited] reward of any creature, he said to him, "Thou shalt be privileged to deliver three of his descendants."[50]

Such angelic actions are reminiscent of the Greek rendering of Daniel 3, where the Angel of the Lord cools the oven of Nebuchadnezzar with dew. It is no coincidence that the tradition of the three Israelites youths and their future fiery tests is openly invoked here. Thus, this passage serves not only as an exegesis of Abraham's fiery trial but also as a novel interpretation of the Danielic story, resolving the puzzle of their otherworldly rescuer.

Authors of various rabbinic midrashic compositions also demonstrate familiarity with the aforementioned motifs. *Genesis Rabbah* 38:13 provides the following lengthy account of Abraham's descent into fire:

> And Haran died in the presence of his father Terah. R. Hiyya said: Terah was a manufacturer of idols. He once went away somewhere and left Abraham to sell them in his place. A man came and wished to buy one. "How old are you?" Abraham asked him. "Fifty years," was the reply. "Woe to such a man!" he exclaimed, "You are fifty years old and worship a day-old object!" At this he became ashamed and departed. On the other occasion a woman came with a plateful

> of flour and requested him, "Take this and offer it to them." So he took a stick, broke them, and put the stick in the hand of the largest. When his father returned he demanded, "What have you done to them?" "I cannot conceal it from you," he rejoined. "A woman came with a plateful of fine meal and requested me to offer it to them. One claimed, 'I must eat first,' while another claimed, 'I must eat first.' Therefore the largest arose, took the stick, and broke them." "Why do you make sport of me," he cried out; "have they then any knowledge!" "Should not your ears listen to what your mouth is saying," he retorted. Thereupon he seized him and delivered him to Nimrod. "Let us worship the fire!" he [Nimrod] proposed. "Let us rather worship water, which extinguishes the fire," replied he. "Then let us worship water!" "Let us rather worship the clouds which bear the water." "Then let us worship the cloud!" "Let us rather worship the winds which disperse the clouds." "Then let us worship the wind!" "Let us rather worship human beings, who withstand the wind." "You are just bandying words," he exclaimed; "we will worship naught but the fire. Behold, I will cast you into it, and let your God whom you adore come and save you from it." Now Haran was standing there undecided. If Abram is victorious, [thought he], I will say that I am of Abram's belief, while if Nimrod is victorious I will say that I am on Nimrod's side. When Abram descended into the fiery furnace and was saved, he [Nimrod] asked him, "Of whose belief are you?" "Of Abram's," he replied. Thereupon he seized and cast him into fire; his inwards were scorched and he died in his father's presence. Hence it is written, and Haran died in the presence of (*ʿal pene*) his father Terah.[51]

This account seems to represent another milestone in the development of the fiery trials tradition. It evokes the memory of some ideas found in the haggadic portion of the *Apocalypse of Abraham*, where the young protagonist is also sent by his father to sell manufactured idols.[52] It also depicts an interesting dispute between Abraham and Nimrod, recalling Abraham's address to Terah in the *Apocalypse of Abraham*.[53] The midrash, however, also brings forward a set of new developments. Haran is here portrayed as a spectator of the dispute between Nimrod and Abraham. His reluctance and unbelief is in stark contrast to the faith and strength of Abraham. Eventually, both characters are thrown into the furnace, but unlike his brother, Haran is not able to survive. Notably, Haran's death overshadows the entire account, forming an *inclusio* around the section.

Other passages in *Genesis Rabbah* also betray the knowledge of the story of Abraham's fiery test while interpreting its details in light of the Danielic blueprint.

Take *Gen. Rab.* 34:9: "The Lord smelled the sweet savour. He smelled the savour of the patriarch Abraham ascending from the fiery furnace; He smelled the savour of Hananiah, Mishael, and Azariah ascending from the fiery furnace."[54] This passage clearly envisions the tests of both Abraham and the Danielic youths as sacrifices. *Gen. Rab.* 44:13 also makes a connection between the ordeal of the three Israelite youths and Abraham's fiery tests: "Michael descended and rescued Abraham from the fiery furnace. . . . And when did Michael descend? In the case of Hananiah, Mishael, and Azariah."[55] Instead of Gabriel, Michael is depicted here as the otherworldly rescuer for both the Danielic martyrs and Abraham. Similar ties to Daniel 3 are found in the *Song of Songs Rabbah* 1:56: "R. Eliezer said: While the supreme King of kings, the Holy One, blessed be He, was still at His table in the firmament, Michael the great prince had already descended and delivered our father Abraham from the fiery furnace. The Rabbis, however, say that God Himself came down and delivered him, as it says, I am the Lord that brought thee out of Ur of the Chaldees (Gen 15:7). And when did Michael come down? In the time of Hananiah, Mishael, and Azariah."[56] *Lev. Rab.* 36:4 adds a new twist to the familiar story by connecting Abraham's tests with Jacob:

> R. Berekiah and R. Levi in the name of R. Samuel b. Nahman said: Abraham was saved from the fiery furnace only for the sake of Jacob. This is like the case of a man who was standing for trial before a governor and sentence was passed upon him by the governor to be burned. The governor looked into his horoscope and saw that the man was destined to beget a daughter who would be married to the king, so he said: "He deserves to be saved for the sake of the daughter whom he is destined to beget." It was so with Abraham. He had been sentenced by Nimrod to be burned, but the Holy One, blessed be He, foresaw that Jacob was destined to spring from him, so he said: "He deserves to be saved for the sake of Jacob."[57]

Avot de R. Nathan A 33 adds yet another exegetical insight by listing the patriarch's fiery ordeals among the ten landmarks of Abraham's spiritual journey:

> With ten trials was Abraham our father tried before the Holy One, blessed be He, and in all of them he was found steadfast, to wit: twice, when ordered to move on; twice, in connection with his two sons; twice, in connection with his two wives; once, on the occasion of his war with the kings; once, at the (covenant) between the pieces; once, in Ur of the Chaldees; and once, at the covenant of circumcision.[58]

Later variants of the narrative found in *Sefer ha-Yashar* and the *Book of Zohar* serve as witnesses to the popularity of the fiery trials motif. These demonstrate a dramatic expansion of the familiar story, especially as reflected in the *Book of Yashar*, combining details found in various rabbinic passages into coherent compositions. Yet despite their extensive additions and reworkings, these versions still reveal the basic elements of the original story. Apropos the reworkings found in the *Book of Yashar*, Geza Vermes notes that "the bulk of this Yashar story of Abraham's ordeal, and also of the death of Haran in the flames, is common tradition in rabbinic literature."[59] These later versions still maintain close ties with their conceptual blueprint—the Book of Daniel.[60]

II. Fiery Trials in Early Christian Martyrdoms

Although the *Apocalypse of Abraham*'s ties with the Jewish traditions of the fiery trials have often been acknowledged, a possible connection with early Christian martyrdom accounts, in which the faithful were tested in flames, is regularly neglected by scholars. A comparative analysis, however, reveals some striking similarities between such accounts and the *Apocalypse of Abraham*. One such features is the tradition of the adepts' ascent and vision during their fiery trials. Taking into account composition dates of these early Christian martyrdoms, some of which are contemporaneous with the *Apocalypse*, these early stories of Christian martyrs will now be closely examined.

Acts of Paul

The *Acts of Paul*, a composition usually dated by scholars before 200 CE,[61] tells about the fiery tribulation of the Christian proto-martyr Thecla.[62] Her ordeal brings to mind some details found in Daniel 3, as well as the accounts of Abraham's own fiery tribulation.[63] *Acta Pauli* 3:21–22 portrays the following failed execution of the female proto-martyr:

> And the Governor was affected greatly, and (on the one hand) he flogged Paul and cast him outside of the city, but (on the other hand), he condemned Thecla to be burned. And immediately the Governor rose up, departing into the theater, and all the crowd went out by necessity to the public spectacle. But Thecla was as a lamb in a desert looking around for the shepherd, so she sought for Paul. And having looked into the crowd, she saw the Lord sitting as Paul, and she said, "As if I am not enduring, Paul gazes upon me." And she held fast to him, gazing intently, but he went away into the heavens. And the

> young ones and virgins brought wood and hay, in order that Thecla might be burned. But as she was brought in, naked, the Governor wept and marveled at the power in her. But the executioners spread the wood and commanded her to go up upon the pyre. But Thecla, making the sign of a cross, went upon the wood. But they set it on fire from underneath. Even though a great fire was shining, it did not touch her. For God who has compassion caused an underground roaring, and a cloud from above full of water and hail, and all of the contents were poured out, so that many were at risk and died, and the fire was extinguished and Thecla was saved.[64]

Several details of Thecla's miraculous escape are also present in Daniel 3, especially in its Greek renderings. The first notable feature is the quenching of fire by water sent from a heavenly being. In the Greek rendering of Daniel 3, the Angel of the Lord cools the oven of Nebuchadnezzar with dew.

A second parallel is the death of the antagonistic spectators, a feature present in the Aramaic version of Daniel 3 and reiterated by various later versions. This theme is also found in Abrahamic accounts of the fiery trials. As we recall, Pseudo-Philo reports that 83,500 bystanders were killed. Yet in contrast to Danielic and Abrahamic accounts, Thecla's spectators are killed not by fire, but water.

The third shared feature is the resistance of the adept's body to the element of fire. Focusing on the phrase "fire did not touch her" (οὐχ ἥψατο αὐτῆς τὸ πῦρ), Stephen Davis argues that Thecla "remains completely impervious to the threatening elements around her."[65]

A fourth similarity is the timing of Thecla's vision, which occurs immediately before the fiery ordeal. This vision takes the form of theophany: the female proto-martyr beholds the deity ("the Lord") in the form of Paul. Such theophanic visions recur in conjunction with the fiery trials in other early Christian martyrdoms and in the *Apocalypse of Abraham.*

A reference to "a noise beneath the earth" initiated by the deity in order to save Thecla is also noteworthy, since in Pseudo-Philo the deity saves Abraham from the furnace by stirring up a great earthquake.

Finally, another pivotal feature is how fire becomes a protective enclosure that saves the martyr during future tribulations.[66] This motif constitutes a curious parallel to the *Martyrdom of Polycarp,* where fire functions as a protective layer that saves the martyr from death.[67] In short, what normally kills becomes the means of preservation.

Martyrdom of Polycarp

The *Martyrdom of Polycarp* is traditionally viewed as the oldest Christian document fully devoted to martyrdom.[68] Estimates of its date range from the end of the second century CE[69] to the middle of the third century CE.[70] The account of Polycarp's martyrdom reveals a curious constellation of familiar motifs already known to us from our previous exploration of Daniel 3 and the Jewish renderings of Abraham's fiery tests. In the climax of the story, Bishop Polycarp is tested by fire and his body miraculously survives the flames. Despite the fact that, unlike his Jewish counterparts, Polycarp is eventually killed by his persecutors, the part of the account pertaining to the fiery ordeal (chapters 11–16) is especially relevant for our investigation. Consider the following excerpts taken from *Martyrdom of Polycarp* 11–16:

> The governor said: "I have wild animals, and I shall expose you to them if you do not change your mind."
>
> And he answered: "Go and call for them! Repentance from a better state to one that is worse is impossible for us. But it is good to change from what is wicked to righteousness." And he said again to him: "Since you are not afraid of the animals, then I shall have you consumed by fire—unless you change your mind." But Polycarp answered: "The fire you threaten me with burns merely for a time and is soon extinguished. It is clear you are ignorant of the fire of everlasting punishment and of the judgement that is to come, which awaits the impious. Why then do you hesitate? Come, do what you will."
>
> . . . Next they decided to shout out altogether that Polycarp should be burnt alive. For the vision he had seen regarding his pillow had to be fulfilled, when he saw it burning while he was at prayer and turned and said to his faithful companions: "I am to be burnt alive." All of this happened with great speed, more quickly than it takes to tell the story: the mob swiftly collected logs and brushwood from workshops and baths, and the Jews (as is their custom) zealously helped them with this. When the fire was prepared, Polycarp took off all his clothing, loosed his belt and even tried to take off his own sandals, although he had never had to do this before: for all the Christians were always eager to be the first to touch his flesh. Even before his martyrdom he had been adorned in every way by reason of the goodness of his life. Straightway then he was attached to the equipment that had been prepared for the fire. When they were on the point of nailing him to it, he said: "Leave me thus. For he who has given me the strength to endure the flames will grant me to remain without flinching in the fire even without the firmness you will give me by using nails." He had uttered his Amen and finished

> his prayer, and the men in charge of the fire started to light it. A great flame blazed up and those of us to whom it was given to see beheld a miracle. And we have been preserved to recount the story to others. For the flames, bellying out like a ship's sail in the wind, formed into the shape of a vault and thus surrounded the martyr's body as with a wall. And he was within it not as burning flesh but rather as bread being baked, or like gold and silver being purified in a smelting-furnace. And from it we perceived such a delightful fragrance as though it were smoking incense or some other costly perfume. At last when these vicious men realized that his body could not be consumed by the fire they ordered a *confector* to go up and plunge a dagger into the body. When he did this there came out such a quantity of blood that the flames were extinguished, and even the crowd marveled that there should be such a difference between the unbelievers and the elect. And one of the elect indeed was the most venerable martyr Polycarp, who was in our day a teacher in the apostolic and prophetic tradition and a bishop of the Catholic Church in Smyrna. Every word that he uttered from his mouth was indeed fulfilled and shall be fulfilled.[71]

One important feature of this narration are the multiple allusions to the Danielic blueprint seeping through several peculiar details of the account. The influence of Daniel 3 has not gone unnoticed by scholarship. Jan Willem van Henten, for example, points out that in both stories the fiery ordeals represent punishment for refusing to show loyalty to the ruler and state religion. He also notices that the similarities between the two accounts are especially striking when compared with the Greek versions of Daniel 3. Like Daniel's companions in the Greek versions (Dan 3:24–27 LXX/Th) in *Mart. Pol.* 14.1–2, Polycarp invokes the Lord in a final prayer that starts with a doxology.[72] Another important correspondence is that Polycarp and the Danielic youths are compared to a burnt offering.[73] Thus, according to the *Martyrdom of Polycarp* 14, "they did not nail him down then, but simply bound him; and as he put his hands behind his back, he was bound like a noble ram chosen for an oblation from a great flock, a holocaust prepared and made acceptable to God."[74] The sacrificial motifs are further developed in Polycarp's prayer when the martyr utters the following words: "May I be received this day among them before your face as a rich and acceptable sacrifice, as you, the God of truth who cannot deceive, have prepared, revealed, and fulfilled beforehand."[75] According to Van Henten,[76] the cultic terminology of this phrase is strongly reminiscent of Dan 3:39–40 (LXX): "May we be accepted, as though it were with whole burnt offering of rams and bulls and with tens of thousands of fat lambs; thus let our sacrifice come before you today."[77] By weaving a cluster of phrases from the *Prayer of Azariah* into the account of Polycarp's execution, the author of the *Martyrdom of Polycarp* was likely comparing the fate of Polycarp to Daniel's companions.[78] The purpose of this analogy, in Van Henten's opinion, does not concern the deity's invocation to rescue the Jewish people, as in the Greek versions of Daniel 3. In line with some other early Christian interpretations of Daniel 3 and 6, the deliverance is individual and posthumous. Van Henten suggests that the analogy underlines Polycarp's postmortem vindication by the resurrection of body and soul (14.2). It implies that Polycarp won a vindication similar to that of the righteous Hananiah, Mishael and Azariah, who were miraculously rescued because of their perfect obedience to God. The analogy is strengthened by details and phrases in chapter 15, depicting Polycarp's body as unable to be burned, which is reminiscent of the rescue of the three Israelite youths in Daniel 3. *Mart. Pol.* 14.2 emphasizes the martyr's wish to be received by God "this day," signifying that Polycarp's resurrection will occur immediately after his death rather than at the end of time.[79] Furthermore, the Greek versions of Dan 3:50 speak about "a moist breeze"[80] made inside the furnace by the Angel of the Lord. Van Henten notes[81] that the description of Polycarp's miracle in the fire refers to a furnace as well as to wind.[82]

Another important aspect of Polycarp's story is the tradition of the adept's transformation into a celestial being. Some have suggested that the *Martyrdom of Polycarp* seems to affirm such a metamorphosis by postulating that the martyrs are "no longer human but already angels."[83] In this regard the prominence of the ascent traditions in the *Martyrdom of Polycarp* also warrants close attention. Candida Moss argues that "the notion of immediate ascension to heaven is further illustrated in a famous speech in the *Martyrdom of Polycarp*, in which the protagonist asks that he be given a share in the cup of Christ and be received that day in heaven."[84] *Mart. Pol.* 14 records the following prayer of the Christian martyr:

> O Lord, omnipotent God and Father of your beloved and blessed child Christ Jesus, through whom we have received our knowledge of you, the God of the angels, the powers, and of all creation, and of all the family of the good who live in your sight: I bless you because you have thought me worthy of this day and this hour, to have a share among the number of the martyrs in the cup of your Christ, for the resurrection unto eternal life of both the soul and the body in the immortality of the Holy Spirit. May I be received this day among them before your face as a rich and acceptable sacrifice, as

> you, the God of truth who cannot deceive, have prepared, revealed, and fulfilled beforehand. Hence I praise you, I bless you, and I glorify you above all things, through that eternal and celestial high priest, Jesus Christ, your beloved child, through whom is glory to you with him and the Holy Spirit now and for all ages to come. Amen.[85]

After examining this prayer, Moss concludes:

> Polycarp's request draws upon the biblical image of the cup of wrath imbibed by Christ in the Gospels. This image associates the death of Polycarp and other martyrs with that of Christ. But he further asks to be received into God's presence that very day. The mechanics of this reception suggest that he will be received into God's presence as a sacrifice, presuming that just as the scent of the burnt offering rose to God, so also Polycarp would ascend to be received by God.[86]

Moss's insights about the sacrificial language of the adept's ascent in the *Martyrdom of Polycarp* are relevant to this study.[87] Elsewhere Moss reiterates this thesis, noting that "in recounting the martyr's admission into heaven, a number of images are employed. In the *Martyrdom of Polycarp*, the martyr is drawn into God's presence in the manner of a burnt offering."[88]

The constellation of motifs (fiery trial, ascent, and sacrifice) found in the *Martyrdom of Polycarp* are especially germane for our study of the *Apocalypse of Abraham* since the story of Abraham's fiery trials also includes a strong sacrificial dimension. This is particularly noticeable in Azazel's warning about the patriarch's imminent demise in fire during his ascent to heaven, which can be found in *Apoc. Ab.* 13:4–5:

> And the impure bird spoke to me and said, "What are you doing, Abraham, on the holy heights, where no one eats or drinks, nor is there upon them food of men? But these will all be consumed by fire and they will burn you up. Leave the man who is with you and flee! Since if you ascend to the height, they will destroy you."[89]

Comparable to the *Martyrdom of Polycarp,* the motif of a fiery trial coincides with those of the adept's ascent and his role as a sacrifice.

Finally, another relevant feature is *Martyrdom of Polycarp's* emphasis on the contrast between the fire of martyrdom and the fire of hell.[90] The same contrast between two types flames—demonic and divine—is found in the *Apocalypse of Abraham,* where the flames of Abraham's trials is contrasted with the fire of Azazel's hell.[91]

Martyrdom of Pionius

In the *Martyrdom of Pionius*, a text likely written shortly after this martyr was executed in Smyrna (ca. 250 CE), following Decius's edict,[92] we again encounter the imagery of a fiery test, along with the martyr's body resisting the fire. Scholars have pointed out some connections between the fiery tests of Pionius and Polycarp. Thus, Moss suggests that "the first text that can confidently be said to have known the *Martyrdom of Polycarp* is the *Martyrdom of Pionius*, a third-century martyr act from Smyrna with literary and thematic connections to the *Martyrdom of Polycarp*."[93] Pionius's connection to Polycarp is accentuated by the date of his death, which takes place "on the anniversary of the blessed martyr Polycarp" (*Mart. Pion.* 2.1).[94] Moss also points out that in a further assimilation to the death of Polycarp, the date of Pionius's arrest is twice referred to as the "great sabbath" (*Mart. Pion.* 2.1; 3.6; cf. *Mart. Pol.* 8.1).[95] We will now explore Pionius's martyrdom more closely. *Mart. Pion.* 21–22 reads:

> After they brought the firewood and piled up the logs in a circle, Pionius shut his eyes so that the crowd thought that he was dead. But he was praying in secret, and when he came to the end of his prayer he opened his eyes. The flames were just beginning to rise as he pronounced his last Amen with a joyful countenance and said: "Lord, receive my soul." Then peacefully and painlessly as though belching he breathed his last and gave his soul in trust to the Father, who has promised to protect all blood and every spirit that has been unjustly condemned. Such was the innocent, blameless, and incorruptible life which blessed Pionius brought to an end, with his mind ever fixed on almighty God and on Jesus Christ our Lord the mediator between God and man of such an end was he deemed worthy. After his victory in the great combat he passed through the narrow gate into the broad, great light. Indeed his crown was made manifest through his body. For after the fire had been extinguished, those of us who were present saw his body like that of an athlete in full array at the height of his powers. His ears were not distorted; his hair lay in order on the surface of his head; and his beard was full as though with the first blossom of hair. His face shone once again wondrous grace!—so that the Christians were all the more confirmed in the faith, and those who had lost the faith returned dismayed and with fearful consciences.[96]

Here, as in the *Martyrdom of Polycarp*, we have a reference to the adept's prayer, which coincides with his tests of flames. The most important detail of the martyrdom, however, is the description of the adept's body after the fiery ordeal. We learn that Pionius "passed through the narrow gate into the broad, great light made manifest through his body." After the fire had been extinguished, Pionius's body was "like that of an athlete in full array at the height of his powers." The narration specifically mentions that "his ears were not distorted; his hair lay in order on the surface of his head; and his beard was full as though with the first blossom of hair." These details seem to underline the resistance of the adept's body to flames. Another important detail of the story is a reference to the shining face of the martyr after the fiery ordeal. The text mentions that Pionius's "face shone once again wondrous grace." In light of other Christological allusions, this detail might postulate the adept's transformation in the course of the trial, since it brings to mind the shining face of Jesus during his transfiguration.

The Martyrdom of Montanus and Lucius

In the *Martyrdom of Montanus and Lucius*, a Christian account probably written in the middle of the third century CE,[97] we again encounter the motif of a fiery trial. It is important to note that, unlike previously explored martyrdoms, this account explicitly connects its protagonist's situation with the deliverance of Hananiah, Azariah, and Mishael.[98] From the third and fourth chapters of this martyrdom, we learn the following testimony of Montanus and Lucius:

> At any rate, imprisoned under the authority of the local magistrates, we got the news of our sentence from the soldiers: the governor had threatened us the day before with fire. Indeed, as we later ascertained, he intended to burn us alive. But the Lord alone can rescue his servants from fire, and in his hand are the words and the heart of the king: he it was who averted from us the insane savagery of the governor. Earnestly devoting ourselves to constant prayer with all our faith, we obtained directly what we had asked for: no sooner had the flame been lit to devour our bodies when it went out again; the fire of the overheated ovens was lulled by the Lord's dew. And it was not difficult for those of faith to believe that modern marvels could equal those of old, in view of the Lord's promise through the spirit, for he who caused that deed of glory in favour of the three youths was also victorious in us. The governor, then, seeing that he had been thwarted in his design by the Lord, ordered us to be put into prison. The soldiers took us there, and we were not terrified by the foul darkness of the place. In fact, the dismal prison soon began to shine with the light of the Spirit, and the ardour of our faith clothed us with the brilliance of day to protect us against the ugly shadows and the pitch-black veil of

> night. And thus we climbed this high tower of torment as though we were climbing up to heaven.[99]

Like the *Martyrdom of Polycarp,* this story brings to mind some details found in the Greek versions of Daniel 3. A reference to "the fire of the overheated ovens lulled by the Lord's dew" evokes the *Prayer of Azariah*; it is therefore not surprising that our author openly mentions the three Israelite youths shortly thereafter. These Danielic connections were previously noticed by scholars. Dennis Tucker, for example, observed that the martyrdom not only mentions the three youths of Daniel 3, but also refers to the overheated ovens and the Lord's dew, thereby connecting the two scenes.[100] Tucker further suggests that, "similar to Hippolytus and Origen, the writer of this account appears to collapse history, understanding the identity of the three youths and the identity of those in prison under Valerian to be nearly identical."[101]

Crucial for our study are the allusions to the adepts' glorification and their ascent in the aftermath of the fiery trial. Both ideas are found at the end of the aforementioned passage and rendered by the following enigmatic formulae: "the ardor of our faith clothed us with the brilliance of day" and "we climbed this high tower of torment as though we were climbing up to heaven."

The theme of the heavenly ascent is then unfolded in greater detail in chapter 7, where Victor encounters "the Lord from heaven" in the form of a luminous child who, while answering the adept's question about the location of heaven, promises him the "sign of Jacob."[102] The "sign of Jacob" evokes memory of Jacob's ladder, and such symbolism is often used in the apocalyptic literature as the metaphor for ascension. Here it might also refer to a possibility of the adept's ascent.

With regard to the possible presence of ascent traditions in this account, Candida Moss notes that in Christian martyrdoms, "the flight of the soul to heaven is sometimes cast in almost naturalistic terms. In a vision in the *Martyrdom of Montanus and Lucius,* the Lord from heaven instructs the presbyter Victor: 'The spirit hastens to its God and the soul, now near her sufferings, has sought her proper place.' "[103]

The themes of the adept's metamorphosis and glorification may further be hinted at in the identification of the day of martyrdom as the day of resurrection. Thus, Outi Lehtipuu draws attention to the fact that "in the *Martyrdom of Montanus and Lucius* the narrator identifies the day of martyrdom as the day of resurrection."[104] We learn from chapter 17 of this martyrdom that "the third day after that interval was endured not as a day of martyrdom but of resurrection."[105]

The Martyrdom of Fructuosus and Companions

In the *Martyrdom of Fructuosus and Companions,* usually dated before 400 CE,[106] one can find again the motif of the preservation of the saint's body in a furnace.

This tradition, similar to other martyrdoms, openly relies on the Jewish blueprint. While describing the death of Fructuosus and his deacons in the fire, the author compares these Christian martyrs to the three Danielic youths in the furnace of the pagan king.[107] The *Martyrdom of Fructuosus and Companions* 4–7 reads:

> Fructuosus the bishop was now at the portal of the amphitheater, and the time was drawing near for him to attain not the final penalty but rather the unfading crown. Even though the staff officers whose names have been mentioned above were standing by, Fructuosus spoke so that they as well as all the brethren could hear, with the inspiration and the words of the Holy Spirit: "You will not long be lacking a shepherd, nor can the love and promises of the Lord fail you either here or in the hereafter. For what you look upon now seems but the weakness of a single hour." Thus then did he console the brethren; they then entered on the way of salvation, worthy in their martyrdom and happy to reap the fruit of the holy Scriptures according to the promises. They were like Ananias, Azarias, and Misael, so that the divine Trinity was visible also in them. For to each at his post in the flames the Father was present, the Son gave his aid, and the Holy Spirit walked in the midst of the fire. When the bands that tied their hands were burnt through, recalling the Lord's prayer and their usual custom, they knelt down in joy assured of the resurrection, and stretching out their arms in memory of the Lord's cross, they prayed to the Lord until together they gave up their souls. . . . After this the usual miracles of the Lord were not lacking. Babylas and Mygdonius, two of our brethren in the household of the governor Aemilianus, saw the heavens open, and this they also revealed to Aemilianus' daughter, their mistress according to the flesh: there was the saintly bishop Fructuosus together with his deacons rising crowned up to heaven, with the stakes to which they had been bound still intact. They summoned Aemilianus and said: "Come and see how those whom you have condemned to death today have been restored to heaven and to their hopes." But when Aemilianus came, he was not worthy to behold them. . . . Fructuosus also appeared to Aemilianus, who had condemned him to death, together with his deacons in robes of glory.[108]

Commenting on this account, Van Henten says that "the death by burning of Fructuosus and his deacons Augurius and Eulogius is compared with the punishment of Daniel's companions. The Father, the Son, and the Holy Spirit are present with them in the fire and Fructuosus starts a prayer as Azariah did in the Greek versions of Daniel 3, being certain of the resurrection and making the form of the Cross with his arms as a sign of victory (*Mart. Fruct.* 4.2–3)."[109]

According to Tucker, the story of the three youths serves here as a cipher for understanding the present event.[110] To this end, the *Martyrdom of Bishop Fructuosus* merges the story of Ananias, Azarias, and Misael with elements that are explicitly Christian, namely, the Trinity and the Lord's Prayer.[111] Yet the Danielic archetype is still visible through these Christian reworkings. Indeed, the *Martyrdom of Bishop Fructuosus* reveals how Daniel 3 was considered to be an important text addressing questions of loyalty and disloyalty to the state. As such, Daniel 3 is analogous to the experiences of early Christians, in many ways creating a narrative base for the retelling of martyrdom stories.[112]

Like previous accounts of Christian martyrs, this text again reveals the motif of the adept's ascent. Aware of this, Arik Greenberg notes that "the individual's placement in heaven is mentioned in 5.2, when two surviving brethren addressing the prefect after the deaths of the martyrs tell him that those whom you have condemned to death today have been restored to heaven and to their hopes."[113] Candida Moss provides additional testimony to this:

> Bishop Fructuosus, martyred under Decius, is similarly eager to arrive in heaven. . . . The vision of the heavenly ascent of the bishop, flanked by two deacons, recalls the crucifixion of Jesus. That they wear crowns indicates that their martyrdom is complete and they have been received into heaven. The immediacy of their ascent is again confirmed by the language used by the martyrdom's chief actors. The two visionaries, emboldened by what they had seen, berate Aemilianus the Roman prefect for his actions and invite him to behold the vision, saying, "Come and see how those whom you have condemned to death today have been restored to heaven and to their hopes." (*Mart. Fruct.* 5.2)[114]

Moss goes on to say that this "invitation is likely an allusion to bodily transfiguration and resurrection, but the point remains the same. As with the other martyrs we have examined, Fructuosus and his companions ascend to heaven on the day of their martyrdom."[115] These insights naturally bring us to the theme of the adept's transformation in this martyrdom. Indeed, the possibility of the protagonist's metamorphosis looms large in this account. Thus, in *Mart. Fruct.* 7.1, the main hero appeared to the prefect in a glorious robe.[116] The glory language coincides with the symbolism of gold. Similar to the *Martyrdom of Polycarp*, *Mart. Fruct.* 7 likens the martyr's test in fire to the perfection of gold: "Ah, blessed martyrs, who were tested in the fire like precious gold."[117]

III. Fiery Trials of Abraham in the *Apocalypse of Abraham*

Our study so far has shown that the tradition of the fiery trials, rooted in the biblical story of Hananiah, Azariah and Mishael, had a rich and multifaceted afterlife in both Jewish and Christian martyrological accounts. Often in the course of such fiery ordeals their adepts experienced ascent and theophany. This fact opens up the possibility that Abraham's ordeals in the *Apocalypse of Abraham*, where the patriarch's fiery trials coincide with his ascent and theophany, might also reveal a similar martyrological dimension. In order to explore this conceptual aspect, previously ignored by students of this text, we now direct attention to the fiery trials traditions in the *Apocalypse of Abraham*.

Although Abraham's fiery tests unfold in the so-called "apocalyptic" chapters of the text, which deal with the patriarch's ascent and theophany, this theme is rooted in the first haggadic portion of the pseudepigraphon, which portrays the idolatrous practices of Abraham's family. There one finds several episodes dealing with the fiery tests of idolaters and their infamous idols, often leading to their fatal demise. Previously, I argued that these fiery ordeals and the later tests of the patriarch in flames during his ascent to the heavenly Holy of Holies are interconnected.[118] In order to better understand the motif of Abraham's own fiery ordeals, we turn now to these accounts.

The Fiery Ordeal of Bar-Eshath

Comparable to Pseudo-Philo and rabbinic accounts, the *Apocalypse of Abraham* closely links fiery tests to the rejection of idolatry. The hero's contest against idols plays an especially prominent role in the haggadic part of the apocalypse. A striking feature of this portion of the text is the detailed descriptions of idols, portrayed as independent characters who rival the human heroes of the story. In the course of the narration, some of these idols become known by their proper names. The story involving one such idol, Bar-Eshath (Slav. Варисать), is closely related to the fiery test motif and may constitute one of the most important cruxes of this theme. The story of this enigmatic character begins in chapter 5, where Terah orders Abraham to gather wooden splinters left from the manufacturing of idols in order to prepare a meal. In the pile of wooden chips, Abraham discovers a small figure whose forehead is decorated with the name Bar-Eshath.[119] Since Abraham already doubts the power of idols, his curiosity is piqued, and he decides to test the supernatural abilities of the wooden statue by putting it near the "heart of the fire." Leaving Bar-Eshath near the heat, Abraham ironically orders him to confine the flames and, in case of emergency, to "blow on the fire to make it flare up."[120]

According to the story, however, the wooden idol failed to control the flames. Upon his return, Abraham discovers the statue fallen with his feet enveloped in the fire and terribly burned. Abraham then sees the destruction of the statue as the flames turn Bar-Eshath into a pile of dust. The important feature of the idol's fiery demise is its theophanic imagery, a peculiar conceptual dimension recalling previously explored fiery trials of Jewish and Christian martyrs which are also overlaid with theophanic symbolism.

I previously argued that the depiction of Bar-Eshath's demise is intentionally fashioned with theophanic symbolism; this is reminiscent of the classical depiction of the divine *Kavod* in biblical and pseudepigraphical accounts. In essence, it represents a theophany, although a mocked one. This tendency is important due to the connections between the fiery ordeals and theophanies frequently found in martyrological accounts, where the martyr's endurance in the flames often coincides with his or her theophanic experience. Often in such tests, a martyr embodies a theophany by manifesting a celestial form in the midst of flames. Although in the haggadic portion of the *Apocalypse of Abraham* this tendency is presented in its polemical dimension, such a conceptual development, in which the fiery ordeal entails a theophany, should be explored more closely.

It is crucial that the authors of the Slavonic apocalypse portray Bar-Eshath with his feet enveloped in fire. In *Apoc. Abr.* 5:9, Abraham conveys that when he returned, he "found Bar-Eshath fallen backwards, *his feet enveloped in fire* [нозѣ его обятѣ огнемь][121] and terribly burned."[122] This detail evokes an important theophanic feature found in several visionary accounts in which the anthropomorphic figure of the deity is depicted with fiery feet or a fiery lower body. For example, in the paradigmatic vision recounted in Ezekiel 1, where the seer beholds the anthropomorphic *Kavod*, he describes the fiery nature of the lower body of the deity. Ezek 1:27 reads:

> I saw that from what appeared to be his waist up he looked like glowing metal, as if full of fire, and I saw that from what appeared to be his waist down he looked like fire; and brilliant light surrounded him.

A similar depiction is found in Ezek 8:2. There the prophet again encounters the celestial anthropomorphic manifestation with a fiery lower body:

> I looked, and there was a figure that looked like a human being; below what appeared to be its loins it was fire, and above the loins it was like the appearance of brightness, like gleaming amber.

Additional testimony for this motif occurs in the first chapter of the Book of Revelation, a text possibly contemporaneous with the *Apocalypse of Abraham* and which in many aspects shares the theophanic paradigm of Ezekiel and Daniel.[123] Rev 1:14–15 reads:

> His head and his hair were white as white wool, white as snow; his eyes were like a flame of fire, and his feet were like burnished bronze, refined as in a furnace, and his voice was like the sound of many waters.[124]

It is apparent that the tradition found in the Book of Revelation is related to the one found in the *Apocalypse of Abraham*, given that it refers to the feet of the deity, or, more precisely, Christ, who is divinized in Revelation as "refined as in a furnace." One substantial difference between the aforementioned theophanic accounts and Bar-Eshath's portrayal is that, unlike God's or a martyr's form, the idol's body is not impervious to the fiery substance. Notably, even polemical depictions of the idol's demise, overlaid with irony, still reveal a connection between the fiery test and theophany, thus underlying the visionary potential of the fiery ordeals.

The annihilation of the wooden idol raises the question of how important this episode is for understanding Abraham's fiery trials later in the apocalypse. It sets the stage for the future fiery ordeals, which all of the story's protagonists will undergo: Terah and Nahor during the demise of their idolatrous house of worship, and Yahoel and Abraham during their ascent to heaven. Some of the characters will survive these ordeals; other will perish. *Apoc. Ab.* 7:2 reminds its readers that fire "mocks with its flames the things which perish easily."[125] The purpose of this statement is to underline the distinction between true and false representations of the deity and the adepts who become otherworldly manifestations impervious to fire, in which the celestial form's endurance against fire testifies to its authenticity. The theological conviction that heavenly bodies are somehow unconsumed by fire—and may even be composed of fiery substance—can be found in several places in the *Apocalypse of Abraham*.[126] Moreover, it appears that the authors of the Slavonic apocalypse believe that fire represents the divine substance surrounding the very presence of God.[127] Here the authors of the *Apocalypse of Abraham* are obviously drawing on an established visionary tradition manifested in several biblical theophanies.

Fiery Annihilation of Terah's Household

Despite its ironic nature, the Bar-Eshath episode still reveals its close ties to the conceptual pattern traced to Daniel 3. As we remember, although some characters of Daniel's account survive the furnace, others are doomed to perish in it. A Danielic echo such as this, albeit polemical, is also found in the final destiny of Terah and Nahor, who in the story are predestined to die in the flames along with their idols.[128] These members of Abraham's family, unlike Shadrach, Meshach, and Abednego, are not able to survive the blazing furnace that turns their bodies into ashes. *Apoc. Ab.* 8:1–6 reads:

> And as I was thinking about these things, here is what happened to my father Terah in the courtyard of his house: The voice of the Mighty One came down from heaven in a stream of fire, saying and calling, "Abraham, Abraham!" And I said, "Here am I!" And he said, "In the wisdom of your heart you are searching for the God of gods and the Creator. I am he! Leave Terah your father, and leave the house, so that you too are not slain for the sins of your father's house!" And I went out. And it came to pass as I was going out, that I had not even gotten as far as going beyond the doors of the courtyard when the sound of thunder came forth and burned him and his house and everything in the house, down to the ground [to a distance of] forty cubits.[129]

The destruction of Terah's house is later reaffirmed in *Apoc. Ab.* 26:3, where the deity inquires: "Why did your father Terah not listen to your voice and abandon the demonic idolatry until he perished, and all his house with him?"[130]

As noted previously, the fiery demise of various members of Abraham's immediate family represented a constant feature in many rabbinic stories about the patriarch's trials. Although the testimony found in Pseudo-Philo does not mention the fiery death of any of Abraham's relatives, this tradition is much earlier than Pseudo-Philo's testimony; it is found, for instance, in the *Book of Jubilees*, where Haran is burned in fire before his father's eyes.[131]

The fiery demise of Haran, who in Gen 11:28 is described as the one who "died before his father Terah in the land of his birth, in Ur of the Chaldeans," is interpreted here as the "fire of the Chaldeans."[132] Concerning this tradition, James Kugel observes that "if *'ur* here means 'flame' or 'fire,' then the implication is that Haran, Abraham's brother, perished in some sort of conflagration before the family left their homeland."[133]

The fiery ordeal of the Terah household brings us again to an important feature found in Daniel 3 and other accounts: namely, a peculiar contrast between the fate of the protagonist who survives the flames, and the fate of his opponents, usually represented by the unjust ruler's servants, who are doomed to perish in the flames.[134] This motif stresses the difference between the perishable bodies of the idolaters and the endurance of the adept's body in the fire. In the stories of Abraham's fiery trials, the Danielic motif of perishing opponents is now extended to the members of Abraham's immediate family—Haran, Nahor, and Terah. Although in the Danielic account of the three Israelite youths the opponents' demise coincides with the miraculous escape of the protagonists, in the *Apocalypse of Abraham* these elements of the archetypal plot are confined to different parts of the pseudepigraphon.

Azazel's Warning

Another important conceptual nexus of the fiery trial traditions, now closely tied to Abraham's own ordeals, is the patriarch's encounter with his demonic adversary. In *Apoc. Ab.* 13, while offering his animal sacrifices to God, Abraham meets his nemesis, the fallen angel Azazel. The demon attempts to discourage the patriarch from ascending into the celestial realm, warning him that he will be destroyed there by fire like his sacrificial animals. As cited earlier, *Apoc. Ab.* 13:4–5 offers the following description of the encounter:

> And the impure bird spoke to me and said, "What are you doing, Abraham, on the holy heights, where no one eats or drinks, nor is there upon them food of men? But these will all be consumed by fire and they will burn you up. Leave the man who is with you and flee! Since if you ascend to the height, they will destroy you."[135]

Several details of this enigmatic episode are important. First, Azazel's comparison between Abraham's sacrifices and his upcoming demise suggests that the passage interprets the upcoming fiery ordeal as a sacrifice. It is intriguing that in some rabbinic passages dealing with the fiery trials of Abraham at the hands of Nimrod, the patriarch himself is likened to a sacrificial animal being thrown into a furnace. In *Eliyahu Rabbah* 27 the following binding ritual can be found: "At once his servants bound Abraham hand and foot and laid him on the ground. Then they piled up wood on all sides of him, but at some distance away, a pile of wood five hundred cubits long to the west, and five hundred cubits long to the east. Nimrod's men then went around and around setting the wood on fire."[136] The tying not only recalls the binding of the fallen angels Asael and Asmodeus in early Jewish demonological accounts, but also that of sacrificial animals. Rabbinic traditions also speak about the sweet savor of Abraham's fiery trials, once again confirming their sacrificial nature.

Attempts to fashion Abraham's fiery ordeal as a sacrifice bring to mind the aforementioned Christian stories in which the fiery demise of a martyr is understood as a sacrificial offering, pointing back to the cultic and martyrological dimension of the *Apocalypse of Abraham*.

Another important detail of Azazel's episode is the juxtaposition of the patriarch's fiery trial with the motif of heavenly ascent. Thus, Azazel specifically informs his opponent, the patriarch Abraham, that "if you *ascend to the height*, they will destroy you." This conceptual constellation underlines the liminal nature of the fiery trials, often occurring, as in the *Apocalypse* and other pseudepigraphical accounts, on the borderlines of realms during the ascent or descent of the hero. In the martyrdom accounts, such liminality is emphasized by the martyr's transition from this life to the next. In our investigation of Christian martyrdoms, crossing the thresholds of mortality and immortality frequently coincides with the adept's ascent.

Azazel's cryptic warning remains one of the most enigmatic portions of the text. In attempting to solve this riddle, it is helpful to recall the significance of the motif of a seer's fiery encounter for authors of the pseudepigraphon, who envision fire as a theophanic substance surrounding the very presence of the deity. Later in the text, for instance, Abraham's transition to the divine realm is described as entering into the fire.[137]

Furthermore, the symbolism of the divine furnace is mirrored in the dualistic framework of the *Apocalypse of Abraham* in the imagery of the furnace of Azazel.[138] Thus, Yahoel's speech in chapter 14 reveals the true location of the chief antagonist, the arch-demon; his abode is designated as a furnace of the earth. Moreover, Azazel himself is depicted as the "burning coal" or the "firebrand" of this infernal kiln. In this respect it is important that the warning about the dangers of the heavenly furnace comes from the antagonist, who himself dwells underground in fiery theophanic abode.

To conclude this section, we should again highlight the significance of the antagonist's warning for clarifying Abraham's fiery trials as a martyrdom event. It turns a safe and steady ascent to the abode of the deity, as it is often portrayed in early Jewish apocalypses, into an imminent threat. This antagonistic framework is typical for martyrological accounts in which the hostile antagonists, represented by otherworldly and earthly characters, often play a major role in the trials of adepts. More specifically, positing the otherworldly antagonist immediately prior to the adept's ascent recalls the *Passion of Perpetua and Felicitas,* where the seer beholds a bronze ladder reaching all the way to the heavens. At the foot of the ladder of ascent, the seer sees an enormous dragon who is prepared to attack those who climb up and tries to prevent them from doing so. Here, the antagonist's purpose is not to destroy the adept but rather to intimidate and discourage her from ascending. This parallels Azazel's address to Abraham in the *Apocalypse,* in which the antagonist attempts to discourage the seer from his journey to the divine presence.

Azazel's address is also noteworthy because it introduces an element of negotiation found in Jewish and Christian martyrological stories but absent from conventional apocalyptic accounts of ascent and vision. This brings the *Apocalypse* even closer to the martyrological template. By way of reminder, in Daniel 3, Pseudo-Philo, and rabbinic lore, the role of the negotiating antagonist is often fulfilled by evil rulers. In the stories of Christian martyrs, Jewish or Roman authorities often take on this role by urging martyrs to abandon their faith. In the *Apocalypse of Abraham,* Azazel assumes this archetypical role of the antagonistic delegate who attempts to conduct negotiation with the fiery trial's recipient.

Azazel's Furnace

As mentioned earlier, the fiery nature of the divine abode parallels Azazel's furnace,[139] since the *Apocalypse of Abraham* depicts both domains as theophanic kilns. While some humans are predestined to be transformed in the upper fire of the divine throne room, others are doomed to perish in the lower furnace of Azazel. Furthermore, in our apocalypse the deity himself designates some human beings as "food" for another, demonic, furnace: namely, "the fire of hell." Thus, for example, according to *Apoc. Ab.* 31:3–5 the deity utters the following:

> Since I have destined them to be food for the fire of hell, and ceaseless soaring in the air of the underground depths, the contents of a worm's belly. For those who do justice, who have chosen my will and clearly kept my commandments, will see them. And they will rejoice with joy at the destruction of the abandoned. And those who followed after the idols and after their murders will rot in the womb of the Evil One—the belly of Azazel, and they will be burned by the fire of Azazel's tongue.

Interestingly, this passage identifies the fiery tongue of Azazel with the fire of hell, that is, the very reality by which the sinners will be destroyed.

Two types of fire, one serving as a vehicle of immortality and the other as a tool of destruction, evoke the imagery of certain Christian martyrological accounts which contrast the transforming fire of the martyrs' ordeal (that turns them into immortal beings) with the final fire of judgment (that destroys). Moreover, the former fiery ordeal is often understood as an escape from the latter. By enduring fiery trials in this life, the protagonists of the martyrological accounts escape the final judgment. This is clear in the *Martyrdom of Polycarp*, where readers learn that Christian martyrs "in one hour [buy] themselves an exemption from the eternal fire . . . [and] the fire applied by their inhuman torturers was cooled: for they kept before their eyes the knowledge that they were escaping that eternal fire never to be extinguished."[140] Arik Greenberg points out that in this passage

> a comparison is made between the fires of perdition and those of the executioner's pyre. It is said that "they despised the tortures of this world, in one hour buying themselves an exemption from the eternal fire. . . . They were escaping that eternal fire never to be extinguished" (2:3). Interestingly, the converse of the immortality earned by Polycarp is torment by eternal fire. Those who bear witness to Christ unto death earn exemption from the consequences of their former sins which otherwise would have condemned them to the eternal fires.[141]

Mart. Pol. 11 again repeats the correspondence between two types of fire. The passage presents a conversation between Polycarp and his tormentors, who, like Azazel in the *Apocalypse of Abraham,* attempt to intimidate the bishop with the threat of fiery punishment:

> And he said again to him: "Since you are not afraid of the animals, then I shall have you consumed by fire—unless you change your mind." But Polycarp answered: "The fire you threaten me with burns merely for a time and is soon extinguished. It is clear you are ignorant of the fire of everlasting punishment and of the judgement that is to come, which awaits the impious. Why then do you hesitate? Come, do what you will."[142]

The bishop, however, reminds his oppressors about the everlasting flames that await them after their earthly life. This is similar to the thirteenth chapter of the *Apocalypse,* which mentions both Azazel's intimidation and Yahoel's speech about the demon's fiery prison.

Martyrdom of Pionius, a text influenced by the *Martyrdom of Polycarp,* attests to a similar parallelism between two fires, one temporary and one eternal. In chapter 7, Pionius tells his persecutors that it is far worse to burn after death than to be burned alive in this life.[143]

Fiery Trials of Abraham as the Martyrological Crisis

It is time for a more detailed analysis of the patriarch's own fiery trials. It is not by chance that such ordeals unfold in the chapters dealing with the ascent of the patriarch and his celestial guide, Yahoel. Thus, chapter 17 depicts the beginning of the celestial journey of Abraham and Yahoel as their entrance into fire.[144] *Apoc. Ab.* 17:1 reports the seer's approach to the heavenly furnace while holding the hand of his angelic helper:

> And the angel took me with his right hand and set me on the right wing of the pigeon and he himself sat on the left wing of the turtle-dove, since they both were neither slaughtered nor divided. And he carried me up to the edge of the fiery flame.[145]

Remember that Pseudo-Philo does not specifically refer to an angelic figure who assists the protagonist during his trials. And yet here the patriarch enters into the furnace firmly grasping the hand of his otherworldly helper, Yahoel, who will not abandon his apprentice until he enters the celestial throne room. Such angelic assistance brings to mind the story of the three Israelite youths who also safely walked in fire along with their otherworldly protector. The Greek version of Daniel 3, which defines the otherworldly protector as the Angel of the Lord,[146] is even closer to the development found in the *Apocalypse of Abraham,* since Yahoel in that account is fashioned as the Angel of the Divine Name, and his function and attributes evoke other biblical traditions about the Angel of the Lord.

In Christian martyrological accounts, Christ or the Trinity appears to be fulfilling the role of the otherworldly protector and guide. In other words, these accounts reinterpret the identity of the otherworldly protector of Daniel 3, envisioning him as either Christ[147] or the Trinity.[148] This interpretation is found, for example, in *Mart. Fruct.* 4: "they were like Ananias, Azarias, and Misael, so that the divine Trinity was visible also in them. For to each at his post in the flames the Father was present, the Son gave his aid, and the Holy Spirit walked in the midst of the fire."[149]

Returning to Abraham's fiery trials in the *Apocalypse,* note that the fire is understood as a boundary separating the heavenly realm from the abode of mortals. And since in his ascent the patriarch immediately reaches the divine throne room without a lengthy journey through the heavens, passing through fire also serves as a distinct marker of his entrance into the divine realm. In this respect, it is noteworthy that the depictions of the fire that envelops the seer and his otherworldly helper are laden with distinctive theophanic details known to us from Ezek 1 and other biblical and extra-biblical theophanies. Such details are clearly discernable, for example, in *Apoc. Ab.* 17:1: "And while he was still speaking, behold, a fire was coming toward us round about, and a sound was in the fire like a sound of many waters, like a sound of the sea in its uproar."[150] This description points to a juxtaposition of fire and water, the symbolic constellation often found in biblical theophanic accounts.

An important feature of Abraham's fiery ascent that links to the aforementioned martyrological accounts is the motif of enveloping fire, a fire that comes "round about." This sounds much like Polycarp's martyrdom, in which the adept is portrayed as being enveloped in a fiery vault during his test: "A great flame blazed up and those of us to whom it was given to see beheld a miracle. And we have been preserved to recount the story to others. For the flames, bellying out like a ship's sail in the wind, formed into the shape of a vault and thus surrounded the martyr's body as with a wall. And he was within it not as burning flesh but rather as bread being baked, or like gold and silver being purified in a smelting furnace."[151] This may point to the fact that the adept's body here is envisioned as a theophany.

The Adept's Preparatory Fast before the Fiery Ordeal

Also important is the motif of the patriarch's fast, which precedes his fiery trials. Such praxis is again reminiscent of some Christian martyrdoms, including the *Martyrdom of Pionius*[152] and the *Martyrdom of Fructuosus,* which tell about the martyrs' fasts preceding their fiery ordeals.[153] The *Apocalypse of Abraham* provides an interesting detail about fasting, which may be an attempt to link this ascetic experience to the fiery ordeals. According to this account, the deity specifically instructs him to abstain from food that issues from the fire.[154]

Adept's Prayer before or during the Fiery Trial

Another feature shared by the *Apocalypse of Abraham* and Christian martyrological accounts is the adept's prayer preceding the fiery trial. Recall that in the *Martyrdom of Polycarp* the bishop prays in preparation of and immediately before the fiery trial. From *Mart. Pol.* 7 we learn the following:

> At any rate Polycarp immediately ordered food and drink to be set before them, as much as they wished, even at this hour, and only requested that they might grant him an hour to pray undisturbed. When they consented, he stood up and began to pray facing the east, and so full was he of God's grace that he was unable to stop for two hours, to the amazement of those who heard him, and many were sorry that they had come out to arrest such a godlike old man.[155]

In *Mart. Pol.* 14, already bound for the holocaust, the martyr again offers a long prayer, and only after he finishes do the executers in charge of the fire start to light it.[156] Scholars have noted how these prayer practices, along with their miraculous outcomes, are reminiscent of the prayers of Azariah and his companions in the Greek versions of Daniel 3.[157] According to Van Henten, "The spectacular aftermath of Polycarp's prayer as described in Chapter 15 . . . echoes the Greek version of Daniel 3."[158]

Furthermore, the practice of prayer is also mentioned in the proleptic rehearsal of the fiery trial that Polycarp beholds in a vision: "Three days before he was captured he fell into a trance while at prayer: he saw his pillow being consumed by fire. He turned and said to his companions: 'I am to be burnt alive.' "[159]

Another Christian martyr, Bishop Fructuosus, also prays before his fiery trial. From *Mart. Fruct.* 1 we learn that, while in prison, Fructuosus "prayed constantly, and there were Christians with him, comforting him and begging him to remember them."[160] Moreover, in *Mart. Fruct.* 4, Bishop Fructuosus and his companions, like Azariah and his friends in the Greek renderings of Daniel 3, raised their prayers in the furnace:

> When the bands that tied their hands were burnt through, recalling the Lord's prayer and their usual custom, they knelt down in joy assured of the resurrection, and stretching out their arms in memory of the Lord's cross, they prayed to the Lord until together they gave up their souls.[161]

The *Martyrdom of Montanus and Lucius* attests to the same motif of adepts' prayer in the fiery furnace, which, in this case, miraculously saves the adepts from flames: "Earnestly devoting ourselves to constant prayer with all our faith, we obtained directly what we had asked for: no sooner had the flame been lit to devour our bodies when it went out again; the fire of the overheated ovens was lulled by the Lord's dew."[162] The reference to the "Lord's dew," which extinguishes the martyr's furnace, closely resembles the Greek versions of Daniel 3.

In chapter 22 of the *Martyrdom of Pionius*, the protagonist prays as his persecutors busily prepare the wood for his furnace, and continues praying even after he is in the flames: "After they brought the firewood and piled up the logs in a circle, Pionius shut his eyes so that the crowd thought that he was dead. But he was praying in secret, and when he came to the end of his prayer he opened his eyes. The flames were just beginning to rise as he pronounced his last Amen with a joyful countenance and said: 'Lord, receive my soul.' "[163]

As seen in this account, the praxis of prayer was an important element of the Christian martyrological accounts. And while Pseudo-Philo's account does not specifically mention any prayer routines of the patriarch, the motif is present in the seventh chapter of the *Apocalypse of Abraham*. There, the patriarch offers the following prayer in the midst of his fiery trial:

> And while he was still speaking, behold, a fire was coming toward us round about, and a sound was in the fire like a sound of many waters, like a sound of the sea in its uproar. And the angel bowed with me

> and worshiped. And I wanted to fall face down to the earth. And the place of elevation on which we both stood <sometimes was on high,> sometimes rolled down. And he said, "Only worship, Abraham, and recite the song which I taught you." Since there was no earth to fall to, I only bowed down and recited the song which he had taught me. And he said, "Recite without ceasing." And I recited, and he himself recited the song: "O, Eternal, Mighty, Holy El, God Autocrat, Self-Begotten, Incorruptible, Immaculate, Unbegotten, Spotless, Immortal, Self-Created, Self-Illuminated, Without Mother, Without Father, Without Genealogy, High, Fiery, <Wise>, Lover Of Men, <Favorable,> Generous, Bountiful, Jealous Over Me, Patient, Most Merciful, Eli that is, my God, Eternal, Mighty, Holy Sabaoth, Most Glorious El, El, El, El, Yahoel. You are he whom my soul has loved, the Guardian, Eternal, Fiery, Shining, <Light-Formed>, Thunder-Voiced, Lightning-Looking, Many-Eyed, receiving the entreaties of those who honor you <and turning away from the entreaties of those who besiege you by the siege of their provocation, releases those who are in the midst of the impious, those who are confused among the unrighteous of the inhabited world in the corruptible life, renewing the life of the righteous>. You make the light shine before the morning light upon your creation <from your face in order to bring the day on the earth>. And in <your> heavenly dwellings there is an inexhaustible other light of an inexpressible splendor from the lights of your face. Accept my prayer, <and let it be sweet to you,> and also the sacrifice which you yourself made to yourself through me who searched for you. Receive me favorably and show to me, and teach me, and make known to your servant as you have promised me."[164]

It is important to note that this song was initially conveyed to the adept by his angelic instructor, who encouraged the patriarch to recite "the song which he taught him." This feature underlines the protective role of this invocation, a feature usually unnoticed in previous studies. The shielding function of the song is further hinted at by certain features of the prayer, for example, by labeling the deity as a "guardian" (Slav. хранитель).[165] The protective prayer given by the angel thus develops the tradition of the fiery trials to a new conceptual level, linking the angelic guardian to the adept's prayer routines.

Martyrological Crisis and Ascent's Topology

Our study has suggested that Abraham's fiery trials are envisioned as an antagonistic event, evoking the memory of Jewish and Christian martyrological accounts. Often in such a dramatic crux of an adept's earthly life, his or her perception is drastically altered, opening the door for ascent and a visionary experience. In short, a martyr sees and experiences reality in a way different from how reality is seen and experienced through ordinary human faculties. In the *Apocalypse of Abraham,* this change is signaled by the novel way in which the seer perceives space and time while progressing through the heavenly furnace.

Thus, in the *Apocalypse of Abraham* 17:3, the visionary suddenly reports unusual changes affecting the spatial features of his surroundings. When Abraham tries to prostrate himself, he suddenly notices that the surface escapes his knees: "And I wanted to fall face down to the earth. And the place of elevation on which we both stood sometimes was on high, sometimes rolled down."[166] A couple of verses later, in 17:5, the visionary reflects again on his unusual spatial situation: "Since there was no earth to fall to, I only bowed down and recited the song which he had taught me."[167] Suddenly, there is no ground beneath Abraham's feet.

Martyrological Crisis and the Adept's Ascent

The majority of Jewish and Christian renderings of Abraham's fiery trials, including Pseudo-Philo's testimony, do not contain any reports about the patriarch's ascent or his vision in conjunction with these ordeals. This does not, however, exclude the possibility that the authors were aware of this tradition. Thus, for example, a passing reference to Abraham's ascent can be discerned in chapter 18 of Pseudo-Philo's *Biblical Antiquities*: "And he said to him (Balaam), 'Was it not concerning this people that I spoke to Abraham in a vision, saying, Your seed will be like the stars of the heaven, when I lifted him above the firmament and showed him the arrangements of all the stars?' "[168] This passage speaks about both the ascent and the vision of the patriarch even though these experiences are not mentioned in *Biblical Antiquities* 6, where we find the story of Abraham's fiery trials.

In contrast, the Christian martyrologia and the *Apocalypse of Abraham* depict the adept's vision and ascent practices as unfolding in the midst of his fiery ordeals. This becomes another significant characteristic that unifies the *Apocalypse of Abraham* with Christian accounts. This tendency of martyrological accounts to appropriate Jewish and Christian ascent and vision traditions has been noticed by scholars.[169]

In respect to these developments, Candida Moss notes that the notion of immediate ascension to heaven is underscored, for example, in a speech in the *Martyrdom of Polycarp*, in which Polycarp asks that he be given a share in the cup of Christ and be received that day in heaven.[170] A similar motif is found also in the *Martyrdom of Bishop Fructuosus,* which describes the heavenly ascent of the bishop flanked by two deacons.[171] Other Christian martyrdoms speak about martyrs' ascensions using well-known biblical allegories. Thus, for example, *Passion of Perpetua and Felicitas* 4:3 contains the following allegory that hints at the protagonist's ascent:

> I saw a ladder of tremendous height made of bronze, reaching all the way to the heavens, but it was so narrow that only one person could climb up at a time. To the sides of the ladder were attached all sorts of metal weapons: there were swords, spears, hooks, daggers, and spikes; so that if anyone tried to climb up carelessly or without paying attention, he would be mangled and his flesh would adhere to the weapons.[172]

Reflecting on this allegory, April DeConick makes the following observation: "Perpetua has visions of climbing up a ladder to heaven, where she, as one of Christ's new children, is given milk to drink by the Lord. But this is not Jacob's innocuous ladder. This ladder is laden with metal implements to rip through the skin of anyone who climbs it."[173] Here the adept's ascent coincides with trials that rip her physical body and, like Abraham's ordeals, transform it into a celestial form. The counterpart to this is not only the metamorphosis of Christian martyrs passing through the flames, but also Abraham's ascension; his movement upward is viewed not as the peaceful progress of a visionary, but rather as a martyrological crisis.

Martyrological Crisis and Theophany

In the *Apocalypse of Abraham,* the protagonist's fiery ordeals are closely linked to his visionary praxis and his experience of God's theophany. In *Apoc. Ab.* 18:1–13, the adept reports his encounter with the divine Chariot in the midst of his fiery test:

> And while I was still reciting the song, the edge of the fire which was on the expanse rose up on high. And I heard a voice like the roaring of the sea, and it did not cease because of the fire. And as the fire rose up, soaring higher, I saw under the fire a throne [made] of fire and the many-eyed Wheels, and they are reciting the song. And under the throne [I saw] four singing fiery Living Creatures. . . . And above the Wheels there was the throne which I had seen. And it was covered with fire and the fire encircled it round about, and an indescribable light surrounded the fiery people.[174]

The peculiar setting of this theophany recalls the aforementioned martyrological accounts, where Christian adepts behold the vision of the divine Chariot during their trials. Scholars have shown that the earliest Christian martyrological testimonies take the form of theophanic encounters. Thus, Philip Munoa reminds us that these early testimonies were frequently fashioned as Merkavah visions, reminiscent of Jewish biblical and extra-biblical theophanic accounts. He notes that the vision of Stephen in the Acts of the Apostles,[175] Revelation, and the *Passion of Perpetua and Felicitas* all illustrate how vision and martyrological crisis went hand in hand in the ordeals of the Christian adepts: "In these passages it is the beleaguered, suffering followers of Jesus, facing martyrdom, who were granted visions of the heavenly throne room and its occupants."[176] Munoa reminds us that the biblical theophanic blueprints, including one found in Daniel 7, often served as the framework for these visions and were adapted to fit the circumstances of each visionary.[177]

Martyrological Crisis and the Adept's Metamorphosis

We have already seen how in the course of fiery tests, the adept's body often undergoes a glorious metamorphosis that turns him or her into a celestial being. Thus, Polycarp's and Fructuosus's earthly bodies are transformed and glorified in the flames of their trials. Although the *Apocalypse of Abraham* does not clearly depict Abraham's transformation during his testing period, the account hints at the possibility of this metamorphosis earlier in the story, when Yahoel pronounces that Azazel's celestial garment is now transferred to its new owner—Abraham. This angelic announcement about the patriarch's changing ontology evokes the memory of some early martyrological accounts in which the martyr's future glorification is conveyed through a proleptic event preceding his final metamorphosis. The tradition of such an anticipating event is already documented in the earliest Christian martyrological account, the vision of Stephen, where the face of the martyr became "like an angel," pointing proleptically to the martyr's future glorification.

It is also instructive that the reception of the heavenly form is often described as the fiery ordeal. One of the most spectacular specimens of such a fiery metamorphosis is the transformation of the seventh antediluvian patriarch into the supreme angel Metatron in *3 Enoch* 15:

> R. Ishmael said: The angel Metatron, Prince of the Divine Presence, the glory of highest heaven, said to me: When the Holy One, blessed be He, took me to serve the throne of glory, the wheels of the chariot and all the needs of the Shekinah, at once my flesh turned to flame, my sinews to blazing fire, my bones to juniper coals, my eyelashes

> to lightning flashes, my eyeballs to fiery torches, the hairs of my head to hot flames, all my limbs to wings of burning fire, and the substance of my body to blazing fire.[178]

It is not coincidental that this fiery metamorphosis coincides with Enoch's promotion to the highest angelic rank. In Jewish accounts angels are often described as being made from fire, which explains why the transformed bodies of Jewish and Christian martyrs, who acquire angelic status, become impervious to flames. This link between the adept's angelic status and his form's resistance to fire appears to be assumed in the aforementioned martyrological accounts. Noting the martyr's transformation in the *Martyrdom of Polycarp*, Greenberg observes:

> The reward for perseverance is described as angelic metamorphosis: "and with the eyes of the soul they looked up to those good things that are saved up for those who have persevered, which neither the ear has heard nor the eye seen, nor has it entered into the heart of man: but to them the Lord revealed it seeing they were no longer men but angels." . . . Those who persevere are given the reward; this is unseen by normal perception. Ultimately, the transformation of human to angel is a way to describe the form of Personal Immortality gained by the martyr.[179]

In the *Apocalypse of Abraham*, passing through the flames may also serve as a metaphor for angelification. The seer's encounter with fire is clearly significant for the authors of this apocalypse, as they often portray fire as the substance of the heavenly forms.

Fiery Ordeal as Sacrifice

As already noted, the symbolism of sacrifice permeates many Jewish and Christian accounts of fiery trials. For instance, the *Martyrdom of Polycarp* informs its readers that, while the bishop was still in the middle of the fiery furnace, spectators perceived "an overwhelming sweet smell, like the smell of frankincense or another of the costly aromatic herbs." According to Van Henten, "a pleasing odor indicates a welcome sacrifice, as passages in the Hebrew Bible suggest (e.g. Exod 29:18, 25; Lev 2:2)."[180] The same author reminds us that rabbinic renderings of the fiery trials similarly refer to a pleasant smell coming from the furnaces containing Abraham and Daniel's companions. We see this in *Gen. Rab.* 34:9: "the Lord smelled the sweet savour. He smelled the savour of the patriarch Abraham ascending from the fiery furnace. He smelled the savour of Hananiah,

Mishael, and Azariah ascending from the fiery furnace."[181] This confirms the fact that the fiery tests were often envisioned in Jewish and Christian materials as sacrificial incidents.

Another important detail that intimates a sacrificial dimension is the peculiar ritual of binding the martyrs, which is reminiscent of tying animals before offering them as sacrifices. This connection between binding and sacrifice might already be present in Daniel 3 when the adepts are tied before their placement in the furnace. The text says that Nebuchadnezzar "ordered some of the strongest guards in his army to bind Shadrach, Meshach, and Abednego and to throw them into the furnace of blazing fire." In later accounts of the fiery trials, binding will become even more evocative of sacrificial practice. The *Martyrdom of Polycarp* explicitly compares the bound protagonist to a sacrificial ram in chapter 14: "he was bound like a noble ram chosen for an oblation from a great flock, a holocaust prepared and made acceptable to God."[182] Commenting on this passage, Elizabeth Castelli notes that the public spectacle of Polycarp's death is explicitly characterized as a sacrifice by its narrator.[183] Drawing on this imagery, scholars suggest that early Christian martyrdoms were envisioned as public sacrifices. Deliberating on this motif in the *Martyrdom of Polycarp*, Robin Darling Young argues that "martyrdom was being shaped . . . into a highly public sacrificial liturgy. Those Christians who seemed to be God's choice for martyrdom trained for this sacrifice."[184]

Martyrs often acknowledge their role as a sacrifice, similar to Polycarp, who uttered the following words: "May I be received this day among them before your face as a rich and acceptable sacrifice, as you, the God of truth who cannot deceive, have prepared, revealed, and fulfilled beforehand."[185] Van Henten points out that "the cultic terminology of *Martyrdom of Polycarp* 14 is strongly reminiscent of Dan 3:39–40."[186] The understanding of martyrdom as sacrifice is summarized by Origen in his *Exhort. Mart.* 30:

> For just as those who served the altar according to the Law of Moses thought they were ministering forgiveness of sins to the people by the blood of goats and bulls [Heb 9:13, 10:4; Ps 50:13], so also the souls of those who have been beheaded for their witness to Jesus [Rev 20:4, 6:9] do not serve the heavenly altar in vain and minister forgiveness of sins to those who pray. At the same time we also know that just as the High Priest Jesus the Christ offered Himself as a sacrifice [cf. Heb 5:1, 7:27, 8:3, 10:12], so also the priests of whom He is High Priest offer themselves as a sacrifice. This is why they are seen near the altar as near their own place. Moreover, blameless priests served the Godhead by offering blameless sacrifices, while those who were blemished and offered blemished sacrifices

> and whom Moses described in Leviticus were separated from the altar [Lev 21:17–21]. And who else is the blameless priest offering a blameless sacrifice than the person who holds fast his confession and fulfills every requirement the account of martyrdom demands?[187]

Castelli suggests that in this passage "the purity of the priests and the wholeness and holiness of their offerings translate into the pure and undefiled character of the Christian martyr's sacrifice."[188] She further notes that more than a century before Origen's exhortation, similar ideas about martyrdom as a sacrifice were expressed by Ignatius of Antioch, who wanted to be "a sacrifice to God through these instruments of torture and execution."[189]

In some Jewish accounts of Abraham's fiery trials, the patriarch is also bound as a sacrificial offering before his placement in the furnace. In one such passage, found in *Eliyahu Rabbah* 27, Abraham is tied as a sacrificial animal, by foot and hand, and is thrown into a furnace:

> Nimrod said, "Nevertheless I will rather worship the god of fire, for behold, I am going to cast you into the midst of fire—let the god of whom you speak of come and deliver you from fire." At once his servants bound Abraham hand and foot and laid him on the ground. Then they piled up wood on all sides of him.[190]

In the *Book of Yashar* we encounter a similar scene, in which the king's servants bind the hands and feet of Abraham and his brother with linen cords before casting them both into the furnace. Such depictions of the patriarch bound hand and foot recall other Jewish accounts where human and otherworldly characters are portrayed as sacrificial animals. The most memorable account, of course, is the binding of Isaac before his attempted sacrifice.[191] Another example is Asael's binding in the *Book of the Watchers*. Some scholars have argued that this leader of the Watchers was understood in the Enochic lore as the atoning sacrifice for the sins of the fallen angels.[192]

In light of these traditions of sacrificial bindings, it is possible that in some Jewish materials, Abraham was envisioned as a cultic offering. This sacrificial dimension is present in the *Apocalypse of Abraham*. Elsewhere I have argued that in this text the patriarch is understood as the immolated goat of the Yom Kippur ritual.[193] One significant aspect of the immolated goat ritual was the destruction of the animal's body by fire.[194] The goat used during the atoning rite is thus reinterpreted in the *Apocalypse of Abraham* as the fiery trials of the patriarch.[195]

Another important detail that might point to Abraham's role as sacrifice is the enigmatic phrase uttered by Yahoel at the very beginning of the angel's encounter with Abraham in chapter 11. There, the great angel tells the young hero of faith that he will be visible *until* the sacrifice, and will be invisible after it. "Come with me and I shall go with you, visible *until* the sacrifice, but after the sacrifice invisible forever."[196] This statement is not related to the animal sacrifices of the patriarch, since Yahoel remains visible after Abraham offered these sacrifices. The angel disappears only after the patriarch and Yahoel enter into the heavenly Holy of Holies—the event that seems, once again, to affirm Abraham's role as the sacrificial offering. Finally, one last detail suggesting this role is situated in the prayer Abraham utters during his ascent into the heavenly Holy of Holies, wherein he offers himself as the sacrifice chosen by the deity:

> Accept my prayer, and also the sacrifice which you yourself made to yourself through me who searched for you (прими молитву мою и такоже и жертву юже себе сам створи мною взискающим тебе).[197]

In the subsequent verse, the patriarch's self-definition as a sacrifice is also noteworthy. Here, the patriarch asks the deity to "receive" him favorably. The formula used, as already noted, is likely related to the patriarch's role as the purification offering.[198]

Conclusion

The *Apocalypse of Abraham*, a text written soon after the destruction of the Second Temple, presents Abraham not merely as a visionary who peacefully travels to the heavenly abode of the deity, but as an adept who undergoes dangerous fiery trials on his way to the divine presence. The embellishment of the familiar apocalyptic journey appears not to be coincidental, as it points to a changing social landscape in which adherents of Jewish and Christian religions faced imminent persecution from the Roman authorities. In this respect an insertion of the fiery trials motif into the fabric of the apocalyptic story itself appears to be purposeful, since some scholars trace the origin of this motif to the period of the Roman persecution, thereby seeing it as a martyrological incident.[199]

The recognition of the martyrological dimension present in the *Apocalypse of Abraham* has several conceptual ramifications. First, it reaffirms a possible date of the text in the second century CE after the destruction of the temple and in the midst of the Roman persecution. In previous studies the tentative date of the pseudepigraphon was often postulated on the basis of the sacerdotal traditions present in the text. Yet the juxtaposition of the ascent to the heavenly sanctuary with the theme of the fiery trials, which is reminiscent of early Christian martyrdoms, provides additional support to the old theory about the text's possible date in the second century CE.

It also provides a bridge to the social practices of martyrdom, which unfold in Jewish and Christian communities in the second century CE, and in which the apocalyptic traditions of ascent and vision received a novel afterlife. Unlike Pseudo-Philo or later rabbinic accounts of Abraham's fiery trials, the *Apocalypse of Abraham* explicitly and unambiguously connects the patriarch's fiery ordeals to his ascent and vision of the deity. These associations reveal a close similarity to Jewish and Christian martyrological stories in which the adepts are transformed through their fiery trials.

In light of these connections, the *Apocalypse of Abraham* should be understood as a new chapter in the history of Jewish apocalypticism. Here the prominent legacy of ancient and contemporary martyrs is extended to one of the most important exemplars of Jewish faith in a manner that identifies him not only as a visionary but also as the protological martyr.

Chapter Three

Leviathan's Knot

The High Priest's Sash as a Cosmological Symbol

Said R. Simeon: "Verily, though the members of the Fellowship are students of the story of Creation, having knowledge of its wonders and perception of the paths of the Holy One, blessed be He, yet even among them there are few who know how to interpret it in connection with the mystery of the great dragon."

—*Zohar* II.34b

Come and see! The likeness of that which is above is that which is below, and what is below is also in the sea, and the likeness of that which is above is that which is in the supernal sea, and what is below is also in the lower sea. As the higher sea has length and width and head and arms and hair and a body, so also the lower sea.

—*Zohar* II.48b

Introduction

Josephus in his *Jewish Antiquities* 3.154–156 provides the following description of the high priest's sash:

> This robe is a tunic descending to the ankles, enveloping the body and with long sleeves tightly laced round the arms; they gird it at the breast, winding to a little above the armpits the sash, which is of a breadth of about four fingers and has an open texture giving it

> the appearance of a serpent's skin. Therein are interwoven flowers of divers[e] hues, of crimson and purple, blue and fine linen, but the warp is purely of fine linen. Wound a first time at the breast, after passing round it once again, it is tied and then hangs at length, sweeping to the ankles, that is so long as the priest has no task in hand, for so its beauty is displayed to the beholders' advantage; but when it behoves him to attend to the sacrifices and perform his ministry, in order that the movements of the sash may not impede his actions, he throws it back over his left shoulder. Moses gave it the name of *abaneth*, but we have learnt from the Babylonians to call it *hemian*, for so is it designated among them.[1]

Several scholars have drawn attention to unusual features associated with the sacerdotal girdle. Crispin Fletcher-Louis, for example, notices several peculiar details in this description, including the comparison of the sash with the skin of the serpent (ὄφις) and the language of "twisting" (ἕλιξ), further supporting serpentine symbolism.[2] Analyzing these features, he concludes that "the language is reminiscent of that used of the 'twisting' serpent in Isa 27:1–2[3] and the parallel passage in the Baal cycle (*CTA* 5.I.1–3) where, as we have seen, there is a reference to an ephod."[4] He also draws attention to another description of the sash in *Ant.* 3.185, in which Josephus again offers a novel interpretation of the priestly sash, though this time comparing it to the ocean which encompasses the earth:

> The *essen*, again, he set in the midst of this garment, after the manner of the earth, which occupies the midmost place; and by the girdle wherewith he encompassed it he signified the ocean, which holds the whole in its embrace.[5]

In light of the sash's associations with the serpent's skin and with the watery substance, which in some mythological traditions was understood to be the traditional domain of the sea monster, Fletcher-Louis suggests that the sacerdotal sash might represent the defeated Leviathan. He also posits that Josephus in his passage likens the high priest to a divine warrior who defeats the sea monster, the sash here symbolizing victory over chaotic forces. Fletcher-Louis finishes his examination by noting the possibility that "the high priest wears a vanquished Leviathan: the sash hanging at his side evokes the image of a limp and defeated serpent in the hand of its conqueror."[6] Several other scholars have found Fletcher-Louis's proposal plausible; Andrew Angel writes that "the serpentine cloth from which the sash is made and its identification as the ocean do suggest that it is to be identified with the Leviathan."[7] Like Fletcher-Louis's research, these studies also attempt to interpret Josephus's description of the sash through the lens of the divine warrior motif. Margaret Barker extends the use of this interpretive framework to her analysis of Christian developments, such as the motif of the defeated waters found in the Book of Revelation. She notes that

> the defeated waters occur, however, in two other places in Revelation: in the vision of the new heaven and the new earth there is "no more sea" (21.1) and in the vision of the risen Lord, when he is described as the heavenly high priest wearing a long robe with a golden girdle around his breast (1.13). Josephus tells us the significance of the high priest's girdle: "This vestment reaches down to the feet and sits close to the body . . . it is girded to the breast a little above the elbows by a girdle often going round, four fingers broad, but so loosely woven that you would think it the skin of a serpent. . . . And the girdle which encompassed the high priest round signified the ocean. . . ." (*Ant.* 3.154, 185). The risen Lord wears the ocean like the skin of a dead snake, the encircler with seven heads![8]

While the images of the divine warrior and the defeated sea monster are important for interpreting Josephus's tradition regarding the high priest's sash, other possibilities, especially ones arising from the sacerdotal dimension of the narrative, have been neglected. For example, there is good reason to think that the enigmatic serpentine sash might be closely related to the traditions of the cosmological temple, which loom large in the third book of Josephus's *Jewish Antiquities*. The sash's association with the ocean suggests such a cosmological significance. In fact, this item may be envisioned as a part of the temple of creation. In the remainder of this chapter, we will examine this cosmological imagery in more detail.

The High Priest as the Microcosmic Temple

In order to better understand a possible cosmological meaning of the priestly sash, we must examine its precise function in the broader context of Josephus's description of the high priest's accoutrement found in the third book of his *Jewish Antiquities*. This task is not easy, since this portion of *Jewish Antiquities* contains one of the most detailed descriptions of the high priestly vestments in early Jewish extra-biblical sources. In this lengthy and elaborate account, Josephus goes beyond the traditional biblical descriptions of the sacerdotal garments by unveiling the cosmological significance of the priestly accessories. It is important for this study to note that in Josephus's narrative, the garments of the high priest are linked both to the imagery of the earthly temple, and to its cosmological counterpart in the form of the so-called "temple of creation." *Ant.* 3.178–187 provides the following interpretation of the sacred vestments:

> Such is the apparel of the high priest. But one may well be astonished at the hatred which men have for us and which they have so persistently maintained, from an idea that we slight the divinity whom they themselves profess to venerate. For if one reflects on the construction of the tabernacle and looks at the vestments of the priest and the vessels which we use for the sacred ministry, he will discover that our lawgiver was a man of God and that these blasphemous charges brought against us by the rest of men are idle. In fact, every one of these objects is intended to recall and represent the universe, as he will find if he will but consent to examine them without prejudice and with understanding. . . . The high priest's tunic . . . signifies the earth, being of linen, and its blue the arch of heaven, while it recalls the lightnings by its pomegranates, the thunder by the sound of its bells. His upper garment, too, denotes universal nature, which it pleased God to make of four elements; being further interwoven with gold in token, I imagine, of the all-pervading sunlight. The *essen*, again, he set in the midst of this garment, after the manner of the earth, which occupies the midmost place; and by the girdle wherewith he encompassed it he signified the ocean, which holds the whole in its embrace. Sun and moon are indicated by the two sardonyxes wherewith he pinned the high priest's robe. As for the twelve stones, whether one would prefer to read in them the months or the constellations of like number, which the Greeks call the circle of the zodiac, he will not mistake the lawgiver's intention. Furthermore, the headdress appears to me to symbolize heaven, being blue; else it would not have borne upon it the name of God, blazoned upon the crown—a crown, moreover, of gold by reason of that sheen in which the deity most delights.[9]

In this passage one finds at least three concepts of the sanctuary that are closely intertwined: first, the earthly shrine represented by the Jerusalem Temple; second, the macrocosmic temple, whose sacred chambers corresponded to heaven, air/earth, and sea; and third, the microcosmic temple embodied by the high priest and his sacerdotal garments. When compared to the biblical narratives, a distinctive feature of this description is Josephus's attempt to interpret the symbolism of the priestly garb not only through the prism of allusions to the earthly tabernacle or temple, but also through their connections with cosmological realities. In this novel cosmological framework, each part of the priestly accouterment is linked not only to particular portions of the tripartite structure of the early sanctuary, but also to the respective sacred chambers of the temple of creation, which in Josephus's worldview correspond to heaven, air/earth, and sea.

These striking connections between elements of the priestly attire and parts of the earthly and cosmological sanctuaries have not gone unnoticed by scholars. Reflecting on these cultic correspondences, for instance, Gregory Beale says, "It is, in fact, discernible that there are broadly three sections of the priest's garment that resemble the three sections of the temple."[10] He further notes that "given all this symbolism, one can easily understand the assertion in the *Letter of Aristeas* that anyone who saw the fully attired high priest 'would think he had come out of this world into another one.' "[11] Beale has drawn attention to the fact that these striking sacerdotal correspondences were not unique to Josephus, but rather hinted at or openly attested to in a broad range of ancient Jewish sources, including the LXX, Philo,[12] and the Wisdom of Solomon, among others.[13] Since the idea of the temple of creation is important for our investigation of the high priest's sash in Josephus, a short excursus into the traditions of the cosmological temple is necessary.

Recent scholarship has demonstrated that a variety of early Jewish and Christian sources pronounce the idea of the cosmological temple, or the so-called temple of creation.[14] Such a macrocosmic sacred structure reflected the tripartite division of the earthly temple wherein heaven was conceived as the universal holy of holies, earth as the holy place, and the underworld (represented by the sea) as the courtyard. This concept of the cosmological temple, connecting creation and cult, is quite ancient, stemming from early Mesopotamian[15] and Egyptian[16] traditions. In early Jewish materials, this conceptual trend is often associated with a cluster of protological motifs in which the Garden of Eden functions as the celestial Holy of Holies[17] where the first human ministered as the high priest.[18] Scholars have noted that a conception of the cosmological temple is already implicit in some biblical materials, including Ezekiel's formative depiction of the eschatological sanctuary—which, paradoxically, juxtaposes cosmological and paradisal imagery.[19]

As this study of Jewish lore has already presented, the chambers of the macrocosmic temple were respectively associated with heaven, earth, and sea. A kabbalistic tradition that circulated in the name of Rabbi Pinhas ben Ya'ir states that "the Tabernacle was made to correspond to the creation of the world. . . . The house of the Holy of Holies was made to correspond to the highest heaven. The outer Holy House was made to correspond to the earth. And the courtyard was made to correspond to the sea."[20] This arcane cosmological speculation is not a late invention, but rather a tradition with ancient roots. Thus, in *Ant.* 3.121–123, Josephus suggests that the tripartite division of the earthly sanctuary was a reflection of the tripartite structure of the entire creation,[21] with its sacred chambers corresponding to heaven, earth, and sea:

> Internally, dividing its length into three portions, at a measured distance of ten cubits from the farther end he set up four pillars, constructed like the rest and resting upon similar sockets, but placed slightly apart. The area within these pillars was the sanctuary; the rest of the tabernacle was open to the priests. Now this partitionment of the tabernacle was withal an imitation of universal nature; for the third part of it, that within the four pillars, which was inaccessible to the priests, was *like heaven* devoted to God, while the twenty cubits' space, even *as earth and sea* are accessible to men, was in like manner assigned to the priests alone.[22]

The idea that cult and creation correspond is also found in another prominent Jewish interpreter, Philo, who says that the holy temple of God represents the whole universe in his *On the Special Laws* 1.66.[23] This belief that the earthly temple is a replica of the entire creation is rooted in biblical texts: the creation of the world in Gen 1–2 is set in conspicuous parallel with the building of the tabernacle in Exod 39–40.[24] According to Moshe Weinfeld, "Gen 1:1–2:3 and Exod 39:1–40:33 are typologically identical. Both describe the satisfactory completion of the enterprise commanded by God, its inspection and approval, the blessing and the sanctification which are connected with it. Most importantly, the expression of these ideas in both accounts overlaps."[25] In view of these parallels, many scholars suggest that the earthly sanctuary is envisioned as a microcosm of the world, imitating the sacerdotal structure of the entire creation.[26]

The Sea as the Cosmological Courtyard

Especially important for this study is that the tripartite structure of the cosmological temple includes the sea, which corresponds in these traditions to the courtyard of the temple of creation. *Numbers Rabbah* 13:19 mentions the court encompassing the sanctuary just as the sea surrounds the world.[27] Likewise, *b. Sukkah* 51b tells how the white and blue marble of the temple walls resembled the waves of the sea.[28] The association between the sacred chamber and the sea may also be suggested by the symbolism of the bronze tank in the courtyard of Israel's Temple, designated in some texts as the "molten sea."[29] Elizabeth Bloch-Smith wrote that "the great size of the tank . . . in conjunction with the fact that no practical application is offered for the 'sea' during the time of Solomon, supports the supposition that the tank served a symbolic purpose.[30] Either the 'cosmic waters,' or the 'waters of life,' which emanated from below the garden of Eden, or the 'great deep' of chaos is most often cited as the underlying symbolism of the molten sea."[31]

The depiction of the eschatological temple in the Book of Ezekiel also contains similar imagery insofar as it connects the sacred courtyard to living water. Viktor Hurowitz highlights the significance of this: "Ezekiel's temple of the future has a river flowing from under the threshold (Ezek 47:1). . . . The river envisioned by Ezekiel seems to replace the basins in Solomon's temple—basins that may have symbolized the rivers of a divine garden."[32] Ezek 47:1–8 offers the following description of the sacred waters:

> Then he brought me back to the entrance of the temple; there, water was flowing from below the threshold of the temple toward the east (for the temple faced east); and the water was flowing down from below the south end of the threshold of the temple, south of the altar. Then he brought me out by way of the north gate, and led me around on the outside to the outer gate that faces toward the east; and the water was coming out on the south side. Going on eastward with a cord in his hand, the man measured one thousand cubits, and then led me through the water; and it was ankle-deep. Again he measured one thousand, and led me through the water; and it was knee-deep. Again he measured one thousand, and led me through the water; and it was up to the waist. Again he measured one thousand, and it was a river that I could not cross, for the water had risen; it was deep enough to swim in, a river that could not be crossed. He said to me, "Mortal, have you seen this?" Then he led me back along the bank of the river. As I came back, I saw on the bank of the river a great many trees on the one side and on the other. He said to me, "This water flows toward the eastern region and goes down into the Arabah; and when it enters the sea, the sea of stagnant waters, the water will become fresh."

The flowing rivers of this passage echo another account of the cosmological temple found in the *Apocalypse of Abraham* in which the sea is depicted alongside rivers and their circles.[33] Like the great prophetic account, the *Apocalypse*'s author is familiar with the paradisal provenance of the sacred waters, connecting the Edenic tree to "the spring, the river flowing from it." In both passages, the waters of paradise are portrayed as "flowing."[34] The origin of the paradisal imagery of the circulating waters appears already in Gen 2:10,[35] where a river flows from Eden to water the garden.[36] In Ezekiel, however, the image of flowing Edenic waters has a further cultic meaning. Yet such an emphasis is not unique to Ezekiel. Gregory Beale points out[37] that similar sacerdotal imagery involving "rivers" can be found in the description of Israel's Temple in Psalm 36:8–9.[38] Scholars have additionally discerned[39] a similar sacerdotal motif of sacred waters associated with the temple settings in various Jewish extra-biblical accounts, including the *Letter of Aristeas* 89–91[40] and *Joseph and Aseneth* 2.[41] Christian sources also display acquaintance with the sacerdotal tradition of flowing waters. Rev 22:1–2, for example, portrays a river of the water of life flowing from the throne of God.[42]

All these testimonies demonstrate that in early biblical and extra-biblical Jewish accounts, rivers, seas, and oceans often conveyed cosmological significance, envisioned as a watery courtyard of the temple of creation that encompasses other, more sacred chambers of the cosmological sanctuary. It is in light of these traditions that the passage from *Ant.* 3.185—in which the high priest's girdle encompassed the priest as "the ocean, which holds the whole in its embrace"[43]—should be understood. Earlier we had noted how various parts of the high priest's accoutrement symbolically corresponded to various chambers in both the earthly and cosmological temples. The middle part of his multilayered attire, composed of several garments and undergarments, represented the Holy Place; this, in turn is symbolized in the cosmological language of the temple of creation as the "earth." Recall here Josephus's description of the priestly vestments:

> The high priest's tunic . . . signifies the earth, being of linen, and its blue the arch of heaven, while it recalls the lightnings by its pomegranates, the thunder by the sound of its bells. . . . The *essen*, again, he set in the midst of this garment, after the manner of the earth, which occupies the midmost place; and by the girdle wherewith he encompassed it he signified the ocean, which holds the whole in its embrace.[44]

Akin to the earthly and cosmological sanctuaries, where the watery courtyards (represented respectively by the molten sea or the actual sea) surrounded the Holy Place (represented in the temple of creation by the earth), in Josephus's description, the belt-ocean encompasses the part of the high priest's attire designated as the "earth." How, though, does the Leviathan imagery fit into this set of sacerdotal traditions?

Leviathan as the *Circuitus Mundi*

As noted at the beginning of this study, scholars are aware of the peculiar parallelism in which Josephus associated the priestly sash first with serpentine imagery and then with the ocean. This juxtaposition led scholars to believe that the serpent is in fact the sea monster—the Leviathan.[45] Both entities are said to encompass the part of the high priest's accoutrement which, in Josephus's description, was associated with the earth. Our study already demonstrated that the ocean, symbolized by the sash, encompasses here the microcosmic temple embodied by the high priest's figure. But could the Leviathan imagery also be part of this sacerdotal symbolic framework? In this respect it is important that Jewish lore envisioned not only the sea or ocean, but also its enigmatic inhabitant, the Leviathan himself, as the sacred courtyard that encompasses the temple of creation. In these traditions, the Leviathan is depicted as the one who encompasses the earth, acting as "*Circuitus Mundi.*"[46]

William Whitney's exhaustive research on the Leviathan legends demonstrates that in later Jewish materials, this idea is most clearly represented by Rashbam in his commentary on *b. Bava Batra* 74b. In his interpretation of the famous talmudic passage dealing with the monsters, Rashbam reveals knowledge of a tradition about a female Leviathan who surrounds the earth.[47] Whitney draws attention to another specimen of this motif, found in *Midrash 'Aseret Had-dibberot* (ca. tenth century CE), which transmits the following portrayal of the Leviathan:

> The Holy One (Blessed be He) wished to create the world. Immediately its length was a journey of five hundred years and its breadth a journey of five hundred years. And the great sea surrounded the whole world like an arch of a great pillar. And the whole world was encircled by the fins of Leviathan, who dwells in the lower waters. In them he was like a little fish in the sea.[48]

The presence of this idea in relatively late Jewish materials does not necessarily mean that the tradition of the Leviathan as the *Circuitus Mundi* represents merely a rabbinic invention. Whitney notes that "the image of a serpent which encircles the cosmos, the *ouroboros* (tail-devourer), so named because it is usually represented with its tail in its mouth, is an ancient iconographic motif in the Mediterranean world occurring frequently in magical amulets and certain texts of the Greco-Roman period."[49]

Alexander Kulik's research on the Leviathan tradition in *3 Baruch* demonstrates that the idea of the primordial reptile as the *Circuitus Mundi* has ancient roots.[50] A passage from Philo of Byblos's work *On Snakes,* preserved in Eusebius's *Praeparatio Evangelica* 1.10.45–53, contains such a concept:

> Moreover the Egyptians, describing the world from the same idea, engrave the circumference of a circle of the color of the sky and of fire, and a hawk-shaped serpent stretched across the middle of it,

> and the whole shape like our Theta, representing the circle as the world, and signifying by the serpent which connects it in the middle the good daemon.[51]

Pistis Sophia 3.126 also attests to this motif of the cosmic serpent that encompasses the entire world: "The outer darkness is a great dragon whose tail is in its mouth, and it is outside the whole world and it surrounds the whole world."[52]

Kulik identifies yet another reference to a cosmic reptile who encompasses the world and is associated with the ocean, found in the *Acts of Thomas* 32:[53]

> The snake says to him: I am a reptile, the son of reptile, and harmer, the son of harmer: I am the son of him, to whom power was given over (all) creatures, and he troubled them. I am the son of him, who makes himself like to God to those who obey him, that they may do his will. I am the son of him, who is ruler over everything that is created under heaven. I am the son of him, who is outside of the ocean, and whose mouth is closed.[54]

A crucial early testimony to the Leviathan as the *Circuitus Mundi* is found in Origen's work, *Contra Celsum* VI.25:

> It contained a drawing of ten circles, which were separated from one another and held together by a single circle, which was said to be the soul of the universe and was called Leviathan. The Jewish scriptures, with a hidden meaning in mind, said that this Leviathan was formed by God as a plaything. For in the Psalms we find: "Thou hast made all things in wisdom; the earth is filled with thy creation. This is the sea great and wide; there go the ships, small animals and great, this serpent which thou didst form to play with him." Instead of the word "serpent" the Hebrew text read "Leviathan." The impious diagram said that the Leviathan, which was clearly so objectionable to the prophet, is the soul that has permeated the universe. We also found that Behemoth is mentioned in it as if it were some being fixed below the lowest circle. The inventor of this horrible diagram depicted Leviathan upon the circumference of the circle and at its centre, putting in the name twice.[55]

Whitney's research underscores the complexity of the Leviathan imagery in this presentation of the Ophite diagram. In his judgment, the "circled" serpent (*ouroboros*) is portrayed as surrounding another "axial" serpent.[56]

Finally, the most important passage suggesting the Leviathan's role as *Circuitus Mundi* can be found in the *Apocalypse of Abraham*, a text usually dated to the second century CE. In this text Abraham is given a vision of the lower regions of creation, where he is able to behold the domain of the Leviathan. *Apoc. Ab.* 21:1–5 reads:

> And he said to me, "Look now beneath your feet at the expanse and contemplate the creation which was previously covered over. On this level there is the creation and those who inhabit it and the age that has been prepared to follow it." And I looked beneath the expanse at my feet and I saw the likeness of heaven and what was therein. And I saw there the earth and its fruits, and its moving ones, and its spiritual ones, and its host of men and their spiritual impieties, and their justifications, and the pursuits of their works, and the abyss and its torment, and its lower depths, and the perdition which is in it. And I saw there the sea and its islands, and its animals and its fishes, and Leviathan and his domain, and his lair, and his dens, and the world which lies upon him, and his motions and the destruction of the world because of him. I saw there the rivers and their overflows, and their circles (круты ихъ).[57]

Two details of this description are important for our study. First is the association of the Leviathan's domain with the water symbolism, including the sea and the rivers. Connecting the Leviathan to the rivers will become a prominent motif in later Jewish mysticism.[58] The second feature is the reference to the rivers' *circles* (Slav. круты).[59] Such a reference might indicate the monster's role as the *Circuitus Mundi* in view of his association with these watery streams.

The High Priest as the Eschatological Adam

It is interesting that Josephus describes the high priest's sash as being somewhat different from the belts of ordinary priests, since it had a mixture of gold interwoven into it. In *Ant.* 3.159 he says:

> The high priest is arrayed in like manner, omitting none of the things already mentioned, but over and above these he puts on a tunic of blue material. This too reaches to the feet, and is called in our tongue *meeir*; it is girt about him with a sash decked with the same gay hues as adorned the first, with gold interwoven into its texture.[60]

This description represents a departure from the biblical patterns, where the sash is not associated with gold.[61] However, the golden sash appears in the portrayal of Christ in Rev 1:13,[62] where some argue he is being depicted as the heavenly high priest.[63]

If Josephus's sash is associated with the symbolism of the protological monster, the golden nature of this priestly item brings to mind some Jewish traditions about the luminosity of the Leviathan's skin. *Pesiqta de Rav Kahana*, for example, describes the Leviathan's skin with the symbolism of shining gold that surpasses the splendor of the sun:

> Lest you suppose that the skin of the Leviathan is not something extraordinary, consider what R. Phinehas the Priest ben Hama and R. Jeremiah citing R. Samuel bar R. Isaac said of it: The reflection of the Leviathan's fins makes the disk of the sun dim by comparison, so that it is said of each of the fins "It telleth the sun that it shines weakly" (Job 9:7). For the [Leviathan's] underparts, the reflections thereof, [surpass] the sun: "where it lieth upon the mire, there is a shining of yellow gold" (Job 41:22). It is said, moreover, that the words "Where it lieth upon the mire, there is a shining of yellow gold *(harus)*" mean [not only that the Leviathan's underparts shine, but] that the very place it lies upon is *harus*—that is, golden. Hence where it lieth upon the mire, there is a shining of yellow gold. Still further it is said: Ordinarily, there is no place more filthy than the one where a fish lies. But the place where the Leviathan lies is purer even than yellow gold. Hence where it lieth upon the mire, there is a shining of yellow gold (Job 41:22).[64]

This depiction of the Leviathan's skin with the imagery of "shining of yellow gold" is important for this study, since the high priest's sash in Josephus and Rev 1 is also described with gold symbolism.

Furthermore, *Pesiqta de Rav Kahana* speaks more specifically about the "glory" of the Leviathan:

> On account of its glory, he [God] brings forth his defenders. (Job 41:7). Because he possesses a celestial glory, the Holy One (Blessed be He) says to the ministering angels, "Go down and wage war with it."[65]

Reflecting on this striking narrative about the glory of the primordial reptile, Irving Jacobs notes that

> The imagery and language employed in the opening lines of this passage require further evaluation, particularly the phrase "celestial glory." This unusual formulation occurs, apparently, only in the above context, from which it is difficult to determine its precise significance. We may assume, however, that our unknown aggadist is alluding to an ancient tradition—possibly biblical in origin—that Leviathan is endowed with a supernatural splendour. According to an early tannaitic source, Leviathan's eyes are great orbs of light illuminating the depths of the sea. *Pesiqta d'Rav Kahana*, from which the quotation is taken, also records the tradition that Leviathan's fins alone could dim the light of the sun with their brilliance. In this respect, the splendour of Leviathan is comparable with that of the primordial light, which, according to rabbinic tradition, emanated from the mantle donned by God at the time of creation. Thus Leviathan radiates a heavenly splendour.[66]

The legends about the glory of the Leviathan in rabbinic literature are not confined solely to these excerpts from *Pesiqta de Rav Kahana*, but also can be found in the talmudic passages. *B. Baba Batra* 74a, when describing the Leviathan's skin, also portrays it as a luminous entity: "The Holy One, blessed be He, will in time to come make a tabernacle for the righteous from the skin of Leviathan . . . The rest [of Leviathan] will be spread by the Holy One, blessed be He, upon the walls of Jerusalem, and *its splendour will shine* from one end of the world to the other; as it is said: And nations shall walk at thy light, and kings at the brightness of thy rising."[67] A reference to the Leviathan's "glory" also appears in Qalliri's description of this primordial reptile: "Great fish dance about beneath him. Angels sing above him. They proclaim his splendor and his glory."[68] Scholars often equate "Leviathan's glory to the celestial splendor of the *pulhu*, the divine garment, and the *melammu*, the divine aureole, in which the dragons of Tiamat's army are garbed in *Enuma Elish*."[69]

One interesting detail that emerges from the aforementioned testimonies about the Leviathan's glory is the comparison of its radiance to the sun. Recall that *Pesiqta de Rav Kahana* informs us how "the reflection of the Leviathan's fins makes the disk of the sun dim by comparison." Irving Jacobs noted that the same association is frequently present in rabbinic descriptions of Adam's glory.[70] Indeed, from *b. Baba Batra* 58a we learn that "his [Adam's] two heels . . . were like two orbs of the sun." Midrashim are also familiar with such comparisons. According to *Leviticus Rabbah* 20:2, "The apple of Adam's heel outshone the globe of the sun; how much more so the brightness of his face!"[71] Something similar is found in *Ecclesiastes Rabbah* 8:1: "The ball of Adam's heel outshone the sun . . . so was it not right that the ball of his heel should outshine the sun, and how much more so the beauty of his face!' "[72]

Such a juxtaposition of the motifs of the luminosity of the Leviathan and the protoplast is relevant for our study of the high priest's sash. In Jewish sacerdotal traditions, the high priest was often envisioned as the eschatological Adam who restores the cultic role of the protoplast, he who once was the high priest of the Garden of Eden. Interestingly, some Jewish traditions suggest the garments of the high priest were literally the protoplast's garments, transmitted through successive generations until they reached Aaron.[73]

The link between the high priestly attire and Adam's clothes is significant for this study of the cultic servant wearing the Leviathan's luminous skin, since it echoes some Jewish traditions in which the first humans were portrayed as God's creatures endowed with the glorious garments of demoted antagonists.[74] The transference of the glory of the demoted antagonist can be found, for example, in the *Primary Adam Books*, where Satan's lament about his lost glory is juxtaposed with the traditions about the glorious garments of the first humans. Of even greater importance for this study, however, is that some of these narratives convey how God made the luminous garments for his beloved protoplasts from the skin of the serpent. This is depicted, for instance, in the *Targum Pseudo-Jonathan* on Gen 3:21, a passage that treats the etiology of the first humans' glorious attire. According to this text, the original humans were endowed with luminous garments that had been stripped from the serpent:

> And the Lord God made garments of glory for Adam and for his wife from the skin which the serpent had cast off (to be worn) on the skin of their (garments of) fingernails of which they had been stripped, and he clothed them.[75]

Later midrashim are also cognizant of the enigmatic provenance of the protoplasts' luminous garments. Thus, for example, *Pirke de Rabbi Eliezer* 20 reads:

> Rabbi Eliezer said: From skins which the serpent sloughed off, the Holy One, blessed be He, took and made coats of glory for Adam and his wife, as it is said, "And the Lord God made for Adam and his wife coats of skin, and clothed them."[76]

Still, other interpretive lines postulate that the clothing was made from the skin of the Leviathan.[77] In relation to this interpretive trajectory, William Whitney notes that "two late texts (*Minhat Yehuda* and *Sefer Hadar-Zeqenim*, both on Gen 3:21) also record a tradition in which the skin of the female Leviathan (preserved for the righteous in the world to come) was used to clothe Adam and Eve."[78]

In light of these traditions, the luminous skin of the Leviathan on the high priest may have additional eschatological and anthropological significance—namely, the re-clothing of the eschatological Adam in the form of the sacerdotal servant with the garment of light stripped from the Leviathan.

Conclusion

Finally, we need to draw attention to the eschatological significance of Leviathan's skin, which again, is curiously linked to its function as the cosmological shell of the temple. Thus, from the Babylonian Talmud, we learn that in the last times the luminous skin of the Leviathan will be used in the building material for the eschatological tabernacle:

> Rabbah in the name of R. Johanan further stated: The Holy One, blessed be He, will in time to come make a tabernacle for the righteous from the skin of Leviathan; for it is said: Canst thou fill tabernacles with his skin. If a man is worthy, a tabernacle is made for him; if he is not worthy [of this] a [mere] covering is made for him, for it is said: And his head with a fish covering. If a man is [sufficiently] worthy a covering is made for him; if he is not worthy [even of this], a necklace is made for him, for it is said: And necklaces about thy neck. If he is worthy [of it] a necklace is made for him; if he is not worthy [even of this] an amulet is made for him; as it is said: And thou wilt bind him for thy maidens. The rest [of Leviathan] will be spread by the Holy One, blessed be He, upon the walls of Jerusalem, and its splendor will shine from one end of the world to the other; as it is said: And nations shall walk at thy light, and kings at the brightness of thy rising.[79]

Here, the already familiar motif of Leviathan's skin is used as the outer shell of the tabernacle of the righteous in the time to come. And not only the tabernacle, but even the wall of the Holy City itself will be covered with the skin of the cosmological reptile.

What is particularly curious in this talmudic excerpt, and something not often noticed by students of the Leviathan tradition, is the comparison between the covering for the worthy and the necklace around the neck for the unworthy. This difference might hint at two functions of the Leviathan's skin: one that surrounds the sacred structure akin to the necklace during the normal time, and one that will become its covering in the messianic time.

This eschatological tradition is important because it reveals how the sacerdotal role of the Leviathan—which was a threating force that surrounded and constantly jeopardized the temple during the course of history—is finally affirmed positively in messianic times.

Chapter Four

Apocalyptic Scapegoat Traditions in the Book of Revelation

> And further the Lord said to Raphael: "Bind Asael by his hands and his feet, and throw him into the darkness. And split open the desert which is in Dudael, and throw him there. And throw on him jagged and sharp stones, and cover him with darkness; and let him stay there forever, and cover his face, that he may not see light, and that on the great day of judgment he may be hurled into the fire."
>
> —*1 Enoch* 10:4–6

The Demise of the Scapegoat in Rabbinic and Patristic Accounts

There are striking differences between the classic description of the scapegoat ritual found in Leviticus 16 and later renderings of this rite in rabbinic and early Christian authors. Several enigmatic additions to the Levitical blueprint of the scapegoat ritual appear in later interpretations of this rite found in mishnaic, targumic, and talmudic accounts, especially in the description of the conclusion of the scapegoat ceremony. Some of these accounts insist that in the final moments of the ritual in the wilderness the crimson band of the scapegoat was removed and then placed back onto the animal. The scapegoat was then pushed off the cliff by its handler. These traditions are not attested in the biblical description of Leviticus, yet they figure into many rabbinic and early Christian interpretations. Take, for example, *Mishnah Yoma* 6:6:

> What did he do? He divided the thread of crimson wool and tied one half to the rock and the other half between its horns, and he

> pushed it from behind; and it went rolling down, and before it had reached half the way down the hill it was broken in pieces.[1]

This account depicts the climax of the scapegoat ceremony, in which the scapegoat's handler strips away the infamous crimson band from the cultic animal and then, according to the Mishnah, divides the band into two pieces, one of which was tied to a rock, and the other bound again around the animal's horns. Scholars have previously suggested that the scarlet band[2] here represents an impure garment, or more specifically, an attire of sins,[3] which the cultic animal was predestined to carry into an uninhabitable realm—in this case, the wilderness.[4] Loosing the cultic band at the end of the rite might signify the forgiveness of the Israelites' sins,[5] since, in some Jewish accounts, the imagery of untying is closely connected to the forgiveness of transgressions.[6]

The aforementioned mishnaic passage also hints at the fact that the final destination of the scapegoat's exile was not merely the desert, as described in Leviticus 16, but rather the underworld or abyss, the descent to which being symbolically expressed through the action of pushing the animal off a cliff. This tradition of the unusual demise of the atoning agent is attested in a panoply of rabbinic sources.[7] Early Christian testimonies reflected in the *Epistle of Barnabas*,[8] Justin Martyr,[9] and Tertullian[10] are also cognizant of the peculiar details of the final demise of the scapegoat in the wilderness.

The Demise of the Eschatological Scapegoat in Jewish Apocalypticism

I previously argued that these additions to the scapegoat ritual found in rabbinic and early Christian sources—including the motifs of the scapegoat's binding, the hurling of the scapegoat off a cliff, and the alteration of its garment of sins represented by the crimson band immediately before its death—all stem from the eschatological reinterpretations of the scapegoat rite found in some early Jewish apocalyptic writings, including, the *Book of the Watchers*, the *Animal Apocalypse*, and the *Apocalypse of Abraham*.[11] In these accounts, which were written earlier than the aforementioned rabbinic and patristic testimonies, one finds a striking refashioning of the traditional atoning rite, where the scapegoat's features are transferred to an otherworldly antagonist bearing the name "Asael" or "Azazel."

One of the earliest apocalyptic reinterpretations of the scapegoat ritual in Jewish tradition can be found in the *Book of the Watchers*, in which the story of the cultic gatherer of impurities receives a novel conceptual makeup. This early Enochic booklet refashions the scapegoat rite in an angelological way, incorporating details from the sacrificial ritual into the story of its main antagonist, the fallen angel Asael. *1 Enoch* 10:4–7 presents a striking depiction laden with familiar sacerdotal details:

> And further the Lord said to Raphael: "Bind Asael by his hands and his feet, and throw him into the darkness. And split open the desert which is in Dudael, and throw him there. And throw on him jagged and sharp stones, and cover him with darkness; and let him stay there forever, and cover his face, that he may not see light, and that on the great day of judgment he may be hurled into the fire. And restore the earth which the angels have ruined, and announce the restoration of the earth, for I shall restore the earth. . . ."[12]

Several scholars have noticed numerous details of Asael's punishment that are reminiscent of the scapegoat ritual as it is reflected in *Mishnah Yoma*. Daniel Olson, for instance, argues that "a comparison of *1 Enoch* 10 with the Day of Atonement ritual . . . leaves little doubt that Asael is indeed Azazel."[13] Additionally, Daniel Stökl Ben Ezra observes that "the punishment of the demon resembles the treatment of the goat in aspects of geography, action, time and purpose."[14] He also notes that "both in the description of the prison of the demon in *1 Enoch* and in traditions about the precipice of the scapegoat ritual an element of ruggedness appears. This ruggedness could reflect an early Midrash on the meaning of גזר (cut, split up) in ארץ גזרה (Lev 16:22) and/or historical memory of the actual cliffs in the mountains of Jerusalem."[15] Furthermore, the place of Asael's punishment designated in *1 Enoch* as Dudael is reminiscent of the terminology used for the designation of the ravine of the scapegoat in later rabbinic interpretations of the Yom Kippur ritual, down which the scapegoat was hurled.[16] This tradition is explicitly attested in *m. Yoma* and *Targum Pseudo-Jonathan*.[17]

The tradition of apocalyptic reinterpretations of the scapegoat ritual reaches its symbolic pinnacle in the *Apocalypse of Abraham*. This Jewish text, which was most likely written during the period in which the mishnaic descriptions of the atoning rite received their conclusive textual codification, provides a unique glimpse into the final stages of the ever-changing scapegoat imagery that began many centuries earlier in the Enochic books. Although the early traits of the Enochic apocalyptic blueprint and the Watchers tradition play a formative role in the *Apocalypse of Abraham*, some novel developments—essential to mishnaic and early Christian versions of the atoning ritual—greatly enhanced this conceptual core. Thus, the imagery of the celestial scapegoat's clothing, only vaguely alluded to in the early Enochic books through the symbolism of covering the antagonist with darkness, now receives its distinctive conceptual expression as the impure vestment of human sins.[18]

The details of the angelic scapegoat's exile into the lower realms found in the Slavonic apocalypse are similarly indebted to the early Enochic blueprint. As with Asael in the Enochic tradition, the antagonist's exile in the *Apocalypse of Abraham* encompasses two movements: first, to the earth,[19] and second, to the fiery abyss of the subterranean realm.[20] Although early versions of the scapegoat ritual found in the Book of Leviticus only attest to a one-step removal of the goat to the wilderness, the tradition of the two-step removal plays a prominent role in later mishnaic versions of the rite, in which the cultic animal is first taken to the wilderness and then pushed from a cliff into the abyss.

The *Apocalypse of Abraham* clearly contains the tradition of sending the scapegoat into the lower realm, since in chapters 13 and 14 the heavenly priest-angel Yahoel banishes Azazel first to the earthly realm and then into the abyss of the subterranean sphere. It is noteworthy that, much like the scapegoat in mishnaic testimonies, the antagonist's exile in the Slavonic apocalypse coincides with his dis-robing and re-robing. The text reports that the fallen angel was first disrobed of his celestial garment and then re-clothed in the ominous attire of human sins; it reads: "For behold, the garment which in heaven was formerly yours has been set aside for him, and the corruption which was on him has gone over to you."[21]

Book of Revelation

The Book of Revelation also belongs to the aforementioned group of apocalyptic writings that offer an eschatological reinterpretation of the scapegoat ritual. The limited scope of this investigation does not allow us to explore all of the Yom Kippur allusions found in the Book of Revelation.[22] Instead, this section will focus on the tradition of the dragon's demise in the Book of Revelation and its possible connection with the scapegoat ritual.

Before proceeding to a close analysis of the conceptual developments found in the Book of Revelation, let us reiterate the main features of the final moments of the scapegoat ritual, as reflected in apocalyptic, mishnaic, and patristic testimonies. They include the following elements:

1. The motif of the scapegoat's removal, represented as a two-stage movement (the antagonist's banishment into the wilderness, and his placement in the abyss or underworld, symbolized in the atoning ritual by pushing the goat off the cliff);
2. The motif of the (angelic) handler who binds and pushes the scapegoat off the cliff;
3. The motif of the scapegoat's binding;

4. The motif of sealing the abyss of the scapegoat;
5. The motif of the temporary healing of the earth;
6. The motif of the scapegoat's temporary unbinding before its final demise;
7. The motif of the scarlet band of the scapegoat.

THE MOTIF OF THE ANTAGONIST'S BANISHMENT

Let us start by exploring the eschatological scapegoat's processions. As mentioned above, in *1 Enoch* 10 the deity orders Raphael to open the pit in the desert and throw Asael into the darkness. The text goes on to describe the celestial scapegoat's fall into the depths of the abyss. Yet the exile of the apocalyptic scapegoat may begin even earlier in the narrative, when the infamous watcher descends from heaven to earth with other members of the rebellious angelic group.

My previous analysis of the otherworldly scapegoat traditions demonstrates that, both in the *Book of the Watchers* and the *Apocalypse of Abraham*, the exile of the apocalyptic scapegoat encompasses a two-stage development. The antagonist first descends to the earth and then into the underground realm, represented by the abyss.[23] Such a two-stage progression of the antagonist's exile corresponds to the two stages of the earthly scapegoat's movements, reflected in later rabbinic and patristic sources by the scapegoat's banishment to the wilderness and its descent into the abyss when the animal was pushed off the cliff.[24]

In the Book of Revelation, a similar two-stage progressive movement shows the main antagonist, the dragon, first banished to the earth in chapter 12, and then to the underground realm, represented by the abyss in chapter 20. This movement merits closer examination.

Revelation 12:9 relates the following tradition: "the great dragon was thrown down . . . he was thrown down to the earth, and his angels were thrown down with him." It is intriguing that here, like in the *Book of the Watchers* and the *Apocalypse of Abraham*, the eschatological scapegoat is demoted along with his "portion."

One important detail of the aforementioned story of the angelic descent in Revelation 12:9 is that the antagonist and his angels did not descend to earth voluntarily, like in the early Enochic booklets, but rather they "were thrown down." This links the tradition found in the Book of Revelation even more closely to the scapegoat ritual, in which the animal was involuntary led out into the wilderness by its handler. It also places the Book of Revelation's rendering of the celestial antagonist's demotion in very close connection to the interpretation found in the *Apocalypse of Abraham*. There, the main antagonist of the story—the fallen angel Azazel—is also forcefully demoted by his angelic handler, Yahoel.

Furthermore, it is noteworthy that the dragon's exile to the earth coincides in Revelation 12 with the wilderness motif, since upon his exile to earth the dragon pursues the woman clothed with the sun in the desert (εἰς τὴν ἔρημον). This is relevant for our study of the imagery of the scapegoat, whose exile to the wilderness represents an important topological marker in many apocalyptic Yom Kippur accounts. Thus, as is written in the *Apocalypse of Abraham,* Yahoel banishes Azazel not simply to the earth, but to "the untrodden parts of the earth." The word "untrodden" (Slav. беспроходна, lit. "impassable")[25] is significant because it designates a place uninhabitable to human beings, reminiscent of the language of Lev 16, where the scapegoat is dispatched to the solitary place in the wilderness.[26]

Second, the "underground" stage of the scapegoat's exile can be identified in Revelation 20:2–3, where the antagonist is thrown into the subterranean chamber: "He seized the dragon . . . and threw him into the pit, and locked and sealed it over him."[27] Here, again, like in the *Book of the Watchers*[28] and the *Apocalypse of Abraham*, this underground imprisonment is temporary, since on the Day of Judgment the antagonist will be thrown for a second time, but this time into the abyss of fire[29]—an event labeled in Revelation as "the second death."[30]

Remember that *1 Enoch* 10:6 describes Asael's second punishment in the following terms: "On the great day of judgment he may be hurled into the fire."[31] In Rev 20:10 this second ordeal is rendered in the following way: "And the devil who had deceived them was thrown into the lake of fire and sulfur, where the beast and the false prophet were, and they will be tormented day and night forever and ever." Both apocalyptic descriptions betray a similar symbolism, namely, the distinctive imagery of fire.

The *Apocalypse of the Abraham* also portrays the pit of the eschatological scapegoat with fiery imagery. There, the underground domain of the antagonist is depicted as the very place of fire. For instance, in Yahoel's speech found in chapter 14, which reveals the true location of the chief antagonist, the archdemon's abode is designated as the furnace of the earth. Azazel himself, moreover, is depicted as the "burning coal" or the "firebrand" of this infernal kiln.

Unlike the Book of Revelation, the *Book of the Watchers* does not describe a temporary release of its antagonist. Yet such an idea might be hinted at in the *Apocalypse of Abraham*, where Azazel, despite his exile into the underground prison, still retains his ability to corrupt humankind.

THE MOTIF OF THE ANGELIC HANDLER

A prominent feature of the mishnaic depiction of the scapegoat ritual is the motif of the scapegoat's handler, who performs ritual actions with regards to the animal by leading it into the wilderness, binding and unbinding its crimson band, and finally throwing the animal into the pit. In the apocalyptic versions of the atoning rite, these sacerdotal actions are performed by angelic figures, namely, Raphael in the *Book of the Watchers* and Yahoel in the *Apocalypse of Abraham*. Similarly, in the Book of Revelation there is an angelic figure that binds and handles the eschatological scapegoat. In Rev 20:1 the seer reports that he saw an angel coming down from heaven, holding in his hand the key to the bottomless pit and a great chain.

Remember that in rabbinic renderings of the scapegoat ritual the animal is thrown into the abyss by its handler. The same order of events can be seen in the *Book of the Watchers*, where Raphael throws Asael into the dark underground pit, and in Rev 20:3, where the angelic figure throws the dragon into the abyss. In the *Apocalypse of Abraham*, the angel Yahoel orders Azazel to be banished into exile to the lower realm, namely, the abyss.

THE MOTIF OF THE SCAPEGOAT'S BINDING

Although the biblical account of the scapegoat ritual found in Leviticus does not mention the binding of the scapegoat, this motif became very prominent in the mishnaic accounts. A passage in *Mishnah Yoma* 4:2 tells how the scapegoat is bound with scarlet thread upon its selection by lottery. Even more important for our study is a tradition found in *Mishnah Yoma* 6:6, which relates that, in the final moments of the scapegoat ceremony, immediately before its demise off the cliff, the go-away goat was unbound and then re-tied with the crimson band.[32] The features that mishnaic authors weave into the fabric of the ancient rite are intriguing and seemingly novel. Yet it should not be forgotten that, several centuries before the composition of the Mishnah, some apocalyptic accounts already linked the scapegoat ritual with the symbolism of binding.[33] In *1 Enoch* 10 we have already seen the handler of the celestial scapegoat, the archangel Rafael, instructed to bind the demon by his hands and feet immediately before throwing him into the subterranean pit. This tradition represents a remarkable parallel to *Mishnah Yoma* 6:6, in which the cultic animal is bound with a crimson band immediately before its demise.

The motif of the antagonist's binding receives its distinctive expression also in the Book of Revelation. In Rev 20:1–2 the seer beholds an angel coming down from heaven, holding in his hand the key to the bottomless pit and a great chain.[34] The angel then seized the dragon and bound him for a thousand years. Robert Henry Charles has noted a parallel between this passage and the tradition of Asael's binding in the *Book of the Watchers*.[35] David Aune,[36] and recently Kelley Coblentz Bautch,[37] also both reaffirm the connection between Revelation 20 and *1 Enoch* 10 by cataloging numerous parallels. Coblentz Bautch concludes that "the binding and imprisonment of Satan in an abyss and a second punishment by fire strongly evoke the fate of the rebellious angels as presented in numerous accounts."[38]Although Aune and Coblentz Bautch do not discuss the relationships between the dragon's binding and the scapegoat motif, Lester Grabbe entertains this implicit connection. He argues that the punishment of the dragon in Revelation has been assimilated to the apocalyptic scapegoat tradition found in *1 Enoch* 10.[39]

THE MOTIF OF SEALING THE SCAPEGOAT'S ABYSS

Another important connection that ties Revelation 20 to *1 Enoch* 10 is the motif of sealing the abyss of the antagonist's first imprisonment. From Rev 20:3 one learns that, after the dragon was thrown into the abyss, the executing angel then locked and sealed the pit over him.

Similarly, in the *Book of the Watchers*, Raphael seals the abyss of the eschatological scapegoat with sharp rocks and darkness. Remember that in *1 Enoch* 10 God commands Raphael to throw onto Asael jagged and sharp stones, and cover him with darkness. The motif of sealing the tomb of the eschatological scapegoat might also be present in the story of another—this time Christian—eschatological scapegoat, namely Jesus, whose temporarily placement in the underground chamber was also accompanied by the sealing of his tomb with a stone.

THE MOTIF OF THE TEMPORARY HEALING OF THE EARTH

In his analysis of the similarities between the punishment of Asael in *1 Enoch* 10 and Yom Kippur traditions, Daniel Stökl ben Ezra argues that the restoration of the earth by the removal of sin in *1 Enoch* 10:7–8 alludes to the cathartic rationale behind Yom Kippur.[40] It is noteworthy that in the *Book of the Watchers*, "the healing of the earth" occurs immediately after Asael's banishment into the abyss but before his fiery demise. This final ordeal will happen much later, on the Day of Judgment, which will occur (as in the case of the other Watchers) after seventy generations of entombment.[41] Such sandwiching of "the healing of the earth" between the antagonist's first and second punishments brings to mind several developments found in the Book of Revelation, where the dragon's first banishment precedes the peace of the millennium, which will later be interrupted by the dragon's brief release. The removal of the antagonist into the bottomless pit appears to accomplish, as in Asael's episode, cathartic and purifying functions that allow the earth to flourish. This context underlines the principal "elimination" aspect of the scapegoat ritual, whereby impurity must be removed from the human *oikoumene* and sent into the uninhabitable realm.[42] This period of prosperity, however, ends with the unchaining of the dragon. Pieter de Villiers has drawn attention to the fact that "the millennium is deliberately framed by the chaining of the dragon and his unchaining which follows in Revelation 20:7–10."[43] The apocalyptic portrayal of earth's healing as a temporary event might be rooted in Yom Kippur traditions, according to which the purification of the land and the community must be repeated on a regular basis.

THE MOTIF OF THE SCAPEGOAT'S TEMPORARY UNBINDING BEFORE HIS FINAL DEMISE

In *m. Yoma* 6:6 we saw that immediately before the scapegoat's final demise its handler briefly removed its crimson band. Such a procedure might signify a short-term release of the antagonist from bondage. It is possible that this theme of the temporary unbinding of the cultic ribbon is also attested in some apocalyptic scapegoat traditions. For example, in addition to the dragon's binding, the Book of Revelation reports his release from captivity. Thus, after the description of the millennium in Rev 20:4–6, during which the dragon remains chained in the bottomless pit, the text discloses the mystery of his release from imprisonment. This event is closely tied to the previous section (pertaining to his imprisonment) through a subtle yet significant terminological link between the chaining and the unchaining, which is formulated by λυθῆναι in Rev. 20:3 and λυθήσεται in Rev 20:7.[44]

THE MOTIF OF THE RED BAND

A particularly important motif, absent in Leviticus 16 but present in mishnaic and early Christian testimonies, is the theme of the scapegoat's crimson band that was put on the animal's head during the ritual of the goats' selection.[45] This scarlet band is regularly reinterpreted in the apocalyptic Yom Kippur traditions as the (red) garment. Thus, for example, the *Apocalypse of Abraham* speaks about Azazel's garment, and the *Epistle of Barnabas* reinterprets the crimson band as a long scarlet robe around Christ's flesh. As evident in apocalyptic scapegoat traditions, the crimson color was often projected onto the entire extent of the eschatological characters.

In light of these developments, special attention should be drawn to Rev 12:3, where the dragon is associated with a fiery red color (πυρρός). Scholarly interpretations of this color symbolism have proffered a panoply of references to various Egyptian,[46] Mesopotamian,[47] and Greek traditions.[48] What is sometimes overlooked in these scholarly debates is that in ancient Jewish lore, the color red was often associated with impurity and defilement. Already Isa 1:18 hints at such an understanding, delivering a promise from the deity that although Israel's "sins are like scarlet, they shall be like snow; though they are red like crimson, they shall become like wool." This passage, associating sin with the color red, was predestined to play a special role in the mishnaic testimonies concerning the crimson band of the scapegoat. Thus, both *m. Yoma* 6:8[49] and *m. Shabbat* 9:3[50] connect the tradition of the crimson band to the aforementioned passage from Isaiah that speaks about the forgiveness of sins. Elsewhere, a connection was made between the scarlet thread and human sins, since Jewish lore often associated the color red with sin, and white with forgiveness. The *Book of Zohar* II.20a–b neatly summarizes this understanding of the color's symbolism:

> Sin is red, as it says, "Though your sins be as scarlet"; man puts the sacrificial animal on fire, which is also red; the priest sprinkles the red blood round the altar, but the smoke ascending to heaven is white. Thus the red is turned to white: the attribute of Justice is turned into the attribute of Mercy.

A very similar appropriation of the color imagery appears to be reflected in the scapegoat ritual. The band's transformation from red to white, signaling the forgiveness of Israel's sins, strengthens the association of the red coloration with sin.[51] Numerous mishnaic and talmudic passages attest to the whitening of the band[52] during the scapegoat ritual, which signifies the removal of sins.[53]

The author of Revelation likely knows of this symbolic conception in which the color red is able to turn white, thus signifying the removal of human transgressions.[54] So, for example, in Rev 7:14 one finds a statement that the righteous had "washed their robes and made them white in the blood of the Lamb."

In light of the aforementioned traditions, it should not be considered coincidental that many antagonists in the Book of Revelation (some of whom had human sins literally heaped upon them) are associated with the color red. Thus, for example, the Scarlet Beast and the Harlot[55] are portrayed in crimson (κόκκινον) garments.[56] These color associations evoke the memory of the scarlet band of the scapegoat.[57] Future investigations into these intriguing details might help clarify the true extent and nature of the Yom Kippur traditions found in the Book of Revelation.

Chapter Five

Azazel's Will

Internalization of Evil in the *Apocalypse of Abraham*

Our forefather Abraham turned the evil instincts into good.

—*y. Ber.* 9:5, 14b

Introduction

The *Apocalypse of Abraham*, a Jewish pseudepigraphon composed several decades after the destruction of the Second Temple, contains a large number of demonological traditions. The profile of the main antagonist of this apocalyptic account, the fallen angel Azazel, is firmly rooted in the Enochic etiology of evil, which was based on the myth of the fallen angels. According to this myth, a group of celestial rebels, called the Watchers, corrupted human beings in the antediluvian period through illicit knowledge and forbidden marital unions. Although the Watchers' corrupting activities in early Enochic booklets were executed through external means—namely, teaching and marriage—the fallen angel of the *Apocalypse of Abraham* is depicted as one who can corrupt human beings even through *internal* means—namely, the faculty of the will. The motif of Azazel's will as an instrument against the human will appears in *Apoc. Ab.* 14:12. There, Abraham's mentor, the angel Yahoel, warns his apprentice about the antagonist's unusual weapon by uttering the following words: "Whatever he says to you, answer him not, lest *his will* (воля его) affect you."[1] The gravity of this internal armament becomes even more apparent in the next verse, where Yahoel explains that this "will" was given to Azazel by God: "God gave him (Azazel) the gravity and *the will* (волю) against those who answer him."[2] Furthermore, the significance of the will for the destiny of a person is reiterated later in the dialogue between God and Abraham in chapter 26 and in other parts of the story.[3]

The motifs of the antagonist's will and the human will are important because they emphasize a crucial human capacity over which Azazel is given some control. The repeated reference to this inner faculty, by which the adversary is able to exercise his influence upon human beings, contributes to a novel demonological setting that can be labeled as an "internalized demonology." Several other details of the text also point to this internalizing of the economy of evil in the *Apocalypse of Abraham*. A short excursus into the process of the internalization of evil in early Jewish lore will elucidate this phenomenon and its impact on the apocalypse's demonology.

I. The Internalization of Evil in Early Jewish Lore

The Internalization of Evil in Early Enochic Materials

As already noted, the fallen angels played an important role in the early Enochic mythology of evil insofar as they were portrayed as the main vehicles of humankind's corruption in the antediluvian period. Yet the "angelic" paradigm had its own limitations for the development of the "internalized" demonologies, since in certain ways it impeded the capacity of the otherworldly antagonist to possess a person or directly influence his or her internal faculties. The fallen angels in the early Enochic story exercised their evil plans externally through illicit instructions or sexual intercourses rather than through direct impact on the human soul.[4] Yet the development of the so-called *yetzer* anthropologies[5] in the Hebrew Bible and Jewish extra-biblical materials demonstrated an urgent need for internalized demonologies in which the antagonists were able to rule inner inclinations of the human heart.[6] The earliest angelological lore attested in the Enochic tradition has another important development, namely, the concept of malevolent spirits. These antagonistic entities, due to their peculiar bodiless ontology, have the potential to take possession of a human being directly, without lengthy instructions or marital commitments.

The *Book of the Watchers* attempts to develop a certain type of demonology in which the adversaries of humankind are envisioned as disembodied spirits who can function inside human bodies and souls. In the *Book of the Watchers*, this conceptual move is closely tied to the Giants' story. The Giants' hybrid anthropology, in which angelic and human were once mingled together, opened a door to a novel psychodemonic synthesis. According to the Enochic myth, although the Giants' bodies perished in the divine punishment, their evil spirits (πνεύματα πονηρά) survived the ordeal, allowing them to harm human beings until the final judgment. Concerning the etiology of malevolent spirits, Loren Stuckenbruck notes:

> The extant textual witnesses to *1 Enoch* 15 do not specify how this change has come about. Nevertheless, the following aetiology may be inferred from a reading of 15:3–16:3 as an elaboration on parts of 10:1–22: As a mixture of heavenly and earthly beings, the Giants were composed of flesh and spirit. When, on account of their destructive activities, they came under divine judgement, the fleshly part of their nature was destroyed, whether through violent conflict among themselves (7:5; 10:12) or through the flood. At this point, spirits or souls emerged from their dead bodies, and it is in this disembodied form that the Giants continue to exist until the final judgement (16:1).[7]

According to *1 Enoch* 10:15, God ordered Michael to "destroy all the spirits of the half-breeds and the sons of the Watchers, because they have wronged men."[8] William Loader has suggested that "this assumes the separate existence of the spirits (πνεύματα, *nafesāta*), independent of the Giants, themselves."[9] Touching on these spirits' nature, Philip Alexander points out that the Giants "consisted of two elements—a mortal, material body, and an immortal spirit. The mortal bodies of the Giants were destroyed, but their immortal spirits were not, and these have continued to inhabit the earth and to afflict mankind."[10] According to Alexander, "unlike the Watchers, who have already been judged and restrained, prior to their final punishment on the day of judgment, the spirits of the Giants will 'go on destroying, uncondemned . . . until the great judgment.' "[11]

The teaching about malevolent spirits is rendered in even greater detail in *1 Enoch* 15.[12] In *1 Enoch* 15:2–15, God orders Enoch to deliver the following message to the fallen Watchers:

> And go, say to the Watchers of heaven who sent you to petition on their behalf: "You ought to petition on behalf of men, not men on behalf of you. Why have you left the high, holy, and eternal heaven, and lain with the women and become unclean with the daughters of men, and taken wives for yourselves, and done as the sons of the earth and begotten giant sons? And you (were) spiritual, holy, living an eternal life, (but) you became unclean upon the women, and begat (children) through the blood of flesh, and lusted after the blood of men, and produced flesh and blood as they do who die and

> are destroyed. And for this reason I gave them wives, (namely) that they might sow seed in them and (that) children might be born by them, that thus deeds might be done on the earth. But you formerly were spiritual, living an eternal, immortal life for all the generations of the world. For this reason I did not arrange wives for you because the dwelling of the spiritual ones (is) in heaven. And now the Giants who were born from body and flesh will be called evil spirits upon the earth, and on the earth will be their dwelling. And evil spirits came out from their flesh because from above they were created; from the holy Watchers was their origin and first foundation. Evil spirits they will be on the earth, and spirits of the evil ones they will be called. And the dwelling of the spirits of heaven is in heaven, but the dwelling of the spirits of earth, who were born on the earth, (is) on earth. And the spirits of the Giants[13] . . . which do wrong and are corrupt, and attack and fight and break on the earth, and cause sorrow; and they eat no food and do not thirst, and are not observed. And these spirits will rise against the sons of men and against the women because they came out (from them)."[14]

In relation to these Enochic traditions, George Nickelsburg points out that "the Giants[15] and the spirits that proceed from their dead bodies are spoken of as the same entities. . . . these are evil spirits."[16] According to Nickelsburg, "This term (πνεύματα πονηρά) is not especially common for demons, but in the literature of this period it always refers to malevolent spirits who cause people to sin or afflict them with evil and disease."[17]

The important quality of these evil spirits of the Giants is that they were able to bridge conventional anthropological boundaries through their ability to "afflict" the human body, possibly even by dwelling inside of a human being. *1 Enoch* 19:1 reflects the malevolent spirits' capacity for embodiment by relating that they are able to assume many forms: "And Uriel said to me: 'The spirits of the angels who were promiscuous with the women will stand here; and they, *assuming many forms, made men unclean* and will lead men astray so that they sacrifice to demons as gods—(that is,) until the great judgment day on which they will be judged so that an end will be made of them.' "[18]

In his thorough and nuanced study about the provenance of the evil spirits, Archie Wright observes that "the evil spirits of the Giants did become the central characters of the story. As a result, Jews may have understood them as the force behind the gentile nations that oppressed Israel, as supernatural powers driving a corrupt leadership, or as spirits that afflicted individuals."[19] *1 Enoch* 15 may contain one of the earliest rationalizations of an internalized demonology in Jewish lore, when the spirits of the external antagonists suddenly were able to control the inner drives and inclinations of humankind. Reflecting on the bridge from external to internal demonological realities, Wright proposes that "the spirits of Giants in the Watcher tradition represent an *external* threat, which operates against the *internal good inclination* of the individual."[20] Wright's use of the term "inclination" begs the question of whether the aforementioned Enochic developments can be seen as a testimony to the *yetzer* tradition. Although *1 Enoch* 15 does not speak directly about *yetzer*, it is likely not coincidental that the very first occurrence of such terminology in the Hebrew Bible is found in a cryptic rendering of the Watchers story attested in Genesis 6.[21] In Gen 6:5, after the *bene elohim*'s descent, "The Lord saw that the wickedness of humankind was great in the earth, and that *every inclination of the thoughts of his heart* was only evil continually."

Internalization of Evil in the Book of Jubilees

Like the early Enochic booklets, the *Book of Jubilees* also traces the origin of evil spirits that torment human beings to the fall of the Watchers.[22] *Jub.* 10:5–7, a passage that speaks about the provenance of demonic spirits, specifically mentions the fallen Watchers as "the fathers of these spirits":[23]

> "You know how your Watchers, the fathers of these spirits, have acted during my lifetime. As for these spirits who have remained alive, imprison them and hold them captive in the place of judgment. May they not cause destruction among your servant's sons, my God, for they are savage and were created for the purpose of destroying. May they not rule the spirits of the living, for you alone know their punishment; and may they not have power over the sons of the righteous from now and forevermore." Then our God told us to tie up each one.[24]

Several scholars have detected a paradigm shift from an angelic to a demonic economy of evil in *Jubilees,* in comparison with the early Enochic booklets.[25] Thus, Annette Reed highlights that "*Jubilees* concurs on one point: the demons are the spirits of the Watchers' hybrid sons. The Watchers, however, *are no longer held responsible for demonic activity on earth* after the time of Noah."[26] Wright also underlines this peculiarity of *Jubilees* by noting that "we are told that the unclean spirits began to lead astray humanity and to destroy them."[27] Deliberating on this important conceptual turn, Loren Stuckenbruck notes:

> The explanation given in *Jubilees* for the origin of evil spirits and demons reflects a shift from the accounts in the *Book of Watchers,*

> *Book of Giants*, and *Animal Apocalypse*. Though the demons are, similar to the *Book of Watchers* and *Book of Giants*, identified as the souls or spirits of the dead Giants (10:5), there is no hint, in contrast to the Enochic traditions, that any of the Giants were actually killed through the flood. The persistence of at least some Giants in the form of spirits beyond the flood is retained by *Jubilees*. However, it seems that in *Jubilees* the Giants have assumed their disembodied state prior to the flood (5:8–9). The Giants' evil character is not articulated explicitly in anthropological terms (*contra 1 Enoch* 15:4, 6–8), that is, as the result of an impure mixture of flesh and spirit on the part of their progenitors.[28]

In *Jubilees* and early Enochic writings, the elaboration of a new class of antagonistic creatures—ones who are different from the fallen angels and who are able, due to their bodiless ontology, to dwell inside human beings—demonstrates a clear tendency toward an internalized demonology. In this respect, the demonology of the evil spirits offered several important benefits for the development of such an internalized option. Concerning the difference between angels and demons,[29] Philip Alexander points out that although

> both demons and angels can be classified as "spirits," since they are both unseen, spiritual forces, but it is evident that they are different in a number of important ways. Thus demons *can invade the human body*, from which they can only be expelled through exorcism, whereas angels cannot. Nowhere do we read of an angel possessing a human. He can reveal himself to the human, and terrify him—but cannot enter his body. The myth of the Giants gives this idea a kind of logic. The demons are part human in origin and so have an affinity with humans, which allows them to penetrate the human body. Indeed, it may be implied that, as disembodied spirits roaming the world, like the human "undead," they particularly seek embodiment, with all its attendant problems for the one whom they possess.[30]

Such a paradigm shift from *embodied* antagonists in the form of (fallen) angels to *bodiless* spiritual entities in the form of demons will serve as an important conceptual avenue for some later *yetzer* anthropologies.

The anthropological limitations of the "angelological" model in advancing various *yetzer* anthropologies led to situations in which the demonological profile of "angelic" antagonists, like Satan or Belial, were supplemented in such a way that they acquired armies of spiritual entities of other kinds who were able to interact directly with human nature or even possess a human being. Such supplementation to the traditional profile of the angelic antagonist with novel demonological capacities can be detected both in *Jubilees* and in the Qumran materials. This shift remains more visible in the *Book of Jubilees* as it portrays its personified angelic[31] antagonist as the leader of the demonic spirits.[32] Stuckenbruck notes that "in *Jubilees* 'Mastema' represents a proper name for the chief demonic power that *has jurisdiction over a contingent of evil spirits*."[33] He further observes that "the most frequent designation of this entity is 'Prince of Mastema/ Animosity' or, better translated, 'Prince Mastema' (*Jub.* 11:5, 11; 18:9, 12; 48:2, 9, 12, 15)" who is understood "as the leader of the spirits requesting permission for a tenth of their number to carry out their work after the Flood."[34]

In Mastema's role as the leader of the demonic spirits in *Jubilees,* Archie Wright detects a departure from a leadership pattern found in early Enochic booklets. According to Wright, "This is a major shift from the role of the evil spirits in the *Book of the Watchers*; there they have no apparent leader, and there is no mention of the figure of Satan (Mastema in *Jubilees*)."[35] He further notes that "the notion of a leader over the realm of evil spirits seems to have been taken up in some of the DSS [Dead Sea Scrolls] that express a demonological interest. The figure in the DSS, identified as Belial, may be connected to Mastema in *Jubilees*."[36]

Another difference is that, while in early Enochic materials both the fallen angels and their evil offspring are portrayed as rogue agents, the rebels corrupting the deity's design of creation, in *Jubilees,* Mastema and his demons represent an essential part of God's plan. As Annette Reed observes, "In *Jubilees* the spirits of the Watchers' sons cause sin, bloodshed, pollution, illness, and famine after the flood (esp. *Jub.* 11:2–6). It is made explicit, however, that they do so as part of God's plan."[37] The antagonist's role in *Jubilees* is reminiscent of Azazel's office in the *Apocalypse of Abraham,* where God also gives the adversary a special will against the sinners.[38]

For this investigation, it is significant that Mastema corrupts humans *through* the army of demons.[39] Thus, according to *Jub.* 11:5, "Prince Mastema was exerting his power in effecting all these actions and, *by means of the spirits*, he was sending to those who were placed under his control (the ability) to commit every (kind of) error and sin and every (kind of) transgression; to corrupt, to destroy, and to shed blood on the earth."[40] In some passages of *Jubilees* these spiritual agents are even called the "spirits of Mastema."[41] Reflecting on this feature, Benne Reynolds suggests that "later Hebrew texts tend to subordinate demons under a chief demon and in many cases strip the evil spirits of any unique, individual identity. This trend . . . is already present in the second century BCE, e.g., *Jubilees*."[42]

Another important aspect is found in *Jub.* 12:20, where Abraham prays to God to save him from "the power of evil spirits who rule the *yetzer of a person's heart*."[43] Here, the evil spirits are unambiguously labeled as the "rulers" of the human *yetzer*. Although in recent years a large amount of ink has been spilled over analyzing the demonological developments found in *Jubilees*, not many scholars have addressed this aspect of the evil spirits' economy that allows them to influence the *yetzer* of the human heart directly.

To summarize this part of our investigation, there are four crucial features of *Jubilees*' demonology. First, in comparison with early Enochic booklets, the evil spirits now replace the fallen angels as the main corrupting force of humankind. Second, these spiritual beings are hierarchized under the leadership of the single angelic antagonist who bears the name Mastema or Belial. Third, this chief angelic antagonist and his demonic army fulfill the will of the deity. Fourth, the evil spirits are able to rule the *yetzer* of the human heart.

Internalization of Evil in the Qumran Materials

Qumran materials contain several demonological molds, so any attempt to speak about a single or unified demonology of the Scrolls will be a mistake.[44] Although systematic demonologies are lacking in Qumran materials, some of these materials have common demonological traits, several of which demonstrate close similarities to the aforementioned demonological tendencies found in early Enochic booklets and the *Book of Jubilees*.

Some Qumran materials contain a familiar consolidation of evil spirits under the leadership of an angelic antagonist, which in some Qumran texts[45] are labeled as "the spirits of Belial."[46] Some texts speak about spirits of the portion or the lot of Belial. From 1QM XIII 2 we learn about "Belial[47] and all the spirits of his lot."[48] 4Q177 IV 14 again speaks about Belial's spiritual army: "to rescue them from all the spirits of [Belial . . .]."[49] CD–A XII 2 also betrays the knowledge of this tradition when it says that "Every /man/ over whom the spirits of Belial dominate."[50] 11Q13 II 12 tells about "Belial and the spirits of his lot."[51] Concerning this tendency to consolidate demonic powers under a single angelic antagonist, Loren Stuckenbruck notes that "over against the Enoch tradition that, in its early received form, presented both Shemihazah and 'Asa'el as leaders of rebellious angels, many of the writings among the Dead Sea Scrolls draw demonic forces together under a single figure."[52] Stuckenbruck's research discerns at least five such main figures: "(a) Melkireša', (b) "Angel of Darkness," (c) "S/satan," (d) Mastema, and (e) Belial."[53]

Another important conceptual tendency is the internalization of evil in the Qumran materials. This conceptual trend is especially noticeable in the *Treatise on the Two Spirits* (1QS III 13–IV 26). Even more important is that, in the Dead Sea Scrolls, like in *Jubilees*, such internalization became closely tied to the *yetzer* imagery. Ishay Rosen-Zvi points out that, in some Qumran materials, *yetzer* appears in two intertwined dimensions: "the anthropological and the demonological. *Yetzer* is the thought/intent/inclination/nature of humans, which . . . is shameful but subject to God, . . . but in the wicked it [*yetzer*] is demonic and under the dominion of Belial."[54] Benjamin Wold also draws attention to this link between external antagonists and *yetzer* in the Qumran materials by noting that "the negative uses of *yēṣer* in the *Rule of the Community* and *Hodayot* relate in one way or another to the activities of Belial. Occurrences of *yetzer* in several of the Scrolls . . . take this a step further when they convey that *yetzer* has demonic connotations."[55] Furthermore, according to Wold, "In the *Plea for Deliverance* (11Ps[a] XIX, 15–16)[56] the *yetzer* appears to move from within the human being to an outward force. The *Plea for Deliverance* has attracted considerable attention because יצר רע occurs in a context alongside 'satan' and an 'unclean spirit,' and could be interpreted as personified external evil."[57] Wold goes on to say:

> In the *Plea for Deliverance* the coupling of "satan" and "unclean spirit" in parallel with יצר רע makes clear that these are not a state of mind, but rather outward forces and demonic in nature. Such personification is part of a broader development demonizing sin, perhaps similar to *Barkhi Nafshi* (4Q436 1 I–II) where יצר רע is rebuked. On the one hand the reference in *Barkhi Nafshi* may be describing the warding off of a demonic being or evil spirit. On the other hand it is described along with negative tendencies (e.g. stiff neck, haughty eyes) and may simply be a personification of vices.[58]

Loren Stuckenbruck sees a possible Enochic background behind the aforementioned passage in the *Plea of Deliverance*. He writes:

> The petition seeks divine help not to come under the rule or power of a demonic being. Here, that being which would have sway over the one praying is designated as both "a satan" and "an unclean spirit." The latter expression may be an echo of Zech 13:2. However, in the present context it may refer to a disembodied spirit, that is, to a being whose origin lies in the illegitimate sexual union between the rebellious angels and the daughters of men which resulted in the birth of the pre-diluvian Giants. If the Enochic background, known to us through the *Book of Watchers* (*1 Enoch* chs. 10 and 15–16) and the *Book of Giants*, lies in the background, the prayer presupposes a wider narrative that negotiates God's decisive intervention against evil in the past (i.e., through the Flood and other acts of punishment) and the final destruction or eradication of evil in the future.[59]

The *Plea of Deliverance* might have a similar anthropology to the one found in the *Book of Jubilees,* where Mastema and his spirits are able to affect the human *yetzer.* In the *Plea of Deliverance*, therefore, Satan may take the place of Mastema as the leader of evil spirits.[60]

Even a preliminary look reveals the striking complexity of Qumran's demonological currents. In order to understand them better, a short overview of these developments is necessary. Philip Alexander has noted that "the belief in demons was central to the Scrolls worldview."[61] According to Alexander, Qumran materials postulate the existence of a rather complex demonic world which includes different species of demons. These include the spirits of the angels of destruction, the spirits of the bastards,[62] demons, Lilith, howlers, and yelpers.[63] Similar to early Enochic literature, some Qumran documents make a distinction between angels, even fallen angels, and demons. Alexander indicates that "the demonology of the Scrolls seems to envisage a clear distinction being drawn between demons and angels, whether fallen or otherwise."[64] He further notes that in the Qumran materials a demon is understood as "a non-corporeal being which is neither human nor angelic, but which causes harm and mischief to humans in a variety of ways."[65]

Alexander points out that "the Qumran inventory of demons, on analysis, turns out to be somewhat vague. It conveys the general impression of a rather diverse demonic world, but seems not to itemize the types of demonic being in any technically precise way. This observation helps to put the Qumran list of demons into perspective. The Qumran list clearly marks an advance on the demonology of the biblical books, which, as has often been noted, are little interested in demons or in creating systematic demonologies."[66]

In Qumran's *Community Rule,* John Collins also detects the paradigm shift from "angelic" to "demonic" etiologies of evil. He writes that "the *Rule* makes no mention of the Watchers, or of any angelic rebellion. Instead, the demonic spirits are subsumed into a new system and given a new origin."[67]

In some Qumran documents, the demons are able to operate on the psychological level. Alexander points out that "there is a marked emphasis in the sectarian scrolls on the view that the harm done to the Community by Belial and the demons is essentially psychological, rather than physical. They lead the Sons of Light into error, sin and doubt. It is appropriate, therefore, that the counter-attack against Belial and the demons should also be largely psychological."[68]

Concerning the interaction between evil spirits and humans in the Qumran materials, Archie Wright notes that, although there are a few references that indicate actual physical possession of the human body in the Dead Sea Scrolls,[69] the language of demonic possession in the Scrolls suggests that the evil spirits influenced humans through evil inclination rather than physical possession of the body. Wright further suggests that "the concept of demonic possession in the

DSS may have its origins in the motif of 'evil inclination.' 1QH 15.3 states, 'for Belial is present when their (evil) inclination becomes apparent' . . . however, this does not necessarily mean physical possession by an evil spirit. It could simply imply the influence of Belial over the human inclination."[70]

In the Dead Sea Scrolls, experts also detect possible examples of *yetzer*'s personification in the form of a spirit. In light of the juxtaposition between anthropological and demonological dimensions, it is often difficult to discern if this spiritual entity represents an external or an internal force. The perplexing nature of these conceptual developments often leads to ambiguity in scholarly conclusions. Thus, reflecting on the few explicit references to an "evil inclination" in the Dead Sea Scrolls, Eibert Tigchelaar suggests that "the Dead Sea Scrolls indicate on the one hand the influence of Gen 6:5, which relates the 'evil inclination' to 'thoughts' and the 'heart,' and on the other hand a new development where the 'evil inclination' *is personified, perhaps in the form of a spirit*."[71] The process of such an ambiguous personification of *yetzer* in the form of a spirit or even an angelic antagonist, which affects the human heart, can be detected in the *Hodayot*. According to Rosen-Zvi, in the *Hodayot* "*yetzer* is indeed inherently evil and is explicitly identified with Belial: 'my heart is horrified at evil plans, for Belial is present when their destructive *yetzer* becomes apparent,' (1QH XV 3–4)."[72]

Rosen-Zvi sees the formative impact of these Qumran developments on later rabbinic beliefs about the evil inclination by arguing that "Qumranic literature helps us identify the context within which we should locate rabbinic *yetzer*. At Qumran *yetzer* is the source of human sinfulness, in both its demonological context—as a counterpart of Satan, Belial, and the spirits of impurity—and in an anthropological one—as a component of human depravity. Rabbinic anthropology and demonology are markedly different—but the role of *yetzer* in both is the prime explanation for human sinfulness."[73]

Tracing possible trajectories of demonic internalization, Rosen-Zvi draws attention to some Christian materials, noting that "while we did find some hints for processes of internalization at Qumran, more complete rejections of external demons, and their replacement with intra-personal powers, are to be found in Jewish Hellenistic and especially early Christian writings."[74] Indeed, some Christian monastic witnesses, including Athanasius of Alexandria's *Life of Anthony*, the works of Evagrius Ponticus, and the Pachomian writings, exhibit some tendencies of an internalized demonology.[75] The conceptual roots of such a trend are already in the corpus of Pauline writings. In respect to these developments, Rosen-Zvi notes that "rabbinic *yetzer* should be located in a process of the internalization of demons that preserves demonic traits while locating them inside the human mind. Such a phenomenon cannot be found in the Philonic corpus, but may be found in the Pauline discourse of sin (ἁμαρτία) as a hypothesized entity, developed most powerfully in Romans 7."[76] According to Rosen-Zvi, "Paul's statement—'sin, using the commandment, seized any opportunity and produced every desire (ἐπιθυμίαν) in me' (Rom 7:8)—should be compared to the rabbinic assertion 'the evil *yetzer* desires (תאב) only what is forbidden for it' (*y. Ned.* 9:1 [41b], *Yom.* 6:5 [43c])."[77]

Geert Cohen Stuart also draws attention to some early Christian documents that attempt to bridge external and internal demonological dimensions. Touching on the process of the internalization of evil in early sources, he notes that "the trend of identifying 'Satan' and 'power of evil in man' is already visible in pre-Rabbinic sources. For instance in Jam 4:7, 8 there is a beginning of that identification, but 'devil' is still used as an outside power, whereas 'double-mindedness' is the inside power. But effectively both seem to be the same. The relation between 'Satan' and 'power of evil' is also found in John and his use of 'Devil' and 'sin as power' in John 8 and 1 John 3. Both seem virtually to be the same there."[78]

In some sources, the evil inclination is sometimes conceptualized as a demon residing inside of a human being. Scholars have suggested that such an understanding is very close to the monastic notion of *daimones*. For example, Rosen-Zvi proposes that "demons residing in the heart, such as the spirits of Belial in the *Testament of Reuben* or the 'Evil heart' in *Fourth Ezra* and, above all, the monastic *daimones*, are thus much closer, in both function and battling techniques, to the rabbinic *yetzer* than Hellenistic appetites."[79] Yet there is an important difference between demons who can be expelled by exorcism and the demonic *yetzer*, which requires different strategies in order to be neutralized or "conquered." Musing on these differences, Rosen-Zvi points out that "being fully internalized, the evil *yetzer* cannot use direct coercion, as other demons do. It is restricted to inner, dialogical means in its attempts to achieve the sinister goal of leading its host astray."[80]

II. The Internalization of Evil in the *Apocalypse of Abraham*

Demonological Developments in the Apocalypse of Abraham

The aforementioned developments which extend the powers of a personified adversary over inner human conditions represent an important step toward the incorporation of angelic and other otherworldly antagonists in the framework of internalized demonologies. These currents are relevant for an understanding of the antihero of the *Apocalypse of Abraham*, the fallen angel Azazel, who, like the personified antagonists of *Jubilees* and the Qumran materials, is able to influence the human will.

It is not surprising that the bedrock of Jewish internalized demonology, exemplified by the Watchers and the Giants story, plays such a significant role in the *Apocalypse of Abraham*. These connections with the foundational Enochic myth are hinted at in the naming of the main antagonist, "Azazel," a term that was often used as a variant of the name of one of the leaders of the fallen Watchers, Asael.[81] Scholars have noted that Azazel's story in this apocalypse is surrounded with a panoply of peculiar Enochic motifs especially related to the fall of the Watchers.[82] According to Ryszard Rubinkiewicz,

> the author of the *Apocalypse of Abraham* follows the tradition of *1 Enoch* 1–36. The chief of the fallen angels is Azazel, who rules the stars and most men. It is not difficult to find here the tradition of Gen 6:1–4 developed according to the tradition of *1 Enoch*. Azazel is the head of the angels who plotted against the Lord and who impregnated the daughters of men. These angels are compared to the stars. Azazel revealed the secrets of heaven and is banished to the desert. Abraham, as Enoch, receives the power to drive away Satan. All these connections show that the author of the *Apocalypse of Abraham* drew upon the tradition of *1 Enoch*.[83]

Several versions of the tradition of fallen angels in the *Apocalypse of Abraham* appear in chapters 13 and 14, where Yahoel delivers lengthy instructions, teaching Abraham how to safeguard himself against his otherworldly enemy. In Yahoel's discourse there are several details of the antihero story that allude to the Watchers and the Giants myth. In *Apoc. Ab.* 13:8, Yahoel says the following to Azazel: "Since *you have chosen it [earth]* to be your dwelling place of your impurity."[84] This passage refers to the voluntary descent of the otherworldly antagonist to the earth, which hints at the Enochic provenance of the tradition rather than its Adamic counterpart. In contrast to the Enochic mythology of evil, the Adamic etiology, reflected in the *Primary Adam Books*, insists that their antihero, Satan, did not descend on his own accord but rather was forcefully deposed by the deity into the lower realms after refusing to venerate Adam.

The reference to Azazel's impurity is also intriguing in view of the defiling nature of the Watchers' activities on earth. Additionally, a hint about Asael/Azazel's punishment in the abyss appears in *Apoc. Ab.* 14:5, where Yahoel offers his human apprentice the following incantation to battle Azazel: "Say to him, 'May you be the fire brand of the furnace of the earth! Go, Azazel, into the untrodden parts of the earth.' "[85] Here is a possible allusion to the story found in *1 Enoch* 10, where the place of Asael/Azazel's punishment is situated in the fiery abyss. I have suggested elsewhere that, similar to *1 Enoch* 10, the *Apocalypse of Abraham* combines traditions about the scapegoat and the fallen angel by referring to the wilderness motif in the form of "the untrodden parts of the earth."[86]

There is also a possible allusion to the Watcher Asael/Azazel's participation in the procreation of the race of the Giants. In *Apoc. Ab.* 14:6, Yahoel teaches Abraham the following protective formula against the "impure bird": "Say to him . . . since *your inheritance* are those who are with you, *with men born with the stars and clouds, and their portion is in you*, and they come into being through your being."[87] The reference to human beings "born with the stars" is intriguing, since the *Animal Apocalypse* of *1 Enoch* conveys the Watchers' descent through the peculiar imagery of the stars falling from heaven and subsequently depicts the Watchers as participants in the procreation of the new race of the Giants.[88]

In light of these Enochic allusions, the question remains: how is Azazel able to control inner human faculties, since his features and roles clearly point to the fact that he is not a demon but rather a fallen angel, similar to Asael and Shemihazah of early Enochic booklets? We have already witnessed the limitations of "angel" demonology in relation to *yetzer* anthropology, the confines which were mitigated in early Enochic texts via the teaching about evil spirits. Rabbinic lore undermines the effectiveness of the "angel" demonology in relation to *yetzer* anthropologies even further, arguing that "the evil impulse has not dominion over the angels."[89] *Gen. Rab.* 48:11 states that "the Tempter has no power over angels."[90] *Lev. Rab.* 26:5 attests to a similar belief:

> It is the same with the celestial beings, where the Evil Inclination is non-existent and so one utterance is sufficient for them; as it says, The matter is by the decree of the watchers, and the sentence by the word of the holy ones (Dan 4:14). But as to the terrestrial beings, in whom the Evil Inclination exists, O that they might resist it after two utterances![91]

According to these sources, unlike the evil spirits who were born from the earthly bodies of the Giants, the former celestial citizens—angels—would not have any experience of *yetzer*, since it does not exist in the upper realm.

The later rabbinic *Midrash of Shemhazai and Azael* provides a possible key for making sense of this perplexing issue by further elaborating the story of the Watchers' descent. It explains how the fallen angels were endowed with the evil inclination *after* their descent to the lower realm, when they became dwellers on the earth. The *Midrash of Shemhazai and Azael* 1–4 offers the following account of the Watchers' fall:

> When the generation of Enosh arose and practiced idolatry and when the generation of the flood arose and corrupted their actions,

> the Holy One—Blessed be He—was grieved that He had created man, as it is said, "And God repented that he created man, and He grieved at heart." Forthwith arose two angels, whose names were Shemhazai and Azael, and said before Him: "O Lord of the universe, did we not say unto Thee when Thou didst create Thy world, Do not create man?" The Holy One—Blessed be He—said to them: "Then what shall become of the world?" They said before Him: "We will suffice (Thee) instead of it." He said: "It is revealed and (well) known to me that if peradventure you had lived in that (earthly) world, the evil inclination would have ruled you just as much as it rules over the sons of man, but you would be more stubborn than they." They said before Him: "Give us Thy sanction and let us descend and dwell among the creatures and then Thou shall see how we shall sanctify Thy name." He said to them: "Descend and dwell ye among them." Forthwith the Holy One allowed the *evil inclination* to rule over them, as soon as they descended. When they beheld the daughters of man that they were beautiful, they began to corrupt themselves with them, as it is said, "When the sons of God saw the daughters of man, they could not restrain their inclination."[92]

Here the motif of the evil inclination becomes linked not to the Giants and their demonic spirits but to the fallen angels—Shemhazai and Azael. This endowment with "evil desire" or "evil inclination" coincides in the *Midrash* with the antagonists' descent, when the former celestial citizens ceased to be angelic beings and became the fallen Watchers. Just as in the case with humans, it is the deity who endows them with *yetzer*. The passage clearly states that it was God who allowed the evil inclination to rule over the fallen angels "as soon as they descended." The statement that God allowed *yetzer hara* to rule over the fallen angels as soon as *they descended* is pertinent to our study, since Azazel's deeds in relation to inner human faculties in the *Apocalypse of Abraham* are also closely connected with his affairs after his exile from heaven.

If Azazel is indeed associated with an internalized demonology in the *Apocalypse of Abraham,* the question remains as to how this external personified adversary is able to control and corrupt the inner faculties of a human being. A look back to the instructions Yahoel gave the seer in chapter 14 will answer this question.

The Antagonist's Control over Humans: Azazel's Lot

The crucial bulk of the Enochic traditions unfolds in chapters 13 and 14. In *Apoc. Ab.* 14:1–14, Yahoel teaches his human apprentice an incantation against

Azazel and his malicious allies. This spell includes the important phrase "your [Azazel's] inheritance is those who are with you, with men born with the stars and clouds." As suggested earlier, this utterance brings to mind the story of the Giants who are, in the symbolic language of the *Animal Apocalypse,* begotten from the union of the "stars" (Watchers) and human women. Not all elements of the Slavonic text, however, are entirely clear. One of the puzzling details is an occurrence of the word "clouds" (Slav. облаки).[93] Although being born with "stars" makes sense in the context of early Enochic traditions, being born with "clouds" is a rather unusual addition. Ryszard Rubinkiewicz offers a solution to this textual puzzle, suggesting that the word "clouds" may be a corruption of the Hebrew נפלים / Greek Ναφηλείμ—the Nephilim, a term which occurs already in Gen 6:4.[94] According to Rubinkiewicz, a Slavic scribe has retained "Nephilim," a Hebrew term used in some texts for the Giants,[95] which later copyists took for Greek νεφέλαι and translated it as "clouds."[96] In light of this emendation, Rubinkiewicz suggests replacing the traditional translation "with the stars and clouds" with "avec les étoiles et avec les Géants."[97] This hypothesis is plausible, but it is more reasonable to assume that the confusion between Ναφηλείμ and νεφέλη occurred already in the Greek *Vorlage* of the *Apocalypse of Abraham.*[98]

If the original text had "Nephilim" instead of "clouds," it is noteworthy that our text designates their progeny both as the "inheritance" and as the "lot" of Azazel: "Since *your inheritance* (достояние твое) are those who are with you, with men born with the stars (the Nephilim) and clouds. And *their portion is you* (ихъже часть еси ты)."[99] The occurrence of the terminology of "inheritance" and "lot" brings to mind demonological developments found in the Dead Sea Scrolls. Some Qumran passages speak about Belial's army of "spirits," assigned to "his lot." This can be found, for example, in 1QM XIII 2, a passage which conveys a tradition about "Belial and all the spirits of his lot,"[100] and in 11Q13 II 12, a tradition which again speaks about the spirits of the antagonist's *goral.*[101]

The imagery of the lots also looms large in the *Apocalypse of Abraham,* where their descriptions are widely dispersed throughout the second, apocalyptic, part of the pseudepigraphon. These renderings are reminiscent of the terminology found in the Qumran materials. Scholars have suggested that the word "lot" (Slav. *часть*) in the Slavonic text appears to be connected to the Hebrew גורל, a term prominent in cultic descriptions found in biblical and rabbinic accounts as well as in the eschatological developments attested in the Qumran materials.[102]

The *Apocalypse of Abraham* shares other similarities with the Qumran materials. At Qumran, the lots are linked to fallen angelic figures or translated heroes (like Belial or Melchizedek). In the *Apocalypse of Abraham,* the portions of humanity are now tied to the main characters of the story—the fallen angel

Azazel[103] and the translated patriarch Abraham.[104] In the *Apocalypse of Abraham*, like the Qumran materials,[105] the positive lot is at times designated as the lot of the deity—"my [God's] lot":[106]

> And the Eternal Mighty One said to me, "Abraham, Abraham!" And I said, "Here am I!" And he said, "Look from on high at the stars which are beneath you and count them for me and tell me their number!" And I said, "Would I be able? For I am [but] a man." And he said to me, "As the number of the stars and their host, so shall I make your seed into a company of nations, set apart for me in *my lot* with Azazel."[107]

A further connection with the Qumran documents is found in *Apoc. Ab.* 14:6, where the concept of the eschatological "lot" or "portion" (Slav. часть)[108] of Azazel is used interchangeably with the notion of "inheritance" (Slav. достояние). The two notions, "inheritance" and "lot," are also used interchangeably in some Qumran passages that contain "lot" imagery. For example, 11Q13 speaks about the "inheritance" of Melchizedek's lot, which will be victorious in the eschatological battle:

> and from the *inheritance* of Melchizedek, fo[r] . . . and they are the inherita[nce of Melchize]dek, who will make them return. And the d[ay of aton]ement is the e[nd of] the tenth [ju]bilee in which atonement shall be made for all the sons of [light and] for the men [of] the lot of Mel[chi]zedek.[109]

In 1QS III 13–IV 26, the idea of inheritance is tied to that of the lot of the righteous:

> They walk in wisdom or in folly. In agreement with man's inheritance in the truth, he shall be righteous and so abhor injustice; and according to his share in the lot of injustice, he shall act wickedly in it, and so abhor the truth.[110]

In 1QS XI 7–8 and CD XIII 11–12, inheritance language is used in connection with participation in the lot of light, also labeled in 1QS as "the lot of the holy ones":[111]

> To those whom God has selected he has given them as everlasting possession; and he has given them an *inheritance in the lot of the holy ones*. (1QS XI 7–8)[112]

> And everyone who joins his congregation, he should examine, concerning his actions, his intelligence, his strength, his courage and his wealth; and they shall inscribe him in his place according to his *inheritance in the lot of* light. (CD XIII 11–12)[113]

In these last two texts, the phrase "inheritance in the lot" seems to imply that "inheritance" is the act of participation in one of the eschatological lots.[114] The same idea is at work in the aforementioned passage from *Apoc. Ab.* 14:6, where "inheritance" is understood as partaking in the lot of Azazel.

The incantation found in the *Apocalypse of Abraham* reveals an interesting constellation of motifs with its reference to the Giants and their "progeny," who are depicted as the "inheritance" of Azazel and the "lot" whom he himself "made." In this respect, the *Apocalypse of Abraham* goes even further than *Jubilees*, which does not directly identify Mastema or Belial as one of the fallen Watchers or as the procreators of the Giants and their malevolent spirits. Here, however, the "parental" link is clearly visible. Additional evidence for this connection is found in *Apoc. Ab.* 14:6b: "And their portion is you [Azazel], and *they come into being through your being.*" The antagonist is depicted as the one who himself begot his own spiritual army. This tradition is a novel development in comparison with the Belial/Mastema trend attested in the *Jubilees* and in the Qumran materials.

If we assume that the original text of *Apoc. Ab.* 14:6 indeed had "Nephilim/Giants" instead of "clouds," the question remains: how are these bastards still alive at the time of Abraham and still able to represent Azazel's lot, despite the fact that the Giants had already perished in the antediluvian period? A possible answer is that these Giants are now functioning not in their bodily form, but rather in their spiritual one,[115] as evil spirits.[116] If so, Azazel, like Mastema or Belial, is now understood as the leader of the malevolent spirits who escaped the Giants after the demise of their material bodies. Although the text does not speak directly about the (evil) spirits of the Giants, other details, like the terminology of "inheritance" and "lot," are used in the *Apocalypse of Abraham* in the description of these allies of the antagonist, make such an interpretation plausible. Another important reference about the lot of Azazel and the Giants/Nephilim is made in the incantation, which the adept must repeat in order to safeguard himself against their harmful influence. This provides additional proof that Azazel's assistants represent a demonic entity that now require such a tool.

Azazel's Will: Backdoor to the Human Nature?

The category of "will" plays a very important role in various passages found in the *Apocalypse of Abraham*. These narratives speak about the "will" of God,[117] the will of Azazel,[118] and possibly the will of Abraham.[119] In the *Apocalypse of Abraham*, "will" is envisioned as a tool by which Azazel is able to influence human choices. It becomes another crucial instrument by which the antagonist of the apocalyptic story is able to exercise his control over inner human conditions, possibly even without the help of his demonic army. Such bridging of demonological and anthropological boundaries through the category of will establishes a new paradigm of the "internalized demonology," which is similar to the one attested in early Enochic writings and the Qumran materials. These materials developed a concept of the demonic spirit with its ability to act internally.[120] According to this new paradigm, a malevolent spiritual entity even has the ability to inhabit a human soul or body, becoming a sort of spiritual parasite on its physical human host. Similar to the *Jubilees* and the Qumran materials, the *Apocalypse of Abraham* shows familiarity with this demonological model when it unveils its tradition about Azazel's demonic lot. Yet, along with this already familiar demonological blueprint, our text also postulates another option for bridging internal and external realities. This option is an ability to corrupt human nature by controlling the human will. In this demonological framework there is no need for the antagonist's capacities to act internally or reside inside the human soul or body, as he can exercise his control over human anthropology "remotely," through a subject's will. But how is the malevolent agent able to influence a human being's free will, given the fact that it was granted to humanity by the deity himself? According to the *Apocalypse of Abraham*, it became possible because God himself gave Azazel a special "will" that allows Azazel to control the inner workings of human beings.

At first glance, this paradigm shift appears to be not entirely novel. The Hebrew *Sirach*,[121] the *Testament of Reuben*,[122] the *Testament of Asher*,[123] the *Testament of Naphtali*[124] and the *Testament of Benjamin*[125] often portray otherworldly figures as in charge of human inclinations. Some of these accounts curiously mention the faculty of the human will in the midst of speculation about the two spirits. Thus, from the *Testament of Judah* 20:1–5 we learn the following:

> So understand, my children, that two spirits await an opportunity with humanity: the spirit of truth and the spirit of error. In between is the conscience of the mind which inclines as it will (οὗ ἐὰν θέλῃ κλῖναι). The things of truth and the things of error are written in the affections of man, each one of whom the Lord knows. There is no moment in which man's works can be concealed, because they are written on the heart in the Lord's sight. And the spirit of truth testifies to all things and brings all accusations. He who has sinned is consumed in his heart and cannot raise his head to face the judge.[126]

The second sentence of this passage thematizes the faculty of the human will.[127] As Robert Henry Charles points out, "we have here an admirable description of man's attitude to good and evil, which are here personified as spirits of good and evil. *His will can determine for either* (ver. 2).[128] The results of his volitions are forthwith written on his heart, [in other words,] on his character, and are ever open to the eyes of God (3–4)."[129] If Charles is correct, the human "will" conditions a human person's "attitude to good and evil."

Although some aforementioned accounts discuss the role of the human will in the process of choosing between good and evil, these accounts are missing one important element that is present in the *Apocalypse of Abraham*. This feature is presented with utmost clarity in *Apoc. Ab.* 14:13, a passage from which we learn that "*God gave him* (Azazel) the gravity and *the will* against those who answer him."[130] I have argued elsewhere that "gravity" or "heaviness," a concept expressed through the Slavonic term тягота, designates here the attribute of the glory bestowed by the deity on the antagonist.[131] But what is the precise meaning of the other quality mentioned in the passage—namely, the mysterious "will" given to Azazel? It is important that the *Apocalypse of Abraham* traces the origins of this "will" to God, who at the same time decided to delegate the power over human volition to the adversary through the enigmatic transferal of this capacity.[132] This situation appears to be different, on the one hand, from the *Testaments of the Twelve Patriarchs* and the Qumran materials and, on the other hand, from later rabbinic accounts, as each of these sources firmly maintains the freedom of human choice in the face of all afflictions.

The gift of "will" received by the adversary becomes a powerful weapon against not only the Gentiles, but the chosen people as well. In *Apoc. Ab.* 14:12, Abraham's mentor, the angel Yahoel, warns his apprentice that Azazel's "will" can affect even him: "And the angel said, 'Now, whatever he says to you, answer him not, lest *his will* (воля его) affect you.' "[133] In this passage there is a significant link between Azazel's will and Abraham's will. This link demonstrates that the deity's gift to the antagonist enables him to control a human being's inclinations, as he is literally able to paralyze Abraham's volitional abilities.

The motif of the antagonist's "weaponization" of will may have its early roots in the *Book of Jubilees*, a writing that shows remarkable similarities to some demonological traditions found in the *Apocalypse of Abraham*. *Jubilees* also speaks about the "will" of its otherworldly adversary, Mastema. In *Jub.* 10:3–7, in response to Noah's plea, the deity orders the angels to bind all the evil spirits.[134] Their leader, Mastema, objects to this action[135] by uttering the following:

> Lord creator, leave some of them before me; let them listen to me and do everything that I tell them, because if none of them is left

> for me I shall not be able to exercise *the authority of my will* among mankind. For they are meant for the purposes of destroying and misleading before my punishment because the evil of mankind is great (*Jub.* 10:8).[136]

Following Noah's plea and Mastema's objections, God decides to leave "one-tenth of the demons unbound" (10:9).[137] An important detail in these negotiations is that the antagonist's ability to exercise *the authority of his will* is connected with the active presence of his demonic army. The text links Mastema's "will" with his demons, as he will not be able "to exercise the authority of his will" without them.[138] Does this mean that Azazel's "will" in the *Apocalypse of Abraham* presumes the ownership of his demonic lot?

Although in his apotropaic prayer Noah prays to God not to give power to Mastema and his demons over human beings, God still grants the adversary this power. In *Apoc. Ab.* 23:13, the deity also speaks about the "power" over human beings given to Azazel: "Hear, Abraham! Those who *desire evil* (иже злаго желают) and whom I have hated as they are doing these [works], over them I gave him (Azazel) *power* (власть), and [he is] to be loved by them."[139] Here God gives Azazel *power* (власть) over humans tormented with evil desires, and he empowers him to be loved by them.

Finally, one more important conceptual cluster pertaining to Azazel's possible connection with an internalized demonology is situated in chapter 13. There, Yahoel teaches the adept about Azazel's tricks by providing crucial information about his nefarious roles. The first aspect is Azazel's role as personified iniquity. *Apoc. Ab.* 13:6 reads: "And it came to pass when I saw the bird speaking I said to the angel, 'What is this, my lord?' And he said, 'This is *iniquity* (бещестие), this is Azazel!' "[140] Commenting on the tradition of scholars seeing Azazel here as the personification of iniquity or evil, Marc Philonenko notes that "dans l'Apocalypse d'Abraham, Azazel est l'impiété personnifiée."[141] In an attempt to clarify the meaning of the Slavonic term "бесчестие," Rubinkiewicz traces it to the Greek ἀσέβεια or Hebrew רשע.[142] Azazel's role as personified "iniquity" is reaffirmed later in the scene of the protological couple's corruption in chapter 23, where the antagonist is also defined as "iniquity": "and he who is between them is the *impiety* (*бесчестие*) of their pursuits for destruction, Azazel himself." (*Apoc. Ab.* 23:11).[143]

Another pertinent role of the adversary, hinted at in Yahoel's instructions, is that of tempter. From *Apoc. Ab.* 13:11 we learn that Azazel has been appointed to tempt people, though not the righteous: "You have been appointed to tempt." This assignment of a certain portion of humankind for temptation and corruption is again reminiscent of *Jubilees*' demonology, according to which Mastema is able to tempt/corrupt only a part of the human race. Another important role is found in Azazel's designation as "the all-evil spirit," mentioned in *Apoc. Ab.* 13:9: "*Through you the all-evil spirit (is) a liar* (и тобою всезлыи духъ лъжив), and through you (are) wrath and trials on the generations of men who live impiously."[144]

The most important verse for establishing Azazel's role as the one who is able to control a human being's nature is *Apoc. Ab.* 13:10, which speaks about his ability to act *through the bodies* of human beings. Alexander Kulik's translation renders this verse in the following way: "since the Eternal Mighty God did not send the righteous, in their bodies, to be in your hand."[145] However, the Slavonic text can be literally translated as "but the Eternal Mighty God did not give the righteous *bodily* (телесѣмъ) in your hand."[146] The meaning of this verse appears to be that God forbids the antagonist to influence the *bodily instincts* of the righteous. Does this implicitly signify that he can influence the bodies of the wicked? If it is indeed so, such interaction between demonological and anthropological realities has great significance for our study.

Another aspect of Azazel's evil economy is that, although the spirits are not mentioned in the speculations about his lot of the Giants, the text still relates the antagonist's possible control over spiritual entities. Such a hint comes from *Apoc. Ab.* 13:9. In Yahoel's rebuke, the adversary is linked with the "wholly-evil spirit": "And because of you [there is] the wholly-evil spirit (всезлый духъ) of the lie."[147] Curiously, Azazel appears to be not the wholly-evil spirit himself but rather the one who secures its existence. Does this signify that the evil spirit serves here, as in the case of the angelic antagonists of the *Book of Jubilees,* as Azazel's agent? Our book unfortunately does not provide an answer to this question.

Conclusion

At the end of this study, it is useful to return again to Philip Alexander's insights, mentioned earlier, that underline a crucial difference between angels (even fallen angels, like Azazel) and demons in relation to human anthropology.[148] While demons can "dwell" inside of a human being, angels are not able to do so. As Alexander puts it, "Demons can invade the human body, from which they can only be expelled through exorcism, whereas angels cannot. Nowhere do we read of an angel possessing a human."[149] Compared with "demon" demonology, this "angel" demonology is clearly less useful for the specific needs of internalized anthropologies. By the peculiarities of its nature and operation, which allow it to indwell or possess a human being, the demon gains immediate access to the inner human nature—access which an angel is not able to attain. Because of this, the overwhelming majority of internalized demonologies appropriate the concept of demonic spirits as the first choice of their malevolent opponents. Yet, as the example of the *Apocalypse of Abraham* indicates, the "angel" demonology, with some important modifications, can still be useful for the purposes of some internalized anthropologies.

Chapter Six

Glorification through Fear in *2 Enoch*

My flesh trembles for fear of you.

—Ps 119:120

Introduction

2 Enoch is an early Jewish apocalypse written in the first century of the Common Era, which begins with the dream of the seventh antediluvian hero, Enoch. While he is sleeping, Enoch sees two angels arrive at his earthly abode in order to bring him into heaven. In the apocalypse, the patriarch's visitors are depicted as enormously large creatures with shining faces. The story immediately transitions from the seer's dream to a vision in an awakened state. The apocalypse reports that when Enoch is awoken by the angels he is terrified because he beholds his guests "in actuality." The seer's fear is no novelty here, as it represents a standard feature in Jewish and Christian apocalyptic accounts—human beings are frightened by their encounters with celestial manifestations.

What is novel, however, is that Enoch's fear appears to lead to his transformation. Both recensions of the Slavonic text report the metamorphosis of the seer's visage. Moreover, both recensions also connect these changes to Enoch's fear. Thus, the longer recension of *2 Enoch* 1:7-8 states that the appearance of the patriarch's face "was changed because of fear."[1] Even more striking is the manner in which Enoch's metamorphosis is attested in the shorter recension. According to this recension, the face of the visionary was not simply changed, but it also became glorified. The shorter recension of *2 Enoch* 1:7-8 provides this puzzling description: "I hurried and stood up and bowed down to them; and the appearance of my face was glittering because of fear (блеща ся привидѣниемъ лице мое от страха)."[2] Francis Andersen previously reflected on the uniqueness of the imagery of glorification through fear. He argued that "the reading of [the manuscripts] A and U, *blestac(a)*, suggests that his [Enoch's] face was shining (or blanched?). The verb really means 'to be radiant,' and it is not part of the vocabulary usual for the terror response to an epiphany of this kind. . . . It would be more appropriate for the visitors."[3]

Despite the oddity of this imagery, it appears that the seer's glorification through fear is not an accidental slip of the author's pen or a mistake made by the translators of this text during its long afterlife in various foreign cultural milieus. Rather, it is a marker of the peculiar theophanic proclivities of the pseudepigraphon that can be detected in other parts of the text as well. In this respect, it appears not coincidental that it is the *face* of the visionary that becomes transformed by fear. Scholars have previously noted the importance of face imagery in the Slavonic apocalypse, arguing that such symbolism often establishes an important theophanic nexus. Thus, one of the high points of the patriarch's story in the Slavonic apocalypse is his luminous metamorphosis in the seventh heaven, where his visage becomes glorified before the frightening face of God. The reference to metamorphosis through the seer's fear in the beginning of Enoch's story proleptically anticipates his future transformation in the seventh heaven.

The purpose of this chapter is to explore the imagery of fear found in *2 Enoch* and its significance for the transformations that Enoch undergoes during his heavenly journey.

The Theophanic Motif of Fear in the Hebrew Bible

In order to clarify the unique role that fear appears to be playing in the glorification of the seventh antediluvian patriarch in the Slavonic apocalypse, we must first turn our attention to the Hebrew Bible, where there is a strong motif of fear in visionary accounts. Since the motif of fear, and especially the fear of God, is quite a popular topic in the Bible, we will limit our exploration to theophanic and angelophanic encounters in which a vision of an otherworldly being provokes human fear. Moreover, this analysis of various theophanic encounters in the Hebrew Bible will only concentrate on a few conceptual traits that exercised crucial formative influences on the traditions found in *2 Enoch*.

It should be noted that fear is a common emotion found in early Jewish accounts when visionaries encounter a divine or an angelic manifestation.[4] Early Pentateuchal stories of the primordial patriarchs' and prophets' encounters with divine manifestations contain references to the fear that otherworldly beings instill in humans. For example, immediately after the protoplast's transgression,

Genesis 3 reports Adam's fear regarding God's visitation to the Garden. The Book of Genesis also recounts the fear of Abraham, Isaac, and Jacob during their encounters with divine and angelic manifestations. The fear of the visionary also becomes a prominent motif in prophetic and apocalyptic accounts in the Hebrew Bible, and especially in the book of Daniel.[5] While there is a stunning plethora of biblical accounts that narrate frightening encounters with divine and angelic beings, it appears that one particular cluster of biblical motifs exercised the most crucial influence on the developments found in the Slavonic apocalypse. This cluster deals with the visionary traditions related to the most prominent visionary of the Hebrew Bible, Moses, a paradigmatic seer who had several very special encounters with the deity. We first hear of Moses's fear early in the prophet's visionary career—during his initial experience with an otherworldly reality in Exod 3:6.[6] In the later record of his encounters with the deity on Mount Sinai, which is attested in various passages from Exodus and Deuteronomy, the motif of Moses's fear is juxtaposed with the imagery of the divine face. This juxtaposition of the danger motif with the tradition of the divine face found in biblical Mosaic accounts would prove to be very important for the authors of *2 Enoch*, wherein the motif of the frightening luminosity of the divine visage occupied an important conceptual place. The formative Mosaic accounts provided specific references for the harmful effect that theophanic experiences have on those mortals who dare to approach the divine *panim*. Thus, for example, in Exod 33:20 the deity warns Moses about the danger of seeing his face: "You cannot see my face, for no one may see me and live." The motif of peril is further reinforced by God's instructions in Exod 33:22, where the deity commands Moses to hide himself in a cleft in the rock and promises to protect the prophet with his hands.

The Slavonic apocalypse also specifically devotes a lengthy account to the dangers of seeing the divine face. I have previously argued that these developments exhibit formative influences of the Mosaic traditions.[7] Thus, scholars have noted that in *2 Enoch* 39:3–6, as in the Mosaic account from Exod 33, the face is closely associated with the divine, and that the face is not simply understood to be a part of the Lord's body, but as a radiant facade of his anthropomorphic form.[8]

Mosaic theophanic accounts found in the Hebrew Bible offer another conceptual contribution that proved to be formative for the theology of *2 Enoch*; namely, that the seer's face is glorified after his encounter with the divine *panim*, and other people who encounter the seer's glorious visage also fear because of the change of the seer's countenance. Thus, Exod 34:29–35 portrays Moses after his encounter with the Lord. The passage reads:

> Moses came down from Mount Sinai. . . . Moses did not know that the skin of his face shone because he had been talking with God.

> When Aaron and all the Israelites saw Moses, the skin of his face was shining, and they were afraid to come near him . . . and Moses would put the veil on his face again, until he went in to speak with him.

The report that Moses's face was glorified is not the only important detail of this passage. The fear that other humans experience when they encounter Moses's metamorphosis is significant as well. *2 Enoch* attests to a very similar constellation of motifs wherein the imagery of the glorified visage of Enoch coincides with the danger motif. *2 Enoch* 37 recounts the unusual procedure performed on Enoch's face at the final stage of his encounter with the deity in the seventh heaven. After the patriarch's transformation and after the utmost mysteries of the universe are revealed to him, Enoch must go back to the human realm in order to convey these revelations to the people of the earth. His glorious celestial visage, however, poses a problem for his communication with other human beings. Anticipating this, God calls one of his senior angels to chill the face of Enoch. The text says that the angel was "terrifying and frightful," and appeared frozen; he was as white as snow, and his hands were as cold as ice. With these cold hands he then chilled the patriarch's face. Right after this chilling procedure, the Lord informs Enoch that if his face had not been chilled, no human being would have been able to look at him. This reference to the dangerous radiance of Enoch's face after his encounter with the deity represents a parallel to the incandescent face of Moses after the Sinai experience in Exodus.[9]

The Motif of the Seer's Fear in Early Enochic Accounts

As previously noted, the primordial patriarchs' and prophets' fear is a recurring theme when they experience the deity in the biblical theophanic accounts of Genesis and Exodus. Often inspired by references to the fear of Adam, Abraham, Jacob, and Moses in these formative biblical accounts, Jewish pseudepigraphical texts strive to further enhance these motifs, often putting them in new visionary contexts.[10]

The motif of the seer's fear was certainly not forgotten in early Enochic lore—a body of materials that represents one of the most extensive early compilations of Jewish visionary traditions. Already in one of the earliest Enochic booklets, the *Book of the Watchers*, the reader learns about the fear of the seventh antediluvian patriarch as he approaches the divine presence. Chapter 14 of this early Enochic work portrays the seer's entrance into what seems to be envisioned as the heavenly temple, the sacred abode of the deity, a very special *topos* that is terrifying not only to human beings, but also to the celestial creatures. *1 Enoch* 14:9-14 offers the following report of the seer's progress into the celestial sanctuary:

> And I proceeded until I came near to a wall which was built of hailstones, and a tongue of fire surrounded it, and it began to make me afraid. And I went into the tongue of fire and came near to a large house which was built of hailstones, and the wall of that house (was) like a mosaic (made) of hailstones, and its floor (was) snow. Its roof (was) like the path of the stars and flashes of lightning, and among them (were) fiery Cherubim, and their heaven (was like) water. And (there was) a fire burning around its wall, and its door was ablaze with fire. And I went into that house, and (it was) hot as fire and cold as snow, and there was neither pleasure nor life in it. Fear covered me and trembling took hold of me. And as I was shaking and trembling, I fell on my face.[11]

It is intriguing and significant that Enoch is not simply frightened by his otherworldly experience, but that he is literally "covered with fear." Scholars have previously noted the unusual strength of these formulae of fear. For example, John Collins notes the text's "careful observation of Enoch's terrified reaction."[12] Another scholar, Martha Himmelfarb, notices the power of the visionary's reaction to the divine presence, which, in her opinion, supersedes some formative biblical visionary accounts, including Ezekiel's visions. She notes that "Ezekiel's prostrations are never attributed to fear; they are reported each time in the same words, without any mention of emotion, as almost ritual acknowledgments of the majesty of God. The *Book of the Watchers*, on the other hand, emphasizes the intensity of the visionary's reaction to the manifestation of the divine."[13] Moreover, in the *Book of the Watchers*, the fear of the visionary becomes a reaction not only to the divine or angelic manifestations but also to the sacred space itself. It reveals a pronounced sacerdotal dimension to human fear. This notion is also prominent in some biblical accounts[14] in which the danger motif has been extended to the sacred abode represented by the Holy of Holies. In this respect, it is then noteworthy that the theme of Enoch's fear unfolding in the *Book of the Watchers* represents an intriguing constellation not only of visionary traditions but also of sacerdotal traditions. Sometimes the sacerdotal dimensions of Enoch's fear take primacy over its visionary dimension. In this respect, Martha Himmelfarb notes:

> Although Enoch catches sight of God on his throne of cherubim from his prostrate position, it is not the sight of God that causes his terror. Rather it is the fearsome experience of standing inside the

> house of hailstones that makes Enoch tremble and quake and finally fall on his face. . . . Thus the *Book of the Watchers* emphasizes the glory of God's heavenly temple by making it, rather than the vision of God himself, the cause of Enoch's fear.[15]

It is also important that, already in the *Book of the Watchers,* the divine manifestation became conspicuously labeled as the "face," a portentous Mosaic allusion that remained a crucial conceptual point in the theophanic encounters found in the Slavonic apocalypse.[16]

Moreover, in early Enochic booklets, and especially in the *Book of the Similitudes*, one finds another tendency that became important in developments found in *2 Enoch*: namely, the juxtaposition of the seer's fearful reaction with the transformation of his physical body. Thus, for example, in the visionary encounter with the deity attested in *1 Enoch* 60, the formula of fear coincides with a reference to the "melting" of Enoch's being.[17]

Fearsome Face

Although it appears that already in the early Enochic booklets the fear of the seventh antediluvian hero might be linked with his metamorphosis, in the Slavonic apocalypse this connection receives an even more striking embodiment. Moreover, in *2 Enoch,* this juxtaposition takes on a new conceptual dimension: it becomes one of the consistent markers of Enoch's metamorphosis, which he undergoes in the course of his celestial journey.

The symbolism of fear therefore appears to be playing an important conceptual role in the Slavonic apocalypse. Scholars have previously noted the intensity of the formula of fear in this text. Thus, Martha Himmelfarb notices that the fear language is more intense in *2 Enoch* than in other Jewish apocalyptic accounts, including even the early Enochic booklets. She reflects on the repeated expressions of fear that Enoch conveys to his celestial guide Gabriel, noting its unusual intensity:

> The distress he expresses to Gabriel, "Alas, my lord, I am paralyzed by fear" (9:10), is a striking contrast to the absence of any emotion in the account of Levi's vision of God in the heavenly temple in the *Testament of Levi*, and it goes beyond the *Book of the Watchers* in emphasizing the terror that the visionary feels upon finding himself in the heavens. The intensity of Enoch's fear at being left without his guides serves to emphasize the magnitude of what takes place next.[18]

Although the language of fear permeates the whole narrative fabric of *2 Enoch,* starting from the very first verses of the apocalypse, the formulae of fear receive their utmost intensity in Enoch's encounter with the divine face—the visionary event that would become the apex of the theophanic theology of the text. The immense fear that the visionary experiences during this momentous encounter became so embedded in Enoch's soul—and even in his newly acquired angelic nature—that it was the very first subject of his revelation to humanity upon his brief return to earth. Thus, the very first lines of Enoch's admonition to his sons report the frightening nature of his meeting with the divine face. The longer recension of *2 Enoch* 39:8 conveys the following account:

> Frightening and dangerous it is to stand before the face of an earthly king, terrifying and very dangerous it is, because the will of the king is death and the will of the king is life. How much more terrifying and dangerous it is to stand before the face of the King of earthly kings and of the heavenly armies, the regulator of the living and of the dead. Who can endure that endless misery?[19]

Without a doubt, this passage in many ways represents one of the conceptual *nexi* of the Slavonic apocalypse. As has been previously mentioned, the imagery of the face is of paramount significance for the conceptual framework of *2 Enoch,* where the vision of the divine *panim* became the pinnacle of the seer's otherworldly experience. With this fixation on the face imagery, the Slavonic apocalypse demonstrates close affinities not only with early Enochic booklets, where the terminology of the "face" is already present, but also, and more importantly, with the later Merkabah and Hekhalot accounts, wherein the seer's contemplation of the face becomes the most significant aspect of revelation. Distinguished experts of early Jewish mysticism have previously reflected on the importance of this imagery, noting that it will become the "center of the divine event" and the teleological objective for the ascension of the *yorde merkabah.* Thus, Peter Schäfer points out that *Hekhalot Rabbati,* for example, considers the countenance of God as "the goal of *yored merkabah* and simultaneously revokes this statement in a puzzling way by stressing at the conclusion that one cannot 'perceive' this face."[20] One can see that here, like in *2 Enoch,* early biblical Mosaic traditions were evoked and reformulated. Schäfer further observes that, for the visionary in the Hekhalot tradition, the countenance of God is the center "not only of overwhelming beauty, and therefore of a destructive nature, but at the same time the center of the divine event."[21] God's face thus becomes the consummation of the heavenly journey, since, according to Schäfer, "everything God wishes to transmit to the *yored merkabah* . . . is concentrated in God's countenance."[22]

Moreover, in the Merkabah tradition, the visionaries not only receive and transmit their knowledge about the divine face, but their nature becomes transformed by the encounter with the divine visage. One can see the similar transformational patterns in the Slavonic apocalypse.

As already demonstrated in our study of *2 Enoch*, the encounter with the fearful divine face transforms the face of the seventh patriarch into a luminous entity. We should remember that the text especially underlines this aspect of the seer's transformation by informing its reader that the deity ordered a special angelic servant to chill the face of the patriarch before his return to the lower realm. It appears that the peculiar details in the description of this angelic servant again point to the prevailing tendency of our apocalypse, which often emphasizes the transformational power of fear.

The "Frightening" Angel

We have already mentioned that one of the prominent conceptual *loci* of the danger motif in the Slavonic apocalypse is connected not only with the imagery of the terrifying face of God, but also with Enoch's own frightening visage that must be tamed before his descent into the earthly abode. It has been previously noticed that this theme in *2 Enoch* is conceptually indebted to the formative Mosaic developments, and especially to the tradition about the prophet's luminous visage found in Exodus 34.[23] While the similarities with the Mosaic account have often been noticed, scholars rarely explain the differences between the two accounts. One of the differences here is that, unlike Moses's face, the visage of the seventh antediluvian hero became reversely transformed right before his journey back to the realm of humanity. More specifically, it was chilled by a special angelic servant. From the longer recension of *2 Enoch* 37:1-2 we learn the following:

> And the Lord called one of the senior angels, *terrifying and frightful* (страшнаа и грозна), and he made him stand with me. And the appearance of that angel was as white as snow, and his hands like ice, having the appearance of great frigidity. And he chilled my face, because I could not endure the terror of the Lord, just as it is not possible to endure the fire of a stove and the heat of the sun and the frost of death. And the Lord said to me, "Enoch, if your face had not been chilled here, no human being would be able to look at your face."[24]

The figure of the mysterious angelic "chiller" deserves closer attention. The text defines this celestial servant as a *terrifying and frightening*[25] creature. On the surface, it is not entirely clear why the text put these characteristics in the description of this angelic character responsible for the reverse metamorphosis of the seer. Yet, in view of the peculiarities of other metamorphoses of the seer's physique, especially his face, that were found earlier in the Slavonic apocalypse, the definition of the transforming angel as a *frightening* creature becomes more obvious. It calls to mind the transformation of the seer before the divine face, when his nature was transformed by the frightening countenance of the deity. Further, it is also reminiscent of the transformation of Enoch's face in the very first verses of our apocalypse. Remember that the symbolism of the seer's metamorphosis also coincides with the fear motif. In both accounts, the transformation of the visionary's face is juxtaposed with his fear. The frightening nature of what is beheld appears to be one of the requirements for the possibility of human metamorphosis. In other words: fear is a necessary prerequisite for transformation. In Enoch's encounter with the angelic "chiller" found in *2 Enoch* 37, we detect a similar constellation of motifs: the fact that the transforming angel is a frightening creature points not merely to the danger motif associated with encountering an otherworldly being, but also indirectly to the fear of the vision's recipient. Enoch's face has now undergone a reverse metamorphosis, turning his glorified visage into the face of a normal human being. Here again one encounters a prime example of the face's metamorphosis through fear, affirming the earlier transformational pattern found in the first chapter of *2 Enoch*.

Incorruptibility by Fear

The changes in the seer's nature reappear in the narrative wherein the patriarch refuses to participate in the family meal. This story takes place during Enoch's short visit to earth, when he is commanded to deliver God's revelations to his children and the people of the earth. Although Enoch's face was chilled by the frightening angel, his transformed nature had not been returned to its previous human condition. The text therefore makes clear that the patriarch is not a human, but an incorruptible celestial being who is no longer sustained and nourished by earthly provisions. Yet, the humans appear to be misguided by the chilled face of the patriarch, erroneously assuming that Enoch is still a human being who receives his nourishment in the conventional way. So the patriarch's son Methuselah invites his father to take part in a family meal. The patriarch politely rejects his son's offer, telling him that human food is no longer agreeable to him. It becomes clear that his human nature had been altered and that he now receives his nourishment in a different, non-human way. In Enoch's address to Methuselah, we find an interesting tradition that is relevant to the subject of our investigation: Enoch attributes his transition to this incorruptible state to the fear that he experienced in the upper realm. The shorter recension of *2 Enoch* 56:2 discloses the following tradition: "And Enoch answered his son and said, "Listen, my child! Since the time when the Lord anointed me with the ointment of my glory, *and I experienced fear* (и страшно бысть мнѣ), and food is not agreeable to me, and I have no desire for earthly food."[26]

This account, where the transformation of the seer is linked to his experience of fear during his encounter with the divine face in the seventh heaven, once again attests to the theological tendency of the Slavonic apocalypse—a tendency that strives to link the seer's fear with his metamorphosis.

The Glorification of the Righteous through the Fear of God

We have already witnessed that the testimonies in *2 Enoch* 1 and *2 Enoch* 56 suggest that Enoch's fear became one of the causes for his transition into a glorified state. Further proof for such a possibility is also hinted at in chapter 43, where the seventh antediluvian hero delivers his final ethical exhortations to his children before he departs to the upper realm. These instructions deal with the norms of righteous behavior, contrasting them with unlawful and evil practices. From the patriarch's admonitions, the reader learns that those who fear the deity will be glorified. The shorter recension of *2 Enoch* 43:3 reads: "But there is no one better than he who fears the Lord; *for those who fear the Lord will be glorious forever* (боящи бо ся Господа славнии будутъ в вѣк)."[27] The longer recension conveys a similar tradition: "Even though these sayings are heard on every side, nevertheless there is no one better than he who fears God. He will be the most glorious in that age."[28]

At first blush, it might appear that this reference to humans being glorified because they fear God, found in the midst of Enoch's ethical instructions, is not laden with any anthropological meaning, nor is it directly connected with the metamorphosis of a human being. Nevertheless, an exploration of the immediate context of the passage reveals its possible anthropological significance. It must not be coincidental that, immediately after this verse, Enoch begins his meditation on the "face" imagery—the symbolism that proved to be so crucial elsewhere in the Slavonic apocalypse, where the motif of fear coincided with human metamorphosis. Thus, *2 Enoch* 44:1-2 reads:

> The Lord with his own two hands created mankind; and in a facsimile of his own face. Small and great the Lord created. Whoever insults a person's face insults the face of the Lord; whoever treats a person's face with repugnance treats the face of the Lord with repugnance. Whoever treats with contempt the face of any person treats the face of the Lord with contempt.[29]

Here, the reader encounters the already familiar correlation between the face of the deity and the visage of the human being—the correspondence that proved to be so crucial in Enoch's glorious metamorphosis.

The conventional division of these chapters often separates the passage about the glorification of those who fear God from speculation concerning the seer's face, placing them in different chapters. Yet, it is possible that in the original design of the apocalypse, the authors of these two passages meant them to be read together, especially in light of the other theophanic encounters found in *2 Enoch*. If this is the case, the familiar conceptual link between fear and glorification, which was revealed in the midst of speculation concerning the divine and the human face, is extended to elect human beings who are also predestined to undergo a similar metamorphosis.

Adam's Fear

Our investigation of the conceptual developments found in the Slavonic apocalypse suggests that fear might be understood there not merely as a human reaction or emotion, but also as an experience that can lead a human into a glorified condition. This transition from the fallen human form to the state of a celestial citizen, achieved through fear, evokes some protological allusions. We have already mentioned that the very first biblical account of human fear occurs in Genesis 3, where the protoplast fears the deity's presence after his transgression in the Garden. Analyzing this Adamic account, some scholars have suggested that the fear of the first human might serve as a sign of the fallen condition of the protoplast. It has also been suggested that this same pattern, in which theophanic fear is connected with transgression and the loss of good standing before God, is likewise observable in Mosaic theophanic accounts that underline Israelite fear of the divine face after the idolatrous Golden Calf incident. Regarding these biblical accounts, Ian Wilson notes "it is possible that the Israelite fear of the divine face—and divine presence in general—stemmed from the biblical account of humanity's fall in the Garden of Eden (Gen 3). Prior to the fall there is no evidence that the man and woman fear Yahweh's presence in any way, but after the fall Yahweh's approach prompts great fear in them (cf. Gen 3:8)."[30]

These connections are important for our study, as they might provide the key for understanding the transformational power of fear in the Slavonic apocalypse. While scholarship has previously attempted to connect the fall of the protoplast with the origin of theophanic fear, another important aspect of the tradition found in Genesis 3 has been overlooked—namely, Adam's nakedness, to which fear is also closely tied in Genesis 3.[31] The symbolism of nakedness found in that text points to an important set of anthropological and transformational motifs. Thus, in Jewish and Christian lore, the nakedness of the protoplasts was often linked to their loss of the so-called "garments of light"—glorious attire that the primordial humans had before their transgression in Eden.[32] Such a loss might be already hinted at in the biblical account of the Fall, where the deity fashions the garments of skin for the primordial couple after their transgression.[33]

If it is indeed possible that the fear which Adam and Eve experienced after the Fall in Genesis 3 is connected with the loss of their luminous anthropological attire, and that this made them feel "naked," then this connection helps clarify some developments that are found in Jewish and Christian apocalyptic accounts, and especially some of the theophanic developments found in *2 Enoch*. It is possible that, in these visionary accounts, theophanic fear serves not only as a reminder of the loss of the luminous garments, but also as a transformational possibility that can return a human seer back to his once-lost glorious condition. The fear that was first manifested at the loss of the glorious garments now serves as a sign of regaining the luminous attire. Eschatology here, as in many other Jewish apocalyptic accounts, attempts to mirror protology.[34]

The fear of the visionary thus serves as an important prerequisite for the reversal of the fallen nature of humanity and as the first step toward the restoration of its nature to the prelapsarian state.[35] In this respect, it is instructive to remember the previously mentioned concept found in the longer recension of *2 Enoch* 43:3, which tells that those who fear the deity "will be glorious forever."[36]

Conclusion

In conclusion, we must again draw our attention to the account of Enoch's glorified face, as it is found in the first chapter of the Slavonic apocalypse. It is possible that this transformational account was designed by its authors not only to proleptically anticipate the seer's glorious metamorphosis before the fearful face in chapter 22, but also to anticipate the eschatological transformation of the righteous.[37] In this respect, it is intriguing that the peculiar structure of the initial chapters of *2 Enoch* mirrors the macrostructure of the entire apocalypse. As we recall, after his encounter with the angels, found in the first chapter of the apocalypse, when the patriarch's face became luminous, he was then ordered by his otherworldly visitors to go to his relatives and tell them "everything that they must do in your house while they are without you on the earth."[38] Enoch then summons his sons and delivers a brief set of ethical exhortations to them. Some themes evoked in the patriarch's short admonition are reminiscent of those found in Enoch's lengthy instructions given in the second part of the pseudepigraphon. The initial chapters thus anticipate the overall structure of the apocalypse, where the hero is first transformed before the divine face and then returns to earth and delivers these revelations to his children. By mirroring the content of the initial chapters and the entire text, the metamorphosis of Enoch's face appears to fit nicely into the conceptual framework of the pseudepigraphon, anticipating the chief transformational event of the entire apocalypse: the glorification of the seer before the divine *panim* in *2 Enoch* 22.[39]

Conclusion

This volume has explored several early Jewish and Christian accounts in which a hero's conflict with an antagonist was a prerequisite for the hero's exaltation. This study enables us to discern several important characteristics of these antagonistic interactions.

Close analysis has demonstrated that apocalyptic conflicts reveal patterns of temporal and spatial symmetry. In the temporal dimension, the antagonistic setting of *Urzeit* is reiterated at *Endzeit,* when the emblematic features of the protological conflict appear again in the eschatological encounter. The mishap of the first, primordial conflict, resulting in the otherworldly antagonist's victory over human beings who were stripped of their prelapsarian condition, was repaired in the final battle, during which the human hero was able to regain his former status and glory. In the course of our investigation, we discerned such temporal symmetrical patterns in both of the leading etiologies of evil prevalent in early Jewish and Christian apocalyptic accounts: the Adamic history of the protoplast's fall and the Enochic myth of the Watchers' fall. While considering Adam's inauguration into the office of the divine image, we saw how the protological conflict of the protoplast with Satan was reinterpreted in several eschatological scenarios wherein the exaltations of various biblical exemplars, including Enoch, Jacob, Moses, the Son of Man, and Jesus, were located in antagonistic settings reminiscent of the first human's story. In these accounts, the primordial conflict with the ancient enemy was paradoxically reiterated, leading the eschatological heroes into their final apotheosis.

The symmetry between protological and eschatological conflicts can also be found in the stories based on the Enochic etiology of evil. In one such account found in the *Apocalypse of Abraham*, the fallen angel Azazel interferes with the ascent of the patriarch Abraham by attempting to impede his exaltation. The memory of the initial corruption caused by the Watchers is clearly present in this account. The mishap is repaired when Abraham's impure attire is placed upon Azazel while the fallen angel's heavenly garment is given to the patriarch.

Just like in the Adamic accounts, where the protoplast's exaltation strips Satan of his former glory, here too Azazel's celestial glory is transferred to a new favorite of the deity. Some Christian accounts also reveal this temporal symmetry by envisioning Jesus as the second Adam. In the synoptic accounts of Jesus's temptation in the wilderness, for example, the antagonistic encounter becomes a pivotal nexus of early Christology, which propels the Christian exemplar into his new role as the personified divine image.

The second important discovery of our study is the recognition of spatial symmetry in the antagonistic interactions according to which the earthly realities conspicuously parallel the heavenly ones. As an outcome of the apocalyptic battle, the human protagonist often takes the exalted celestial place of his antagonist while the defeated enemy is demoted to the lower realm.

This spatial correspondence is also manifested in the peculiar exchange of attributes between human protagonists and otherworldly antagonists during the course of their eschatological ordeals. The features of the defeated antagonists often become a part of the new eschatological accoutrement of the human heroes. We can clearly see this tendency in the tradition of the high priest's belt, which evokes the serpentine qualities of the defeated sea monster. This distinctive feature of the cultic attire proleptically anticipates the final defeat of evil.

The demotion of the seer's opponent plays a significant role in the apocalyptic drama. Like the protagonist's story, the ordeal of the antagonist culminates in a striking metamorphosis in the midst of conflict. This metamorphosis, however, is a reversed one. In a stunning change of fortune, the former winner of the protological ordeal is now defeated during the eschatological battle. Furthermore, in Jewish and Christian apocalypticism, the antagonists become the inverse mirrors of the exalted heroes, often surrendering their personal treasures to them upon defeat, including their supernatural attire. The theme of the garment's transference from the demoted angelic antagonist to an exalted human protagonist plays an equally important role in Adamic and Enochic mythologies of evil. Thus, antagonistic interaction not only becomes a prerequisite for the adept's metamorphosis but itself provides crucial elements which make such a transformation possible. In this framework, the defeated party's former condition, status, or garment becomes a "trophy" of the eschatological battle's winner.

This study explored another important characteristic of the apocalyptic conflict, namely, its sacerdotal dimension. The accounts of antagonistic interactions often contain peculiar cultic motifs of pollution and cleansing. In this cultic framework, the heroes and the antiheroes of antagonistic interactions often assume familiar sacerdotal offices, including the roles of priests and sacrificial animals. This tendency is especially noticeable in our study of the eschatological scapegoat in the Book of Revelation and in our analysis of Azazel's role in the

Apocalypse of Abraham. In both of these accounts, antagonistic interactions take the form of the familiar rituals of Yom Kippur.

Finally, this study traced out some Jewish and Christian developments in which the eschatological conflict was internalized. Through these developments, the human heart becomes the seat of the eschatological battle in which otherworldly entities eventually fight for the human's final destiny. This internalization of the conflict goes hand in hand with another important tendency—the internalization of the adept's metamorphosis. Close attention to the realities of the internalized conflict demonstrates that in early Jewish and Christian traditions, such antagonistic interactions became a part of the complex anthropologies closely tied to gendered, national, and sexual roles and identities. This connection between internalized mythologies of evil and social realities can assist scholars in better understanding not only features of early Jewish and Christian apocalypticism, but also various *yetzer* anthropologies of the rabbinic corpora and ascetic psychologies of the patristic authors.

Our investigation of the antagonistic settings of the adept's apotheosis has demonstrated that eschatological conflicts are closely connected with social and ideological realities that stand behind these apocalyptic ordeals. In this respect, close attention to the peculiar details of these conflicts can elucidate contemporary social and ideological tensions that lurk behind these stories. This is especially useful for understanding the social contexts of the Jewish and Christian martyrological accounts, which help to establish more precise dates and milieus for these compositions.

Notes

Introduction

1. H. Gunkel, *Schöpfung und Chaos in Urzeit und Endzeit: Eine religionsgeschichtliche Untersuchung über Gen. 1 und Ap. Joh. 12* (Göttingen: Vandenhoeck & Ruprecht, 1895). English translation: H. Gunkel, *Creation and Chaos in the Primeval Era and the Eschaton* (tr. K. W. Whitney; Grand Rapids: Eerdmans, 2006).

2. One of the critics of Gunkel's methodology argues that the problem with Gunkel's theory is that it did not simply identify mythological elements, "it also imposed on them a structure dictating the relationships among the elements—a structure that was based on inadequate knowledge and the forced interpretation of his sources. In other words, Gunkel wrote a myth, his own myth, that I would argue is essentially false. False in two ways: It fits the *Zeitgeist* of his own time rather than the time frame of his study and, indeed, was intended to do so because Gunkel was avowedly looking for the primordial tradition from which his historical present had evolved. Moreover, in its fullest formulation, Gunkel's myth corresponds to no real myth of either his own time or the ancient world writ large, including Greece and Rome and extending into the Christian era. I do not need to add that Gunkel also required all myths of the ancient Near East to be telling essentially the same story—the sort of analysis I believe we have long outgrown." J. Scurlock, Introduction to *Creation and Chaos: A Reconsideration of Hermann Gunkel's Chaoskampf Hypothesis* (eds. J. Scurlock, and R. H. Beal; Winona Lake, IN: Eisenbrauns, 2013), ix–x.

3. J. J. Collins, "The Mythology of Holy War in Daniel and the Qumran War Scroll: A Point of Transition in Jewish Apocalyptic," *VT* 25 (1975) 596–612 at 598.

4. P. Machinist, Foreword to Gunkel, *Creation and Chaos*, ix–xx.

5. Yarbro Collins defines "combat myth" as the pattern shared by a number of narratives in circulation in the first century CE that share common features. Accordingly, "the use of the term does not imply any particular theory of historical origin and interrelationship of the individual versions of the myth." A. Yarbro Collins, *The Combat Myth in the Book of Revelation* (HDR, 9; Missoula: Scholars, 1976), 58.

6. Yarbro Collins, *The Combat Myth*, 57.

7. Yarbro Collins, *The Combat Myth*, 57.

8. Yarbro Collins, *The Combat Myth*, 57.

9. F. M. Cross, *Canaanite Myth and Hebrew Epic: Essays in the History of the Religion of Israel* (Cambridge, MA: Harvard University Press, 2009), 162–3.

10. Apropos Marduk's weaponry, Eric Nels Ortlund notes that "the extended description of Marduk's weapons in his fight with cosmic chaos includes thunderbolts, storm-winds, raging fire (with which he covers his body), the deluge, his chariot, as well as his accompanying warriors and radiant aura. . . . The awesome radiance of the warrior storm-god is thus part-and-parcel both his weaponry and of his recognition as king." E. N. Ortlund, *Theophany and Chaoskampf: The Interpretation of Theophanic Imagery in the Baal Epic, Isaiah, and the Twelve* (GUS, 5; Piscataway, NJ: Gorgias, 2010), 97.

11. Ortlund, *Theophany and Chaoskampf*, 102.

12. As Ortlund puts it, "binding of theophany and the divine defeat of chaos is so widespread in Hebrew poetry that any occurrence of a theophany in a poetic context without such conflict leaps out by contrast." Ortlund, *Theophany and Chaoskampf*, 2.

13. Collins, "The Mythology of Holy War in Daniel and the Qumran War Scroll: A Point of Transition in Jewish Apocalyptic," 601. See also A. Angel, *Chaos and the Son of Man.: The Hebrew Chaoskampf Tradition in the Period 515 BCE to 200 CE* (LSTS, 60; London: T&T Clark, 2006).

14. Collins argues that "for Daniel the four beasts which come out of the sea collectively take the place of the sea-monster in the Ugaritic myth." Collins, "The Mythology of Holy War in Daniel and the Qumran War Scroll: A Point of Transition in Jewish Apocalyptic," 602.

15. A. C. M. Willis, *Dissonance and the Drama of Divine Sovereignty in the Book of Daniel* (Library of Hebrew Bible/Old Testament Studies; London: T&T Clark, 2010), 76.

16. On the *Chaoskampf* motif and theophany, see, among others, Cross, *Canaanite Myth and Hebrew Epic: Essays in the History of the Religion of Israel*, 14–177; J. Day, *God's Conflict with the Dragon and the Sea* (OP, 35; Cambridge: Cambridge University Press, 1985), 30, 105–108; A. Green, *The Storm-God in the Ancient Near East* (BJSUC, 8; Winona Lake, IN: Eisenbrauns, 2003), 15–84; J. Jeremias, *Theophanie: Die Geschichte einer alttestamentlichen Gattung* (WMANT, 10; Neukirchen-Vluyn, Neukirchener Verlag, 1965), 73–89; T. W. Mann, *Divine Presence and Guidance in Israelite Traditions: The Typology of Exaltation* (Johns Hopkins Near Eastern Studies; Baltimore: Johns Hopkins University, 1977), 9ff.; P. D. Miller, *The Divine Warrior in Early Israel* (HSM, 5; Leiden: Brill, 1973), 86, 107; T. R. Y. Neufeld, *"Put on the Armour of God": The Divine Warrior from Isaiah to Ephesians* (JSNTSS, 140; Sheffield: Sheffield Academic Press, 1997), 50ff; J. Niehaus, *God at Sinai: Covenant and Theophany in the Bible and Ancient Near East* (SOTBT; Grand Rapids: Zondervan, 1995), 81–141; Ortlund, *Theophany and Chaoskampf*; M. Weinfeld, " 'Rider of the Clouds' and 'Gatherer of the Clouds,' " *JANES* 5 (1973): 421–25; K. W. Whitney, *Two Strange Beasts: Leviathan and Behemoth in Second Temple and Early Rabbinic Judaism* (HSM, 63; Winona Lake, Indiana: Eisenbrauns, 2006), 42, 156–158; N. Wyatt, "Arms and the King: The Earliest Allusions to the *Chaoskampf* Motif and their Implications for the Interpretation of the Ugaritic and Biblical Traditions," in *"Und Mose schrieb dieses Lied auf": Studien zum Alten Testament und zum Alten Orient. Festschrift für Oswald Loretz zur Vollendung seines 70* (AOAT, 250; Münster: Ugarit-Verlag, 1998), 834–47; Wyatt, *Space and Time in the Religious Life of the Near East* (BS, 85; Sheffield: Sheffield Academic Press, 2001), 95–113.

17. On the Divine Warrior motif, see C. Kloos, *Yhwh's Combat with the Sea* (Amsterdam: G. A. van Oorschot; Leiden: Brill, 1986); Neufeld, *"Put on the Armour of God"*; M. Klingbeil, *Yahweh Fighting from Heaven: God as Warrior and as God of Heaven in the Hebrew Psalter and Ancient Near Eastern Iconography* (OBO, 169; Göttingen: Vandenhoeck & Ruprecht, 1999); D. S. Ballentine, *The Conflict Myth and the Biblical Tradition* (Oxford: Oxford University Press, 2015), 73–123.

18. Already in the ancient Near Eastern materials, the tradition of the theophany in battle was extended to human beings: "the radiant appearance of the Divine Warrior in battle was not, however, limited only to gods and goddesses in Mesopotamia. Mesopotamian royal annals give abundant examples of description of Assyrian kings who engage in battle with historical enemies with thunder, lightning, flood and fire, to tumultuous effect." Ortlund, *Theophany and Chaoskampf*, 98.

19. Debra Scoggins Ballentine points out that "the logic of the legitimating ideology exhibited in these texts is fully grounded in the signification of Leviathan and the sea/waters within occurrences of the conflict motif such as those preserved in the Hebrew Bible, in which Leviathan and the sea/waters have been defeated and tamed by Yahweh." Ballentine, *Conflict Myth,* 157.

20. Ballentine, *Conflict Myth,* 157.

21. N. Cohn, *Cosmos, Chaos, and the World to Come* (New Haven, CT: Yale University Press, 1993), 214.

22. A. Yarbro Collins, *Crisis and Catharsis: The Power of the Apocalypse* (Philadelphia: Westminster Press, 1984), 99.

23. Yarbro Collins, *Crisis and Catharsis,* 153.

Chapter One. Between God and Satan

1. Apropos the ancient roots of this story, Fletcher-Louis notes that:

> Besides its appearance in the Latin, Georgian, and Armenian versions of the *Life of Adam and Eve*, the Worship of Adam Story is attested in both Jewish and Christian sources in a way that suggests a nonsectarian provenance and wide circulation in the first century of the Christian era (if not earlier). In the Christian environment, the story is attested in diverse pseudepigraphical sources, but the church fathers themselves do not quote from it. Because their theology was Christocentric, not anthropocentric, it is unsurprising that they did not make direct use of it. This also means it is unlikely that early Christians created the story, even if they found it useful when appropriated through a Christological lens. We know that the rabbis were aware of it because they preserve a similar story that says when the angels began to worship the first human being, God took steps to ensure that in the future they would not mistake Adam for his Creator. This is clearly designed to refute the Worship of Adam Story and is best taken as evidence that "certain people in the first centuries CE maintained that Adam, although created, was a divine or at least semi-divine being who deserved to be worshipped, and

> the rabbis vehemently opposed such a 'heretical' idea." It is possible that the rabbis are reacting to a story dear to Christians, but several considerations make this unlikely. At no point do the rabbinic texts explicitly polemicize against Christians for believing that Adam was worshipped as a divine being. And given the way the Adam story is marginalized in mainstream patristic theology, it is more likely that the rabbis are reacting to a story that had been doing the rounds in their own Jewish environment.

C. H. T. Fletcher-Louis, *Jesus Monotheism, vol. 1, Christological Origins: The Emerging Consensus and Beyond* (Eugene, OR: Cascade Books, 2015), 259–260.

2. Although the story is not found in the Greek version of the *Primary Adam Books*, scholars argue that its author "must have known it in some form, but he has chosen not to narrate it." For example, Johannes Magliano-Tromp notes:

> In the Greek *Life of Adam and Eve* 16:3, it is told that the devil invited the serpent to be his companion in seducing Adam to sin, "so that he will be cast out of paradise, just as we have been cast out by him." This must be a reference to the story of the devil's fall from heaven, a story that is narrated at length in the Armenian, Georgian, and Latin versions of the writing. The author of the Greek *Life of Adam and Eve* must have known it in some form, but he has chosen not to narrate it.

J. Magliano-Tromp, "Adamic Traditions in *2 Enoch* and in the Books of Adam and Eve," in *New Perspectives on 2 Enoch: No Longer Slavonic Only* (eds. A. A. Orlov, G. Boccaccini, and J. Zurawski; SJS, 3; Leiden: Brill, 2012), 283–304 at 298. See also M. Stone, "The Fall of Satan and Adam's Penance: Three Notes on The Books of Adam and Eve," *JTS* 44 (1993): 153–56.

Fletcher-Louis explains the absence of the story in some versions as the result of Christian censorship. He argues that:

> Because the story does not fit well with the belief that it is Jesus Christ who is the image of God, the fact that it is fully told in the Latin, Armenian, and Georgian, but not in the extant Greek and the Slavonic is best explained as textual evidence for its suppression in Christian transmission. Either the Greek and Slavonic tradents disapproved of the story altogether or they were concerned that it should only be handled with extreme care, and it should not be widely known among the uneducated or the laity, who might misunderstand it. The fact that some Greek manuscripts refer to the story, but do not lay it out fully, suggests this second explanation.

Fletcher-Louis, *Jesus Monotheism*, 260.

3. G. Anderson and M. Stone, *A Synopsis of the Books of Adam and Eve. Second Revised Edition* (EJL, 17; Atlanta: Scholars Press, 1999), 16E.

4. Anderson and Stone, *A Synopsis of the Books of Adam and Eve*, 16E.

5. The Latin version of the *Primary Adam Books* 13:2–14:1 reads: "The Lord God then said: 'Behold, Adam, I have made you in our image and likeness.' Having gone forth[,] Michael called all the angels[,] saying: 'Worship the image of the Lord God, just as the Lord God has commanded.'" The Armenian version of the *Primary Adam Books* 13:2–14:1 reads: "God said to Michael, 'Behold I have made Adam in the likeness of my image.' Then Michael summoned all the angels, and God said to them, 'Come, bow down to god whom I made.'" Anderson and Stone, *A Synopsis of the Books of Adam and Eve*, 16E.

6. Fletcher-Louis, *Jesus Monotheism*, 265. Fletcher-Louis further notes that "indeed, this is clear even at a cursory reading of the Greek and Latin versions of the *Primary Adam Books*. Later on in the story of Adam's life, when Seth and Eve go in search of healing oil to help Adam, Seth is attacked by a wild animal (*Synopsis* §12). He is able to rebuke and overcome the beast because he is the image of God to whom the animal creature should submit. That story would not work quite so well if Seth were made according to God's image." Fletcher-Louis, *Jesus Monotheism*, 265.

7. Anderson and Stone, *A Synopsis of the Books of Adam and Eve*, 16E.

8. Anderson and Stone, *A Synopsis of the Books of Adam and Eve*, 16E.

9. Anderson and Stone, *A Synopsis of the Books of Adam and Eve*, 16E. Corrine Patton observes that "Adam's role as the effective symbol of God's presence in heaven is the result of a divine command." C. Patton, "Adam as the Image of God," *SBLSP* 33 (1994): 294–300 at 299. She goes on to say that "because this image of God was created and ordained as such by God, Satan's refusal to worship Adam is paramount to Satan's refusal to worship God." Patton, "Adam as the Image of God," 299–300.

10. "*adora imaginem dei Jehova*." Anderson and Stone, *A Synopsis of the Books of Adam and Eve*, 16–16E. See also Latin *Vita* 15:2: "Worship the image of God. If you do not worship, the Lord God will grow angry with you." Anderson and Stone, *A Synopsis of the Books of Adam and Eve*, 17E.

11. The Latin version of the *Primary Adam Books* 14:2–15:1 reads: "Michael himself worshipped first then he called me and said: 'Worship the image of God Jehovah.' I answered: 'I do not have it within me to worship Adam.' When Michael compelled me to worship, I said to him: 'Why do you compel me? I will not worship him who is lower and later than me. I am prior to that creature. Before he was made, I had already been made. He ought to worship me.' Hearing this, other angels who were under me were unwilling to worship him." The Armenian version of the *Primary Adam Books* 14:2–15:1 reads: "Michael bowed first. He called me and said, 'You too, bow down to Adam.' I said, Go away, Michael! I shall not bow [down] to him who is posterior to me, for I am former. Why is it proper [for me] to bow down to him? The other angels, too, who were with me, heard this, and my words seemed pleasing to them and they did not prostrate themselves to you, Adam." Anderson and Stone, *A Synopsis of the Books of Adam and Eve*, 16E–17E.

12. The motif of angelic opposition has been regularly marginalized in previous studies of the story, while the motif of angelic worship has been exaggerated. Such an approach is evident in the peculiar labeling of the account as "Worship of Adam Story" (Fletcher-Louis, *Jesus Monotheism*, 256) or "Exaltation of Adam" (G. Anderson, "The

Exaltation of Adam and the Fall of Satan," in *Literature on Adam and Eve. Collected Essays* [eds. G. Anderson, M. E. Stone, J. Tromp; SVTP, 15; Leiden: Brill, 2000], 83–110).

13. Fletcher-Louis argues for the early pre-Christian provenance of this motif by noting that "Philo is almost certainly a witness to it in his treatise *On the Creation of the World*, where he says that when man was created the other creatures were so amazed at the sight of him that they worshipped (*proskynein*) him as one by nature ruler and master (§83)." Fletcher-Louis, *Jesus Monotheism*, 262.

14. The deification of Adam is especially evident in the Armenian version of the *Primary Adam Books* 14:1: "Then Michael summoned all the angels, and God said to them, 'Come, bow down *to god* whom I made.'" Anderson and Stone, *A Synopsis of the Books of Adam and Eve*, 16E.

15. With regard to the motif of angelic veneration, Steenburg argues that "the worship of the image of God, insofar as it is a visible or physical manifestation of God, is within the bounds of Torah." S. Steenburg, "The Worship of Adam and Christ as the Image of God," *JSNT* 39 (1990): 95–109 at 95.

16. Fletcher-Louis, *Jesus Monotheism*, 270. Later he notes that "the story does not portray Adam as a thoroughly separate, individuated, divine being. He is not 'a god' or 'demigod.' He exists solely at the service of God; as God's image and likeness." Fletcher-Louis, *Jesus Monotheism*, 271.

17. A. A. Orlov, *Dark Mirrors: Azazel and Satanael in Early Jewish Demonology* (Albany: State University of New York Press, 2011), 105.

18. Anderson and Stone, *A Synopsis of the Books of Adam and Eve*, 16E.

19. The LXX version of Gen 2:7 reads: "And God formed man, dust from the earth, and breathed into his face (εἰς τὸ πρόσωπον αὐτοῦ) a breath of life, and the man became a living being."

20. Anderson and Stone, *A Synopsis of the Books of Adam and Eve*, 16–16E.

21. Steenburg, "The Worship of Adam and Christ as the Image of God," 96. In Steenburg's opinion, "'Face' relates more specifically to physical, visual appearance, just as the angelic worship of Adam in *Vit. Ad.* is peculiar to Adam alone. . . . To be adequate to the text in its irregular usage of 'face,' however, we are probably meant to understand that Adam is not just a representative by virtue of his patriarchy, but that he is also the best representative and that his superiority in this regard pertains to his physical or visible likeness to God." Steenburg, "The Worship of Adam and Christ," 97.

22. Fletcher-Louis, *Jesus Monotheism*, 270.

23. On the date of *2 Enoch*, see R. H. Charles, and W. R. Morfill, *The Book of the Secrets of Enoch* (Oxford: Clarendon Press, 1896), xxvi; R. H. Charles and N. Forbes, "The Book of the Secrets of Enoch," in *The Apocrypha and Pseudepigrapha of the Old Testament* (2 vols.; ed. R. H. Charles; Oxford: Clarendon Press, 1913), 2.429; J. T. Milik, *The Books of Enoch: Aramaic Fragments of Qumrân Cave 4* (Oxford: Clarendon Press, 1976), 114; C. Böttrich, *Das slavische Henochbuch* (JSHRZ, 5; Gütersloh: Gütersloher Verlaghaus, 1995), 813; A. A. Orlov, *The Enoch-Metatron Tradition* (TSAJ, 107; Tübingen: Mohr Siebeck, 2005), 323–328; Orlov, "The Sacerdotal Traditions of 2 Enoch and the Date of the Text," in *New Perspectives on 2 Enoch: No Longer Slavonic Only* (eds. A. A. Orlov, G. Boccaccini, and J. Zurawski; SJS, 4; Leiden: Brill, 2012), 103–116.

24. F. Andersen, "2 (Slavonic Apocalypse of) Enoch," in *The Old Testament Pseudepigrapha* (2 vols.; ed. J. H. Charlesworth; New York: Doubleday, 1983–1985), 1.138.

25. The Adamic story of the angelic veneration of Adam and Satan's disobedience is attested in many Jewish, Christian, and Muslim materials. See e.g. Slavonic version of *3 Bar.* 4, *Gos. Bart.* 4, Coptic *Enthronement of Michael*; *Cave of Treasures* 2:10–24, and *Qur'an* 2:31–39; 7:11–18; 15:31–48; 17:61–65; 18:50; 20:116–123; 38:71–85.

26. Charles and Morfill, *The Book of the Secrets of Enoch*, 28.

27. M. E. Stone, "The Fall of Satan and Adam's Penance," in *Literature on Adam and Eve. Collected Essays* (eds. G. Anderson, M. E. Stone, J. Tromp; SVTP, 15; Brill: Leiden, 2000), 43–56 at 47.

28. Stone, "The Fall of Satan and Adam's Penance," 48.

29. Stone, "The Fall of Satan and Adam's Penance," 48.

30. Stone, "The Fall of Satan and Adam's Penance," 48.

31. Stone, "The Fall of Satan and Adam's Penance," 48. For Stone, "The conclusion seems quite clear. The author of *2 Enoch* 21–22 knew a story of the rebellion of Satan that strongly resembled that which is found in chaps. 11–17 of the *Primary Adam Books*, in its Latin, Armenian, and Georgian forms. It is particularly interesting that this form of the tradition does not occur in the Slavonic recension of the *Primary Adam Books*. This situation seems to invite us to conclude that this material entered *2 Enoch* in Greek. Certainly, the story of Satan's rebellion did not enter *2 Enoch* from the Slavonic *Vita*." Stone, "Fall of Satan," 48.

32. Anderson, "The Exaltation of Adam and the Fall of Satan," 100.

33. Anderson, "The Exaltation of Adam and the Fall of Satan," 100.

34. Anderson, "The Exaltation of Adam and the Fall of Satan," 101.

35. Anderson, "The Exaltation of Adam and the Fall of Satan," 101.

36. Anderson, "The Exaltation of Adam and the Fall of Satan," 101.

37. Andersen, "2 Enoch," 1.138.

38. Andersen, "2 Enoch," 1.114.

39. Andersen, "2 Enoch," 1.117.

40. Anderson and Stone, *A Synopsis of the Books of Adam and Eve*, 45E (Armenian version).

41. Anderson and Stone, *A Synopsis of the Books of Adam and Eve*, 45E (Armenian version).

42. *PAB* 43(13): "The Lord said, 'I will admit them into the Garden and I will anoint them with that unction.'" Anderson and Stone, *A Synopsis of the Books of Adam and Eve*, 45E (Georgian version).

43. M. E. Stone, "The Angelic Prediction in the *Primary Adam Books*," in *Literature on Adam and Eve. Collected Essays* (eds. G. Anderson, M. E. Stone, J. Tromp; SVTP, 15; Brill: Leiden, 2000), 111–131 at 127.

44. H. E. Gaylord, "3 (Greek Apocalypse of) Baruch," in *The Old Testament Pseudepigrapha* (2 vols; ed. J. H. Charlesworth; New York: Doubleday, 1983–1985), 1.658.

45. Stone, "Angelic Prediction in the Primary Adam Books," 126.

46. E. C. Quinn, *The Quest of Seth for the Oil of Life* (Chicago: University of Chicago Press, 1962), 59.

47. Anderson and Stone, *A Synopsis of the Books of Adam and Eve*, 40E.

48. Stone, "Angelic Prediction in the Primary Adam Books," 126.

49. Andersen, "2 Enoch," 1.163.

50. The longer recension of *2 Enoch* 64:4–5 reads: "O our father, Enoch! May you be blessed by the Lord, the eternal king! And now, bless your sons, and all the people, so that we may be glorified in front of your face today. For you will be glorified in front of the face of the Lord for eternity, because you are the one whom the Lord chose in preference to all the people upon the earth; and he appointed you to be the one who makes a written record of all his creation, visible and invisible, and the one who carried away the sin of mankind." Andersen, "2 Enoch," 1.190.

51. A. A. Orlov, *The Glory of the Invisible God: Two Powers in Heaven Traditions and Early Christology* (JCTCRS, 31; London: Bloomsbury, 2019), 35.

52. Andersen, "2 Enoch," 1.171; N. Deutsch, *The Gnostic Imagination: Gnosticism, Mandaeism, and Merkabah Mysticism* (Leiden: Brill, 1995), 102.

53. The interchangeability between the notions of *tselem* and *panim* is observable, for example, in later Jewish lore about Jacob's image engraved on the divine throne. Several texts replace the notion of Jacob's *tselem* with the imagery of his *panim*. For example, *Hekhalot Rabbati* (*Synopse* §164): "And testify to them. What testimony? You see Me—what I do to the visage of the face of Jacob your father which is engraved for Me upon the throne of My glory. For in the hour that you say before Men 'Holy,' I kneel on it and embrace it and kiss it and hug it and My hands are on its arms three times, corresponding to the three times that you say before Me, 'Holy,' according to the word that is said, Holy, holy, holy (Isa 6:3)." J. R. Davila, *Hekhalot Literature in Translation: Major Texts of Merkavah Mysticism* (SJJTP, 20; Leiden: Brill, 2013), 86; P. Schäfer, with M. Schlüter and H. G. von Mutius, *Synopse zur Hekhaloth-Literatur* (TSAJ, 2; Tübingen: Mohr Siebeck, 1981), 72. Here, the deity embraces and kisses Jacob's heavenly identity engraved on His Throne. Yet, the striking difference in comparison with other rabbinic accounts is that now it is not the image, but instead Jacob's face, that is said to be engraved on the throne. It appears that this shift is not merely a slip of a Hekhalot writer's pen, but a deliberate conceptual turn, since it is also attested in other rabbinic materials. For example, a testimony is found in *Pirke de Rabbi Eliezer* 35 which also attempts to replace the *tselem* imagery with the symbolism of Jacob's *panim* by arguing that the angels went to see the face of the patriarch, and that his heavenly countenance was reminiscent of a visage of one of the Living Creatures of the divine Throne: "Rabbi Levi said: In that night the Holy One, blessed be He, showed him all the signs. He showed him a ladder standing from the earth to the heaven, as it is said, "And he dreamed, and behold a ladder set up on the earth, and the top of it reached to heaven" (Gen 28:12). And the ministering angels were ascending and descending thereon, and they beheld the face of Jacob, and they said: This is the face—like the face of the *Chayyah*, which is on the Throne of Glory. Such (angels) who were (on earth) below were ascending to see the face of Jacob among the faces of the *Chayyah*, (for it was) like the face of the *Chayyah*, which is on the Throne of Glory." *Pirke de Rabbi Eliezer* (tr. G. Friedlander; London: Bloch, 1916), 265. Such peculiar terminological exchanges between *tselem* and *panim* are significant for our study.

54. Andersen, "2 Enoch," 1.170.

55. According to Nathaniel Deutsch:

> The key to understanding this passage has been provided by F. I. Andersen, who notes in his edition of *2 Enoch*, that its form imitates that of Gen 1:27, which states that "God created man in His image, in the image of God he created him, male and female he created them." Instead of the "image" of God, in *2 Enoch* we find God's "face," and in place of "male and female He created them," we read "small and great the Lord created." In light of the Jewish, Gnostic, and Mandaean traditions which treated the image of God in Gen 1:27 hypostatically, often identifying it with the Cosmic Adam, the substitution of the divine image in Gen 1:27 with the divine face is early evidence that God's face was perceived hypostatically, as well.

Deutsch, *The Gnostic Imagination*, 102.

56. Andersen, "2 Enoch," 1.171, note b. As previously indicated, in other Jewish materials the concept of the divine image is often rendered through the symbolism of the divine Face. See M. Idel, "The Changing Faces of God and Human Dignity in Judaism," in *Moshe Idel: Representing God* (eds. H. Tirosh-Samuelson and A. W. Hughes; LCJP, 8; Leiden: Brill, 2014), 103–122.

57. In relation to the formation of the Hekhalot corpus as a distinct class of texts, Ra'anan Boustan observes that:

> This loose body of texts, written primarily in Hebrew and Aramaic with a smattering of foreign loan words, took shape gradually during Late Antiquity and early Middle Ages (c. 300–900), and continued to be adapted and reworked by Jewish scribes and scholars throughout the Middle Ages and into the early Modern period (c. 900–1500). While Heikhalot literature does contain some material that dates to the "classic" rabbinic period (c. 200–500 CE), this literature seems to have emerged *as a distinct class of texts* only at a relatively late date, most likely after 600 CE and perhaps well into the early Islamic period.

R. S. Boustan, "The Study of Heikhalot Literature: Between Mystical Experience and Textual Artifact," *CBR* 6.1 (2007): 130–160 at 130–131. Later Boustan elaborates on this further: "Heikhalot literature—and its constituent parts—cannot simply be divided into stable 'books' or 'works,' but must be studied within the shifting redactional contexts reflected in the manuscript tradition. In particular, the dynamic relationships among single units of tradition as well as the relationships of those units to the larger whole should be considered. In light of this complex transmission-history, scholars have not always been able to agree on a single definition of what constitutes a Heikhalot text or on how the corpus might best be delimited." Boustan, "The Study of Heikhalot Literature," 139.

58. For a comprehensive analysis of the rabbinic texts and traditions dealing with the angelic opposition to humanity, see P. Schäfer, *Rivalität zwischen Engeln und*

Menschen: Untersuchungen zur rabbinischen Engelvorstellung (SJ, 8; Berlin: Walter de Gruyter, 1975). Schäfer's research demonstrates that the idea of angelic opposition was expressed explicitly in rabbinic literature on three decisive occasions: at the creation of Adam, at the moment of the giving of the Torah, and at the descent of the Shekinah in the Sanctuary. On all three occasions angels speak enviously against humanity in an attempt to prevent God from creating humanity, giving the Torah to Israel, or coming to dwell among humans. Schäfer, *Rivalität zwischen Engeln und Menschen: Untersuchungen zur rabbinischen Engelvorstellung*, 219.

59. P. Alexander, "3 (Hebrew Apocalypse of) Enoch," in *The Old Testament Pseudepigrapha* (2 vols.; ed. J. H. Charlesworth; New York: Doubleday, 1983–1985), 1.258–9; Schäfer et al., *Synopse*, 6–7.

60. Anderson, "The Exaltation of Adam and the Fall of Satan," 83–110. On the Adamic traditions in rabbinic literature, see also A. Altmann, "The Gnostic Background of the Rabbinic Adam Legends," *JQR* 35 (1945): 371–391; B. Barc, "La taille cosmique d'Adam dans la littérature juive rabbinique des trois premiers siècles apres J.-C.," *RSR* 49 (1975): 173–85; J. Fossum, "The Adorable Adam of the Mystics and the Rebuttals of the Rabbis," in *Geschichte-Tradition-Reflexion. Festschrift für Martin Hengel zum 70. Geburtstag* (2 vols; eds. H. Cancik, H. Lichtenberger and P. Schäfer; Tübingen: Mohr Siebeck, 1996), 1.529–39; G. Quispel, "Der gnostische Anthropos und die jüdische Tradition," *ErJb* 22 (1953): 195–234; Quispel, "Ezekiel 1:26 in Jewish Mysticism and Gnosis," *VC* 34 (1980): 1–13; A. Segal, *Two Powers in Heaven: Early Rabbinic Reports about Christianity and Gnosticism* (SJLA, 25; Leiden: Brill, 1977), 108–115.

61. Anderson, "The Exaltation of Adam and the Fall of Satan," 107.

62. Anderson, "The Exaltation of Adam and the Fall of Satan," 108.

63. Alexander, "3 Enoch," 1.259.

64. Anderson, "The Exaltation of Adam and the Fall of Satan," 105.

65. E. R. Wolfson, *Through a Speculum That Shines: Vision and Imagination in Medieval Jewish Mysticism* (Princeton, NJ: Princeton University Press, 1994), 20.

66. Ludwig Köhler and Moshe Weinfeld argue that the phrase, "in our image, after our likeness" precludes the anthropomorphic interpretation that the human being was created in the divine image. L. Köhler, "Die Grundstelle der *Imago Dei* Lehre, Genesis I, 26," *ThZ* 4 (1948): 16; M. Weinfeld, *Deuteronomy and the Deuteronomic School* (Oxford: Clarendon Press, 1972), 199. In relation to these conceptual developments, Wolfson notes that:

> It seems that the problem of God's visibility is invariably linked to the question of God's corporeality, which, in turn, is bound up with the matter of human likeness to God. . . . Although the official cult of ancient Israelite religion prohibited the making of images or icons of God, this basic need to figure or image God in human form found expression in other ways, including the prophetic visions of God as an anthropos, as well as the basic tenet of the similitude of man and divinity. The biblical conception is such that the anthropos is as much cast in the image of God as God is cast in the image of the anthropos. This is stated in the very account of the creation

> of the human being in the first chapter of Genesis (attributed to P) in the claim that Adam was created in the image of God.

Wolfson, *Through a Speculum*, 20–21.

67. A similar motif is entertained in the encounter between Seth and the beast in the *PAB*.

68. In this context, the metamorphoses of some Danielic theriomorphic antagonists, including the first beast who attempts to emulate a human posture by standing on two feet, can be seen as arrogations against the divine authority. On this, see Willis, *Dissonance and the Drama of Divine Sovereignty*, 76.

69. Amy Merrill Willis points out that "Daniel's description of the Ancient of Days signals incomparable honor, glory, and power. Daniel clearly borrows from Ezek 1:26–28, where the description of the deity emphasizes Yahweh's holiness and glory, which is seated on a mobile throne and surrounded by hybrid creatures. Moreover, one finds in the vision cycle Ezekiel's language of brilliant light, fire, and the wheeled throne (Ezek 1:15, 27–28/Dan 7:9–10)." Willis, *Dissonance and the Drama of Divine Sovereignty*, 74–5.

70. Willis, *Dissonance and the Drama of Divine Sovereignty*, 75.

71. Willis, *Dissonance and the Drama of Divine Sovereignty*, 75.

72. Dan 7:4: "The first was like a lion and had eagles' wings. Then, as I watched, its wings were plucked off, and it was lifted up from the ground and made to stand on two feet like a human being; and a human mind was given to it." All biblical quotations are taken from the New Revised Standard Version (NRSV) unless otherwise indicated.

73. Willis, *Dissonance and the Drama of Divine Sovereignty*, 76.

74. Fletcher-Louis, *Jesus Monotheism*, 197. See also P. Owen, "Aramaic and Greek Representations of the 'Son of Man' and the Importance of the Parables of Enoch," in *Parables of Enoch: A Paradigm Shift* (eds. D. L. Bock and J. H. Charlesworth; JCTCRS, 11; London: Bloomsbury, 2013), 114–123 at 115, footnote 5.

75. Fletcher-Louis, *Jesus Monotheism*, 197.

76. Fletcher-Louis, *Jesus Monotheism*, 280.

77. Regarding this passage, Hurtado states the following:

> The effects of the heavenly divine agent concept may be seen especially in *1 Enoch* 46:1–3, where, employing imagery from Dan 7:9–14, the writer pictures the "Son of Man"/"Chosen One" in a heavenly scene, prominently associated with God, possessing an angelic aspect, and privy to all heavenly secrets. In this theophanic scene, the writer pictures God and "another," man-like in appearance, whose face was "full of grace, like one of the holy angels," who "will reveal all the treasures of that which is secret." The writer of *1 Enoch* 46 apparently saw the figure in Dan 7:13–14 as a real being bearing heavenly (angelic) qualities and as God's chosen chief agent of eschatological deliverance. Whether this interpretation reflects the meaning intended by the author of Daniel 7 or was a later development, in either case I suggest that such an interpretation is evidence of the concept of a heavenly divine agent, a figure next to God in authority who acts as God's chief representative.

L. W. Hurtado, *One God, One Lord: Early Christian Devotion and Ancient Jewish Monotheism* (London: SCM, 1988), 54.

78. M. Knibb, *The Ethiopic Book of Enoch: A New Edition in the Light of the Aramaic Dead Sea Fragments* (2 vols.; Oxford: Clarendon, 1978), 2.131–132.

79. Nickelsburg and VanderKam bring attention to this feature by noting that in comparison with Dan 7:13, *1 Enoch* 46:1c mentions the face of the Son of Man. G. Nickelsburg and J. VanderKam, *1 Enoch 2: A Commentary on the Book of 1 Enoch: Chapters 37–82* (Hermeneia; Minneapolis: Fortress, 2012), 156.

80. Nickelsburg and VanderKam, *1 Enoch 2*, 157.

81. Fletcher-Louis, *Jesus Monotheism*, 250.

82. S. L. Herring, *Divine Substitution: Humanity as the Manifestation of Deity in the Hebrew Bible and the Ancient Near East* (FRLANT, 247; Göttingen: Vandenhoeck & Ruprecht, 2013), 216.

83. Analyzing these witnesses, Herring points out that "in at least two passages [the Son of Man] figure appears to receive worship. Thus, 48:5 states that the entire earth will 'fall down and worship before him.' This is given more detail in 62:6–9, which states that 'the kings,' 'the mighty,' 'all who possess the earth,' 'the exalted,' and 'those who rule the earth' will 'bless,' 'glorify,' 'extol,' 'fall on their faces,' 'worship,' and 'set their hope upon the Son of Man.'" Herring, *Divine Substitution*, 216–17.

84. C. H. T. Fletcher-Louis, "The Worship of Divine Humanity as God's Image and the Worship of Jesus," in *The Jewish Roots of Christological Monotheism. Papers from the St. Andrews Conference on the Historical Origins of the Worship of Jesus* (eds. C. Newman et al.; JSJSS, 63; Leiden: Brill, 1999), 112–128 at 113.

85. Fletcher-Louis, *Jesus Monotheism*, 279–280. In another part of his study, he says, that although "there is no literary connection between the *Primary Adam Books* and the *Similitudes* . . . the Adamic contours to the Enochic Son of Man suggest that the worship of the Enochic figure may not be unconnected to wider traditions in which Adam was himself worshipped." Fletcher-Louis, *Jesus Monotheism*, 268.

86. W. Meeks, *The Prophet-King. Moses Traditions and the Johannine Christology* (NovTSup, 14; Leiden: Brill, 1967), 149.

87. The Greek text of the passage was published in several editions including: A.-M. Denis, *Fragmenta pseudepigraphorum quae supersunt Graeca* (PVTG, 3; Leiden: Brill, 1970), 210; B. Snell, *Tragicorum Graecorum Fragmenta I* (Göttingen: Vandenhoeck & Ruprecht, 1971), 288–301; H. Jacobson, *The Exagoge of Ezekiel* (Cambridge: Cambridge University Press, 1983), 54; C. R. Holladay, *Fragments from Hellenistic Jewish Authors* (3 vols.; SBLTT, 30; Pseudepigrapha Series 12; Atlanta: Scholars, 1989), 2.362–66.

88. Jacobson, *Exagoge of Ezekiel*, 54–55.

89. S. N. Bunta, "Moses, Adam and the Glory of the Lord in Ezekiel the Tragedian: On the Roots of a Merkabah Text" (Ph.D. diss.; Marquette University, 2005), 89–92.

90. Bunta, "Moses, Adam and the Glory of the Lord," 86.

91. Moses's enthronement can be also read as an Adamic motif. In this respect Fletcher-Louis reminds us that "In the *Testament of Abraham* A 11:4–12, the first formed Adam sits on a gilded throne at the gate of heaven, most marvelous and adorned with glory, with a form like that of God himself ('the Master')." Fletcher-Louis, *Jesus Monotheism*, 252.

92. On the possibility of angelic veneration of Moses in the *Exagoge*, see Bunta, *Moses, Adam and the Glory of the Lord*, 167–183. Bunta presents four similarities between the portrayal of Moses in the *Exagoge* and traditions about the angelic veneration of Adam: "1. In both traditions the human heroes are appropriately venerated by angels; 2. In both traditions the veneration reflects the human's attainment of a privileged status within the divine entourage; 3. Both traditions reflect an ironic polemic against angels; 4. Within this imagery, both traditions construct a complex dialectic of identity which emphasizes the dichotomous condition of humanity. On one hand, humanity is reminded of its earthliness, its mortal substance, and on the other hand, the body's divine likeness deserves angelic veneration." Bunta, *Moses, Adam, and the Glory of the Lord*, 183.

93. Jacobson, *Exagoge of Ezekiel*, 54–55.

94. As John Collins explains, "the stars had long been identified with the angelic host in Israelite tradition. . . . Ultimately this tradition can be traced back to Canaanite mythology where the stars appear as members of the divine council in the Ugaritic texts." Collins, *Apocalyptic Vision*, 136. See, for example, Judg 5:20: "The stars fought from heaven, from their courses they fought against Sisera"; Job 38:7: "When the morning stars sang together and all the heavenly beings shouted for joy?"; Dan 8:10: "It grew as high as the host of heaven. It threw down to the earth some of the host and some of the stars, and trampled on them"; *1 Enoch* 86:3–4: "And again I saw in the vision and looked at heaven, and behold, I saw many stars, how they came down and were thrown down from heaven to that first star, and amongst those heifers and bulls; they were with them, pasturing amongst them. And I looked at them and saw, and behold, all of them let out their private parts like horses and began to mount the cows of the bulls, and they all became pregnant and bore elephants and camels and asses." Knibb, *The Ethiopic Book of Enoch*, 197; *1 Enoch* 88:1: "And I saw one of those four who had come out first, how he took hold of that first star which had fallen from heaven, and bound it by its hands and its feet, and threw it into an abyss; and that abyss was narrow, and deep, and horrible, and dark." Knibb, *Ethiopic Book of Enoch*, 2.198; *1 Enoch* 90:24: "And the judgment was held first on the stars, and they were judged and found guilty; and they went to the place of damnation, and were thrown into a deep (place), full of fire, burning and full of pillars of fire." Knibb, *The Ethiopic Book of Enoch*, 2.215.

95. Hurtado, *One God, One Lord*, 59. See also L. W. Hurtado, *At the Origins of Christian Worship: The Context and Character of Earliest Christian Devotion* (Grand Rapids, MI: Eerdmans, 2000), 73.

96. Fletcher-Louis, "Worship of Divine Humanity," 113, footnote 3. See also C. H. T. Fletcher-Louis, *All the Glory of Adam. Liturgical Anthropology in the Dead Sea Scrolls* (STDJ, 42; Leiden: Brill, 2002), 7, 70, 101, 344.

97. E. A. W. Budge, *The Book of the Cave of Treasures* (London: The Religious Tract Society, 1927), 52–54.

98. See also St. Ephrem, *Commentary on Genesis* II.15: "For Adam, who had been set in authority and control over animals, was wiser than all the animals, and he who gave names to them all was certainly more astute than them all. For just as Israel could not look upon the face of Moses, neither were the animals able to look upon the radiance of Adam and Eve: at the time when they received names from him they passed in front of Adam with their eyes down, since their eyes were incapable of taking in his

glory." S. Brock, *St. Ephrem the Syrian, Hymns on Paradise* (Crestwood, NY: St. Vladimir's Seminary Press, 1990), 207.

99. Anderson, "The Exaltation of Adam and the Fall of Satan," 88.

100. It is possible that Moses's coronation in the *Exagoge* also represents his endowment with the divine image. Wayne Meeks points out that in some Jewish and Samaritan traditions, Moses's "crown of light was nothing less than the visual symbol for the image of God. Jacob Jervell, moreover, has shown that in Jewish Adam-speculation the image of God was typically regarded as 'gerade auf dem Antlitz eingepragt.' Jervell argues that this conception of the *imago* was especially connected with the notion that Adam had been God's vice-regent, the first 'king of the world.' When the *imago* is identified with Moses' divine crown of light, it is quite clear that the same kind of connection is implied. The similarity is not accidental, for further examination of the enthronement traditions about Moses shows that these stories link Moses very closely with Adam." W. Meeks, "Moses as God and King," in *Religions in Antiquity: Essays in Memory of Erwin Ramsdell Goodenough* (ed. J. Neusner; SHR, 14; Leiden: Brill, 1968), 354–371 at 363. On this tradition, see also M. Smith, "The Image of God. Notes on the Hellenization of Judaism, with Especial Reference to Goodenough's Work on Jewish Symbols," *BJRL* 40 (1958): 473–512; J. Jervell, *Imago Dei. Gen 1, 26f. im Spätjudentum, in der Gnosis und in den paulinischen Briefen* (FRLANT, 76; Göttingen: Vandenhoeck & Ruprecht, 1960), 45.

101. On the role of Jacob as the image of God in rabbinic literature and Jewish mysticism, see A. A. Orlov, *The Greatest Mirror: Heavenly Counterparts in the Jewish Pseudepigrapha* (Albany: State University of New York Press, 2017), 61–118. On the Adamic background of this Jacob's role, see S. Bunta, "The Likeness of the Image: Adamic Motifs and *Tselem* Anthropology in Rabbinic Traditions about Jacob's Image Enthroned in Heaven," *JSJ* 37.1 (2006): 55–84.

102. A total of nine Greek sentences of this pseudepigraphon were preserved in the writings of Origen (c.185–c.254 CE). Fragment A is quoted in Origen's *In Ioannem* II.31.25. Fragment B, a single sentence, is cited in Gregory and Basil's compilation of Origen, the *Philokalia*. This fragment is also quoted in Eusebius, *The Preparation of the Gospel* and in the Latin *Commentary on Genesis* by Procopius of Gaza. Fragment C, which is also found in the *Philokalia*, quotes Fragment B and paraphrases Fragment A. Smith, "Prayer of Joseph," 2.699. Pieter van der Horst and Judith Newman note that "according to the ancient *Stichometry* of Nicephorus, the text originally contained 1100 lines. The extant portions totaling only nine Greek sentences or 164 words thus reflect a small fraction of the original composition." Van der Horst and Newman, *Early Jewish Prayers in Greek*, 249.

103. J. Z. Smith, "The Prayer of Joseph," in *Religions in Antiquity: Essays in Memory of Erwin Ramsdell Goodenough* (ed. J. Neusner; SHR, 14; Leiden: Brill, 1968), 253–93 at 255.

104. Jonathan Z. Smith proposed that "the *Prayer* is most likely to be situated within . . . [the] first-century Jewish groups, both in Palestine and in the Diaspora, both before and after the destruction of the Temple." Smith, "Prayer of Joseph," 2.701. This proposal fits with the judgment of van der Horst and Newman that "the composition must likely have been in circulation for a good period for Origen to have recognized it by title." Van der Horst and Newman, *Early Jewish Prayers in Greek*, 249.

105. Wolfson observes that "the notion of an angel named Jacob-Israel is also known from Jewish Christian texts, as reported mainly by Justin, and appears as well in Gnostic works such as the Nag Hammadi treatise *On the Origin of the World*, and in Manichaean texts." He further suggests that "such a tradition, perhaps through the intermediary of Philo, passed into Christian sources wherein the celestial Jacob or Israel was identified with Jesus who is depicted as the Logos and Son of God." E. Wolfson, "The Image of Jacob Engraved upon the Throne," in Wolfson, *Along the Path: Studies in Kabbalistic Myth, Symbolism, and Hermeneutics* (Albany: State University of New York Press, 1995) 1–62 at 5.

106. The *Book of Jubilees* appears to be also cognizant about the heavenly identity of Jacob. Thus, *Jubilees* 35:17 reads: "Now you are not to be afraid for Jacob because Jacob's guardian is greater and more powerful, glorious, and praiseworthy than Esau's guardian." J. C. VanderKam, *The Book of Jubilees* (2 vols., CSCO, 510–11; Scriptores Aethiopici, 87–88; Louvain: Peeters, 1989), 2.235–236. On this tradition, see also *Targum Pseudo-Jonathan* on Gen 33:10: "And Jacob said, 'Do not speak thus, I pray; if now I have found mercy in your eyes, you must accept my gift from my hand; because it is for this I have seen your countenance, and it seems to me like seeing the face of your angel; and behold, you have received me favorably.'" *Targum Pseudo-Jonathan: Genesis* (tr. M. Maher; ArBib, 1B; Collegeville: Liturgical Press, 1992), 116.

107. This verse appears to be pointing to the demiurgic role of Jacob-Israel. References to the demiurgic quality of Jacob may be found also in a number of rabbinic passages, including *Lev. Rab.* 36:4 and *Gen. Rab.* 98:3. Cf. *Gen. Rab.* 98:3: "R. Phinehas interpreted it: Your father Israel is as a god: as God creates worlds, so does your father create worlds; as God distributes worlds, so does your father distribute worlds." H. Freedman and M. Simon, *Midrash Rabbah* (10 vols.; London: Soncino, 1961), 2.947–948. *Lev. Rab.* 36:4: "R. Phinehas in the name of R. Reuben explains this to mean that the Holy One, blessed be He, said to His world: 'O My world, My world! Shall I tell thee who created thee, who formed thee? Jacob has created thee, Jacob has formed thee'; as is proved by the text, 'He that created thee is Jacob and he that formed thee is Israel.'" Freedman and Simon, *Midrash Rabbah*, 4.460.

108. J. Z. Smith, "Prayer of Joseph," in *The Old Testament Pseudepigrapha* (ed. J. H. Charlesworth; 2 vols.; New York: Doubleday, 1983–85), 2.699–714 at 713–714. For the primary texts, see Denis, *Fragmenta pseudepigraphorum quae supersunt Graeca*, 61–64; A. Resch, *Agrapha: Aussercanonische Schriftfragmente* (Leipzig: J. C. Hinrichs, 1906), 295–298; C. Blanc, ed., Origène, *Commentaire sur Saint Jean. Tome I (Livres I–V)* (SC, 120; Paris: Cerf, 1966), 334–37; J. A. Robinson, ed., Origen, *Philocalia* (Cambridge: Cambridge University Press, 1893); K. Mras, ed., Eusebius, *Praeparatio Evangelica* (GCS, 43:1–2; Leipzig: J. C. Hinrichs, 1954–56).

109. Despite some striking similarities with a Christian understanding of "spirit" as the seer's heavenly identity, one can detect a key conceptual difference between the heavenly state of the *Protoktistoi* of the Christian accounts and Jacob's celestial stand in the *Prayer*. While the seven angels are first-created, similar to Abraham and Isaac who "were created before any work," Jacob's heavenly Self is born. The difference between the celestial origins of Abraham and Isaac on the one hand and Jacob on the other is noteworthy, since it might point to some polemical developments.

110. Pieter van der Horst and Judith Newman note that "the word used for 'pre-created,' προεκτίσθησαν, is a prefixed form of the more frequently appearing κτίζω. The word is used to emphasize the idea that Jacob existed before the creation of the world and its order. The Greek term is found in later Christian literature to refer to the status of Christ as pre-existent, yet the idea resonates with rabbinic traditions that posit the preexistence of certain items before creation, variously among them the Torah, the temple, the heavenly throne, repentance, and wisdom." Van der Horst and Newman, *Early Jewish Prayers in Greek*, 250–251.

111. Van der Horst and Newman note that "the LXX of Exod 4:22 speaks of Israel as God's πρωτότοκος, 'first-born son.' This word is not found elsewhere in scripture, but Philo uses the term to refer both to the Logos (*Conf.* 63, 146; *Somn.* I. 215) and to Israel as a first-born (*Post.* 63; *Fug.* 208), or to Israel in the character of the Logos (*Agr.* 51). This idea of Jacob being 'the firstborn' is also mentioned in the *Prayer of Joseph* in which Jacob is . . . the 'firstborn of all living.'" Van der Horst and Newman, *Early Jewish Prayers in Greek*, 256.

112. Richard Hayward notes that "Philo uses this word only six times in his writings, always to speak of the Logos (*De Conf. Ling.* 63, 146; *De Som.* I. 215), Israel as a first-born (*De Post.* 63; *De Fuga* 208), or Israel in the character of the Logos (*De Agr.* 51)." C. T. R. Hayward, *Interpretations of the Name Israel in Ancient Judaism and Some Early Christian Writings* (Oxford: Oxford University Press, 2005), 200. He further notes that "when Philo calls Israel πρωτόγονος therefore, it may be that he has in mind once again a being who belongs both on earth and in heaven. . . ." Hayward, *Interpretations of the Name,* 200.

113. H. Schwartz, *Tree of Souls: The Mythology of Judaism* (Oxford: Oxford University Press, 2004), 366.

114. H. Windisch, "Die göttliche Weisheit der Juden und die paulinische Christologie," in *Neutestamentliche Studien für G. Heinrici* (eds. A. Deissmann and H. Windisch; UNT, 6; Leipzig: J. C. Heinrichs, 1914), 225, n. 1.

115. J. Fossum, *The Image of the Invisible God: Essays on the Influence of Jewish Mysticism on Early Christology* (NTOA, 30; Fribourg: Universitätsverlag Freiburg Schweiz; Göttingen: Vanderhoeck & Ruprecht, 1995), 24.

116. "He envied me and fought with me and wrestled with me saying that his name and the name that is before every angel was to be above mine." Smith, "Prayer of Joseph," 2.713.

117. Hayward, *Interpretations of the Name,* 205.

118. Cf. the Latin version of the *Primary Adam Books* 12:1: "Groaning, the Devil said: 'O Adam, all my enmity, jealousy, and resentment is towards you, since on account of you I was expelled and alienated from my glory, which I had in heaven in the midst of the angels. On account of you I was cast out upon the earth.'" Anderson and Stone, *A Synopsis of the Books of Adam and Eve*, 15E.

119. Cf. the Latin and the Armenian versions of the *Primary Adam Books* 14:2–15:1.

120. With regard to this verse, James Kugel emphasizes,

> Anyone who knows the Hebrew text of Gen 28:12 will immediately recognize the source of this image. For though the Bible says that in his dream

> Jacob saw a ladder whose top reached to the Heavens, the word for "top," in Hebrew, *rosh*, is the same word normally used for "head." And so our Slavonic text—or, rather, the Hebrew text that underlies it—apparently takes the biblical reference to the ladder's "head" as a suggestion that the ladder indeed had a head, a man's head, at its very top. The fact, then, of this biblical text's wording—"a ladder set up on the earth, and its head reached to heaven"—engendered the heavenly "head" in our pseudepigraphon.

J. Kugel, *In Potiphar's House: The Interpretive Life of Biblical Texts* (San Francisco: Harper Collins, 1990), 118.

121. H. G. Lunt, "Ladder of Jacob," in *The Old Testament Pseudepigrapha* (ed. J. H. Charlesworth; 2 vols.; New York: Doubleday, 1983–85), 2.407.

122. Lunt, "Ladder of Jacob," 2.406.

123. Elliot Wolfson points to a possible connection of this imagery with the conceptual developments found in the targumim: "It is worthwhile to compare the targumic and midrashic explanation of Gen 28:12 to the words of the apocryphal text the *Ladder of Jacob*. . . . 'And the top of the ladder was the face as of a man, carved out of fire.'" Wolfson, "Image of Jacob," 114.

124. Alexander Kulik and Sergey Minov demonstrate the connection of the face with the *Kavod* imagery. They note that "the theophanic associations of the fiery face in 1:4–7 are strengthen even more by the fact that in several rabbinic sources the vision of the ladder of Jacob is explicitly linked to the notion of God's glory." A. Kulik and S. Minov, *Biblical Pseudepigrapha in Slavonic Tradition* (Oxford: Oxford University Press, 2016), 301.

125. Fossum, *The Image of the Invisible God*, 135–51, esp. 143.

126. On these traditions, see Orlov, *Greatest Mirror*, 61–72.

127. Lunt, "Ladder of Jacob," 2.403.

128. Kugel, *In Potiphar's House*, 119.

129. Rachel Neis observes, "It is conceivable that the 'face of Jacob' is used in a more generic sense for Jacob's image or likeness and could include a representation of his entire figure or bust. The bust, or portrait medallion, was ubiquitous in civic, funerary and religious art in Late Antiquity and Byzantine periods, and while emphasizing the face of the person portrayed could portray the upper torso and arms." R. Neis, "Embracing Icons: The Face of Jacob on the Throne of God," *Images: A Journal of Jewish Art and Visual Culture* 1 (2007): 36–54 at 42.

130. Kugel, *In Potiphar's House*, 119.

131. Kugel, *In Potiphar's House*, 119.

132. See also C. C. Rowland, "John 1:51, Jewish Apocalyptic and Targumic Tradition," *NTS* 30 (1984): 498–507; C. H. von Heijne, *The Messenger of the Lord in Early Jewish Interpretations of Genesis* (BZAW, 42; Berlin/New York: Walter de Gruyter, 2010), 177–8.

133. Fossum, *The Image of the Invisible God*, 143, n. 30. I also previously argued for the existence of the heavenly counterpart traditions in the *Ladder of Jacob*. For my arguments, see A. A. Orlov, "The Face as the Heavenly Counterpart of the Visionary in the Slavonic Ladder of Jacob," in *Of Scribes and Sages: Early Jewish Interpretation and Transmission of Scripture* (2 vols.; ed. C. A. Evans; SSEJC, 9; London: T&T Clark, 2004), 2.59–76; Orlov, *Greatest Mirror*, 93–104.

134. Freedman and Simon, *Midrash Rabbah*, 2.626.
135. I. Epstein, *The Babylonian Talmud. Hullin* (London: Soncino, 1935–1952), 91b.
136. Wolfson, "Image of Jacob," 4.
137. Lunt, "Ladder of Jacob," 2.409.
138. In relation to these connections Kugel observes that

> The same motif [of four empires] apparently underlies the *Ladder of Jacob*. Here too, it is Jacob's vision of the ladder that serves as the vehicle for a revelation of the "kings of the lawless nations" who will rule over Israel, and if this text does not specifically mention how many such nations there will be, it does go on to speak (as we have seen) of four "ascents" or "descents" that will bring Jacob's progeny to grief. Indeed, the continuation of our text alludes specifically to the last of the four empires, Rome: "The Most High will raise up kings from the grandsons of your brother Esau, and they will receive the nobles of the tribes of the earth who will have maltreated your seed." As is well known, Esau frequently represents Rome in Second Temple writings.

J. Kugel, "The Ladder of Jacob," *HTR* 88 (1995): 214.
139. Kugel, "The Ladder of Jacob," 214.
140. Freedman and Simon, *Midrash Rabbah*, 4.370. See also *Exod. Rab.* 32:7: "God showed Jacob the guardian angels of every empire, for it says, And he dreamed, and behold a ladder set up on the earth (Gen 28:12). He showed him how many peoples, governors, and rulers would arise from each kingdom, and just as He displayed their rise, so he showed their fall, as it says, And behold, the angels of God ascending and descending on it. . . ." Freedman and Simon, *Midrash Rabbah*, 3.411.
141. W. G. Braude, *The Midrash on Psalms* (2 vols.; YJS, 13; New Haven, CT: Yale University Press, 1959), 2.26–27. *Pesiqta de-Rab Kahana* 23 contains an almost identical tradition:

> R. Nahman applied it to the episode in Jacob's life when He dreamed, and beheld a ladder . . . and angels of God (Gen 28:12). These angels, according to R. Samuel bar R. Nahman, were the princes of the nations of the earth. Further, according to R. Samuel bar Nahman, this verse proves that the Holy One showed to our father Jacob the prince of Babylon climbing up seventy rungs the ladder, then climbing down; the prince of Media climbing up fifty-two rungs and no more; the prince of Greece, one hundred and eighty rungs and no more; and the prince of Edom climbing and climbing, no one knows how many rungs. At the sight of Edom's climbing our father Jacob grew afraid said: Is one to suppose that this prince will have no come-down? The Holy One replied: Be not dismayed, O Israel (Jer 30:10): Even if—as though such a thing were possible!—thou were to see him seated next to Me, I would have him brought down thence.

W. G. Braude and I. J. Kapstein, *Pesikta de-Rab Kahana. R. Kahana's Compilation of Discourses for Sabbaths and Festal Days* (Philadelphia: Jewish Publication Society of America, 1975), 353. See also *Zohar* I.149b:

> And behold, the angels of God ascending and descending on it; this alludes to the Chieftains who have charge of all the nations, and who ascend and descend on that ladder. When Israel is sinful, the ladder is lowered and the Chieftains ascend by it; but when Israel are righteous, the ladder is removed and all the Chieftains are left below and are deprived of their dominion. Jacob thus saw in this dream the domination of Esau and the domination of the other nations. According to another explanation, the angels ascended and descended on the top of the ladder; for when the top was detached, the ladder was lowered and the Chieftains ascended, but when it was attached again, the ladder was lifted and they remained below.

H. Sperling and M. Simon, *The Zohar* (5 vols; London and New York: Soncino, 1933), 2.79–80.

142. On this, see J. Kugel, *Traditions of the Bible: A Guide to the Bible as It Was at the Start of the Common Era* (Cambridge, MA: Harvard University Press, 1998), 363.

143. Kugel, "The Ladder of Jacob," 215.

144. Fletcher-Louis, *Jesus Monotheism*, 263.

145. Fletcher-Louis, *Jesus Monotheism*, 263.

146. D. C. Allison, Jr. "The Magi's Angel (Matt. 2:2, 9–10)," in D. C. Allison, Jr., *Studies in Matthew: Interpretation Past and Present* (Grand Rapids, MI: Baker Academic, 2005), 17–41. Cf. also D. C. Allison Jr., "What Was the Star That Guided the Magi?" *BR* 9 (1993): 24; B. G. Bucur, *Angelomorphic Pneumatology: Clement of Alexandria and Other Early Christian Witnesses* (SVC, 95; Leiden: Brill, 2009), 93.

147. Cf. Gen 2:8: "And the Lord God planted a garden in Eden, in the east; and there he put the man whom he had formed."

148. With respect to the cultic functions of frankincense and myrrh, like ingredients in incense, Dale Allison notes that "frankincense was an odoriferous gum resin from various trees and bushes which had a cultic usage in the ancient world. According to Exod 30:34–8, it was a prescribed ingredient of sacred incense. According to Lev 24:7, it was to be offered with the bread of the Presence. According to Lev 2:1–2, 14–6; 6:14–8, it was added to cereal offerings. . . . Myrrh was a fragrant gum resin from trees . . . a component of holy anointing oil, and an ingredient in incense." D. C. Allison, Jr., *Matthew: A Shorter Commentary* (London: T&T Clark, 2004), 27. The magi's gifts also include gold, a material which is mentioned in the description of Eden in Gen 2:11. In relation to this, Gordon Wenham observes that "if Eden is seen as a super sanctuary, this reference to gold can hardly be accidental for the most sacred items of tabernacle furniture were made of or covered with 'pure gold.'" G. J. Wenham, "Sanctuary Symbolism in the Garden of Eden Story," in *Proceedings of the Ninth World Congress of Jewish Studies, Division A: The Period of the Bible* (Jerusalem: World Union of Jewish Studies,

1986), 19–25 at 22. With respect to the connections between the gold of Eden and the materials used for the decoration of the tabernacle and priestly vestments in the Book of Exodus, see also D. Chilton, *Paradise Restored: A Biblical Theology of Dominion* (Ft. Worth: Dominion Press, 1985).

149. Jacques van Ruiten argues that, in *Jubilees*, "the Garden of Eden is seen as a Temple, or, more precisely as a part of the Temple: the room which is in the rear of the Temple, where the ark of the covenant of the Lord is placed, and which is often called 'Holy of Holies.'" Such an understanding of Eden as the temple presupposes the protoplast's role as a sacerdotal servant. In relation to this, van Ruiten suggests that, according to the author of *Jubilees*, Adam is acting as a prototypical priest as he burns incense at the gate of the Garden of Eden. Van Ruiten puts this description in parallel with a tradition found in Exodus, in which the incense was burned in front of the Holy of Holies. J. van Ruiten, "Visions of the Temple in the Book of Jubilees," in *Gemeinde ohne Tempel/Community without Temple: Zur Substituierung und Transformation des Jerusalemer Tempels und seines Kults im Alten Testament, antiken Judentum und frühen Christentum* (eds. B. Ego et al.; WUNT, 1.118; Tübingen: Mohr Siebeck, 1999), 215–228; Van Ruiten, "Eden and the Temple: The Rewriting of Genesis 2:4–3:24 in the Book of Jubilees," in *Paradise Interpreted: Representations of Biblical Paradise in Judaism and Christianity* (ed. G. P. Luttikhuizen; TBN, 2; Leiden: Brill, 1999), 76.

150. *Jub.* 3:27 reads: "On that day, as he was leaving the Garden of Eden, he burned incense as a pleasing fragrance—frankincense, galbanum, stacte, and aromatic spices—in the early morning when the sun rose at the time when he covered his shame." VanderKam, *Jubilees*, 2.20. Regarding the Edenic incense, see also *1 Enoch* 29–32: "And there I saw . . . vessels of the fragrance of incense and myrrh," Knibb, *The Ethiopic Book of Enoch*, 2.117–123; Sir 24:15: "like cassia and camel's thorn I gave forth perfume, and like choice myrrh I spread my fragrance, like galbanum, onycha, and stacte, and like the odor of incense in the tent"; Armenian version of the *Primary Adam Books* 29:3 reads: "Adam replied and said to the angels, 'I beseech you, let (me) be a little, so that I may take sweet incenses with me from the Garden, so that when I go out of here, I may offer sweet incenses to God, and offerings, so that, perhaps, God will hearken to us.'" Anderson and Stone, *A Synopsis of the Books of Adam and Eve*, 72E.

151. Previous studies have identified the connection between the magi story and the birth of a priestly child (Noah, Melchizedek, and Moses) in some Jewish accounts. These studies see sacerdotal items in the gifts that the magi brought to the child. Thus, for example, Fletcher-Louis observes that, "[I]t is noteworthy that at the birth of Jesus, of course, there is signaled the child's priestly identity in the gift of gold, frankincense and myrrh (cf. Exod 30:23; 28:5, 6, 8, etc.) from the magi (Matt 2:11)." Fletcher-Louis, *All the Glory of Adam*, 53.

152. Concerning this tradition, Allison and Davies note that:

> Of the many legends that later came to surround the magi and their gifts, one of the most pleasing is found in the so-called *Cave of Treasures* (6th cent. AD). Adam, we are told, had many treasures in paradise, and when he was expelled therefrom he took what he could with him—gold, frankincense,

and myrrh. Upon his death, Adam's sons hid their father's treasures in a cave, where they lay undisturbed until the magi, on their way to Bethlehem, entered the cave to get gifts for the Son of God. In this legend, Matthew's story has become the vehicle for a very Pauline idea, namely, that Jesus is the second Adam.

W. D. Davies and D. C. Allison Jr., *A Critical and Exegetical Commentary on the Gospel According to Saint Matthew* (ICC; 3 vols.; Edinburgh: T&T Clark, 1991), 1.251.

153. Cf. Matt 2:8: "Πορευθέντες ἐξετάσατε ἀκριβῶς περὶ τοῦ παιδίου· ἐπὰν δὲ εὕρητε ἀπαγγείλατέ μοι, ὅπως κἀγὼ ἐλθὼν προσκυνήσω αὐτῷ."

154. Matt 17:6: "καὶ ἀκούσαντες οἱ μαθηταὶ ἔπεσαν ἐπὶ πρόσωπον αὐτῶν καὶ ἐφοβήθησαν σφόδρα."

155. Matt 2:11: "και πεσόντες προσεκύνησαν αὐτω"; Matt 4:9: "πεσὼν προσκυνήσῃς μοι"; Matt 17:6: "ἔπεσαν ἐπὶ πρόσωπον αὐτῶν." Concerning this terminology, see Davies and Allison, *The Gospel According to Saint Matthew,* 1.248.

156. The motif of the disciples' veneration is reminiscent of the one performed by the magi. Thus, Allison and Davies note that "the magi do not simply bend their knees (cf. 17:14; 18:29). They fall down on their faces. This is noteworthy because there was a tendency in Judaism to think prostration proper only in the worship of God (cf. Philo, *Leg. Gai.* 116; *Decal.* 64; Matt 4:9–10; Acts 10:25–6; Rev 19:10; 22:8–9)." Davies and Allison, *The Gospel According to Saint Matthew,* 1.248. See also Robert Gundry: "they [the magi] knelt down before him with heads to the ground." R.H. Gundry, *Matthew: A Commentary on His Handbook for a Mixed Church under Persecution* (Grand Rapids, MI: Eerdmans, 1994), 31.

157. Another unique Matthean occurrence of this motif is found in Matt 18:26, in which one can find the familiar constellation of "πεσών" and "προσεκύνει." Gundry observes that, besides the magi story, "Matthew inserts the same combination of falling down and worshiping in 4:9 and uses it in unique material at 18:26." He further notes that, "[I]n particular, πεσόντες sharpens Matthew's point, for in 4:9 falling down will accompany worship in the alternatives of worshiping God and worshiping Satan, and without parallel it describes the response of the disciples who witnessed the transfiguration (17:6)." Gundry, *Matthew: A Commentary on His Handbook for a Mixed Church under Persecution*, 31–32.

158. On this, see A. A. Orlov, "The Veneration Motif in the Temptation Narrative of the Gospel of Matthew: Lessons from the Enochic Tradition," in A. A. Orlov, *Divine Scapegoats: Demonic Mimesis in Early Jewish Mysticism* (Albany: State University of New York Press, 2015), 153–166.

159. Fletcher-Louis also detects the memory of such motifs in Philo's treatise *On the Creation of the World* and 4Q381 frag. 1, lines 10–11. On this, see Fletcher-Louis, *Jesus Monotheism*, 262–3.

160. Dealing with the story of the angelic adoration of Adam in the various versions of the *Primary Adam Books,* Fletcher-Louis says that in these accounts, "Adam was created to bear divine presence as God's physical and visual image." Fletcher-Louis, *Jesus Monotheism*, 272–3. See also Fletcher-Louis, "Worship of Divine Humanity," 112–128; Fletcher-Louis, *All the Glory of Adam*, 101–102.

161. In *3 Enoch* 45:1–4 we find the following tradition about the *Pargod*: "R. Ishmael said: Metatron said to me: Come and I will show you the curtain of the Omnipresent One which is spread before the Holy One, blessed be he, and on which are printed all the generations of the world and their deeds, whether done or to be done, till the last generation. . . . the kings of Judah and their generations, their deeds and their acts; the kings of Israel and their generations, their deeds and their acts; the kings of the gentiles and their generations, their deeds and their acts." Alexander, "3 Enoch," 1.295–298.

> 162. Then Moses went up from the plains of Moab to Mount Nebo, to the top of Pisgah, which is opposite Jericho, and the Lord showed him the whole land: Gilead as far as Dan, all Naphtali, the land of Ephraim and Manasseh, all the land of Judah as far as the Western Sea, the Negeb, and the Plain—that is, the valley of Jericho, the city of palm trees—as far as Zoar. The Lord said to him, "This is the land of which I swore to Abraham, to Isaac, and to Jacob, saying, I will give it to your descendants; I have let you see it with your eyes, but you shall not cross over there."

163. J. Dupont, "L'arrière-fond biblique du récit des tentations de Jésus," *NTS* 3 (1957): 287–304 at 297.

164. Already the earliest Christian interpreters, including Justin (*Dial.* 103) and Irenaeus (*Adv. Haer.* 5.21.2), saw the temptation of Jesus as the reversal of Adam's sin. On this, see D. C. Allison, "Behind the Temptations of Jesus: Q 4:1–13 and Mark 1:12–13," in *Authenticating the Activities of Jesus* (eds. B. D. Chilton and C. Evans; NTTS, 28.2; Leiden: Brill, 2002), 196.

165. W. A. Schultze, "Der Heilige und die wilden Tiere. Zur Exegese von Mc 1,13b," *ZNW* 46 (1955): 280–83; A. Feuillet, "L'épisode de la tentation d'après l'évangile selon saint Marc (I,12–13)," *EstBib* 19 (1960): 49–73; J. Jeremias, "Nachwort zum Artikel von H.-G. Leder," *ZNW* 54 (1963): 278–79; J. Jeremias, "Adam," in *Theological Dictionary of the New Testament* (ed. G. Kittel, tr. G. W. Bromiley; 10 vols.; Grand Rapids, MI: Eerdmans, 1964), 1.141–143; A. Vargas-Machuca, "La tentación de Jesús según Mc. 1, 12–13 ¿Hecho real o relato de tipo haggádico?" *EE* 48 (1973): 163–190; P. Pokorný, "The Temptation Stories and Their Intention," *NTS* 20 (1973–74): 115–27; J. Gnilka, *Das Evangelium nach Markus* (2 vols; EKKNT, 2.1–2; Zürich: Benziger; Neukirchen-Vluyn: Neukirchener Verlag, 1978–79), 1.58; R. A. Guelich, *Mark 1–8:26* (WBC, 34A; Dallas: Word, 1989), 38–39; R. Bauckham, "Jesus and the Wild Animals (Mark 1:13): A Christological image for an Ecological Age," in *Jesus of Nazareth: Lord and Christ: Essays on the Historical Jesus and New Testament Christology* (eds. J. B. Green and M. Turner; Grand Rapids, MI: Eerdmans, 1994), 3–21; J. Gibson, *Temptations of Jesus in Early Christianity* (JSNTSS, 112; Sheffield: Sheffield Academic Press, 1995), 65–66; Allison, "Behind the Temptations of Jesus: Q 4:1–13 and Mark 1:12–13," 196–199.

166. J. Jeremias, *New Testament Theology* (London: SCM Press, 2012), 69. The theme of alienation between humanity and animals already looms large in the *Book of Jubilees*. This theme receives further development in the *Primary Adam Books* in which Eve and Seth are predestined to encounter a hostile beast.

167. Jeremias, *New Testament Theology*, 69–70.

168. Jeremias, *New Testament Theology*, 70.

169. Bauckham, "Jesus and the Wild Animals," 6.

170. Davies and Allison suggest that "in Mark 1:12–13 Jesus is probably the last Adam (cf. Rom 5:12–21; 1 Cor 15:42–50; Justin, *Dial.* 103; *Gospel of Philip* 71.16–21; Irenaeus, *Adv. haer.* 5.21.2). He, like the first Adam, is tempted by Satan. But unlike his anti-type, he does not succumb, and the result is the recovery of paradise (cf. *Testament of Levi* 18:10) the wild beasts are tamed and once again a man dwells with angels and is served by them." Davies and Allison, *The Gospel According to Saint Matthew*, 1.356.

171. Allison, "Behind the Temptations of Jesus: Q 4:1–13 and Mark 1:12–13," 198.

172. Fletcher-Louis suggested that the reference to the angels serving Jesus in Mark 1:13 and Matt 4:11 can be an allusion to the story of the angelic worship of Adam. Fletcher-Louis, *Jesus Monotheism*, 263. Commenting on Mark 1:13, Joel Marcus notes that "*Diakonein* can also, like Heb. *'bd*, mean 'worship' (see e.g. Josephus, *Ant.* 7.365), and this may be a secondary nuance in our passage, in view of the legend in which Adam is worshiped by angels." J. Marcus, *Mark 1–8: A New Translation with Introduction and Commentary* (AB, 27; New York: Doubleday, 2000), 168–71.

173. The absence of this tradition in Mark remains a debated issue. Cranfield proposes that "in view of the parallels it is surprising that Mark does not mention Jesus' face. That a reference to it has dropped out of the text by mistake at a very early stage, as Streeter suggested, is conceivable; but perhaps it is more likely that Matt and Luke have both introduced the reference independently under the influence of Exod 34:29 ff." C. E. B. Cranfield, *The Gospel According to St. Mark* (Cambridge: Cambridge University Press, 1983), 290.

174. On this imagery in the transfiguration story, see B. G. Bucur, *Scripture Re-envisioned: Christophanic Exegesis and the Making of a Christian Bible* (The Bible in Ancient Christianity, 13; Leiden: Brill, 2019), 122–124.

175. The correlation between *panim* and *iqonin* is also discernible in *Joseph and Aseneth*. On this, see Orlov, *Greatest Mirror*, 141–148.

176. J. van Ruiten, "The Old Testament Quotations in the Apocalypse of Peter," in *The Apocalypse of Peter* (eds. J. N. Bremmer and I. Czachesz; Leuven-Paris: Peeters, 2003), 158–73 at 169.

177. D. D. Buchholz, *Your Eyes Will Be Opened. A Study of the Greek (Ethiopic) Apocalypse of Peter* (SBLDS, 97; Atlanta: Scholars, 1988), 242.

178. On the tradition of God/Jacob's face in the *Apocalypse of Peter*, see Van Ruiten, "Old Testament Quotations," 171–2.

179. *Targum Neofiti 1 and Pseudo-Jonathan: Exodus* (eds. M. J. McNamara, R. Hayward, and M. Maher; ArBib, 2; Collegeville: Liturgical Press, 1994), 260.

180. McNamara et al., *Targum Neofiti 1 and Pseudo-Jonathan: Exodus*, 261.

181. McNamara et al., *Targum Neofiti 1 and Pseudo-Jonathan: Exodus*, 261.

182. See L. L. Belleville, *Reflections of Glory: Paul's Polemical Use of the Moses-Doxa Tradition in 2 Corinthians 3.1–18* (JSNTSS, 52; Sheffield: Sheffield Academic Press, 1991), 50.

183. See Davies and Allison, *The Gospel According to Saint Matthew*, 2.705.

184. Freedman and Simon, *Midrash Rabbah*, 7.173. I previously argued that in 4Q504 the glory of Adam and the glory of Moses's face were already creatively juxtaposed. The luminous face of the prophet serves in this text as an alternative to the lost luminosity of Adam and as a new symbol of God's glory once again manifested in the human body. On this, see A. A. Orlov, "Vested with Adam's Glory: Moses as the Luminous Counterpart of Adam in the Dead Sea Scrolls and the Macarian Homilies," *Christian Orient* 4.10 (2006): 498–513.

185. A. Goshen-Gottstein, "The Body as Image of God in Rabbinic Literature," *HTR* 87 (1994): 183. Speaking about this passage, Linda Belleville observes that "*Midrash Tadshe* 4 associates Moses' glory with being created in the image of God, stating that God created man in his own image, first in the beginning and then in the wilderness." Belleville, *Reflections of Glory*, 65.

186. According to Jewish sources, the image of God was especially reflected in the radiance of Adam's face. On this, see J. Fossum, *The Name of God and the Angel of the Lord. Samaritan and Jewish Concepts of Intermediation and the Origin of Gnosticism* (WUNT, 36; Tübingen: Mohr Siebeck, 1985), 94.

187. Freedman and Simon, *Midrash Rabbah*, 4.252.

188. Freedman and Simon, *Midrash Rabbah*, 1.81.

189. Meeks observes that in the early Mosaic accounts, "Moses' elevation at Sinai was treated not only as a heavenly enthronement, but also as a restoration of the glory lost by Adam. Moses, crowned with both God's name and his image, became in some sense a 'second Adam,' the prototype of a new humanity." Meeks, "Moses as God and King," 365.

190. Meeks, "Moses as God and King," 364–65.

191. Philo, *Questions and Answers on Exodus* (tr. R. Marcus; LCL; Cambridge, MA: Harvard University Press/London: Heinemann, 1949), 91–92.

192. U. Luz, *Matthew 8–20* (Hermeneia; Minneapolis: Fortress, 2001), 395.

193. Thus, Leroy Huizenga argues the following: "In the Matthean version, however, it is the divine voice which declares that Jesus is the beloved Son and commands Peter to remember the prior passion prediction which precipitates the fear." L. A. Huizenga, *The New Isaac: Tradition and Intertextuality in the Gospel of Matthew* (NovTSup, 131; Leiden: Brill, 2009), 218.

194. Loren Stuckenbruck notes that "The expression 'Do not fear' was frequently used in biblical and ancient Near Eastern literature to communicate a message of divine comfort." L. Stuckenbruck, *Angel Veneration and Christology: A Study in Early Judaism and in the Christology of the Apocalypse of John* (WUNT, 2.70; Tübingen: Mohr Siebeck, 1995), 88.

195. See also *3 Enoch* 15B:5: "At once Metatron, Prince of the Divine Presence, said to Moses, 'Son of Amram, fear not! for already God favors you. Ask what you will with confidence and boldness, for light shines from the skin of your face from one end of the world to the other.'" Alexander, "3 Enoch," 1.304.

196. Andersen, "2 Enoch," 1.106–108.

197. Andersen, "2 Enoch," 1.136–138.

198. Davies and Allison, *The Gospel According to Saint Matthew*, 2.703.

199. Cf. *2 Enoch* 22:5: "And the Lord, with his own mouth, said to me, 'Be brave, Enoch! Don't be frightened! Stand up, and stand in front of my face forever.' " Andersen, "2 Enoch," 1.136–138.

200. In the Georgian version of the *Primary Adam Books*, the affirmation mentions Adam's unique role as the divine image: "Bow down before the likeness and the image of the divinity." The Latin version also speaks about the divine image: "Worship the image of the Lord God, just as the Lord God has commanded." In the Armenian version too Adam's name is not mentioned and the new created protoplast seems to understood now as the divine manifestation: "Then Michael summoned all the angels, and God said to them, 'Come, bow down to god whom I made.' " Anderson and Stone, *A Synopsis of the Books of Adam and Eve*, 16E.

201. Fletcher-Louis, *Jesus Monotheism*, 256.

Chapter Two. Furnace that Kills and Furnace that Gives Life

1. N. W. Porteous, *Daniel. A Commentary* (OTL; Philadelphia: The Westminster Press, 1965), 55.

2. Porteous, *Daniel*, 55.

3. M. Dulaey, "Les trois hébreux dans la fournaise (Dn 3) dans l'interprétation symbolique de l'église ancienne," *RSR* 71 (1997): 33–59; P. B. Munoa, "Jesus, the Merkavah, and Martyrdom in Early Christian Tradition," *JBL* 121 (2002): 303–25; D. Tucker, "The Early Wirkungsgeschichte of Daniel 3: Representative Examples," *JTI* 6 (2012): 295–306.

4. Another important biblical specimen in which martyrdom coincides with theophany is the Book of Job, where the suffering of a righteous person culminates in the vision of God.

5. P. Middleton, *Radical Martyrdom and Cosmic Conflict in Early Christianity* (LNTS, 307; London: T&T Clark, 2006), 107.

6. Middleton, *Radical Martyrdom*, 107.

7. Tucker, "The Early Wirkungsgeschichte of Daniel 3," 297–298. Tucker discerns the echoes of Dan 3 in another early account devoted to the martyrdom, namely, Origen's *Exhortation to Martyrdom*. Tucker notes that:

> In his exhortation, Origen makes a number of critical hermeneutical moves in his appropriation of Dan 3. In Mattathias' speech in 1 Macc 2:59, the story of the three youths appears within a larger list of faithful ancestors who had been delivered by God. In *Exhortation to Martyrdom*, Origen has made the connection between Dan 3 and martyrdom all the more specific. Prior to the section read above, Origen recounts the story of 2 Macc 7, and then provides a lengthy discourse on the chalice as a symbol of martyrdom and Jesus' comments in the Garden about the chalice passing from before him. He concludes that Jesus was not avoiding martyrdom but only wanting that

> perfect form that would bring universal good to all people. Having discussed both the Maccabean account and the Garden scene in the Gospels, and the instructive nature of each for understanding martyrdom, Origen shifts to the story of the three youths. In so doing, Origen collapses history in some sense, refusing to differentiate between the affairs articulated in Dan 3 and those currently being experienced by Ambrose and Protoctetus.

Tucker, "The Early Wirkungsgeschichte of Daniel 3," 298–299.

8. Dan 3:25: "like a son of the gods." With regard to the identity of this character, John Collins observes that:

> The story assumes that the furnace was large enough to permit movement and the appearance of the fourth is like a divine being: "Divine being" rendered literally would be "a son of a god," that is, in Semitic idiom, a member of the class "gods." Such a polytheistic designation is quite appropriate on the lips of Nebuchadnezzar. . . . This designation is obviously rooted in Near Eastern polytheistic mythology. In Jewish and Christian tradition, the "sons of God" are treated as angels; thus Dan 3:28 attributes the deliverance of the youths to an angel in the furnace. Christian tradition typically identified the "son of God" here as Christ.

J. J. Collins, *Daniel: A Commentary on the Book of Daniel* (Hermeneia; Minneapolis: Fortress Press, 1993), 190.

9. C. L. Seow, *Daniel* (Westminster Bible Companion; Louisville: Westminster John Knox Press, 2003), 59; Bucur, *Scripture Re-envisioned,* 248ff.

10. E. Yassif, *The Hebrew Folktale. History, Genre, Meaning* (Bloomington: Indiana University Press, 1999), 83–84.

11. Seow, *Daniel,* 60.

12. Seow, *Daniel,* 59.

13. See A. DeConick, "Traumatic Mysteries: Pathways of Mysticism among the Early Christians," in *Jewish Roots of Eastern Christian Mysticism: Studies in Honor of Alexander Golitzin* (ed. A. A. Orlov; SVC, 160; Leiden: Brill, 2020), 11–51.

14. On Abraham's fiery trials traditions, see W. Adler, "Abraham and the Burning of the Temple of Idols," *JQR* 77 (1986–1987): 95–117; G. N. Bonwetsch, *Die Apokalypse Abrahams. Das Testament der vierzig Martyrer* (Leipzig: J. C. Hinrichs, 1897), 41–55; G. H. Box and J. I. Landsman, *The Apocalypse of Abraham* (TED, 1.10; London: The Macmillan Company, 1919), 88–96; B. G. Bucur, "Christophanic Exegesis and the Problem of Symbolization: Daniel 3 (The Fiery Furnace) As a Test Case," *JTI* 10 (2016): 227–44; Bucur, *Scripture Re-envisioned,* 248–254; L. Ginzberg, *The Legends of the Jews* (7 vols.; Philadelphia: Jewish Publication Society, 1909–38), 1.198–201 and 5.212–213; J. Gutmann, "Abraham in the Fire of the Chaldeans: A Jewish Legend in Jewish, Christian and Islamic Art," *FS* 7 (1973): 342–52; M. Kister, "Observations on Aspects of Exegesis, Tradition, and Theology in Midrash, Pseudepigrapha, and Other Jewish Writings," in *Tracing the Threads: Studies in the Vitality of Jewish Pseudepigrapha* (ed. J. C. Reeves; EJL, 6; Atlanta: Scholars, 1994), 1–34;

J. L. Kugel, *The Bible As It Was* (Cambridge, MA: Harvard University Press, 1997), 143ff.; Kugel, *Traditions of the Bible*, 268–270; S. L. Lowin, *The Making of a Forefather: Abraham in Islamic and Jewish Exegetical Narratives* (IHC, 65; Leiden: Brill, 2006); E. Spicehandler, "Shāhin's Influence on Bābāi ben Lotf: The Abraham-Nimrod Legend," in *Irano-Judaica II* (eds. S. Shaked and A. Netzer; Jerusalem: Ben Zvi Institute, 1990), 158–65 at 162; G. Vermes, *Scripture and Tradition in Judaism. Haggadic Studies* (SPB, 4; Leiden: Brill, 1973), 85–90.

15. Menahem Kister notes that "we cannot state with certainty when the tradition of the martyrology of Abraham begins. It may be quite early." Kister, "Observations on Aspects of Exegesis," 25.

16. *Traditions about the Early Life of Abraham* (eds. J. A. Tvedtnes et al.; Provo: FARMS, 2001), 5, note 2.

17. C. Holladay, *Fragments from Hellenistic Jewish Authors* (4 vols.; Chico, CA: Scholars, 1983–96), 2.235.

18. Kugel, *Traditions of the Bible*, 268.

19. Kugel, *Traditions of the Bible*, 268. On the possibility of such an interpretation, see also Holladay, *Fragments*, 2.258; Tvedtnes et al., *Traditions about the Early Life of Abraham*, 6, note 3.

20. *LAB*'s date is a debated issue. Deliberating about various possibilities, Howard Jacobson states that there has been a general consensus which postulates the date of *LAB* between 50 CE and 150 CE. In recent years, however, scholars favor the earlier date, although support for the post-70 period still remains. Jacobson himself advocates for the post-70 date, after the destruction of the Second Jerusalem Temple, by arguing that "the general tone of *LAB* suggests a time of catastrophe and gloom. It is not impossible that the work postdates not only the fall of Jerusalem and the destruction of the Temple, but the failure of the Bar-Cochba revolt as well." H. Jacobson, *A Commentary on Pseudo-Philo's Liber Antiquitatum Biblicarum, with Latin Text and English Translation* (2 vols.; AGAJU, 31; Leiden: Brill, 1996), 1.208.

21. Jacobson, *A Commentary on Pseudo-Philo's Liber Antiquitatum Biblicarum*, 1.97–100. *Chronicles of Jerahmeel* 29 contains a Hebrew retroversion of this account. On this late account, see M. Gaster, *The Chronicles of Jerahmeel* (OTF, 4; London: Royal Asiatic Society, 1899), 60–63.

22. VanderKam, *Jubilees*, 2.67–70.

23. Maher, *Targum Pseudo-Jonathan: Genesis*, 51, n. 17.

24. Vermes, *Scripture and Tradition*, 88.

25. Vermes, *Scripture and Tradition*, 88–89.

26. Vermes, *Scripture and Tradition*, 90.

27. Indeed, several structural and narrative elements in Pseudo-Philo are reminiscent of details found in Daniel 3. These include the following: an evil earthly leader and his erected idol; a tower/idol that reaches heaven; the leader issues an order to find apostates; the protagonist is brought by complicit people; the evil leader throws the protagonist into the fire; the fiery demise of bystanders; the protagonist is rescued by the deity, unharmed by the fire.

28. Collins, *Daniel*, 186. Craig Evans also sees Dan 3 behind Abraham's fiery trials. He notes:

> These exegeses also follow the lead of the famous story in Daniel. The allusion to fire in Genesis 11 suggested comparison with the furnace of fire in Daniel 3, the furnace into which Shadrach, Meshach, and Abednego were cast. These three men, who refused to worship the golden image erected by Nebuchadnezzar the Chaldean, were spared by God and "came out from the fire" (Dan 3:26). Their reason for being cast into the fire gave interpreters of Genesis 11 the reason why Abraham had been cast into the fire of the Chaldeans. Even the fantastic claim in Pseudo-Philo's version, that 83,500 men were killed by the flames of the furnace, probably owes its inspiration to Dan 3:22, which says the intense heat of the furnace killed the men who threw the three Israelites into the fire.

C. A. Evans, "Abraham in the Dead Sea Scrolls: A Man of Faith and Failure," in *The Bible at Qumran: Text, Shape, and Interpretation* (ed. P. W. Flint; Grand Rapids, MI: Eerdmans, 2001), 149–58 at 154.

29. On Abraham's martyrdom in rabbinic lore, see A. Gross, *Spirituality and Law: Courting Martyrdom in Christianity and Judaism* (Lanham, MD: University Press of America, 2005), 33ff.

30. Jacobson, *A Commentary on Pseudo-Philo's Liber Antiquitatum Biblicarum*, 2.359.

31. Jacobson, *A Commentary on Pseudo-Philo's Liber Antiquitatum Biblicarum*, 2.359.

32. Kugel, *Traditions of the Bible*, 269. In connection with the motif of the patriarch's fiery trials, Abraham Gross notes that "we cannot rule out the possibility that this story represents peripheral Jewish circles who had radical attitudes to martyrdom." Gross, *Spirituality and Law*, 34.

33. M. Wadsworth, "Making and Interpreting Scripture," in *Ways of Reading the Bible* (Sussex: Harvester Press, 1981), 7–22 at 11; F. J. Murphy, "Retelling the Bible: Idolatry in Pseudo-Philo," *JBL* 107 (1988): 275–87 at 276. Others disagree with this opinion. On this, see Jacobson, *A Commentary on Pseudo-Philo's Liber Antiquitatum Biblicarum*, 1.355–356. Jacobson argues that "both in the Bible and in *LAB* (also Josephus *AJ* 1.113–15) the very erection of such a tower—or at least the thoughts that inspire it—is seen as a hybristic act of rebellion against God—and so must be punished. But neither idolatry per se nor the idea of storming the heaven plays a role in *LAB*." Jacobson, *A Commentary on Pseudo-Philo's Liber Antiquitatum Biblicarum*, 2.356.

34. Sometimes, in rabbinic accounts, Nimrod poses under the name of Amraphel. Cf., for example, *Pesikta Rabbati* 33:4: "Of course you may not know what I did to all who engaged with the three Patriarchs—to Amraphel who first engaged with Abraham by casting him into a fiery furnace." *Pesikta Rabbati* (ed. W. Braude; 2 vols.; YJS, 18; New Haven, CT: Yale University Press, 1968), 2.637.

35. The previously mentioned interpretation of אור as "fire" in Gen 15:7 strengthens the link between Abraham's rescue from the fire of the Chaldeans and the deliverance of the three Jewish youths in Daniel. Vermes points to this connection in *Gen. Rab.* 44:13: "R. Liezer b. Jacob said: Michael descended and rescued Abraham from the fiery furnace. The Rabbis said: The Holy One, blessed be He, rescued him; thus it is written, 'I am the

Lord that brought thee out of Ur of the Chaldees.' And when did Michael descend? In the case of Hananiah, Mishael, and Azariah." Freedman and Simon, *Midrash Rabbah*, 1.369. Vermes asserts that "the exegetical association between Genesis 15:7 and Daniel 3 is not mere hypothesis, as *Genesis Rabbah* 44:13 demonstrates." Vermes, *Scripture and Tradition*, 90.

36. In Vermes's opinion, the influence of Nebuchadnezzar's typology is especially strong in the tradition found in the *Book of Yashar,* because there, "like Nebuchadnezzar, Nimrod is forced to recognize for a time the God of Israel." Vermes, *Scripture and Tradition*, 90.

37. M. Dods, "St. Augustine's City of God," in *A Select Library of the Nicene and Post-Nicene Fathers of the Christian Church. First Series. Vol. 2* (ed. P. Schaff; New York: Christian Literature Company, 1887), 1–511 at 320.

38. C. T. R. Hayward, *Saint Jerome's Hebrew Questions on Genesis* (Oxford Early Christian Studies; Oxford: Clarendon, 1995), 43–44.

39. M. Gaster, *The Asatir: The Samaritan Book of the "Secrets of Moses" Together with the Pitron or Samaritan Commentary and the Samaritan story of the Death of Moses* (OTF, 26; London: The Royal Asiatic Society, 1927), 246. On these traditions, see also Kister, "Observations on Aspects of Exegesis," 25.

40. Reflecting on the development of the fiery trials traditions in rabbinic literature, Menahem Kister notes the martyrological aspects of some specimens of this story, arguing that "forms and themes of this tradition vary from version to version and from period to period (Abraham as setting fire to the shrine of the idols, Abraham as a martyr). It is these shifting themes that gave life to the legend and made it so popular in Jewish sources." Kister, "Observations on Aspects of Exegesis," 7. Kister further notes that "included at times in these descriptions are reflections of other biblical stories, such as the rescue of Hananiah, Mishael, and Azariah from the fire, for which the midrash explicitly employs Abraham as a prototype." Kister, "Observations on Aspects of Exegesis," 25.

41. Maher, *Targum Pseudo-Jonathan: Genesis*, 51.

42. Maher, *Targum Pseudo-Jonathan: Genesis*, 55.

43. "He said to him, 'I am the Lord who brought you out of the fiery furnace of the Chaldeans to give you this land to inherit.' " Maher, *Targum Pseudo-Jonathan: Genesis*, 60.

44. "Sarai said to Abram, . . . 'we will not need the children of Hagar, the daughter of Pharaoh, the son of Nimrod, who threw you into the furnace of fire.' " Maher, *Targum Pseudo-Jonathan: Genesis*, 62.

45. *Targum Neofiti 1: Genesis* (ed. M. McNamara; ArBib, 1A; Collegeville: Liturgical Press, 1992), 85–86.

46. McNamara, *Targum Neofiti 1: Genesis,* 95. Cf. also *Targum Neofiti* to Gen 16:5: "And Sarai said to Abram . . . 'we will not need the son of Hagar the Egyptian, who belongs to the children of the sons of the people who gave you into the furnace of fire of the Chaldeans.' " McNamara, *Targum Neofiti 1: Genesis,* 98–99.

47. *The Two Targums of Esther* (ed. B. Grossfeld; ArBib, 18; Edinburgh: T&T Clark, 1991), 67.

48. *Targums of Ruth and Chronicles* (eds. D. R. G. Beattie and J. S. Mclvor; ArBib, 19; Collegeville: Liturgical Press, 1994), 212.

49. Epstein, *The Babylonian Talmud. Eruvin*, 53a.

50. Epstein, *The Babylonian Talmud. Pesahim,* 118a. On this tradition, see Bucur, *Scripture Re-envisioned,* 249.

51. Freedman and Simon, *Midrash Rabbah,* 1.310–311.

52. *Eliyahu Rabbah* 27 elaborates this theme in even greater detail:

> How did Abraham come in this world to merit a life with no distress, with no inclination to evil—a life, indeed, such as God bestows upon the righteous only in the world-to-come? Because for the sake of Heaven he was willing to give up his life in the fire of the Chaldees. . . . Keep in mind that the household of Abraham's father, idolaters all, used to make idols and go out to sell them in the marketplace. . . . He [Nimrod] sent men to fetch Abraham and had him appear before him. Nimrod then said to him, "Son of Terah, make a beautiful god for me, one which will be uniquely mine." So Abraham went back to his father's house and said, "Make a beautiful idol for Nimrod." When Terah's household got the idol finished, they put a cincture around it and painted it a variety of colors. [After Abraham brought the image to Nimrod, he said to him, "You are a king, and yet you are so lacking in a king's wisdom as to worship this thing which my father's household has just turned out!"] Thereupon Nimrod had Abraham taken out [to be consumed] in a fiery furnace. In tribute to Abraham's righteousness, however, the day turned cloudy, and presently rain came down so hard that Nimrod's men could not get the fire started. Next, as Nimrod sat [in his throne room], surrounded by the entire generation that was to be dispersed [for its transgressions], Abraham was brought in and put in their midst. He approached Nimrod and again voiced his contempt of the king's idol. "If not this idol, whom shall I worship?" Nimrod asked. Abraham replied, "The God of gods, the Lord of lords, Him whose kingdom endures in heaven and earth and in uppermost heaven of heavens." Nimrod said, "Nevertheless I will rather worship the god of fire, for behold, I am going to cast you into the midst of fire—let the god of whom you speak come and deliver you from fire." At once his servants bound Abraham hand and foot and laid him on the ground. Then they piled up wood on all sides of him, [but at some distance away], a pile of wood five hundred cubits long to the west, and a five hundred cubits long to the east. Nimrod's men then went around and around setting the wood on fire. . . . At once the compassion of the Holy One welled up, and the holiness of His great name came down from the upper heaven of heavens, from the place of His glory, His grandeur, and His beauty and delivered our father Abraham from the taunts and the jeers and from the fiery furnace, as is said, I am the Lord that brought thee out of the fire of the Chaldees (Gen 15:7).

Braude and Kapstein, *Tanna Debe Eliyyahu: The Lore of the School of Elijah* (trs. W. G. Braude and I. J. Kapstein; Philadelphia: Jewish Publication Society of America, 1981), 102–103.

53. *Eliyyahu Zuta* 25 preserves the remnants of a similar tradition of disputation between the patriarch and the evil king:

> When Nimrod came and found him there, he asked: Are you Abraham the son of Terah? Abraham replied: Yes. Nimrod asked: Do you not know that I am lord of all things? Sun and moon, stars and planets, and human beings go forth only at my command. And now you have destroyed my divinity, the only thing that I revere. . . . Then Nimrod summoned Terah, Abraham's father, and said: You know what is to be the sentence of this one who has burned my divinities? His sentence must be death by fire. At once Nimrod seized Abraham and put him in prison. Then his servants spent ten years building the furnace in which Abraham was to be burned and hauling and bringing wood for furnace. When they finally took him out to burn him in the fiery furnace, at once the Holy One came down to deliver him.

Braude and Kapstein, *Tanna Debe Eliyyahu*, 525–526.

54. Freedman and Simon, *Midrash Rabbah*, 1.273.

55. Freedman and Simon, *Midrash Rabbah* 1.369. See also *Exod. Rab.* 23:4: "He delivered Abraham from the fiery furnace and from the kings." Freedman and Simon, *Midrash Rabbah*, 3.281.

56. Freedman and Simon, *Midrash Rabbah*, 9.78. See also *Song of Songs Rabbah* 2:16 "Stay ye me with dainties: with many fires—with the fire of Abraham, and of Moriah, and of the bush, with the fire of Elijah and of Hananiah, Mishael, and Azariah." Freedman and Simon, *Midrash Rabbah*, 9.104.

57. Freedman and Simon, *Midrash Rabbah*, 4.461. A similar motif is developed in *Song of Songs Rabbah* 8:8:

> R. Berekiah interpreted the verse as applying to our father Abraham. We have a little sister (*ahot*): this is Abraham, as it says, Abraham was one (*ehad*) and he inherited the land (Ezek 33:24); he, as it were, stitched together (*iha*) all mankind in the presence of the Holy One, blessed be He. Bar Kappara said: Like a man who stitches up a rent little: while he was still a child, he occupied himself with religious observances and good deeds. And she hath no breast; though as yet he was under no obligation to perform religious duties and good deeds. What shall we do for our sister in the day when she shall be spoken for: the day when the wicked Nimrod sentenced him to be thrown into the fiery furnace.

Freedman and Simon, *Midrash Rabbah*, 9.311.

58. J. Goldin, *The Fathers According to Rabbi Nathan* (YJS, 10; New Haven, CT: Yale University Press, 1955), 132. *Pirke de R. Eliezer* 26 continues the theme of Abraham's trials: "The second trial was when he [Abraham] was put into prison for ten years—three years in Kithi, seven years in Budri. After ten years they sent and brought him forth and cast him into the furnace of fire, and the King of Glory put forth His right hand

and delivered him from the furnace of fire, as it is said, 'And he said to him, I am the Lord who brought thee out of the furnace of the Chaldees' (Gen 15:7). Another verse (says), 'Thou art the Lord the God, who didst choose Abram, and broughtest him forth out of the furnace of the Chaldees' (Neh 9:7)." Friedlander, *Pirke de Rabbi Eliezer*, 188.

59. Vermes, *Scripture and Tradition*, 85.

60. The story of Abraham's fiery trial has received new afterlife in the Islamic tradition, where it also became closely linked to the theme of idolatry. From *Qur'an* 21.51–71 we learn the following rendering of the story:

> Long ago We bestowed right judgement on Abraham and We knew him well. He said to his father and his people, "What are these images to which you are so devoted?" They replied, "We found our fathers worshipping them." He said, "You and your fathers have clearly gone astray." They asked, "Have you brought us the truth or are you just playing about?" He said, "Listen! Your true Lord is the Lord of the heavens and the earth, He who created them, and I am a witness to this. By God I shall certainly plot against your idols as soon as you have turned your backs!" He broke them all into pieces, but left the biggest one for them to return to. They said, "Who has done this to our gods? How wicked he must be!" Some said, "We heard a youth called Abraham talking about them." They said, "Bring him before the eyes of the people, so that they may witness [his trial]." They asked, "Was it you, Abraham, who did this to our gods?" He said, "No, it was done by the biggest of them—this one. Ask them, if they can talk." They turned to one another, saying, "It is you who are in the wrong," but then they lapsed again and said, "You know very well these gods cannot speak." Abraham said, "How can you worship what can neither benefit nor harm you, instead of God? Shame on you and on the things you worship instead of God. Have you no sense?" They said, "Burn him and avenge your gods, if you are going to do the right thing." But We said, "Fire, be cool and safe for Abraham." They planned to harm him, but We made them suffer the greatest loss.

Haleem, *Qur'an* (tr. M. A. S. Abdel Haleem; Oxford: Oxford University Press, 2004), 205–206. For other Muslim versions of the story, see C. Bakhos, *The Family of Abraham: Jewish, Christian, and Muslim Interpretations* (Cambridge, MA: Harvard University Press, 2014), 96ff.; Lowin, *The Making of a Forefather: Abraham in Islamic and Jewish Exegetical Narratives*; Spicehandler, "Shāhin's Influence on Bābāi ben Lotf: The Abraham-Nimrod Legend," 162.

61. Tertullian's *De Baptismo*, written between 196 and 206 C.E., mentions the *Acta Pauli* and provides the *terminus ante quem*. *Terminus post quem* is a debated issue. On the date of the *Acts of Paul*, see *New Testament Apocrypha* (trs. A. Higgins et al.; eds. E. Hennecke and W. Schneemelcher; 2 vols.; Philadelphia: Westminster Press, 1963–66), 2.235; J. N. Bremmer, "Magic, Martyrdom and Women's Liberation in the Acts of Paul and Thecla," in *The Apocryphal Acts of Paul and Thecla* (ed. J. N. Bremmer; Kampen:

Kok Pharos, 2000), 36–59 at 57; Bremmer, "The Five Major Apocryphal Acts: Authors, Place, Time and Readership," in *The Apocryphal Acts of Thomas* (Leuven: Peeters, 2001), 153; J. W. Barrier, *The Acts of Paul and Thecla: A Critical Introduction and Commentary* (WUNT, 2.270; Tübingen: Mohr Siebeck, 2009), 23.

62. Stephen Davis argues that "Thecla's perseverance amidst the fire earned her early acclaim as a 'proto-martyr' of the Christian church." S. Davis, *The Cult of Saint Thecla: A Tradition of Women's Piety in Late Antiquity* (Oxford: Oxford University Press, 2001), 156.

63. I am thankful to Jennifer Henery for bringing my attention to these traditions.

64. Barrier, *Acts of Paul and Thecla*, 121–124.

65. Davis, *The Cult of Saint Thecla*, 26.

66. Cf. *Acts of Paul* 4:9: "And there was a cloud of fire (νεφέλη πυρός) around her, so that neither the beasts could touch her, nor could they see her naked." Barrier, *Acts of Paul and Thecla*, 160–161.

67. Cf. *Mart. Pol.* 15: "For the flames, bellying out like a ship's sail in the wind, formed into the shape of a vault and thus surrounded the martyr's body as with a wall." H. Musurillo, *The Acts of the Christian Martyrs. Introduction, Texts, and Translations* (Oxford: Oxford University Press, 1972), 15.

68. J. W. van Henten, "Martyrs, Martyrdom, and Martyr Literature," in *Oxford Encyclopedia of Ancient Greece and Rome* (ed. M. Gagarin; 7 vols; Oxford: Oxford University Press, 2010), 1.365.

69. Herbert Anthony Musurillo notes that "it would seem correct to infer that Polycarp's martyrdom at the age of 86 would have taken place close to the last quarter of the second century, but the precise date has been widely controverted." Musurillo, *Acts of the Christian Martyrs*, xiii.

70. Candida Moss argues that "there are historical, literary, and conceptual reasons which suggest that the *Martyrdom of Polycarp* was composed sometime after the events described in it, potentially as late as the middle of the third century." C. R. Moss, *Ancient Christian Martyrdom. Diverse Practices, Theologies, and Traditions* (The Anchor Yale Bible Reference Library; New Haven, CT: Yale University Press, 2012), 62.

71. Musurillo, *Acts of the Christian Martyrs*, 11–15.

72. J. W. Van Henten, "Daniel 3 and 6 in Early Christian Literature," in *The Book of Daniel: Composition and Reception I–II* (eds. J. J. Collins and P. W. Flint; 2 vols.; VetTSup, 83; Leiden: Brill, 2001), 1.149–69 at 1.156–158.

73. Van Henten, "Daniel 3 and 6 in Early Christian Literature," 156–158.

74. Musurillo, *Acts of the Christian Martyrs*, 13. In Dan 3 the adepts of the fiery ordeal are also bound before their placement in the furnace: "He ordered the furnace heated up seven times more than was customary, and ordered some of the strongest guards in his army to bind Shadrach, Meshach, and Abednego and to throw them into the furnace of blazing fire. So the men were bound, still wearing their tunics, their trousers, their hats, and their other garments, and they were thrown into the furnace of blazing fire."

75. Musurillo, *Acts of the Christian Martyrs*, 13.

76. Van Henten, "Daniel 3 and 6," 156–158.

77. *A New English Translation of the Septuagint* (tr. A. Pietersma and B. G. Wright; New York and Oxford: Oxford University Press, 2007), 1001.

78. Van Henten, "Daniel 3 and 6," 156–158. Van Henten notes that "in Dan 3 an angel moves the fire in the furnace upward so that Daniel's companions at the furnace's bottom can even enjoy a cool morning breeze (Dan 3:46–50 in the Greek versions). The description of Polycarp's miracle in the fire refers to a furnace as well as to wind. The fire does not affect the martyr's body, in the same way that Daniel's companions' bodies were not affected. The fire surrounds Polycarp like a vault or a sail bellying out. The wind may be an indirect reference to God's interference." J. W. van Henten and F. Avemarie, *Martyrdom and Noble Death: Selected Texts from Graeco-Roman, Jewish, and Christian Antiquity* (New York: Routledge, 2002), 115.

79. Van Henten, "Daniel 3 and 6," 156–158.

80. Pietersma and Wright, *New English Translation of the Septuagint*, 1001.

81. Van Henten, *Martyrdom and Noble Death*, 114–115.

82. *Mart. Pol.* 15: "for the flames, bellying out like a ship's sail in the wind."

83. *Mart. Pol.* 2.3. See also *Mart. Pol.* 14.2.

84. C. Moss, *The Other Christs: Imitating Jesus in Ancient Christian Ideologies of Martyrdom* (Oxford: Oxford University Press, 2010), 127.

85. Musurillo, *Acts of the Christian Martyrs*, 13–15.

86. Moss, *Other Christs*, 127. Moss later notes that "like Jesus, Christian martyrs were believed to ascend directly to heaven at the moment of their death, their martyrdom serving as their passport to the throne of God. The extent to which the rapidity of the ascension of martyrs to heaven is part of an *imitatio Christi* hinges upon contemporary notions about resurrection as it was more generally construed." Moss, *Other Christs*, 118.

87. Bruce Chilton also suggests that "the *Martyrdom of Polycarp* glorifies the martyr as a complete sacrifice." B. Chilton, *Abraham's Curse: Child Sacrifice in the Legacies of the West* (New York: Doubleday, 2008), 109.

88. Moss, *Other Christs*, 129.

89. A. Kulik, *Retroverting Slavonic Pseudepigrapha: Toward the Original of the Apocalypse of Abraham* (TCS, 3; Atlanta: Scholars, 2004), 20.

90. N. T. Wright notes that *Mart. Pol.* compares "the short-lived fire they face at the stake with the fire of hell which is everlasting, never to be quenched." N. T. Wright, *The Resurrection of the Son of God* (Minneapolis: Fortress, 2003), 487.

91. Cf. *Apoc. Ab.* 14:5, which reads: "May you be the fire brand of the furnace of the earth! Go, Azazel, into the untrodden parts of the earth."

92. On the dating of the *Martyrdom of Pionius*, see R. Lane Fox, *Pagans and Christians: In the Mediterranean World from the Second Century AD to the Conversion of Constantine* (London: Penguin, 2006), 460; L. Robert, *Le Martyre de Pionios Prêtre de Smyrne* (Washington, DC: Dumbarton Oaks, 1994), 2–9.

93. Moss, *Ancient Christian Martyrdom*, 73. For an in-depth discussion of the literary dependence of *Mart. Pion.* upon *Mart. Pol.*, see J. M. Kozlowski, "Pionius Polycarpi Imitator: References to Martyrium Polycarpi in Martyrium Pionii," *Science et Esprit* 67 (2015): 417–434.

94. Moss, *Ancient Christian Martyrdom*, 73.

95. Moss, *Ancient Christian Martyrdom*, 73.

96. Musurillo, *Acts of the Christian Martyrs*, 165.

97. Musurillo suggests that "the date would in all likelihood be in the spring of the year 259, either 24 February, with the Roman martyrology, or 23 May, following the *kalendarium Carthaginiense*." Musurillo, *Acts of the Christian Martyrs*, xxxv.

98. Van Henten, "Daniel 3 and 6," 158.

99. Musurillo, *Acts of the Christian Martyrs*, 215–217.

100. Tucker, "The Early Wirkungsgeschichte of Daniel 3," 299–300.

101. Tucker, "The Early Wirkungsgeschichte of Daniel 3," 299–300.

102. *Mart. Mont. Luc.* 7 reads: " 'I saw a child enter the prison here,' he said, 'whose face shone with a brilliance beyond description.' . . . Now this was the Lord from heaven, and Victor asked him where heaven was. 'It is beyond the world,' said the child. 'Show it to me,' said Victor. He said to Victor: 'Where then would your faith be?' Victor, out of human weakness, said to him: 'I cannot hold fast to your charge. Give me a sign that I can tell them.' To this the Lord replied, 'Give them the sign of Jacob.' " Musurillo, *Acts of the Christian Martyrs*, 219.

103. Moss, *Other Christs*, 130.

104. O. Lehtipuu, *Debates Over the Resurrection of the Dead: Constructing Early Christian Identity* (Oxford: Oxford University Press, 2015), 170.

105. Musurillo, *Acts of the Christian Martyrs*, 231.

106. Musurillo notes that, "known to Augustine and Prudentius at least in substance, the *acta* surely existed before 400, and were perhaps composed shortly after the peace of the Church." Musurillo, *Acts of the Christian Martyrs*, xxxii.

107. Greenberg notes that "the names of the three men in the fiery furnace from the Book of Daniel (1:6–7; 3:13–26) are invoked here, in the Latin forms of their names, to remind the reader of the power of faith in God and obedience unto death." L. A. Greenberg, *"My Share of God's Reward": Exploring the Roles and Formulations of the Afterlife in Early Christian Martyrdom* (SBL, 121; New York: Peter Lang, 2009), 180.

108. Musurillo, *Acts of the Christian Martyrs*, 181–185.

109. Van Henten, "Daniel 3 and 6," 158. Greenberg notes that "during the death scene, after their bonds are burned away by the fire, 'they knelt down in joy assured of the resurrection, and stretching out their arms in memory of the Lord's cross, they prayed to the Lord until together they gave up their souls' (4.3)." Greenberg, *My Share of God's Reward*, 180.

110. Tucker, "The Early Wirkungsgeschichte of Daniel 3," 300–301.

111. Tucker, "The Early Wirkungsgeschichte of Daniel 3," 300–301.

112. Tucker, "The Early Wirkungsgeschichte of Daniel 3," 300–301.

113. Greenberg, *My Share of God's Reward*, 180.

114. Moss, *Other Christs*, 128.

115. Moss, *Other Christs*, 128.

116. "Fructuosus also appeared to Aemilianus, who had condemned him to death, together with his deacons in robes of glory. And he scolded and mocked him, saying that it was of no use for him to believe vainly that, stripped of their bodies, they would

remain in the earth, now that he could see them in glory." Musurillo, *Acts of the Christian Martyrs*, 185.

117. Musurillo, *Acts of the Christian Martyrs*, 185. Cf. *Mart. Pol.* 15: "And he was within it not as burning flesh but rather as bread being baked, or like gold and silver being purified in a smelting-furnace." Musurillo, *Acts of the Christian Martyrs*, 15.

118. A. A. Orlov, *Heavenly Priesthood in the Apocalypse of Abraham* (Cambridge: Cambridge University Press, 2013), 11–44.

119. Kulik, *Retroverting Slavonic Pseudepigrapha*, 12.

120. Kulik, *Retroverting Slavonic Pseudepigrapha*, 12–13.

121. B. Philonenko-Sayar and M. Philonenko, *L'Apocalypse d'Abraham. Introduction, texte slave, traduction et notes* (Semitica, 31; Paris: Librairie Adrien-Maisonneuve, 1981), 46.

122. Kulik, *Retroverting Slavonic Pseudepigrapha*, 13.

123. It should be noted that the Book of Daniel and the Book of Revelation refer to fiery feet of not only divine but also angelic manifestations. Cf. Dan 10:5–6: "I looked up and saw a man clothed in linen, with a belt of gold from Uphaz around his waist. His body was like beryl, his face like lightning, his eyes like flaming torches, his arms and legs like the gleam of burnished bronze, and the sound of his words like the roar of a multitude." Rev 10:1: "And I saw another mighty angel coming down from heaven, wrapped in a cloud, with a rainbow over his head; his face was like the sun, and his legs like pillars of fire."

124. This tradition is then reaffirmed in Rev 2:18: "These are the words of the Son of God, who has eyes like a flame of fire, and whose feet are like burnished bronze."

125. Kulik, *Retroverting Slavonic Pseudepigrapha*, 15.

126. See *Apoc. Ab.* 18:2; 18:3; 18:12; 19:4; 19:6.

127. See *Apoc. Ab.* 8:1; 18:2.

128. Concerning the circulation of this motif in Byzantine chorographical accounts, see Adler, "Abraham and the Burning of the Temple of Idols," 95–117.

129. Kulik, *Retroverting Slavonic Pseudepigrapha*, 16.

130. Kulik, *Retroverting Slavonic Pseudepigrapha*, 30.

131. VanderKam, *The Book of Jubilees*, 2.67–70. On this tradition, see J. van Ruiten, *Abraham in the Book of Jubilees: The Rewriting of Genesis 11:26–25:10 in the Book of Jubilees 11:14–23:8* (JSJSS, 161; Leiden: Brill, 2012), 32. Another interesting version of the fiery demise of Terah's household is found in the *Palaea Historica* 26:1–9:

> Concerning Abraham: In those days, [a man] was born [by the name] of Abraham. He was given the name by his father and was taught astronomy. He used to seek for God the creator of heaven and earth and the stars, the sun and the moon, but he was unable to find knowledge of him. Now his father was an idolater. When Abraham saw the gods of [his] father, he said [to] himself, "Why is my father, who builds homes for gods and invents new ones, unable to explain to me about the creator of heaven and earth, as well as the sun, moon and stars?" While turning these questions over in his mind, he was in deep reflection. Then one day he rose up early in

> the morning and set fire to the building where the gods of his father were housed; and the building, together with the gods, went up in flames. Terah, who was his brother and the father of Lot, got up and retrieved his so-called gods. He was consumed in the flames, he together with his gods.

W. Adler, "Palaea Historica," in *Old Testament Pseudepigrapha: More Noncanonical Scriptures* (eds. R. Bauckham et al.; Grand Rapids, MI: Eerdmans, 2013), 609–610.

132. Kugel notes that the *Targum Neophiti* to Gen. 11:28 apparently preserves an echo of this tradition: "And his father Terah was still alive when Haran died in the land of his birth, in the fiery furnace of the Chaldeans." Kugel, *Traditions of the Bible*, 268.

133. Kugel, *Traditions of the Bible*, 267. Kugel rightly differentiates the fiery trials of Abraham from the ordeals of his immediate family, noting that

> The motif "Haran Perished in the Furnace" is quite separate from "Abraham Saved from Fire"; although the two depend on the same pun (Ur = fire). Which came first? The very fact that "Haran Perished in the Furnace" is found in an ancient work like *Jubilees*, whereas nary a hint of "Abraham Saved from Fire" is found in that text, nor in Ben Sira or the Wisdom of Solomon, might suggest that the latter motif is more recent. Whatever the date of these motifs' earliest attestations, it seems likely that "Abraham Saved from Fire" developed out of "Haran Perished in the Furnace" rather than vice versa. The original purpose of "Haran Perished in the Furnace" was to clarify the troubling biblical assertion cited earlier, "Haran died before his father Terah in the land of his birth, in Ur of the Chaldeans" (Gen 11:28). Interpreters certainly must have found it strange that Haran should live to adulthood and yet die before his father. Stranger still was the fact that the Bible tells us nothing of the circumstances in which this (apparently unnatural) death occurred. Given this void, the otherwise gratuitous pun, Ur = fire, seemed to offer one valuable piece of information: it supplied at least a hint about how Haran died—he perished in a fire. This was enough to allow interpreters to fill in the remaining details, connecting this "fire of the Chaldeans" to Abraham's zealous campaign against idolatry.

Kugel, *Traditions of the Bible*, 268–269.

134. Recall Dan 3: "Because the king's command was urgent and the furnace was so overheated, the raging flames killed the men who lifted Shadrach, Meshach, and Abednego."

135. Kulik, *Retroverting Slavonic Pseudepigrapha*, 20.

136. Braude and Kapstein, *Tanna Debe Eliyyahu*, 62–63.

137. Cf. *Apoc. Ab.* 15:3: "And he carried me up to the edge of the fiery flame." *Apoc. Ab.* 17:1: "And while he was still speaking, behold, a fire was coming toward us round about, and a sound was in the fire like a sound of many waters, like a sound of the sea in its uproar." Kulik, *Retroverting Slavonic Pseudepigrapha*, 22.

138. Orlov, *Dark Mirrors*, 18–19.

139. Orlov, *Dark Mirrors,* 18–19.

140. Musurillo, *Acts of the Christian Martyrs,* 3–5.

141. Greenberg, *My Share of God's Reward,* 153.

142. Musurillo, *Acts of the Christian Martyrs,* 11.

143. "Pionius said: 'Would that I were able to persuade you to become Christians.' The men laughed aloud at him. 'You have not such power that we should be burnt alive,' they said. 'It is far worse,' said Pionius, 'to burn after death.'" Musurillo, *Acts of the Christian Martyrs,* 145.

144. Here the fire appears to embody a special substance that reshapes the seer's mortal body.

145. Kulik, *Retroverting Slavonic Pseudepigrapha,* 22.

146. Greek versions of Dan 3:49–50 read: *Old Greek*: "But an angel of the Lord came down into the furnace to be with Azarias and his companions and shook the flame of the fire out of the furnace and made the inside of the furnace as if a moist breeze were whistling through. And the fire did not touch them at all and caused them no pain or distress." *Theodotion*: "But the angel of the Lord came down into the furnace to be with Azarias and his companions and shook the flame of the fire out of the furnace and made the inside of the furnace as though a moist breeze were whistling through. And the fire did not touch them at all and caused them no pain or distress." Pietersma and Wright, *New English Translation of the Septuagint,* 1001.

147. Bucur points out that "early Christian writers, from Irenaeus to Romanos the Melodist and from Tertullian to Prudentius, consistently identified Christ, the Logos, as the heavenly agent . . . who entered the furnace and saved the three youths." Bucur, *Scripture Re-envisioned,* 250.

148. On this, see Bucur, *Scripture Re-envisioned,* 256–258.

149. Musurillo, *Acts of the Christian Martyrs,* 181. See also the *Martyrdom of Montanus and Lucius* 3: "Indeed, as we later ascertained, he intended to burn us alive. But the Lord alone can rescue his servants from fire, and in his hand are the words and the heart of the king: he it was who averted from us the insane savagery of the governor . . . the fire of the overheated ovens was lulled by the Lord's dew." Musurillo, *Acts of the Christian Martyrs,* 215–217.

150. Kulik, *Retroverting Slavonic Pseudepigrapha,* 22.

151. Musurillo, *Acts of the Christian Martyrs,* 15. In the *Acts of Thecla* 34 a cloud of fire forms around Thecla "so that neither could the beasts touch her nor could she be seen naked." It appears that fire plays a protective role here like in the *Apocalypse of Abraham* and the *Martyrdom of Polycarp.*

152. *Mart. Pion.* 2: "Now Pionius knew on the day before Polycarp's anniversary that they were all to be seized on that day. Being together with Sabina and Asclepiades and fasting, as he realized that they were to be taken on the following day." Musurillo, *Acts of the Christian Martyrs,* 137.

153. *Mart. Fruct.*: "Many out of brotherly affection offered him a cup of drugged wine to drink, but he said: 'It is not yet the time for breaking the fast.' For it was still in the fourth hour, and in gaol they duly observed the stational fast on Wednesdays." Musurillo, *Acts of the Christian Martyrs,* 179.

154. Thus, *Apoc. Ab.* 9:7 reports the following command: "But for forty days abstain from every food which issues from fire, and from the drinking of wine, and from anointing [yourself] with oil." Kulik, *Retroverting Slavonic Pseudepigrapha*, 17.

155. Musurillo, *Acts of the Christian Martyrs*, 7.

156. *Mart. Pol.* 14–15 reads: "They did not nail him down then, but simply bound him; and as he put his hands behind his back, he was bound like a noble ram chosen for an oblation from a great flock, a holocaust prepared and made acceptable to God. Looking up to heaven, he said: 'O Lord, omnipotent God and Father of your beloved and blessed child Christ Jesus.' . . . He had uttered his Amen and finished his prayer, and the men in charge of the fire started to light it. A great flame blazed up and those of us to whom it was given to see beheld a miracle." Musurillo, *Acts of the Christian Martyrs*, 13–15.

157. Although the original Aramaic text of Dan 3 does not mention the adepts' prayer, the Greek versions of Dan 3 speak in detail about the Israelite youths' prayer routines before or during the fiery ordeal. It begins with the portrayal of the protagonists "singing hymns to God and blessing the Lord" in the flames of furnace. Greek versions of Dan 3:24 read: *Theod.* "So, therefore, Ananias and Azarias and Misael prayed and sang hymns to the Lord." *Old Greek*: "And they were walking around in the middle of the flames, singing hymns to God and blessing the Lord." Pietersma and Wright, *New English Translation of the Septuagint*, 999. Greek versions of Dan 3:51: *Theod.* "Then the three as though from one mouth were singing hymns and glorifying and blessing God." *Old Greek*: "Now, the three resuming, as though from one mouth, were singing hymns and glorifying and blessing and exalting God." Pietersma and Wright, *New English Translation of the Septuagint*, 1001.

158. Van Henten and Avemaria, *Martyrdom and Noble Death*, 115.

159. Musurillo, *Acts of the Christian Martyrs*, 7. Another description of this episode is found in *Mart. Pol.* 12, where the fiery ordeal also coincides with the prayer: "For the vision he had seen regarding his pillow had to be fulfilled, when he saw it burning while he was at prayer and turned and said to his faithful companions: 'I am to be burnt alive.'" Musurillo, *Acts of the Christian Martyrs*, 13.

160. Musurillo, *Acts of the Christian Martyrs*, 177.

161. Musurillo, *Acts of the Christian Martyrs*, 181–183.

162. Musurillo, *Acts of the Christian Martyrs*, 215–217.

163. Musurillo, *Acts of the Christian Martyrs*, 165.

164. Kulik, *Retroverting Slavonic Pseudepigrapha*, 22–23.

165. Philonenko-Sayar and Philonenko, *L'Apocalypse d'Abraham*. 74.

166. Kulik, *Retroverting Slavonic Pseudepigrapha*, 22.

167. Kulik, *Retroverting Slavonic Pseudepigrapha*, 22.

168. Jacobson, *A Commentary on Pseudo-Philo's Liber Antiquitatum Biblicarum*, 118. On this tradition, see Kugel, *Traditions of the Bible*, 262.

169. James VanderKam and William Adler point out that "one form in which millennialist apocalypticism expressed itself in Egypt, as in Asia Minor and North Africa, was the ideology of martyrdom." J. C. VanderKam and W. Adler, *The Jewish Apocalyptic Heritage in Early Christianity* (CRINT, 3.4; Assen: Van Gorcum; Minneapolis: Fortress, 1996), 168.

170. Moss, *Other Christs*, 127.
171. Moss, *Other Christs*, 128.
172. Musurillo, *Acts of the Christian Martyrs*, 111.
173. DeConick, "Traumatic Mysteries," 37–38.
174. Kulik, *Retroverting Slavonic Pseudepigrapha*, 23–24.
175. Analyzing Stephen's vision recorded in Acts 7, Philip Munoa argues that

> The author of Acts appears to have used Dan 7 when describing Stephen's martyrdom. Like Daniel, Stephen is described as a captive visionary, having been seized by a hostile crowd of Jews who have him under their control (Acts 6:8–12). Stephen's words according to Acts 7:56, "I see the Son of Man standing at the right hand of God," go on to imply that, like Daniel, he sees both God on his throne, recalling Daniel's "Ancient of Days," who was seated on a throne, and the "one like a son of man," who was in the presence of the enthroned "Ancient of Days" (Dan 7:9–13). Acts 7 is in this way an implicit Merkavah vision.

Munoa, "Jesus, the Merkavah, and Martyrdom," 305–306.
176. Munoa, "Jesus, the Merkavah, and Martyrdom," 323–324.
177. Munoa, "Jesus, the Merkavah, and Martyrdom," 323–324.
178. Alexander, "3 Enoch," 1.267. On this motif, see also T. L. Putthoff, *Ontological Aspects of Early Jewish Anthropology: The Malleable Self and the Presence of God* (BRLJ, 53; Leiden: Brill, 2016), 191.
179. Greenberg, *My Share of God's Reward*, 153–154.
180. Van Henten and Avemaria, *Martyrdom and Noble Death*, 116.
181. Freedman and Simon, *Midrash Rabbah*, 1.273.
182. Musurillo, *Acts of the Christian Martyrs*, 13. In Dan 3 the protagonists are also bound before their placement in the crematory.
183. E. Castelli, *Martyrdom and Memory: Early Christian Culture Making* (New York: Columbia University Press, 2004), 53.
184. R. D. Young, *Procession before the World. Martyrdom as Public Liturgy in Early Christianity* (The Père Marquette Lecture in Theology 2001; Milwaukee: Marquette University Press, 2001), 24.
185. Musurillo, *Acts of the Christian Martyrs*, 13.
186. Van Henten, "Reception of Dan 3 and 6," 157.
187. *Origen: An Exhortation to Martyrdom, Prayer, and Selected Works* (tr. R. Greer; New York: Paulist Press, 1979), 62.
188. Castelli, *Martyrdom and Memory*, 53.
189. Castelli, *Martyrdom and Memory*, 53.
190. Braude and Kapstein, *Tanna Debe Eliyyahu*, 62–63.
191. On this motif, see Kugel, *Traditions of the Bible*, 322; W. J. Van Bekkum, "The Aqedah and Its Interpretations in Midrash and Piyyut," in *The Sacrifice of Isaac: The Aqedah (Genesis 22) and Its Interpretations* (eds. E. Noort and E. Tigchelaar; TBN, 4; Leiden: Brill, 2002), 91; M. Harl, "La 'ligature' d'Isaac (Gen. 22, 9) dans la Septante et

chez les Pères grecs," in *Hellenica et Judaica: Homage à Valentin Nikiprowetzky* (eds. A. Caquot, M. Hadas-Lebel, and J. Riaud; Leuven-Paris: Peeters, 1986), 457–472.

192. Milik, *The Books of Enoch,* 313.

193. A. A. Orlov, *The Atoning Dyad: The Two Goats of Yom Kippur in the Apocalypse of Abraham* (SJS, 8; Leiden: Brill, 2016), 148–153.

194. Cf. Lev 16:27; 11Q19 col. xxvi 3–9; *m. Yoma* 6:7. Regarding this rite, Daniel Stökl Ben Ezra notes that "the carcasses of the bull and the sacrificial goat, whose blood was sprinkled in the holy of holies, are then burned by an adjutant at a special holy place outside the temple." D. Stökl Ben Ezra, *The Impact of Yom Kippur on Early Christianity: The Day of Atonement from Second Temple Judaism to the Fifth Century* (WUNT, 1.163; Tübingen: Mohr Siebeck, 2003), 32.

195. Orlov, *Atoning Dyad,* 148.

196. Kulik, *Retroverting Slavonic Pseudepigrapha,* 19.

197. Kulik, *Retroverting Slavonic Pseudepigrapha,* 23; Philonenko-Sayar and Philonenko, *L'Apocalypse d'Abraham,* 76.

198. See *Apoc. Ab.* 17:21: "Receive me favorably." Kulik, *Retroverting Slavonic Pseudepigrapha,* 23.

199. Kugel, *Traditions of the Bible,* 269.

Chapter Three. Leviathan's Knot

1. H. S. J. Thackeray, *Josephus* (LCL; 10 vols.; Cambridge, MA: Harvard University Press/London: Heinemann, 1967), 4.388–389.

2. C. H. T. Fletcher-Louis, "The High Priest as Divine Mediator in the Hebrew Bible: Dan 7:13 as a Test Case," *SBLSP* 36 (1997): 161–93 at 191. See also C. H. T. Fletcher-Louis, "Priests and Priesthood," in *Dictionary of Jesus and the Gospels* (2nd ed.; eds. J. B. Green, J. K. Brown, and N. Perrin; Downers Grove, IL: IVP Academic, 2013), 698.

3. Isa 27:1 reads: "On that day the Lord with his cruel and great and strong sword will punish Leviathan the fleeing serpent, Leviathan the twisting serpent, and he will kill the dragon that is in the sea."

4. Fletcher-Louis, "High Priest as Divine Mediator," 191.

5. Thackeray, *Josephus,* 4.405.

6. Fletcher-Louis, "High Priest as Divine Mediator," 191. Elsewhere he reiterates the same thesis by arguing that "the high priest's ephod is probably the same kind of garment which Ba'al wears when he slays Leviathan (*CTA* 5.I.1–5). A passage in Josephus (*Ant.* 3.154–6) suggests his sash was worn to evoke the image of a slain Leviathan hanging limp at its conqueror's side." C. H. T. Fletcher-Louis, "Alexander the Great's Worship of the High Priest," in *Early Jewish and Christian Monotheism* (eds. L. T. Stuckenbruck and W. E. S. North; London: T&T Clark, 2004), 71–102 at 87.

7. Angel, *Chaos and the Son of Man,* 183.

8. M. Barker, *The Revelation of Jesus Christ: Which God Gave to Him to Show to His Servants What Must Soon Take Place (Revelation 1.1)* (Edinburgh: T&T Clark, 2000), 220.

9. Thackeray, *Josephus,* 4.403–407. In relation to Josephus's interpretation of the Temple imagery, Jon Levenson argues the following: "the affinity of Josephus's method of interpreting the Temple with Hellenistic allegory, Jewish and Gentile, and ultimately with Platonic philosophy, is unmistakable. This granted, however, it would be an error to see this allegory as the aberration of a Jew writing in Greek largely for the benefit of a mixed Hellenistic intelligentsia. For this sort of allegorical reading of the Tabernacle/Temple is also abundant in Rabbinic literature, written in Hebrew for a Jewish readership." J. D. Levenson, *Creation and the Persistence of Evil. The Jewish Drama of Divine Omnipotence* (San Francisco: Harper & Row, 1988), 96.

10. G. Beale, *The Temple and the Church's Mission* (NSBT, 15; Downers Grove, IL: InterVarsity Press, 2004), 39.

11. Beale, *The Temple and the Church's Mission,* 39–40.

12. Philo, *Mos.* II.117: "Such was the vesture of the high priest. But I must not leave untold its meaning and that of its parts. We have in it as a whole and in its parts a typical representation of the world and its particular parts." *Philo* (eds. F. H. Colson and G. H. Whitaker; 10 vols.; LCL; Cambridge, MA: Harvard University Press, 1929–1964), 5.505; *Spec.* 1.84: "The high priest is bidden to put on a similar dress when he enters the inner shrine to offer incense, because its fine linen is not, like wool, the product of creatures subject to death, and also to wear another, the formation of which is very complicated. In this it would seem to be a likeness and copy of the universe. This is clearly shewn by the design." Colson and Whitaker, *Philo,* 7.149.

13. Beale, *The Temple and the Church's Mission,* 39.

14. On this, see M. Barker, *The Gate of Heaven: The History and Symbolism of the Temple in Jerusalem* (London: SPCK, 1991), 104–132; Beale, *The Temple and the Church's Mission,* 29–79; A. A. de Silva, "A Comparison Between the Three-Levelled World of the Old Testament Temple Building Narratives and the Three-Levelled World of the House Building Motif in the Ugaritic Texts KTU 1.3 and 1.4," in *Ugarit and the Bible* (eds. G. J. Brooke, A. H. W. Curites, and J. F. Healy; Münster: Ugarit-Verlag, 1994), 11–23; C. H. T. Fletcher-Louis, *Luke-Acts: Angels, Christology and Soteriology* (WUNT, 2.94; Tübingen: Mohr Siebeck, 1997), 156–162; C. T. R. Hayward, *The Jewish Temple: A Non-Biblical Sourcebook* (London and New York: Routledge, 1996); V. Hurowitz, *I Have Built You an Exalted House: Temple Building in the Bible in Light of Mesopotamian and North-West Semitic Writings* (Sheffield: JSOT Press, 1992), 335–337; R. C. Koester, *The Dwelling of God: the Tabernacle in the Old Testament, Intertestamental Jewish Literature, and the New Testament* (CBQMS, 22; Washington: Catholic Biblical Association, 1989), 59–63; J. D. Levenson, "The Temple and the World," *JR* 65 (1984): 283–298; Levenson, *Sinai and Zion: An Entry into Jewish Bible* (Minneapolis: Winston, 1985), 111–184; Levenson, *Creation and the Persistence of Evil,* 87–88; R. Patai, *Man and Temple in Ancient Jewish Myth and Ritual* (2nd ed.; New York: KTAV, 1967), 54–139; J. H. Walton, *Genesis* (NIVAC; Grand Rapids, MI: Zondervan, 2001), 148.

15. B. Janowski, "Der Tempel als Kosmos—Zur kosmologischen Bedeutung des Tempels in der Umwelt Israels," in *Egypt—Temple of the Whole World / Ägypten—Tempel der Gesamten Welt. Studies in Honour of Jan Assmann* (ed. S. Meyer; Leiden: Brill, 2003), 163–186 at 165–175. Jon Levenson notes that "the association of the Temple in Jerusalem with 'heaven and earth' is not without Near Eastern antecedents, nor is it limited in the

Hebrew Bible to texts whose subject is creation. At Nippur and elsewhere in ancient Sumer, the temple held the name Duranki, 'bond of heaven and earth,' and we hear of a shrine in Babylon called Etemenanki, 'the house where the foundation of heaven and earth is.'" Levenson, *Creation and the Persistance of Evil*, 90.

16. Janowski, "Der Tempel als Kosmos," 175–184.

17. Cf. *Jub*. 8:19: "He knew that the Garden of Eden is the holy of holies and is the residence of the Lord." VanderKam, *Jubilees*, 2.53.

18. Understanding Eden as the temple presupposes the protoplast's role as a sacerdotal servant. Van Ruiten suggests that the author of *Jubilees* sees Adam acting as a prototypical priest who burns incense at the gate of the Garden of Eden. Van Ruiten draws a parallel between this description and a tradition found in Exodus: "[T]he incense is burned in front of the Holy of Holies. The burning of incense is a privilege given to the priests, namely the sons of Aaron." Van Ruiten also calls attention to another important detail related to the function of Adam as priest, namely, the covering of nakedness. He reminds us that covering one's nakedness is a condition for offering, since the priests are explicitly bidden to cover their nakedness. The author of *Jubilees* likewise lays emphasis on covering nakedness. Van Ruiten, "Eden and the Temple," 77–78. On sacerdotal Edenic traditions, see also J. Davila, "The Hodayot Hymnist and the Four Who Entered Paradise," *RevQ* 17/65–68 (1996): 457–78; F. García Martínez, "Man and Woman: Halakhah Based upon Eden in the Dead Sea Scrolls," in *Paradise Interpreted: Representations of Biblical Paradise in Judaism and Christianity* (ed. G. Luttikhuizen; TBN, 2; Leiden: Brill, 1999), 95–115 at 112–113; E. Noort, "Gan-Eden in the Context of the Mythology of the Hebrew Bible," in *Paradise Interpreted: Representations of Biblical Paradise in Judaism and Christianity* (ed. G. Luttikhuizen; TBN, 2; Leiden: Brill, 1999), 25; D. W. Parry, "Garden of Eden: Prototype Sanctuary," in *Temples of the Ancient World: Ritual and Symbolism* (ed. D. W. Parry; Provo, UT: Deseret, 1994), 126–151; Van Ruiten, "Visions of the Temple," 215–228; Wenham, "Sanctuary Symbolism," 21–22; M. Wise, "4QFlorilegium and the Temple of Adam," *RevQ* 15/57–58 (1991): 103–132.

19. Beale notes that "Ezekiel 32 explicitly calls Eden the first sanctuary, which substantiates that Eden is described as a temple because it is the first temple, albeit a 'garden-temple.'" Beale, *The Temple and the Church's Mission*, 80. Some scholars argue that Solomon's temple was an intentional replication of the Garden of Eden, especially in its arboreal likeness. For this, see Beale, *The Temple and the Church's Mission*, 72; L. Stager, "Jerusalem and the Garden of Eden," in *Festschrift for F. M. Cross* (Eretz Israel, 26; Jerusalem: Israel Exploration Society, 1999), 183–193; Stager, "Jerusalem as Eden," *BAR* 26 (2000): 36–4.

20. Patai, *Man and Temple*, 108–109.

21. Regarding the tripartite structure of the entire creation in the Jewish tradition, see L. Stadelman, *The Hebrew Conception of the World—A Philological and Literary Study* (Analecta Biblica, 39; Rome: Biblical Institute, 1970), 9.

22. Thackeray, *Josephus*, 4.373–375.

23. *Spec*. I.66 reads: "The highest, and in the truest sense the holy, temple of God is, as we must believe, the whole universe, having for its sanctuary the most sacred part of all existence, even heaven. . . ." Colson and Whitaker, *Philo*, 7.137. *Zohar* II.149a conveys a similar tradition: "Said R. Isaac: 'We are aware that the structure of the Tabernacle

corresponds to the structure of heaven and earth.'" Sperling and Simon, *The Zohar*, 4.22. Cf. also *Zohar* II.231a:

> Now, the Tabernacle below was likewise made after the pattern of the supernal Tabernacle in all its details. For the Tabernacle in all its works embraced all the works and achievements of the upper world and the lower, whereby the Shekinah was made to abide in the world, both in the higher spheres and the lower. Similarly, the Lower Paradise is made after the pattern of the Upper Paradise, and the latter contains all the varieties of forms and images to be found in the former. Hence the work of the Tabernacle, and that of heaven and earth, come under one and the same mystery.

Sperling and Simon, *The Zohar*, 4.289; *Zohar* II.235b:

> Now, the lower and earthly Tabernacle was the counterpart of the upper Tabernacle, whilst the latter in its turn is the counterpart of a higher Tabernacle, the most high of all. All of them, however, are implied within each other and form one complete whole, as it says: "that the tabernacle may be one whole." The Tabernacle was erected by Moses, he alone being allowed to raise it up, as only a husband may raise up his wife. With the erection of the lower Tabernacle there was erected another Tabernacle on high. This is indicated in the words "the tabernacle was reared up (*hukam*)," reared up, that is, by the hand of no man, but as out of the supernal undisclosed mystery in response to the mystical force indwelling in Moses that it might be perfected with him.

Sperling and Simon, *The Zohar*, 4.303.

24. Levenson notes that "collectively, the function of these correspondences is to underscore the depiction of the sanctuary as a world, that is, an ordered, supportive, and obedient environment, and the depiction of the world as a sanctuary, that is, a place in which the reign of God is visible and unchallenged, and his holiness is palpable, unthreatened, and pervasive. Our examination of the two sets of Priestly texts, one at the beginning of Genesis and the other at the end of Exodus, has developed powerful evidence that, as in many cultures, the Temple was conceived as a microcosm, a miniature world." Levenson, *Creation and the Persistence of Evil*, 86.

25. M. Weinfeld, "Sabbath, Temple and the Enthronement of the Lord: The Problem of the Sitz im Leben of Genesis 1:1–2:3," in *Mélanges bibliques et orientaux en l'honneur de M. Henri Cazelles* (eds. A. Caquot and M. Delcor; AOAT, 212; Neukirchen-Vluyn: Neukirchener Verlag, 1981), 501–503. See S. E. Balentine, *The Torah's Vision of Worship* (Minneapolis: Fortress, 1999), 67–68; Beale, *The Temple and the Church's Mission*, 60–61; J. Blenkinsopp, "The Structure of P," *CBQ* 38 (1976): 283–86; M. Fishbane, *Text and Texture* (New York: Schocken, 1979), 12; V. Hurowitz, "The Priestly Account of Building the Tabernacle," *JAOS* 105 (1985): 21–30; P. J. Kearney, "Creation and Liturgy: The P Redaction of Ex 25–40," *ZAW* 89.3 (1977): 375–387 at 375; Levenson, *Sinai and Zion*, 143; Levenson, *Creation and the Persistence of Evil*, 85–86; Ch. Nihan, *From Priestly Torah to Pentateuch: A Study in the Composition of the Book of Leviticus* (FAT, 25; Tübingen: Mohr

Siebeck, 2007), 54–58; Walton, *Genesis*, 149; P. Weimar, "Sinai und Schöpfung: Komposition und Theologie der priesterschriftlichen Sinaigeschichte," *RB* 95 (1988): 337–85; Wenham, "Sanctuary Symbolism," 19–25.

26. Jon Levenson suggests that "world building and Temple building seem to be homologous activities. In fact, some of the same language can be found in the description of the establishment of the sanctuary in the land and the distribution of the land among the tribes in Joshua 18–19." J. Levenson, "The Jerusalem Temple in Devotional and Visionary Experience," in *Jewish Spirituality. Vol. I: From the Bible through the Middle Ages* (ed. A. Green; New York: Crossroad, 1987), 32–61 at 52.

27. "His offering was one silver dish, etc. The dish was in allusion to the court which encompassed the Tabernacle as the sea encompasses the world." Freedman and Simon, *Midrash Rabbah*, 6.546. Concerning a similar tradition in *Midrash Tadshe*, see G. MacRae, "Some Elements of Jewish Apocalyptic and Mystical Tradition and Their Relation to Gnostic Literature" (2 vols.; Ph.D. diss.; University of Cambridge, 1966), 55.

28. "The reference is to the building of Herod. Of what did he build it?—Rabbah replied, Of yellow and white marble. Some there are who say, with yellow, blue and white marble. The building rose in tiers in order to provide a hold for the plaster. He intended at first to overlay it with gold, but the Rabbis told him, Leave it alone for it is more beautiful as it is, since it has the appearance of the waves of the sea." Epstein, *The Babylonian Talmud: Sukkah*, 51b.

29. 1 Kgs 7:23–25 reads: "Then he made the molten sea; it was round, ten cubits from brim to brim, and five cubits high, and a line of thirty cubits measured its circumference. Under its brim were gourds, for thirty cubits, compassing the sea round about; the gourds were in two rows, cast with it when it was cast. It stood upon twelve oxen, three facing north, three facing west, three facing south, and three facing east; the sea was set upon them, and all their hinder parts were inward." See also 2 Kgs 16:17; 2 Kgs 25:13; 1 Chr 18:8; 2 Chr 4:2; Jer 52:17.

30. Elizabeth Bloch-Smith observes that "the exaggerated size of the structures of the Solomonic Temple courtyard would suggest that they were not intended for human use, but belonged to the realm of the divine." E. Bloch-Smith, "'Who Is the King of Glory?' Solomon's Temple and Its Symbolism," in *Scripture and Other Artifacts. Essays on the Bible and Archeology in Honor of Philip J. King* (eds. M. Coogan et al.; Louisville: Westminster, 1994), 19–31 at 21.

31. Bloch-Smith, "'Who Is the King of Glory?'" 20. See also C. L. Meyers, "Sea, Molten," in *Anchor Bible Dictionary* (ed. D. N. Freedman; 6 vols.; New York: Doubleday, 1992), 5.1061–62.

32. V. Hurowitz, "Inside Solomon's Temple," *Bible Review* 10.2 (1994): 24–36. Jon Levenson also draws attention to the creational symbolism of the molten sea by arguing that "the metal 'Sea' (*yam*) in its courtyard (1 Kgs 7:23–26) suggests the Mesopotamian *apsu*, employed both as the name of the subterranean fresh-water ocean . . . and as the name of a basin of holy water erected in the Temple. As the god of the subterranean freshwater ocean, *apsu* played an important role in some Mesopotamian cosmogonies, just as the Sea (*yam*) did in some Israelite creation stories (e.g., Ps 74:12–17; Isa 51:9–11). This suggests that the metal Sea in the Temple courtyard served as a continual testimony to the act of creation." Levenson, "Jerusalem Temple," 51.

33. On the temple of creation in the *Apocalypse of Abraham,* see A. A. Orlov, "The Cosmological Temple in the *Apocalypse of Abraham*," in Orlov, *Divine Scapegoats: Demonic Mimesis in Early Jewish Mysticism* (Albany, NY: State University of New York Press, 2016), 37–54.

34. *Apoc. Ab.* 21:5: "I saw there the rivers and their overflows, and their circles;" Ezek 47:1: "water was flowing from below the threshold of the temple."

35. Regarding this biblical passage, Wenham observes that "the brief account of the geography of the garden in 2:10–14 also makes many links with later sanctuary design. 'A river flows out of Eden to water the garden.' . . . Ps 46:5 speaks of 'a river whose streams make glad the city of God' and Ezekiel 47 describes a great river flowing out of the new Jerusalem temple to sweeten the Dead Sea." Wenham, "Sanctuary Symbolism," 22.

36. "A river flows out of Eden to water the garden, and from there it divides and becomes four branches." Regarding the rivers of paradise, see also *2 Enoch* 8, 1QH 14 and 16.

37. Beale, *The Temple and the Church's Mission*, 72.

38. "They feast on the abundance of your house, and you give them drink from the river of your delights. For with you is the fountain of life; in your light we see light."

39. Beale, *The Temple and the Church's Mission*, 74.

40.

> There is an uninterrupted supply not only of water, just as if there were a plentiful spring rising naturally from within, but also of indescribably wonderful underground reservoirs, which within a radius of five stades from the foundation of the Temple revealed innumerable channels for each of them, the streams joining together on each side. All these were covered with lead down to the foundation of the wall; on top of them a thick layer of pitch, all done very effectively. There were many mouths at the base, which were completely invisible except for those responsible for the ministry, so that the large amounts of blood which collected from the sacrifices were all cleansed by the downward pressure and momentum. Being personally convinced, I will describe the building plan of the reservoirs just as I understood it. They conducted me more than four stades outside the city, and told me to bend down at a certain spot and listen to the noise at the meeting of the waters. The result was that the size of the conduits became clear to me, as has been demonstrated.

R. J. H. Shutt, "Letter of Aristeas," in *The Old Testament Pseudepigrapha* (ed. J. H. Charlesworth; 2 vols.; New York: Doubleday, 1983–1985), 2.7–34 at 18–19.

41. An image of overflowing water surrounding the Temple courtyard is found also in *Jos. Asen.* 2:17–20: "And there was in the court, on the right hand, a spring of abundant living water. . . ." Scholars have noted that "detailed description of [Aseneth's] garden clearly echoes Ezekiel's account of what he saw in his celebrated temple-vision (Ezek 40–8)." G. Bohak, *Joseph and Aseneth and the Jewish Temple in Heliopolis* (Atlanta: Scholars, 1996), 68.

42. "Then the angel showed me the river of the water of life, bright as crystal, flowing from the throne of God and of the Lamb through the middle of the street of the city."

43. Thackeray, *Josephus*, 4.405.

44. Thackeray, *Josephus*, 4.405.

45. Fletcher-Louis, "High Priest as Divine Mediator," 698.

46. W. Whitney, *Two Strange Beasts: Leviathan and Behemoth in Second Temple and Early Rabbinic Judaism* (HSM, 63; Winona Lake, IN: Eisenbrauns, 2006), 118.

47. Whitney, *Two Strange Beasts*, 118.

48. Whitney, *Two Strange Beasts*, 117; *Beth ha-Midrasch* (Jellinek) I:63.

49. Whitney, *Two Strange Beasts*, 119. Whitney points out that an early example of the *ouroboros* motif appears in a silver Phoenician bowl found in an Etruscan warrior burial of ca. ninth-eighth century BCE at Praeneste in Italy. Whitney, *Two Strange Beasts*, 119.

50. A. Kulik, "The Mysteries of Behemoth and Leviathan and the Celestial Bestiary of 3 Baruch," *Le Muséon* 122 (2009): 291–329 at 299.

51. E. H. Gifford, *Eusebius, Praeparatio Evangelica (Preparation for the Gospel)* (2 vols.; Grand Rapids, MI: Baker, 1981), 1.43.

52. *Pistis Sophia* (eds. C. Schmidt and V. MacDermot; NHS, 9; Leiden: Brill, 1978), 317.

53. Kulik, "The Mysteries of Behemoth and Leviathan," 299.

54. A. F. J. Klijn, *The Acts of Thomas: Introduction, Text, and Commentary* (2nd ed.; NovTSup, 108; Leiden: Brill, 2003), 92–93.

55. H. Chadwick, *Origen, Contra Celsum* (Cambridge: Cambridge University Press, 1953), 340.

56. Whitney, *Two Strange Beasts*, 122.

57. Kulik, *Retroverting Slavonic Pseudepigrapha*, 26; Philonenko-Sayar and Philonenko, *L'Apocalypse d'Abraham*, 82–84.

58. See, for example, *Zohar* I.52a.

59. Philonenko-Sayar and Philonenko, *L'Apocalypse d'Abraham*, 84.

60. Thackeray, *Josephus*, 4.390–391.

61. Exod 39:29: "and the sash of fine twisted linen, and of blue, purple, and crimson yarns, embroidered with needlework; as the Lord had commanded Moses."

62. Rev 1:13: "And in the midst of the lampstands I saw one like the Son of Man, clothed with a long robe and with a golden sash across his chest."

63. See R. Winkle, "'You Are What You Wear': The Dress and Identity of Jesus as High Priest in John's Apocalypse," in *Sacrifice, Cult, and Atonement in Early Judaism and Christianity: Constituents and Critique* (eds. H. L. Wiley and C. A. Eberhart; Atlanta: SBL, 2017), 344–345.

64. Braude and Kapstein, *Pesikta de-Rab Kahana*, 467.

65. While Jacobs and Whitney render this passage with the formulae of "glory," Braude and Kapstein prefer use the term "pride" by rendering the passage in the following way: "The rows of his shields are his pride (Job 41:7). The Leviathan has the pride which is proper only to Him who is on high, and so the Holy One says to the ministering angels: Go down and wage war against him." Braude and Kapstein, *Pesikta de-Rab Kahana*, 468.

66. I. Jacobs, *The Midrashic Process: Tradition and Interpretation in Rabbinic Judaism* (Cambridge: Cambridge University Press, 1995), 160–162. Jacobs traces this attribute of glory to some Mesopotamian traditions, noting that the "interpretation of this obscure

phrase is supported by a much older source, which may preserve the prototype for the awesome, luminous monster of Jewish tradition. The Babylonian creation epic contains a description of the dreadful dragons provided for Tiamat's army by Mother Hubur. These monsters are garbed with a *pulhu*, the awesome, fiery garment of the gods, and are crowned with a *melammu*, a dazzling, divine aureole, so that when they rear up—like Leviathan—none can withstand them." Jacobs, *The Midrashic Process*, 162. Shawn Zelig Aster defines *melammu* as:

> A quality of overwhelming and overpowering strength, and it can be defined as "the covering, outer layer, or outward appearance of a person, being, or object, or rays emanating from a person or being, that demonstrate the irresistible or supreme power of that person, being, or object." A god who possesses *melammu* is sovereign, a person who possesses *melammu* is unbeatable, and a force which possesses *melammu* cannot successfully be stopped. In second-millennium mythic texts the *melammu* is portrayed as a cloak or covering, which is often radiant. But many texts ascribe *melammu* to objects that are not radiant, and radiance is not an intrinsic element of *melammu* in most periods. Beginning in the Sargonid period (late eight century BCE), *melammu* can be used as a synonym for terms meaning "radiance," but it can also be used in its more traditional meaning. When used with this traditional meaning (the standard definition of which is given above), *melammu* does not necessarily indicate a radiant phenomenon.

S. Z. Aster, "The Phenomenon of Divine and Human Radiance in the Hebrew Bible and in Northwest Semitic and Mesopotamian Literature: A Philological and Comparative Study" (Ph. D. diss.; University of Pennsylvania, 2006), 512–513. On the terminology of *melammu* and its application to the monsters and other antagonists, see L. Oppenheim, "Akkadian *pul(u)h(t)u* and *melammu*," *JAOS* 63 (1943): 31–34; E. Cassin, *La splendeur divine: Introduction à l'étude de la mentalité mésopotamienne* (Civilisations et Sociétés, 8; Paris and La Haye: Mouton, 1968); Aster, "The Phenomenon of Divine and Human Radiance," 80–82; S. Z. Aster, *The Unbeatable Light: Melammu and Its Biblical Parallels* (AOAT, 384; Münster: Ugarit-Verlag, 2012).

67. Epstein, *The Babylonian Talmud. Baba Bathra,* 75a.

68. Whitney, *Two Strange Beasts,* 134–5.

69. Whitney, *Two Strange Beasts,* 137.

70. Jacobs, *The Midrashic Process,* 162.

71. Freedman and Simon, *Midrash Rabbah,* 4.252.

72. Freedman and Simon, *Midrash Rabbah,* 8.213–214. See also *Zohar* I.142b: "Said R. Jose: 'Can it really be so, that Jacob's beauty equaled that of Adam, seeing that, according to tradition, the fleshy part of Adam's heel outshone the orb of the sun? Would you, then, say the same of Jacob?' " Sperling and Simon, *The Zohar,* 2.57.

73. *Num. Rab.* 4:8: "Adam was the world's firstborn. When he offered his sacrifice, as it says: And it pleased the Lord better than a bullock that hath horns and hoofs—he donned high priestly garments; as it says: And the Lord God made for Adam and for his wife garments of skin, and clothed them (Gen 3:21). They were robes of honor which

subsequent firstborn used. When Adam died he transmitted them to Seth. Seth transmitted them to Methusaleh. When Methusaleh died he transmitted them to Noah." Freedman and Simon, *Midrash Rabbah*, 5.101. A similar tradition is also found in *Pirke de Rabbi Eliezer* 24: "Rabbi Jehudah said: The coats which the Holy One, blessed be He, made for Adam and his wife, were with Noah in the ark." Friedlander, *Pirke de Rabbi Eliezer*, 175.

74. For discussions about the luminous garments of the protoplasts, see D. Aaron, "Shedding Light on God's Body in Rabbinic Midrashim: Reflections on the Theory of a Luminous Adam," *HTR* 90 (1997): 299–314; S. Brock, "Clothing Metaphors as a Means of Theological Expression in Syriac Tradition," in *Typus, Symbol, Allegorie bei den östlichen Vätern und ihren Parallelen im Mittelalter* (ed. M. Schmidt; EB, 4; Regensburg: Friedrich Pustet, 1982), 11–40; A. D. DeConick and J. Fossum, "Stripped before God: A New Interpretation of Logion 37 in the Gospel of Thomas," *VC* 45 (1991): 123–50 at 141; N. A. Dahl and D. Hellholm, "Garment-Metaphors: The Old and the New Human Being," in *Antiquity and Humanity: Essays on Ancient Religion and Philosophy: Presented to Hans Dieter Betz on His 70th Birthday* (eds. A. Yarbro Collins and M. M. Mitchell; Tübingen: Mohr Siebeck, 2001), 139–58; Goshen-Gottstein, "The Body as Image of God," 171–95; B. Murmelstein, "Adam, ein Beitrag zur Messiaslehre," *WZKM* 35 (1928): 242–75 at 255; N. Rubin and A. Kosman, "The Clothing of the Primordial Adam as a Symbol of Apocalyptic Time in the Midrashic Sources," *HTR* 90 (1997): 155–74; J. Z. Smith, "The Garments of Shame," *HR* 5 (1965/1966): 217–38.

75. Maher, *Targum Pseudo-Jonathan: Genesis*, 29. Later rabbinic traditions also hold that the glorious garments of Adam and Eve were made from the skin of the female Leviathan.

76. Friedlander, *Pirke de Rabbi Eliezer*, 144.

77. In relation to this tradition, Lambden notes that

> In his *Legends of the Jews* . . . Ginzberg drew attention to a probably early and "unknown Midrash" recorded in mediaeval Jewish sources to the effect that the first couple's garments were made from the skin of Leviathan, a creature which figures in a rich variety of myths and traditions recorded in ancient Near Eastern and biblical texts as well as in certain rabbinic, Christian, Gnostic, magical and other ancient literatures. This tradition is of considerable interest in the light of Leviathan's being pictured in rabbinic sources as a creature of great glory . . . and the possibility that there existed an early (tannaitic [?]) branch of Jewish mysticism surrounding Behemoth and Leviathan (reflected in such Gnostic texts as the cosmological Diagram of the Ophians mentioned in Origen's *Contra Celsum* [6.25] [?]). There appears to be some connection between rabbinic Adam speculation and the traditions about Leviathan. Garment imagery and eschatological themes are connected with this complex of traditions.

S. N. Lambden, "From Fig Leaves to Fingernails: Some Notes on the Garments of Adam and Eve in the Hebrew Bible and Select Early Postbiblical Jewish Writings," in *A Walk in the Garden: Biblical, Iconographical and Literary Images of Eden* (eds. P. Morris and D. Sawyer; JSOTSS, 136; Sheffield: Sheffield Academic Press, 1992), 74–90 at 87–88.

78. Whitney, *Two Strange Beasts*, 137. On this, see also Ginzberg, *The Legends of the Jews*, 5.42, note 123.

79. Epstein, *The Babylonian Talmud. Baba Bathra*, 75a.

Chapter Four. Apocalyptic Scapegoat Traditions in the Book of Revelation

1. H. Danby, *The Mishnah* (Oxford: Oxford University Press, 1992), 170.

2. The tradition of the scarlet band is also reflected in *m. Shekalim* 4:2: "The [Red] Heifer and the scapegoat and the crimson thread were bought with the *Terumah* from the Shekel-chamber." Danby, *The Mishnah*, 155; *m. Shabbat* 9:3: "Whence do we learn that they tie a strip of crimson on the head of the scapegoat? Because it is written, though your sins be as scarlet they shall be as white as snow." Danby, *The Mishnah*, 108.

3. *m. Yoma* 4:2 attests to the initial "clothing" of the two goats of the Yom Kippur ritual, in which one crimson band is tied around the horns of the scapegoat, while the other is tied around the neck of the immolated goat: "He bound a thread of crimson wool on the head of the scapegoat and he turned it towards the way by which it was to be sent out; and on the he-goat that was to be slaughtered [he bound a thread] about its throat." Danby, *The Mishnah*, 166.

4. A. Dorman, " 'Commit Injustice and Shed Innocent Blood': Motives behind the Institution of the Day of Atonement in the Book of *Jubilees*," in *The Day of Atonement: Its Interpretation in Early Jewish and Christian Traditions* (eds. T. Hieke and T. Nicklas; TBN, 15; Leiden: Brill, 2012), 57; Orlov, *Divine Scapegoats*, 24–28.

5. R. Hiers, " 'Binding and Loosing': The Matthean Authorizations," *JBL* 104 (1985): 233–250 at 233. It also can be understood as release from the oath placed on the cultic animal by the high priest, following later rabbinic usage. Hiers, "Binding and Loosing," 233.

6. C. H. T. Fletcher-Louis, "The Revelation of the Sacral Son of Man," in *Auferstehung-Resurrection* (eds. F. Avemarie and H. Lichtenberger; WUNT, 1.135; Tübingen: Mohr Siebeck, 2001), 284; J. A. Emerton, "Binding and Loosing—Forgiving and Retaining," *JTS* 13 (1962): 325–31 at 329–30.

7. See *b. Yoma* 67a: "What did he do? He divided the thread of crimson wool, and tied one half to the rock, the other half between its horns, and pushed it from behind. And it went rolling down and before it had reached half its way down hill it was dashed to pieces. He came back and sat down under the last booth until it grew dark. And from when on does it render his garments unclean? From the moment he has gone outside the wall of Jerusalem. R. Simeon says: from the moment he pushes it into the Zok." Epstein, *The Babylonian Talmud: Yoma*, 67a; *y. Yoma* 6:3: "All during Simeon the Just's lifetime he [the scapegoat] did not fall down half the mountain before he dissolved into limbs; after Simeon the Just's death he fled to the desert and was eaten by the Saracens." *The Jerusalem Talmud. Second Order: Mo'ed. Tractates Pesahim and Yoma* (ed. and trans. H. W. Guggenheimer; SJ, 74; Berlin: Walter de Gruyter, 2013), 559; *Targum Pseudo-Jonathan* on Lev. 16:21–22:

> Aaron shall lay both his hands on the head of the live goat, in this fashion: his right hand upon his left. He shall confess over it all the iniquities of the children of Israel and all their rebellions, whatever their sins; he shall put them on the head of the goat with a declared and explicit oath by the great and glorious Name. And he shall let (it) go, in charge of a man who has been designated previously, to go to the desert of Soq, that is Beth Haduri. The goat shall carry on himself all their sins to a desolate place; and the man shall let the goat go into the desert of Soq, and the goat shall go up on the mountains of Beth Haduri, and the blast of wind from before the Lord will thrust him down and he will die.

Targum Neofiti 1, Leviticus; Targum Pseudo-Jonathan, Leviticus (eds. M. McNamara et al.; ArBib, 3; Collegeville, MN: Liturgical Press, 1994), 169.

8. *Barnabas* 7:6–11.

9. Justin Martyr's *Dialogue with Trypho* 40:4–5.

10. Tertullian's *Against Marcion* 3:7 and *Against the Jews* 14:9.

11. Orlov, *Divine Scapegoats,* 9–36.

12. Knibb, *The Ethiopic Book of Enoch*, 2.87–88.

13. D. Olson, *Enoch: A New Translation: The Ethiopic Book of Enoch, or 1 Enoch* (North Richland Hills, TX: Bibal Press, 2004), 34.

14. Stökl Ben Ezra, *The Impact of Yom Kippur,* 87; Olson, *Enoch:A New Translation*, 38.

15. Stökl Ben Ezra, *The Impact of Yom Kippur*, 88.

16. A. Geiger, "Einige Worte über das Buch Henoch," *JZWL* 3 (1864): 196–204 at 200.

17. See *Targum Pseudo-Jonathan* to Lev 16:10: "The goat on which the lot of Azazel fell shall be set alive before the Lord to make atonement for the sinfulness of the people of the house of Soq, that is Beth Haduri." McNamara et al., *Targum Neofiti 1, Leviticus; Targum Pseudo-Jonathan: Leviticus*, 167.

18. In *Apoc. Ab.* 13:7–14, the following mysterious encounter between the heavenly high priest Yahoel and the celestial scapegoat Azazel takes place:

> Reproach is on you, Azazel! Since Abraham's portion is in heaven, and yours is on earth, since you have chosen it and desired it to be the dwelling place of your impurity. Therefore the Eternal Lord, the Mighty One, has made you a dweller on earth. And because of you [there is] the wholly-evil spirit of the lie, and because of you [there are] wrath and trials on the generations of impious men. Since the Eternal Mighty God did not send the righteous, in their bodies, to be in your hand, in order to affirm through them the righteous life and the destruction of impiety. . . . Hear, adviser! Be shamed by me, since you have been appointed to tempt not all the righteous! Depart from this man! You cannot deceive him, because he is the enemy of you and of those who follow you and who love what you desire. For behold, the garment which in heaven was formerly yours has been set aside for him, and the corruption which was on him has gone over to you.

Kulik, *Retroverting Slavonic Pseudepigrapha,* 20.

19. *Apoc. Ab.* 13:8: "Since Abraham's portion is in heaven, and yours is *on earth,* since you have chosen it and desired it to be the dwelling place of your impurity." Kulik, *Retroverting Slavonic Pseudepigrapha,* 20.

20. *Apoc. Ab.* 14:5: "May you be the fire brand of the *furnace of the earth*!" Kulik, *Retroverting Slavonic Pseudepigrapha,* 21.

21. Kulik, *Retroverting Slavonic Pseudepigrapha,* 20.

22. On Yom Kippur traditions in the Book of Revelation, see P. Carrington, *The Meaning of Revelation* (London: SPCK, 1931), 348, 392; D. T. Niles, *As Seeing the Invisible* (New York: Harper and Brothers, 1961), 110–113; A. Farrer, *A Rebirth of Images* (Gloucester, MA: Peter Smith, 1970), 177–178; J. M. Ford, *Revelation* (AB, 38; Garden City, NY: Doubleday, 1975), 277, 287; G. L. Carey, "The Lamb of God and Atonement Theories," *Tyndale Bulletin* 32 (1981): 97–122; K. A. Strand, "An Overlooked Old Testament Background to Rev 11:1," *AUSS* 22 (1984): 317–325; B. Snyder, "Combat Myth in the Apocalypse: The Liturgy of the Day of the Lord and the Dedication of the Heavenly Temple" (PhD diss.; Graduate Theological Union, 1991); D. Davis, *The Heavenly Court Judgment of Revelation 4–5* (Lanham, MD: University Press of America, 1992), 220–226; A. R. Treiyer, *The Day of Atonement and the Heavenly Judgment* (Siloam Springs, AR: Creation Enterprises International, 1992); J. Paulien, "The Role of the Hebrew Cultus, Sanctuary, and Temple in the Plot and Structure of the Book of Revelation," *AUSS* 33 (1995): 245–64 at 255–256; E. Lupieri, "Apocalisse, sacerdozio e Yom Kippur," *ASE* 19/1 (2002): 11–21; R. Stefanovic, *Revelation of Jesus Christ: Commentary on the Book of Revelation* (Berrien Springs, MI: Andrews University Press, 2002), 31–32; J. Ben-Daniel and G. Ben-Daniel, *The Apocalypse in the Light of the Temple: A New Approach to the Book of Revelation* (Jerusalem: Beit Yochanan, 2003); R. S. Boustan, *From Martyr to Mystic: Rabbinic Martyrology and the Making of Merkavah Mysticism* (TSAJ, 112; Tübingen: Mohr Siebeck, 2005), 197.

23. Orlov, *Divine Scapegoats,* 66.

24. Orlov, *Divine Scapegoats,* 73–4.

25. Philonenko-Sayar and Philonenko, *L'Apocalypse d'Abraham,* 68.

26. Lev 16:22: "The goat shall bear on itself all their iniquities to a barren region; and the goat shall be set free in the wilderness."

27. The biblical roots of the motif of the incarceration of heavenly beings in the subterranean realm can be found in Isa 24:21–22: "On that day the Lord will punish the host of heaven in heaven, and on earth the kings of the earth. They will be gathered together like prisoners in a pit; they will be shut up in a prison, and after many days they will be punished." Regarding this tradition, see D. D. Aune, *Revelation 17–22* (WBC, 52C; Nashville: Nelson, 1998), 1078.

28. In relation to this tradition, Patrick Tiller suggests that "the temporary rocky prison of Asael may be somehow related to the offering of a live goat, which bears the sins of Israel, to Azazel on the Day of Atonement (Leviticus 16)." P. A. Tiller, *A Commentary on the Animal Apocalypse of 1 Enoch* (EJL, 4; Atlanta: Scholars, 1993), 371.

29. Scholars note that the complex nature of the imagery of angelic imprisonment in early Enochic materials operates with various types of subterranean/desert prisons,

temporary as well as permanent. Sometimes these separate entities are combined into a single prison. With respect to this, Tiller observes that

> In both the *Book of the Watchers* and the *Animal Apocalypse*, there are two prisons into which the Watchers will be cast. The first, a temporary prison, is described as two separate places in 10:4–5 (=88.1) and 10:12 (=88:3). In 18:12–16 and 21:1–6 these two places are combined into a single prison for both the wandering and the fallen angels. In the later part of the *Book of the Watchers* (18:12–16; 21:1–6), this prison is not an abyss at all but a dark, desert wasteland. In chapters 6–12, it is not clear whether the temporary prisons are abysses or not. The permanent prison, the abyss of fire, is described in 10:6, 13; 18:9–11; and 21:7–10 in the *Book of the Watchers* and in 90:24–25 in the *Animal Apocalypse*. The abyss described by Jude seems to be a composite of all of these prisons: it is dark (10:4–5; 88:1); it is reserved for the wandering stars (18:12–16; 21:1–6); and it is eternal (10:6, 13; 21:7–10).

Tiller, *A Commentary on the Animal Apocalypse*, 252–254.

30. Rev 20:14: "Then Death and Hades were thrown into the lake of fire. This is the second death, the lake of fire."

31. Knibb, *The Ethiopic Book of Enoch*, 2.88.

32. It is possible that the loosing of the band at the end of the ritual signified the forgiveness of the Israelite sins. Some studies point to the connection of the formulae of loosing with the theme of forgiveness. On this, see Hiers, "Binding and Loosing," 234.

33. Scholars have noted that the binding motif was very prominent in the tradition of the fall of the Watchers. On this, see R. Bauckham, *Jude, 2 Peter* (WBC, 50; Waco, TX: Word Books, 1983), 53. On the binding motif, see also *1 Enoch* 13:1; 14:5; 18:16; 21:3–6; 54:3–5; 56:1–4; 88:1; 4QEnGiants 8:14; *Jub.* 5:6; 10:7–11; *2 Enoch* 7:2; *2 Bar.* 56:13; *Sib. Or.* 2.289; Origen, *Contra Celsum* 5:52.

34. A curious parallel to the motif of a great chain can be found in *1 Enoch* 54, where Enoch sees iron chains of "immeasurable weight" that are prepared for "the hosts of Asael/Azazel." *1 Enoch* 54:3–5 reads: "And there my eyes saw how they made instruments for them—iron chains of immeasurable weight. And I asked the angel of peace who went with me, saying: 'These chain-instruments—for whom are they being prepared?' And he said to me: 'These are being prepared for the hosts of Azazel, that they may take them and throw them into the lowest part of Hell; and they will cover their jaws with rough stones, as the Lord of Spirits commanded.'" Knibb, *The Ethiopic Book of Enoch*, 2.138. The peculiar details of the punishment, which includes the motif of "rough stones," brings to mind Asael's demise in *1 Enoch* 10.

35. Charles argued that:

> This idea of binding the powers of evil in prison for an undefined period is already found in Isa 24:22, and of their final judgment in xxiv. These powers consist of the host of heaven and the kings of the earth. This idea of the angels and the kings of the earth being judged together reappears in *1*

> *Enoch* 53:4–54:5, and the idea of the binding of the fallen angels in a place of temporary punishment till the day of the final judgment is found in *1 Enoch* 18:12–16, 19:1–2, 21:1–6, from which the final place of their punishment an abyss of fire is carefully distinguished, 10:13–15, 18:11, 21:7–10, 54:6, 90:24–25. Their leader Azazel is bound in a place by himself (10:4–5) as a preliminary punishment, but at the final judging is to be cast into a place of everlasting punishment (10:6). In nearly all cases the evil spirits are spoken of in *1 Enoch* as being "bound" in a preliminary place of punishment, just as in Isa 24:22 and in our text.

R. H. Charles, *A Critical and Exegetical Commentary on the Revelation of St. John* (ICC; 2 vols.; Edinburgh: T&T Clark, 1920), 2.141–142.

36. David Aune notes that in Rev 20:1–3, 7–10:

> (1) An angel descends from heaven with a key and a chain (v. 1). (2) The angel seizes and binds Satan (v. 2a). (3) Satan will be imprisoned one thousand years (v. 2b). (4) Satan is cast into a pit that is locked and sealed (v. 3). (5) Satan is released for an unspecified period (vv. 3b, 7–9). (6) Satan and his associates are cast into the lake of fire for eternal torment (v 10). *1 Enoch* 10:4–6 contains the following motifs: (1) God sends an angel (Raphael). (2) Azazel (an alias for Satan) is bound by the angel. (3) Azazel is thrown into darkness and imprisoned "forever." (4) The time of imprisonment, however, will actually end at the great day of judgment. (5) On the great day of judgment Azazel is thrown into the fire. A similar sequence is evident in *1 Enoch* 10:11–13: (1) God sends an angel (Michael). (2) The angel binds Semyaza (another alias for Satan) and his associates. (3) They are imprisoned under the earth. (4) The period of imprisonment is limited to seventy generations. (5) On the day of judgment they are thrown into the abyss of fire.

Aune, *Revelation 17–22*, 1078. Aune concludes his comparative analysis with the following: "Since the narrative pattern found twice in Rev 20:1–10 (i.e., in vv. 1–3 and 7–10) also occurs twice in *1 Enoch*, it seems likely that both authors are dependent on a traditional eschatological scenario. The enumeration of motifs found in these three passages exhibits a striking similarity, though John has introduced the innovation of the temporary release of Satan." Aune, *Revelation 17–22*, 1078–1079.

37. K. C. Bautch, "The Fall and Fate of Renegade Angels: The Intersection of Watchers Traditions and the Book of Revelation," in *The Fallen Angels Traditions* (eds. A. Kim Harkins et al.; CBQMS, 53; Washington, DC: The Catholic Biblical Association of America, 2014), 69–93.

38. Bautch, "The Fall and Fate of Renegade Angels," 83.

39. For Grabbe,

> Although there is no explicit reference to the scapegoat ceremony, Rev 20:1–3 has clear connections with *1 Enoch* 10:4–5. Note the common features: Asael is bound prior to the judgment just as is Satan. This binding

> seems to include chains, according to *1 Enoch* 54:3–5, though the exact date of the Parables is disputed. Just as Satan is cast into the abyss, so are Asael and others according to Syncellus' version of *1 Enoch* 9:4: "Then the Most High commanded the holy archangels, and they bound their leaders [sc. of the fallen angels] and threw them into the abyss until the judgment." In the final judgment, just as Satan is cast into a "lake of fire" . . . so Asael and his companions are cast into an "abyss of fire". . . . Thus, the punishment of Satan has been assimilated to the Asael tradition of *1 Enoch*.

L. L. Grabbe, "The Scapegoat Tradition: A Study in Early Jewish Interpretation," *JSJ* 18 (1987): 165–79 at 160–61.

40. Stökl Ben Ezra, *The Impact of Yom Kippur,* 88.

41. Concerning the punishment of Asael and other fallen angels in the *Book of the Watchers*, Archie Wright notes that:

> *1 Enoch* 10:4–15 describes the punishment of the Watchers for their crimes against God and His creation. Asa'el is first to face his punishment for his role in the Instruction motif of *BW* (10:4–6, 8). He will be bound and cast into the darkness where he will be entombed until the Day of Judgment at which time he will be destroyed in the fire. The angels from the Shemihazah tradition face a similar punishment in 10:11–14. They will first view the death of their offspring (10:12) and secondly, they shall be bound under the earth until their judgment (10:12). The judgment occurs after seventy generations of entombment at which time they shall be cast into the fire where they will be destroyed (10:13–14).

A. T. Wright, *The Origin of Evil Spirits: The Reception of Genesis 6.1–4 in Early Jewish Literature* (WUNT, 2.198; Tübingen: Mohr Siebeck, 2005), 145–146. Other Enochic booklets reaffirm the same pattern:

> The pattern recurs in the *Animal Apocalypse* as the Watchers are first consigned to an abyss (*1 Enoch* 88:1, 3) described as deep, dark and of the earth. At the time of the eschaton, the angels are brought forward for judgment (*1 Enoch* 90:21) and then thrown into a fiery abyss along with other sinners (*1 Enoch* 90:24–26). The *Book of Parables* describes a similar fate: chains are prepared for the host of Azazel (a later rendering of Asael and a reference to one of the Watchers) so that they might be thrown into an abyss of complete judgment and covered with jagged stones (cf. *1 Enoch* 10:5). On the day of judgment, we are told, the archangels will throw the rebels into a burning furnace because they became servants of Satan and led astray humankind (54:3–6).

Bautch, "The Fall and Fate of Renegade Angels," 84.

42. In relation to the dynamics of the scapegoat ritual, Jacob Milgrom points out that "purgation and elimination rites go together in the ancient world. Exorcism of

impurity is not enough; its power must be eliminated. An attested method is to banish it to its place of origin (the wilderness or the netherworld) or to some place where its malefic powers could work in the interest of the sender." J. Milgrom, *Leviticus. A Book of Ritual and Ethics. A Continental Commentary* (Minneapolis; Fortress, 2004), 172.

43. P. de Villiers, "Prime Evil and its Many Faces in the Book of Revelation," *Neotestamentica* 34 (2000): 57–85 at 62.

44. De Villiers, "Prime Evil," 63–4.

45. *m. Yoma* 4:2: "He bound a thread of crimson wool on the head of the scapegoat and he turned it towards the way by which it was to be sent out; and on the he-goat that was to be slaughtered [he bound a thread] about its throat." Danby, *The Mishnah*, 166.

46. E. Lohmeyer, *Die Offenbarung des Johannes* (HNT, 16; Tübingen: Mohr, 1970), 99; Yarbro Collins, *The Combat Myth*, 79.

47. Charles, *Revelation*, 1.318–319; Yarbro Collins, *The Combat Myth*, 77.

48. D. D. Aune, *Revelation 6–16* (WBC, 52B; Nashville: Nelson, 1998), 683; C. R. Koester, *Revelation: A New Translation with Introduction and Commentary* (AYB, 38A; New Haven, CT: Yale University Press, 2014), 545.

49. *m. Yoma* 6:8: "R. Ishmael says: Had they not another sign also?—a thread of crimson wool was tied to the door of the Sanctuary and when the he-goat reached the wilderness the thread turned white; for it is written, Though your sins be as scarlet they shall be as white as snow." Danby, *The Mishnah*, 170.

50. *m. Shabbat* 9:3: "Whence do we learn that they tie a strip of crimson on the head of the scapegoat? Because it is written, Though your sins be as scarlet they shall be as white as snow." Danby, *The Mishnah*, 108.

51. *b. Yoma* 39a: "Our Rabbis taught: Throughout the forty years that Simeon the Righteous ministered, the lot ['For the Lord'] would always come up in the right hand; from that time on, it would come up now in the right hand, now in the left. And [during the same time] the crimson-colored strap would become white. From that time on it would at times become white, at others not." Epstein, *The Babylonian Talmud. Yoma*, 39a; *b. Yoma* 39b: "Our Rabbis taught: During the last forty years before the destruction of the Temple the lot ['For the Lord'] did not come up in the right hand; nor did the crimson-colored strap become white." Epstein, *The Babylonian Talmud. Yoma*, 39b.

52. *b. Yoma* 67a:

> But let him tie the whole [thread] to the rock?—Since it is his duty [to complete his work with] the he-goat, perhaps the thread might become fast white, and he would be satisfied. But let him tie the whole thread between its horns?—At times its head [in falling] is bent and he would not pay attention. Our Rabbis taught: In the beginning they would tie the thread of crimson wool on the entrance of the Ulam without: if it became white they rejoiced; if it did not become white, they were sad and ashamed. Thereupon they arranged to tie it to the entrance of the Ulam within. But they were still peeping through and if it became white, they rejoiced, whereas, if it did not become white, they grew sad and ashamed. Thereupon they arranged to tie one half to the rock and the other half between its horns. R. Nahum b. Papa said in the name of R. Eleazar ha-Kappar: Originally they used to

> tie the thread of crimson wool to the entrance of the Ulam within, and as soon as the he-goat reached the wilderness, it turned white. Then they knew that the commandment concerning it had been fulfilled, as it is said: If your sins be as scarlet, they shall be as white wool.

Epstein, *The Babylonian Talmud. Yoma*, 67a.

53. Cf. also *m. Shabbat* 9:3: "Whence do we learn that they tie a strip of crimson on the head of the scapegoat? Because it is written, Though your sins be as scarlet they shall be as white as snow." Danby, *The Mishnah*, 108.

54. Lupieri, "Apocalisse, sacerdozio e Yom Kippur," 19.

55. Rev 17:3–4: "So he carried me away in the spirit into a wilderness, and I saw a woman sitting on a scarlet beast (ἐπὶ θηρίον κόκκινον) that was full of blasphemous names, and it had seven heads and ten horns. The woman was clothed in purple and scarlet (κόκκινον), and adorned with gold and jewels and pearls, holding in her hand a golden cup full of abominations and the impurities of her fornication." The *Epistle of Barnabas* uses the same terminology in its descriptions of scarlet band: *Barn.* 7:8: "and wrap a piece of scarlet wool (τὸ ἔριον τὸ κόκκινον) around its head."

56. The red colored attributes of the antagonists present a striking contrast with the white attributes of the sinless and the righteous (Rev 2:17; 3:4–5; 6:11; 7:9–14) and their eschatological leaders (Rev 1:14; 4:4). Scholars previously noted that "in Revelation the color 'white' consistently denotes purity." L. T. Stuckenbruck and M. D. Mathews, "The Apocalypse of John, *1 Enoch*, and the Question of Influence," in *Die Johannesapokalypse. Kontexte—Konzepte—Rezeption* (eds. J. Frey et al.; WUNT, 1.287. Tübingen: Mohr Siebeck, 2012), 191–234 at 198. See also D. D. Aune, *Revelation 1-5* (WBC, 52A; Dallas, TX: Word Books, 1997), 222–223.

57. Carrington, *The Meaning of Revelation*, 348, 392; Ford, *Revelation*, 277, 287.

Chapter Five. Azazel's Will

1. Kulik, *Retroverting Slavonic Pseudepigrapha*, 21; R. Rubinkiewicz, *L'Apocalypse d'Abraham en vieux slave. Introduction, texte critique, traduction et commentaire* (ŹM, 129; Lublin: Towarzystwo Naukowe Katolickiego Uniwersytetu Lubelskiego, 1987), 150.

2. Kulik, *Retroverting Slavonic Pseudepigrapha*, 21. Rubinkiewicz, *L'Apocalypse d'Abraham en vieux slave*, 150.

3. *Apoc. Ab.* 26:5: "Hear, Abraham! As the will of your father is in him, as your will is in you, so also the will desired by me is inevitable in coming days." Kulik, *Retroverting Slavonic Pseudepigrapha*, 30.

4. Athenagoras's *Legatio pro christianis* makes this distinction: "These angels, then, who fell from heaven busy themselves about the air and the earth and are no longer able to rise to the realms above the heavens. The souls of the giants are the demons (δαίμονες) who wander about the world. Both angels and demons produce (ποιέω) movements (κινήσεις)—demons movements which are akin to the natures they received, and angels movements which are akin to the lusts (ἐπιθυμίαι) with which they were possessed." *Athenagoras: Legatio and De resurrectione* (ed. W. R. Schoedel; Oxford: Clarendon, 1972), 60–61.

5. The notion of "inclination" or "*yetzer*" is often considered to be one of the most complex and misunderstood concepts of the Jewish religious tradition. *Yetzer* was especially important in the rabbinic corpora where it became "a fundamental category through which rabbis expressed their conceptions of desire, emotions, and particularly impulses to transgress their own norms." J. W. Schofer, "The Redaction of Desire: Structure and Editing of Rabbinic Teachings Concerning 'Yeṣer' ('Inclination')," *JJS* 12 (2003): 19–53 at 19.

6. On various *yetzer* anthropologies in Jewish and Christian writings, see E. S. Alexander, "Art, Argument, and Ambiguity in the Talmud: Conflicting Conceptions of the Evil Impulse in b. Sukkah 51b–52a," *HUCA* 73 (2002): 97–132; G. H. Cohen Stuart, *The Struggle in Man between Good and Evil. An Inquiry into the Origin of the Rabbinic Concept of Yeṣer Hara* (Kampen: Kok, 1984); N. Ellis, *The Hermeneutics of Divine Testing* (WUNT, 2.296; Tübingen: Mohr Siebeck, 2015), 125–152; Y. Kiel, *Sexuality in the Babylonian Talmud: Christian and Sasanian Contexts in Late Antiquity* (Cambridge: Cambridge University Press, 2016); M. Kister, "The Yetzer of Man's Heart," in *Meghillot: Studies in the Dead Sea Scrolls VIII–IX* (eds. M. Bar-Asher and D. Dimant; Jerusalem: Bialik Institute and Haifa University Press, 2010) [Hebrew], 243–284; F. C. Porter, "The Yeçer Hara: A Study in the Jewish Doctrine of Sin," in *Biblical and Semitic Studies* (Yale Historical and Critical Contributions to Biblical Science; New York: Charles Scribner's Sons, 1901), 93–156; I. Rosen-Zvi, *Demonic Desires: Yetzer Hara and the Problem of Evil in Late Antiquity* (Philadelphia: University of Pennsylvania Press, 2011); Schofer, "The Redaction of Desire," 19–53; P. W. van der Horst, "A Note on the Evil Inclination and Sexual Desire in Talmudic Literature," in *Jews and Christians in their Graeco-Roman Context: Selected Essays on Early Judaism, Samaritanism, Hellenism, and Christianity* (WUNT, 1.196; Tübingen: Mohr Siebeck, 2006), 59–65;

7. L. T. Stuckenbruck, "The Origins of Evil in Jewish Apocalyptic Tradition: Interpretation of Genesis 6:1–4 in the Second and Third Centuries BCE," in *The Fall of the Angels* (eds. Ch. Auffarth and L. T. Stuckenbruck; TBN, 6; Leiden: Brill, 2004), 87–118 at 102. Stuckenbruck further observes that "this reconstructed aetiology explains how it is that the Giants could become so openly identified as demons at a later stage." Stuckenbruck, "The Origins of Evil in Jewish Apocalyptic Tradition," 103.

8. G. W. E. Nickelsburg, *1 Enoch 1: A Commentary on the Book of Enoch, Chapters 1–36, 81–108* (Minneapolis: Fortress, 2001), 215.

9. W. Loader, *Enoch, Levi, and Jubilees on Sexuality: Attitudes Towards Sexuality in Early Enoch Literature, the Aramaic Levi Document, and the Book of Jubilees* (Grand Rapids, MI: Eerdmans, 2007), 24.

10. P. Alexander, "Demonology of the Dead Sea Scrolls," in *The Dead Sea Scrolls after Fifty Years* (eds. P. W. Flint and J. C. VanderKam; 2 vols.; Leiden: Brill, 1999), 339.

11. Alexander, "Demonology of the Dead Sea Scrolls," 339.

12. Commenting on the development of the Giants/evil spirits theme in this chapter of *1 Enoch*, James VanderKam notes that:

> The spirits of the Giants receive greater attention in *1 Enoch* 15:8–16:1. There they are usually distinguished from the Giants, although 15:8 sounds as if it is identifying the Giants as spirits. *1 Enoch* 15:9 makes the distinction

> explicit: "And evil spirits came out from their flesh because from above they were created; from the holy Watchers was their origin and first foundation. Evil spirits they will be on the earth, and spirits of the evil ones they will be called." The activities of these spirits are detailed: they do wrong, are corrupt, attack, fight, break, and cause sorrow (v. 11). According to v. 12, these "spirits will rise against the sons of men and against the women because they came out from them." *1 Enoch* 16:1 may add, though there is a textual problem, that the spirits will carry out their evil work until the judgment.

J. C. VanderKam, "The Demons in the Book of Jubilees," in *Die Dämonen: Die Dämonologie der israelitisch-jüdischen und frühchristlichen Literatur im Kontext ihrer Umwelt* (ed. A. Lange et al.; Tübingen: Mohr Siebeck, 1997), 339–364 at 349.

13. Nickelsburg points out that:

> Because they were begotten on earth, these spirits must remain on earth. Here they constitute an empire of evil spirits who wreak all manner of havoc on the human race, as the author describes in vv. 11–12. The presupposition of this passage is a belief in such a demonic realm. Its function is to explain the origins of that realm. The author employs the story in chaps. 6–11 to this end, and he uses the generational metaphor to explain the proliferation and continued existence of malevolent spirits. Here he differs from *Adam and Eve* 12–16, where the devil leads a revolt against God and is cast from heaven with his angels.

Nickelsburg, *1 Enoch 1*, 273.

14. Knibb, *The Ethiopic Book of Enoch*, 2.100–102.

15. In some traditions, the spirits of the Giants as well as the spirits of the Watchers are depicted as harming people. In relation to this, Loren Stuckenbruck says the following:

> For all its emphasis on the spirits of the Giants, the *Book of Watchers* in the visions suggests that their progenitors, fallen angels, also continue to exert their influence following the flood. Whereas according to the separate tradition of 10:12 the fettered Watchers are consigned [for] seventy generations to a place "below the hills of the ground," in the account of Enoch's journey through the cosmos they are said to lead people to sacrifice to demons until the time of their eschatological judgement (19:1). The Greek recension in Codex Panopolitanus adds that the spirits of these angels "will harm people" (λυμαίνεται τοὺς ἀνθρώπους), a function that is generically reminiscent of what the spirits of the Giants do (cf. 15:11).

Stuckenbruck, "The Origins of Evil," 104.

16. Nickelsburg, *1 Enoch 1*, 272. Wright points out that, in comparison with the human spirit, which is created directly by God, "the spirit of the giant is a corrupted spirit that evolved from the fallen angels." He further notes that "the Spirit of God (רוח) within humans results in the existence of 'good' within creation, while the spirit of the

Watchers (רוח) within the Giants results in the origin of evil." A. T. Wright, *The Origin of Evil Spirits*, 164.

17. Nickelsburg, *1 Enoch 1*, 272.

18. Knibb, *The Ethiopic Book of Enoch*, 2.106.

19. Wright, *The Origin of Evil Spirits*, 223. He further elaborates that:

> The death of the Giants reveals something about the nature of their spirits. They are considered evil spirits because they were born on the earth; they are a mixed product of a spiritual being (Watcher angel) and a physical, and a somewhat spiritually undefined human. The resulting entities are identified in *I Enoch* 15:8 as "strong spirits," "evil spirits," which come out of their bodies at their death. The spirit of the Giant is in a class similar to the spirit of a Watcher, but with distinct differences. There are two main points that identify important characteristics of the nature of the Giants' spirits in relation to the angelic Watchers. First, we find no evidence that upon the death of their physical body the spirits of the Giants are able to transform themselves into human form in order to have intercourse with the women, as did their fathers. The second point involves the necessity for the Watchers to be bound in Tartarus in order to halt their activity, while the spirits of the Giants, following the death of their physical body, are allowed to roam freely upon the earth. The ability to roam about the earth links the nature of the evil spirits of the Giants to the spiritual nature of the Watchers prior to their fall. What is not clear is why these beings are given that freedom. However, the Watcher tradition in *Jubilees* indicates that this semi-freedom was required in order for them to operate within the divine economy.

Wright, *The Origin of Evil Spirits*, 148–149.

20. Wright, *The Origin of Evil Spirits*, 214.

21. Such a connection can also be seen in the Qumran materials. John Collins points out that "the Damascus Document cites the story of the Watchers in the course of an admonition to 'walk perfectly on all his paths and not follow after thoughts of the guilty inclination and lascivious eyes' (CD II 15–16)." J. J. Collins, *Apocalypticism in the Dead Sea Scrolls* (London & New York: Routledge, 2002), 36.

22. In relation to the conceptual developments found in *Jubilees,* Annette Reed observes that:

> *Jubilees* takes a similar approach to the issue of angelic culpability for human suffering. As in *1 Enoch* 15:8–16:1 (*BW*), the demons that plague humankind are the spirits of the Watchers' hybrid sons (*Jub.* 10:5), and, as in *1 Enoch* 19:1 (*BW*), the demons help to spread idolatry (*Jub.* 11:4–5). Yet, the meaning of these traditions has changed with their displacement into a different narrative context. When the "polluted demons began to lead astray the children of Noah's sons," Noah pleads with God to bind them in the "place of judgment" so that they may not "rule over the spirits of the

> living" (10:1–6). This occasions *Jubilees*' rather off-handed revelation of a link between the Watchers and present-day demons, inasmuch as Noah's petition alludes to the Watchers as "the fathers of these spirits" (10:5). In response to the petition, God orders the angels to bind all the evil spirits (10:7). Just then, an objection is raised by Mastema, the "leader of the spirits": Lord creator, leave some of them before me; let them listen to me and do everything that I tell them, because if none of them is left for me I shall not be able to exercise the authority of my will among humankind. For they are meant for destroying and misleading before my punishment, because the evil of humankind is great (*Jub.* 10:8). Taking both petitions into account, God arrives at a compromise. He leaves one-tenth of the demons unbound (10:9), and He orders the angels to teach Noah "all their medicines" (10:10) so that "he could cure by means of the earth's plants" (10:12).

A. Y. Reed, *Fallen Angels and the History of Judaism and Christianity: The Reception of Enochic Literature* (Cambridge: Cambridge University Press, 2005), 93–94.

23. Concerning the differences between this passage and *1 Enoch* 15, Chad Pierce notes that

> while *Jubilees* is not primarily concerned with the giant offspring of the watchers, it does place significant emphasis on the role of the spirits that emanated from the Giants, especially concerning how they interact with humans. Unlike *1 Enoch* 15, *Jubilees* never directly states that evil spirits are the beings that emanated from the Giants upon their mutual destruction. However, if *Jub.* 5:1, which states that the watchers are the fathers of the Giants is combined with 10:5, which names the watchers as the father of evil spirits, it appears that *Jubilees* assumes the etiology of evil spirits from the *Book of Watchers*. One main difference, however, is that the Giants seem to have assumed their disembodied state and begun their leading astray prior to the flood (5:8–9; 7:5).

C. T. Pierce, *Spirits and the Proclamation of Christ: 1 Peter 3:18–22 in Light of Sin and Punishment Traditions in Early Jewish and Christian Literature* (WUNT, 2.305; Tübingen: Mohr Siebeck, 2011), 116.

24. VanderKam, *Jubilees*, 2.59.

25. In relation to *Jubilees*' etiology, Ellis observes that "*Jubilees* moves beyond Enoch to construct a supernatural paradigm in which the demonic offspring of the Watchers become the cause of seduction and then the destruction of humankind both before (*Jub.* 7:27–28) and after the Flood narrative (*Jub.* 10:1–11)." Ellis, *The Hermeneutics*, 63.

26. Reed, *Fallen Angels*, 94. Reed further notes that "the *Book of the Watchers* was clearly a privileged source and intertext for the author of *Jubilees*, and his description of Enoch's composition of this text (4:21–22) suggests that he granted it an authority akin to Genesis itself." Reed, *Fallen Angels*, 94.

27. Wright, *The Origin of Evil Spirits*, 155.

28. Stuckenbruck, "The Origins of Evil," 112. Stuckenbruck further notes that

> the demonic spirits which, after the time of the flood, continue to bring afflictions to humanity represent only one tenth of their original number. Their post-diluvian activity is made possible through the petitions of their chief Mastema, who asked that God, though having commanded the angels to bind all the spirits for judgement, allow a small proportion of the evil spirits to corrupt humans, lead them astray, and to cause suffering through illness (10:8, 12). Evil, identified with activities of the spirits of Giants, is characterized as something which only operates by divine permission; therefore, evil powers are ultimately limited (10:13) and their ultimate defeat is assured (10:8).

Stuckenbruck, "The Origins of Evil in Jewish Apocalyptic Tradition," 112.

29. Clarifying the distinction between angels and demons, Kevin Sullivan also points to the angels' inability "to possess human beings." Sullivan notes that

> as otherworldly beings, angels and demons have some similarities. Their common traits are mentioned in many ancient texts: immortality, special knowledge, and so on, but the distinguishing characteristic of demons from the New Testament period onward seems to be their ability to possess human beings. Angels are not said to possess humans, so the better parallel for demons is spirits, while angels may be something of a class unto themselves. The Watchers, then, do not fit one of the key criteria for being considered demons as they came to be known in New Testament and later writings, that is, they do not possess human beings. . . . The demons' invasion of the human being, causing mental or physical illness seems to be a key difference between them and angels.

K. Sullivan, "The Watchers Traditions in 1 Enoch 6–16: The Fall of Angels and the Rise of Demons," in *The Watchers in Jewish and Christian Traditions* (eds. A. Kim Harkins, K. C. Bautch, and J. C. Endres; Minneapolis: Fortress, 2014), 91–103 at 99. On this, see also K. Sullivan, "Spiritual Inhabitation in the Gospel of Mark: A Reconsideration of Mark 8:33," *Henoch* 32 (2010): 401–19.

30. Alexander, "Demonology of the Dead Sea Scrolls," 339.

31. Some scholars point to a possible angelic status of Mastema. Thus, Archie Wright notes that "it seems likely that the origin of Mastema as the leader of the demonic realm began in *Jubilees* and the Qumran literature. . . . It seems unlikely that he is the fallen angel of later Christian tradition, but rather an angel or entity that did the work of God in the area of the punishment of the enemies of God and testing the faith of the people of God (see Job 1:6; 2:1)." Wright, *The Origin of Evil Spirits*, 158. Jacques van Ruiten points out that in *Jubilees* "the demons are put under the authority of Mastema (10:8; 11:5; 19:28; 49:2; cf. 11:11; 17:16; 18:9, 12; 48:2, 3–4, 9, 12–18). This leader of

the demons is probably no demon himself, but a sort of evil angel. He is, however, not one of the watchers, because they are tied up in the depths of the earth until the great day of judgment (5:6–11)." J. van Ruiten, "Abram's Prayer: The Coherence of the Pericopes in Jubilees 12:16–27," in *Enoch and the Mosaic Torah: The Evidence of Jubilees* (eds. G. Boccaccini and G. Ibba; Grand Rapids, MI: Eerdmans, 2009), 211–228 at 228. Segal notes "Mastema himself is not one of the spirits, but rather, he is accorded a higher status, presumably that of an angel." M. Segal, *The Book of Jubilees: Rewritten Bible, Redaction, Ideology and Theology* (JSJSS, 117; Leiden: Brill, 2007), 176. In another part of his study, Segal again suggests that "Mastema is presumably an angel, as can be discerned from his opposition to the angel of the presence (chs. 17–18 and 48), and against God (ch. 10)." Segal, *The Book of Jubilees,* 178.

32. *Jub.* 10:8: "Mastema, the leader of the spirits." VanderKam, *Jubilees,* 2.52. Van Ruiten notes that "the demons do everything Mastema tells them, so that he is able to exercise the authority of his will among mankind to punish them for their evil (cf. 10:8)." Van Ruiten, "Abram's Prayer," 228. A similar situation is seen in Athenagoras's *Legatio pro christianis* which speaks about the "ruler" of the "the souls of the giants":

> The souls of the giants are the demons (δαίμονες) who wander about the world. . . . The prince (ἄρχων) of matter, as may be seen from what happens, directs and administers things in a manner opposed to God's goodness . . . But since the demonic impulses and activities (δαιμονικαὶ κινήσεις καὶ ἐνέργειαι) of the hostile spirit (πνεῦμα) bring these wild attacks—indeed we see them move men from within and from without, one man one way and another man another, some individually and some as nations, one at a time and all together, because of our kinship (συμπάθεια) with matter and our affinity with the divine. . . . But to the extent that it depends on the reason peculiar to each individual and the activity (ἐνέργεια) of the ruling prince (ἄρχοντος) and his attendant demons (δαιμόνων), one man is swept along one way, another man another way, even though all have the same rationality (λογισμός) within.

Schoedel, *Athenagoras,* 60–3. On this tradition, see D. Giulea, "The Watchers' Whispers: Athenagoras's Legatio 25,1–3 and the Book of the Watchers," *VC* 61 (2007): 258–281.

33. L. T. Stuckenbruck, *The Myth of Rebellious Angels: Studies in Second Temple Judaism and New Testament Texts* (WUNT, 1.335; Tübingen: Mohr Siebeck, 2014), 96. *Jubilees* appears to intentionally maintain a distance between Mastema and "spirits." In this respect, Michael Segal suggests that "Mastema refers to the spirits as a crystallized group, to which he does not belong: 'leave some of them before me; let them listen to me and do everything that I tell them. . . .' (10:8)." Segal, *The Book of Jubilees,* 176.

34. Stuckenbruck, *The Myth of Rebellious Angels,* 97. With respect to Mastema's leading role, James VanderKam notes that "*Jubilees* connects the demons / evil spirits with many kinds of sin, but bloodshed and idolatry are prominently consistent among them. In general the demons / evil spirits are the agents of Mastema in causing evil of

every sort in human society—evils that remind one of what happened before the flood." VanderKam, "The Demons in the Book of Jubilees," 345.

35. Wright, *The Origin of Evil Spirits*, 157.

36. Wright, *The Origin of Evil Spirits*, 157. Ellis also notes that "*Jubilees* extends the tradition of the Watchers, derived from the Enoch tradition, into a combination of demonic enemies and a Satanic prosecutorial figure active in the heavenly court." Ellis, *The Hermeneutics*, 63.

37. A. Y. Reed, "Enochic and Mosaic Traditions in Jubilees: The Evidence of Angelology and Demonology," in *Enoch and the Mosaic Torah: The Evidence of Jubilees* (eds. G. Boccaccini and G. Ibba; Grand Rapids, MI: Eerdmans, 2009), 353–68 at 357–358.

38. Ellis notes that "in a number of places Mastema serves as a substitute for God in potentially compromised roles. This occurs in *Jub.* 49:2 where Mastema takes the place of the angel of death, as well as in *Jub.* 48:2 where God's attempt to put Moses to death in Exod 5:24 is recast as the actions of Mastema." Ellis, *The Hermeneutics*, 63.

39. Stuckenbruck notes that "the *Book of Jubilees* presents demonic activity under the leadership of Mastema as an inevitable characteristic of this age until the final judgment." Stuckenbruck, *The Myth of Rebellious Angels*, 99.

40. VanderKam, *Jubilees*, 2.65.

41. For example, *Jub.* 19:28: "May the spirits of Mastema not rule over you and your descendants to remove you from following the Lord who is your God from now and forever." VanderKam, *Jubilees*, 2.115. See also *Jub.* 49:2, "all the forces of Mastema were sent to kill every first-born in the land of Egypt." VanderKam, *Jubilees*, 2.315.

42. B. H. Reynolds, "Understanding the Demonologies of the Dead Sea Scrolls: Accomplishments and Directions for the Future," *Religion Compass* 7 (2013): 103–14 at 108.

43. VanderKam, *Jubilees*, 1.75; 2.72.

44. Thus, Stuckenbruck's research highlights some distinctions between the Aramaic documents found at Qumran and the literature composed in Hebrew and between earlier "nonsectarian" and later "sectarian" literature. On these distinctions, see L. T. Stuckenbruck, "Demonic Beings and the Dead Sea Scrolls," in *Explaining Evil. Vol. 1. Definitions and Development* (ed. H. J. Ellens; 3 vols.; Santa Barbara, CA: Praeger, 2011), 121–44 at 140–41.

45. Stuckenbruck points out that "most of the extant occurrences of Belial are to be found among the sectarian, that is, the proto-Yahad texts (i.e., Damascus Document) and Yahad documents (Serek ha-Yahad, Serek ha-Milhamah, Hodayot, pesharic interpretations, and 4QCatena, 4QBerakot, and 11QMelchizedek)." Stuckenbruck, "Demonic Beings and the Dead Sea Scrolls," 137.

46. Stuckenbruck, *The Myth of Rebellious Angels*, 98.

47. Stuckenbruck notes that statistics indicate that

> Belial is by far the most frequent designation used for an evil being in the Dead Sea Scrolls. Like Mastema, there must have been a close connection between the figure and the meaning of the name, in this case "worthlessness." However, unlike Mastema, the word Belial never appears in a text affixed to the definite article, even in the position of nomen rectum. Therefore, phrases such as "dominion of Belial," "lot of Belial," "army of Belial,"

> "spirits of Belial," "congregation of Belial," and "child" or "children of Belial" and "men of Belial" all suggest that, in many cases at least, we have to do with a term that has become a proper name.

Stuckenbruck, "Demonic Beings and the Dead Sea Scrolls," 137.

48. *The Dead Sea Scrolls Study Edition* (eds. F. García Martínez and E. Tigchelaar; 2 vols.; Leiden: Brill, 1997), 132–3.

49. García Martínez and Tigchelaar, *The Dead Sea Scrolls Study Edition*, 366–7.

50. García Martínez and Tigchelaar, *The Dead Sea Scrolls Study Edition*, 570–571.

51. García Martínez and Tigchelaar, *The Dead Sea Scrolls Study Edition*, 1206–7.

52. Stuckenbruck, "Demonic Beings and the Dead Sea Scrolls," 131. Stuckenbruck, however, cautiously warns against the extension of this conceptual tendency on the entire corpus of the scrolls by noting that "it is not clear how much the widely divergent texts allow us to infer that any of the writers identified a figure designated by one name with a figure designated by another. Moreover, we cannot assume that when single figures are referred to, their designations always function as proper names rather than as descriptions." Stuckenbruck, "Demonic Beings and the Dead Sea Scrolls," 131.

53. Stuckenbruck, "Demonic Beings and the Dead Sea Scrolls," 132.

54. Rosen-Zvi, *Demonic Desires*, 50.

55. B. Wold, "Sin and Evil in the Letter of James in Light of Qumran Discoveries," *NTS* 65 (2019): 1–20 at 7.

56. *Plea for Deliverance* (11Q5 XIX, 15–16) reads: "Let not Satan rule over me, nor an evil spirit; let neither pain nor evil purpose take possession of my bones." García Martínez and Tigchelaar, *The Dead Sea Scrolls Study Edition*, 1174–5. Dealing with this passage, Stuckenbruck mentions that "here we have to do with the most classic example of a prayer against the demonic." L. Stuckenbruck, "Prayers of Deliverance from the Demonic in the Dead Sea Scrolls and Related Early Jewish Literature," in *The Changing Face of Judaism, Christianity, and Other Greco-Roman Religions in Antiquity* (eds. I. H. Henderson and G. S. Oegema; JSHRZ, 2; Gütersloh: Gütersloher Verlagshaus, 2006), 146–165 at 148.

57. Wold, "Sin and Evil in the Letter of James," 7.

58. Wold, "Sin and Evil in the Letter of James," 7–8.

59. Stuckenbruck, *The Myth of Rebellious Angels*, 201.

60. In relation to Satan's figure in this passage, Stuckenbruck suggests that

> it is not clear whether the writer has a chief demonic ruler in view (i.e., "Satan"), or uses the term functionally to refer to a being that plays an adversarial role. Its juxtaposition with "unclean spirit" may suggest that "satan" is not a proper name. . . . What is clear, nonetheless, is that the use of the term reflects a development that has gone well beyond its use in the Hebrew Bible where it denotes an angelic being that is subservient to God (cf. Num 22:22, 32; Ps 109:6; even Job 1–2 and Zech 3:1–2) or functions as a general designation for one's enemies (1 Kgs 11:23, 25; Ps 71:13; 109:20, 29).

Stuckenbruck, *The Myth of Rebellious Angels*, 202.

61. Alexander, "Demonology of the Dead Sea Scrolls," 331.

62. Apropos this category, Alexander observes that the expression "spirits of the bastards" suggests that Qumran demonology relies on the etiology of demons found in the *Book of the Watchers*. Alexander, "Demonology of the Dead Sea Scrolls," 337–338.

63. Alexander, "Demonology of the Dead Sea Scrolls," 333. On various classes of these spiritual beings in Qumran materials, see also Stuckenbruck, *The Myth of Rebellious Angels*, 83; Alexander, "Demonic Beings and the Dead Sea Scrolls," 125–131.

64. Alexander, "Demonology of the Dead Sea Scrolls," 332.

65. Alexander, "Demonology of the Dead Sea Scrolls," 332.

66. Alexander, "Demonology of the Dead Sea Scrolls," 336.

67. J. J. Collins, *Seers, Sybils and Sages in Hellenistic-Roman Judaism* (JSJSS, 54; Leiden: Brill, 1997), 293.

68. Alexander, "Demonology of the Dead Sea Scrolls," 345–6.

69. Wright further notes:

> Some of the DSS do offer examples of physical possession. It could be understood from 1QS III 20 that the sons of injustice were afflicted by evil/unclean spirits (physically possessed as were the Giants) and thus required an exorcism of the spirit. 1QS IV 20–21, although in eschatological and cosmic language, perhaps suggests such an exorcism. These lines describe, in very graphic language, the removal of the "spirit of injustice" from the structure of a man. Garcia Martinez translates the verse "ripping out all spirit of injustice from *the innermost part of his flesh*." The spirit of injustice can be related to the unclean spirit that causes defilement (see line 22), but the question that remains is: what is the innermost part of his flesh? It may be possible that this phrase is alluding to Lev 17:11, 14 with the understanding that the human soul is in the blood, which, if I may suggest, could be understood as the "innermost part of his flesh." This would imply then that the influence of an evil spirit might be upon the soul or upon the intellect of the individual. Demonic possession in the DSS then could be understood as something that affects the ethical behavior of an individual, rather than in a strict sense, denoting an invasion of the physical body.

Wright, *The Origin of Evil Spirits*, 178–9.

70. Wright, *The Origin of Evil Spirits*, 178.

71. E. Tigchelaar, "The Evil Inclination in the Dead Sea Scrolls, with a Re-Edition of 4Q468i (4QSectarian Text?)" in *Empsychoi Logoi. Religious Innovations in Antiquity. Studies in Honour of Pieter Willem van der Horst* (eds. A. Houtman, A. de Jong, and M. Misset-van der Weg; AJEC, 73; Leiden: Brill, 2008), 352.

72. Rosen-Zvi, *Demonic Desires*, 49.

73. Rosen-Zvi, *Demonic Desires*, 52.

74. Rosen-Zvi, *Demonic Desires*, 53–54.

75. On this, see D. Brakke, *Demons and the Making of the Monk: Spiritual Combat in Early Christianity* (Cambridge, MA: Harvard University Press, 2006).

76. Rosen-Zvi, *Demonic Desires*, 54.

77. Rosen-Zvi, *Demonic Desires*, 54.

78. Cohen Stuart, *The Struggle in Man*, 217.

79. Rosen-Zvi, *Demonic Desires*, 84. In another place of his study, Rosen-Zvi reminds us that "rabbinic *yetzer* should therefore not be read in the tradition of the Hellenistic quest for control over the lower parts of the psyche, but rather in the tradition of ancient Jewish and Christian demonology." Rosen-Zvi, *Demonic Desires*, 6. Rosen-Zvi thus firmly locates the *yetzer* inside the Jewish demonological tradition, "alongside entities such as Satan, Mastema, and Belial . . . reading it as a component of the ontology of evil." Rosen-Zvi, *Demonic Desires*, 6.

80. Rosen-Zvi, *Demonic Desires*, 87.

81. Loader points out that, "as in the *Parables of Enoch* and 4QAges of Creation, here Asael of the *Book of the Watchers* has become Azazel and assumed primary responsibility for their descent and sexual wrongdoing and its effects." W. Loader, *The Pseudepigrapha on Sexuality: Attitudes towards Sexuality in Apocalypses, Testaments, Legends, Wisdom, and Related Literature* (Grand Rapids, MI: Eerdmans, 2011), 107.

82. Philonenko-Sayar and Philonenko, *L'Apocalypse d'Abraham*, 31–33; Rubinkiewicz, *L'Apocalypse d'Abraham en vieux slave*, 50.

83. R. Rubinkiewicz and H. Lunt, "Apocalypse of Abraham," in *The Old Testament Pseudepigrapha* (ed. J. H. Charlesworth; 2 vols. New York: Doubleday, 1983–1985), 1.681–705 at 685. Marc Philonenko also sees Azazel's connections with the fallen angel traditions by observing that "dans le livre d'Hénoch, Azazel est l'un des deux chefs des anges déchus. Il a enseigné aux hommes toutes les iniquités commises sur la terre et révélé les mystères éternels célébrés dans le ciel. Un texte découvert dans la grotte IV de Qoumrân concerne Azazel et le mythe de la chute des anges. On peut suivre Azazel, accompagné parfois de son inquiétant acolyte Shemhazai, dans le *Targum du Pseudo-Jonathan* sur Genèse 6, 4, dans le *Livre des Géants*, dans le midrash et jusque dans la littérature mandéenne." Philonenko-Sayar and Philonenko, *L'Apocalypse d'Abraham*, 32.

84. Kulik, *Retroverting Slavonic Pseudepigrapha*, 20.

85. Kulik, *Retroverting Slavonic Pseudepigrapha*, 21.

86. Orlov, *Divine Scapegoats*, 13.

87. Kulik, *Retroverting Slavonic Pseudepigrapha*, 21.

88. Loader observes that the *Apocalypse of Abraham* "makes reference to the sexual wrongdoing of the Watchers. In doing so it uses what appears to be Enochic tradition from the *Book of the Watchers* about their defilement and binding in fiery depth of the earth and from the *Animal Apocalypse*, depicting them as stars, and about Azazel, in particular." Loader, *The Pseudepigrapha on Sexuality*, 111.

89. G. F. Moore, *Judaism in the First Centuries of the Christian Era: The Age of the Tanaaim* (3 vols; Cambridge, MA: Harvard University Press, 1924), 1.484.

90. Freedman and Simon, *Midrash Rabbah* 1.413.

91. Freedman and Simon, *Midrash Rabbah*, 4.330. See also *Lev. Rab.* 24:8: "It is the same with the celestial beings. As the Evil Inclination is non-existent among them they have but one sanctity; as it says, And the sentence by the word of the holy ones (Dan 4:14). But as for the terrestrial beings, seeing that the Evil Inclination sways them." Freedman and Simon, *Midrash Rabbah*, 4.310.

92. Milik, *The Books of Enoch: Aramaic Fragments of Qumrân Cave 4*, 327.

93. Philonenko-Sayar and Philonenko, *L'Apocalypse d'Abraham*, 68.

94. Rubinkiewicz, *L'Apocalypse d'Abraham en vieux slave*, 148.

95. On the Nephilim and their identification with the Giants, see L. T. Stuckenbruck, *The Book of Giants from Qumran. Texts, Translation, and Commentary* (TSAJ, 63; Tübingen: Mohr Siebeck, 1997), 111–112. Stuckenbruck argues that "the Septuagintal and Aramaic targum traditions (*Onqelos* and *Neophyti*) have coalesced the 'nephilim' in Genesis 6:4a into their respective terms for the Giants." Stuckenbruck, *The Book of Giants from Qumran*, 111.

96. Rubinkiewicz, *L'Apocalypse d'Abraham en vieux slave*, 149. A similar corruption can be found in the Greek and Ethiopic renderings of *1 Enoch* 15:11, where the giants's spirits are associated with clouds (νεφέλας). Reflecting on the clouds imagery, Johannes Flemming and Ludwig Radermacher suggest that "νεφέλας ist Missverständnis für Ναφηλείμ." J. Flemming and L. Radermacher, *Das Buch Henoch* (GCS; Leipzig: Hinrichs, 1901), 43. This hypothesis was later supported by Michael Knibb (*The Ethiopic Book of Enoch*, 2.101) and Matthew Black (*The Book of Enoch or 1 Enoch: A New English Edition* [SVTP, 7; Leiden: Brill, 1985], 153). Black argues that "νεφέλας is a misreading of Ναφηλείμ: the expression is correctly reproduced by Sync. at 16.1 τῶν γιγάντων Ναφηλείμ = גברין ונפילין (ד״). . . . The 'spirits of the giants, the Nephilim' are, in this context, clearly the 'evil spirits' which issued from the 'bodies of flesh' of the giants." Black, *The Book of Enoch*, 153.

97. Rubinkiewicz, *L'Apocalypse d'Abraham en vieux slave*, 149.

98. On the Greek *Vorlage* of the *Apocalypse of Abraham*, see Kilik, *Retroverting Slavonic Pseudepigrapha*, 37–60.

99. Kulik, *Retroverting Slavonic Pseudepigrapha*, 21; Philonenko-Sayar and Philonenko, *L'Apocalypse d'Abraham*, 68.

100. García Martínez and Tigchelaar, *The Dead Sea Scrolls Study Edition*, 132–3.

101. "Its interpretation concerns Belial and the spirits of his lot." García Martínez and Tigchelaar, *The Dead Sea Scrolls Study Edition*, 1206–7.

102. Philonenko-Sayar and Philonenko, *L'Apocalypse d'Abraham*, 33. See also B. Philonenko-Sayar and M. Philonenko, *Die Apokalypse Abrahams* (JSHRZ, 5.5; Gütersloh: Mohn, 1982), 413–460 at 418; Rubinkiewicz, *L'Apocalypse d'Abraham en vieux slave*, 54.

103. *Apoc. Ab.* 13:7: "And he said to him, 'Reproach is on you, Azazel! Since *Abraham's portion* (часть Аврамля) is in heaven, and *yours* is on earth.'" Kulik, *Retroverting Slavonic Pseudepigrapha*, 20; Philonenko-Sayar and Philonenko, *L'Apocalypse d'Abraham*, 66.

104. *Apoc. Ab.* 10:15: "Stand up, Abraham, go boldly, be very joyful and rejoice! And I am with you, since *an honorable portion* (часть вѣчная) has been prepared for you by the Eternal One." Kulik, *Retroverting Slavonic Pseudepigrapha*, 18; Philonenko-Sayar and Philonenko, *L'Apocalypse d'Abraham*, 60.

105. This identification of the positive lot with the lot of God is also present in the Qumran materials. Cf. 1QM XIII 5–6: "For they are the lot of darkness but the lot of God is for [everlast]ing light." García Martínez and Tigchelaar, *The Dead Sea Scrolls Study Edition*, 135.

106. This idea can be compared to *Jub.* 15:30–32, where the spirits rule over the nations while God rules over Israel. On this motif, see VanderKam, "The Demons in the Book of Jubilees," 352–4. *Jub.* 15:30–32 reads: "For the Lord did not draw near to himself either Ishmael, his sons, his brothers, or Esau. He did not choose them (simply) because they were among Abraham's children, for he knew them. But he chose Israel to be his people. He sanctified them and gathered (them) from all mankind. For there are many nations and many peoples and all belong to him. He made spirits rule over all in order to lead them astray from following him. But over Israel he made no angel or spirit rule because he alone is their ruler. He will guard them and require them for himself from his angels, his spirits, and everyone, and all his powers so that he may guard them and bless them and so that they may be his and he theirs from now and forever." VanderKam, *Jubilees*, 2.93.

107. *Apoc. Ab.* 20:1–5. Kulik, *Retroverting Slavonic Pseudepigrapha*, 25.

108. Although here and in *Apoc. Ab.* 10:15 the Slavonic word часть is used for the designation of "lots," *Apoc. Ab.* 20:5 and *Apoc. Ab.* 29:21 use the Slavonic word жребий for their designation of "lot." Cf. Philonenko-Sayar and Philonenko, *L'Apocalypse d'Abraham*, 82 and 102.

109. García Martínez and Tigchelaar, *The Dead Sea Scrolls Study Edition*, 1207–1209.

110. García Martínez and Tigchelaar, *The Dead Sea Scrolls Study Edition*, 75–79.

111. In 1QM XIV 9 the terminology of inheritance is invoked again. There, the remnant predestined to survive is called "the rem[nant of your inheritance] during the empire of Belial." García Martínez and Tigchelaar, *The Dead Sea Scrolls Study Edition*, 137.

112. García Martínez and Tigchelaar, *The Dead Sea Scrolls Study Edition*, 97.

113. García Martínez and Tigchelaar, *The Dead Sea Scrolls Study Edition*, 573.

114. García Martínez and Tigchelaar, *The Dead Sea Scrolls Study Edition*, 572.

115. On נפלים as spirits, see D. Dimant, "'The Fallen Angels' in the Dead Sea Scrolls and in the Apocryphal and Pseudepigraphic Books Related to Them" (PhD diss.; Hebrew University of Jerusalem, 1974) 48–49; Segal, *The Book of Jubilees*, 174. Another tradition found in *Jubilees* envisions spirits/demons as emanations from angels themselves. Touching on this detail, VanderKam notes that

> *Jubilees* also adds the element of the evil spirits, although it does not claim that they emanated from the carcasses of the Giants. Rather, in 10:5 Noah says in his prayer: "You know how your Watchers, the fathers of these spirits, have acted during my lifetime. As for these spirits who have remained alive. . . ." It does appear from this verse as if the demons are emanations from the angels themselves, but, since *Jubilees* also knows of the Giants and identifies them as the sons of the watchers (5:1, 6–10), it perhaps means by calling the watchers "the fathers of these spirits" that they were their ancestors. They are definitely presented as the ones who continue the work of the watchers who are themselves imprisoned in the nether places and thus precluded from active involvement in earthly matters.

VanderKam, "The Demons in the Book of Jubilees," 349.

116. Apropos to the Giants' survival after their physical bodies were destroyed, Stuckenbruck notes,

> Although the Giants are not spared, neither is it the case that they are completely annihilated; though not escaping divine wrath, they end up surviving in a radically altered state: they are "evil spirits" (*1 Enoch* 15:8–9). The preserved textual witnesses to *1 Enoch* 15 do not state how this alteration of existence has occurred, but it is possible to reconstruct an aetiology behind the existence of demons based on 15:3–16:3 and the *Book of Giants* that may have been elaborating on parts of *1 Enoch* 10. When the Giants came under God's judgment, their physical nature was destroyed while their spirits or souls emerged from their dead bodies. In this disembodied state, they continue to exist until the final triumph of God at the end of history as we know it (16:1). After the Great Flood they engaged in the sorts of activities that they had previously done. In particular, as before, they wished to afflict human beings (15:12). Why? We may infer that they were jealous of humanity who had managed to escape the deluge with their bodies intact.

Stuckenbruck, *The Myth of Rebellious Angels*, 181.

117. *Apoc. Ab.* 26:5: "Hear, Abraham! As the will of your father is in him, as your will is in you, so also the will desired by me is inevitable in coming days. . . ." Kulik, *Retroverting Slavonic Pseudepigrapha*, 30.

118. *Apoc. Ab.* 14:13: "God gave him (Azazel) the gravity and the will (*и* волю) against those who answer him." Kulik, *Retroverting Slavonic Pseudepigrapha*, 21.

119. *Apoc. Ab.* 14:10–13: "And the angel said to me, 'Answer him not!' And he spoke to me a second time. And the angel said, 'Now, whatever he says to you, answer him not, lest his *will* affect you. Since God gave him the gravity and the *will* against those who answer him. Answer him not.'" Kulik, *Retroverting Slavonic Pseudepigrapha*, 21.

120. On demonic possession in the Qumran texts, see P. Alexander, "Wrestling Against Wickedness in High Places: Magic in the Worldview of the Qumran Community," in *The Scrolls and Scriptures Qumran Fifty Years After* (eds. S. E. Porter and C. A. Evans; JSPSS, 26; Sheffield: Sheffield Academic Press, 1997), 324; M. Brand, *Evil Within and Without: The Source of Sin and Its Nature as Portrayed in Second Temple Literature* (JAJS, 9; Göttingen: Vandenhoeck & Ruprecht, 2013); E. Eshel, "Demonology in Palestine during the Second Temple Period" (PhD diss., Hebrew University of Jerusalem, 1999) [Hebrew]; M. Kister, "Demons, Theology and Abraham's Covenant (CD 16:4–6 and Related Texts)," in *The Dead Sea Scrolls at Fifty: Proceedings of the 1997 Society of Biblical Literature Qumran Section Meetings* (eds. R. A. Kugler and E. M. Schuller; EJL, 15; Atlanta: Scholars, 1999), 167–84 at 172–5; L. T. Stuckenbruck, "Jesus' Apocalyptic Worldview and His Exorcistic Ministry," in *Pseudepigrapha and Christian Origins: Essays from the Studiorum Novi Testamenti Societas* (eds. G. S. Oegema and J. H. Charlesworth; JCTCRS, 4; London: T&T Clark International, 2008), 77–79; Wright, *The Origin of Evil Spirits*, 178–9.

121. Hebrew Sir 15:14: "For God created man from the beginning; and *put him into the hand of him that would spoil him*; and gave him into the hand of his inclination." P. C. Beentjes, *The Book of Ben Sira in Hebrew* (VetTSup, 58; Leiden: Brill, 1997), 142.

122. *Testament of Reuben* 4:8–9: "You heard how Joseph protected himself from a woman and purified his mind from all promiscuity: He found favor before God and men. For the Egyptian woman did many things to him, summoned magicians, and brought potions for him, but his soul's inclination (τὸ διαβούλιον) rejected evil desire (ἐπιθυμίαν πονηράν). For this reason the God of our fathers rescued him from every visible or hidden death. For if promiscuity does not triumph over your reason, then neither can Beliar conquer you." H. C. Kee, "Testaments of the Twelve Patriarchs," in *The Old Testament Pseudepigrapha* (ed. J. H. Charlesworth; 2 vols.; New York: Doubleday, 1983–1985), 1.783–4; M. de Jonge et al., *The Testaments of the Twelve Patriarchs. A Critical Edition of the Greek Text* (PVTG, 1,2; Leiden: Brill, 1978), 8.

123. *Testament of Asher* 1:8–9: "But if the mind is disposed toward evil (ἐν πονηρῷ κλίνῃ τὸ διαβούλιον), all of its deeds are wicked; driving out the good, it accepts the evil and is overmastered by Beliar, who, even when good is undertaken, presses the struggle so as to make the aim of his action into evil, since the devil's storehouse is filled with the venom of the evil spirit." Kee, "Testaments of the Twelve Patriarchs," 1.816–7; de Jonge, *The Testaments of the Twelve Patriarchs. A Critical Edition of the Greek Text*, 135–136.

124. *Testament of Naphtali* 2:2–7 reads:

> For just as a potter knows the pot, how much it holds, and brings clay for it accordingly, so also the Lord forms the body in correspondence to the spirit, and instills the spirit corresponding to the power of the body. And from one to the other there is no discrepancy, not so much as a third of a hair, for all the creation of the Most High was according to height, measure, and standard. And just as the potter knows the use of each vessel and to what it is suited, so also the Lord knows the body to what extent it will persist in goodness, and when it will be dominated by evil. For there is no inclination (πλάσμα) or conception which the Lord does not know since he created every human being according to his own image. As a person's strength, so also is his work; as is his mind, so also is his skill. As is his plan, so also is his achievement; as is his heart, so is his speech; as is his eye, so also is his sleep; as is his soul, so also is his thought, whether on the Law of the Lord or on the law of Beliar. As there is a distinction between light and darkness.

Kee, "Testaments of the Twelve Patriarchs," 1.811; de Jonge, *The Testaments of the Twelve Patriarchs: A Critical Edition of the Greek Text*, 114.

125. *Testament of Benjamin* 6:1–4: "The inclination (τὸ διαβούλιον) of the good man is not in the power of the deceitful spirit, Beliar, for the angel of peace guides his life. . . . The good inclination (τὸ διαβούλιον τοῦ ἀγαθοῦ) does not receive glory or dishonor from men." de Jonge, *The Testaments of the Twelve Patriarchs: A Critical Edition of the Greek Text*, 172.

126. Kee, "Testaments of the Twelve Patriarchs," 1.800; de Jonge, *The Testaments of the Twelve Patriarchs: A Critical Edition of the Greek Text*, 73.

127. Robert Henry Charles suggests that "the faculty of the will is here referred to." R. H. Charles, *The Testaments of the Twelve Patriarchs: Translated from Editor's Greek Text and Edited, with Introduction, Notes, and Indices* (London: Adam and Charles Black, 1908), 89.

128. Some studies on the *Testaments of the Twelve Patriarchs* connect *yetzer* with "will." For instance, reflecting on the meaning of διαβούλιον in the *Testaments of the Twelve Patriarchs*, Hollander and De Jonge argue that "in the *Testaments* where διαβούλιον is used it denotes the center of the personality, *the will* where actions find their origin (see, e.g., *T. Reu.* 4:9; *T. Jud.* 13:2 [cf. 11:1]; 18:3; *T. Iss.* 6:2; *T. Dan* 4:2–7; *T. Gad* 5:3–7; 7:3, and, particularly, *T. Benj.* 6:1–4)." H. W. Hollander and M. De Jonge, *The Testaments of the Twelve Patriarchs. A Commentary* (SVTP, 8; Leiden: Brill, 1985), 339.

129. Charles, *The Testaments of the Twelve Patriarchs*, 89.

130. Kulik, *Retroverting Slavonic Pseudepigrapha*, 21. Rubinkiewicz, *L'Apocalypse d'Abraham en vieux slave*, 150. Furthermore, *Apoc. Ab.* 14:10–13 clearly connects the "will" given to Azazel by God with his ability to control a human being: "And the angel said to me, 'Answer him not!' And he spoke to me a second time. And the angel said, 'Now, whatever he says to you, answer him not, lest *his will affect you* (како притечеть к тебѣ воля его). Since God gave him the gravity and the *will against those who answer him* (волю на отвѣщавающая ему). Answer him not.'" Kulik, *Retroverting Slavonic Pseudepigrapha*, 21; Philonenko-Sayar and Philonenko, *L'Apocalypse d'Abraham*, 68.

131. A. A. Orlov, "'The Likeness of Heaven': The *Kavod* of Azazel in the Apocalypse of Abraham," in Orlov, *Dark Mirrors*, 11–26.

132. Azazel may here fulfil the role of "the dark side of God." Alexander notes that "certain negative actions towards humanity, rather than being attributed directly to God himself, are sometimes transferred to an angel." Alexander, "Demonology of the Dead Sea Scrolls," 342. Furthermore, in the Dead Sea Scrolls "Satan/Belial, for all his evil intent, operates ultimately under divine authority." Alexander, "Demonology of the Dead Sea Scrolls," 343. In this respect, Azazel's role is very similar to the role of Mastema in *Jubilees* or Belial in some Qumran materials. Deliberating on these demonological patterns, Archie Wright notes that

> The author of *Jubilees* (10:8) has followed a similar pattern of expanding the story concerning the evil spirits in the Watcher tradition as the author of *BW* had done with the *bene elohim* in Genesis. Mastema is introduced in a leadership role over the evil spirits similar to the role of Shemihazah over the Watchers. In addition, he has limited the autonomy of the evil spirits. The author of *BW* makes no mention of the spirits being under a leader or as a part in the economy of God (*1 Enoch* 16:1). *Jubilees* has placed the evil spirits within in the economy of God and under a central leader who, in the biblical tradition, must answer to God.

Wright, *The Origin of Evil Spirits*, 160.

133. Kulik, *Retroverting Slavonic Pseudepigrapha,* 21; Rubinkiewicz, *L'Apocalypse d'Abraham en vieux slave,* 150.

> 134. [Noah] prayed before the Lord his God and said: "God of the spirits . . . You know how your Watchers, the fathers of these spirits, have acted during my lifetime. As for these spirits who have remained alive, imprison them and hold them captive in the place of judgment. May they not cause destruction among your servant's sons, my God, for they are savage and were created for the purpose of destroying. May they not rule the spirits of the living for you alone know their punishment; and may they not have power over the sons of the righteous from now and forevermore." Then our God told us to tie up each one.

VanderKam, *Jubilees*, 2.58–9.

135. Michael Segal notes that "Mastema can negotiate with God, similar to the role of Satan in the narrative framework of Job. In Job, Satan belongs to a divine council, composed of the sons of god (Job 1:6)." Segal, *The Book of Jubilees*, 176.

136. VanderKam, *Jubilees*, 2.29.

137. Reflecting on God's decision, James VanderKam notes that "God's response to Mastema's self-serving request is truly surprising and presents the major puzzle regarding the demons in the *Book of Jubilees*: 'Then he said that a tenth of them should be left before him, while he would make nine parts descend to the place of judgment.' (10:9). For some reason the author has here departed dramatically from his source, the *Book of the Watchers*, which says nothing about limiting the number of the demons or evil spirits." VanderKam, "The Demons in the Book of Jubilees," 344. Wright draws attention to this aspect of limited demonic activity in *Jubilees* in comparison to *1 Enoch* by noting that

> *1 Enoch* 15:12 states that the spirits of the Giants "will rise against the sons of men and women because they came forth from them." The context of this verse, established in 15:11, seems to indicate little restraint is placed upon the activity of the Giants' spirits; their end will come only in the eschaton. The author of *Jubilees* 10 further develops this element of the Watcher tradition by limiting the autonomy of the evil spirits. It is possible from Charles' reading of 10:6 that, up to this point, the spirits had free reign over humanity (similar to what we find in *1 Enoch* 15:11–12), "for you [God] alone can exercise dominion over them. And let them not have power over the sons of the righteous."

Wright, *The Origin of Evil Spirits*, 157.

138. Segal notes that "Mastema has his own agenda (v. 8: 'the authority of my will among mankind'), which is not dependent upon the existence of the spirits. . . . The spirits no longer act according to their own needs, and do not make any decisions for themselves, but rather implement the authority of Mastema's will." M. Segal, *The Book of Jubilees*, 176–7.

139. Kulik, *Retroverting Slavonic Pseudepigrapha,* 28; Philonenko-Sayar and Philonenko, *L'Apocalypse d'Abraham*, 88.

140. *Apoc. Ab.* 13:6. Kulik, *Retroverting Slavonic Pseudepigrapha,* 20; Philonenko-Sayar and Philonenko, *L'Apocalypse d'Abraham*, 64.

141. Philonenko-Sayar and Philonenko, *L'Apocalypse d'Abraham*, 32.

142. Rubinkiewicz, *L'Apocalypse d'Abraham en vieux slave,* 143.

143. Kulik, *Retroverting Slavonic Pseudepigrapha,* 27; Philonenko-Sayar and Philonenko, *L'Apocalypse d'Abraham*, 88.

144. Rubinkiewicz and Lunt, "The Apocalypse of Abraham," 1.695; Philonenko-Sayar and Philonenko, *L'Apocalypse d'Abraham*, 66.

145. Kulik, *Retroverting Slavonic Pseudepigrapha,* 20. Rubinkiewicz and Lunt translate it in the following way: "For the Eternal, Mighty One did not allow the bodies of the righteous to be in your hand." Rubinkiewicz and Lunt, "The Apocalypse of Abraham," 1.695.

146. Philonenko-Sayar and Philonenko, *L'Apocalypse d'Abraham*, 66.

147. Kulik, *Retroverting Slavonic Pseudepigrapha,* 20. Philonenko-Sayar and Philonenko, *L'Apocalypse d'Abraham*, 66.

148. According to Philip Alexander, the Dead Sea Scrolls maintain the strict distinction between angels and demons. He notes that "the demonology of the Scrolls seems to envisage a clear distinction drawn between demons and angels, whether fallen or otherwise." Alexander, "Demonology of the Dead Sea Scrolls," 332. Deliberating on strict deliniation between angels and demons in Jewish lore, Dale Martin notes that

> We find evil angels in company with Lilith, *šēdîm*, and other "demonic" beings. But in none of these materials do we find the equation *šēdîm* = angels. And, of course, we find no identification of fallen angels with Greek *daimons.* One might expect to find an identification of demons with angels in a few other sources from "postbiblical" Judaism, but that seems not to be the case. In Tobit, the angel Raphael helps Tobias defeat the demon Asmodeus, but they are not presented as the same species. In 6:8, demons are mentioned alongside "evil spirits," but again the two kinds of beings are not identified; they may be just two similarly troubling species.

D. Martin, "When Did Angels Become Demons," *JBL* 129 (2010): 657–77 at 670. Such a strict borderline between two types of spiritual beings is also maintained in early Christian materials. Martin notes that "nowhere in the NT are demons equated with angels, fallen or otherwise." Martin, "When Did Angels Become Demons," 673.

149. Alexander, "Demonology of the Dead Sea Scrolls," 339.

Chapter Six. Glorification through Fear in *2 Enoch*

1. Andersen, "2 Enoch," 1.106.

2. Andersen, "2 Enoch," 1.107. G. Macaskill, *The Slavonic Texts of 2 Enoch* (SJS, 6; Leiden: Brill, 2013), 43.

3. Andersen, "2 Enoch," 1.108. Cf. also Böttrich, *Das slavische Henochbuch*, 835, footnote c.

4. On fear as a human response to theophany, see J. C. VanderKam, *From Revelation to Canon: Studies in Hebrew Bible and Second Temple Literature* (Leiden: Brill, 2000), 343; J. Becker, *Gottesfurcht im Alten Testament* (Analecta Biblica, 25; Rome: St. Martin's, 1965), 22.

5. See, for example, Dan 8:17–18: "So he came near where I stood; and when he came, I became frightened and fell prostrate. But he said to me, 'Understand, O mortal, that the vision is for the time of the end.' As he was speaking to me, I fell into a trance, face to the ground; then he touched me and set me on my feet"; Dan 10:7–9: "I, Daniel, alone saw the vision; the people who were with me did not see the vision, though a great trembling fell upon them, and they fled and hid themselves. So I was left alone to see this great vision. My strength left me, and my complexion grew deathly pale, and I retained no strength. Then I heard the sound of his words; and when I heard the sound of his words, I fell into a trance, face to the ground."

6. Exod 3:6: "He said further, 'I am the God of your father, the God of Abraham, the God of Isaac, and the God of Jacob.' And Moses hid his face, for he was afraid to look at God."

7. Orlov, *The Enoch-Metatron Tradition*, 254–303.

8. Orlov, *The Enoch-Metatron Tradition*, 280–281.

9. It should be noted that this constellation of motifs involving the glorified face of the visionary and fear was not forgotten even in the later Enochic traditions. *3 Enoch*, for example, reports that the transformed Enoch was predestined to comfort the frightened Moses, telling him about his luminous face. Thus, *3 Enoch* 15B:5 states: "At once Metatron, Prince of the Divine Presence, said to Moses, 'Son of Amram, fear not! for already God favors you. Ask what you will with confidence and boldness, for light shines from the skin of your face from one end of the world to the other.'" Alexander, "3 Enoch," 1.304.

10. Cf., for example, *Exagoge* 1:82; *Apoc. Ab.* 10:2; 16:1–2; *4 Ezra* 5:14; 10:29–30; 12:3; 13:14; *Lad. Jac.* 2:1–3; *3 Bar.* 7:5.

11. Knibb, *The Ethiopic Book of Enoch*, 2.98.

12. J. J. Collins, *The Apocalyptic Imagination: An Introduction to Jewish Apocalyptic Literature* (Grand Rapids, MI: Eerdmans, 1998), 55.

13. M. Himmelfarb, *Ascent to Heaven in Jewish and Christian Apocalypses* (New York/Oxford: Oxford University Press, 1993), 16.

14. On this, see B. J. Bamberger, "Fear and Love of God in the Old Testament," *HUCA* 6 (1929): 39–53 at 43–47.

15. Himmelfarb, *Ascent to Heaven*, 16.

16. Thus, from *1 Enoch* 14:20–21 one learns that "no angel could enter, and at the appearance of the face (*gaṣṣ*) of him who is honored and praised no (creature of) flesh could look." Knibb, *The Ethiopic Book of Enoch*, 2.99.

17. *1 Enoch* 60:2–3 reads: "And then I saw the Head of Days sitting on the throne of his glory, and the angels and the righteous were standing around him. And a great trembling seized me, and fear took hold of me, and my loins collapsed and gave way, and my whole being melted, and I fell upon my face." Knibb, *The Ethiopic Book of Enoch*, 2.142. The "melting" of Enoch's body during the theophany is also attested in another

passage from the *Book of the Similitudes* (*1 Enoch* 71:9–11) where the patriarch was transformed into the Son of Man: "And Michael and Raphael and Gabriel and Phanuel, and many holy angels without number, came out from that house; and with them the Head of Days, his head white and pure like wool, and his garments indescribable. And I fell upon my face, and my whole body melted, and my spirit was transformed; and I cried out in a loud voice in the spirit of power, and I blessed and praised and exalted." Knibb, *The Ethiopic Book of Enoch*, 2.166.

18. Himmelfarb, *Ascent to Heaven*, 40. In her other book, Himmelfarb reiterates the same position, noting the following in relation to *2 Enoch*: "Overcome by fear, Enoch falls on his face, not once as in the *Book of the Watchers* but twice, clearly an effort to mark Enoch's experience before the throne as even more terrifying than the one described in the *Book of the Watchers*." M. Himmelfarb, *The Apocalypse: A Brief History* (Blackwell Brief Histories of Religion; Malden, MA: Wiley-Blackwell, 2010), 77.

19. Andersen, "2 Enoch," 1.164. The shorter recension of *2 Enoch* 39:8 attests to the similar vocabulary: "It is dangerous and perilous to stand before the face of an earthly king, terrifying (and very perilous) it is, because the will of the king is death and the will of the king is life. To stand before the face of the King (of kings), who will be able to endure the infinite terror (of that), or of the great burnings?" Andersen, "2 Enoch," 1.165.

20. P. Schäfer, *The Hidden and Manifest God: Some Major Themes in Early Jewish Mysticism* (Albany, NY: State University of New York Press, 1992), 18.

21. Schäfer, *The Hidden and Manifest God*, 18.

22. Schäfer, *The Hidden and Manifest God*, 20.

23. Orlov, *The Enoch-Metatron Tradition*, 285–286.

24. Andersen, "2 Enoch," 1.160; Macaskill, *The Slavonic Texts*, 142. The shorter recension of *2 Enoch* 37:1–2 provides a very similar description: "But the Lord called (one) of his senior angels, *a terrifying one* (грозна), and he made him stand with me. And the appearance of that angel (was) snow, and his hands ice, and he refreshed my face, because I could not endure the terror of the burning of the fire. And it is thus that the Lord spoke to me all his words." Andersen, "2 Enoch," 1.161; Macaskill, *The Slavonic Texts*, 143.

25. Slav. страшнаа и грозна. Macaskill, *The Slavonic Texts*, 142.

26. Andersen, "2 Enoch," 1.183. Macaskill, *The Slavonic Texts*, 193. In contrast to the shorter recension, the longer recension does not refer to the motif of transformation through fear: "Listen, child! Since the time when the Lord anointed me with the ointment of his glory, food has not come into me, and earthly pleasure my soul does not remember; nor do I desire anything earthly." Andersen, "2 Enoch," 1.182.

27. Andersen, "2 Enoch," 1.171; Macaskill, *The Slavonic Texts*, 163.

28. Andersen, "2 Enoch," 1.170.

29. Andersen, "2 Enoch," 1.171.

30. I. D. Wilson, " 'Face to Face' with God: Another Look," *ResQ* 51 (2009): 107–114 at 109. On this connection, see also Niehaus, *God at Sinai*, 27.

31. Gen 3:10: "He said, 'I heard the sound of you in the garden, and I was afraid, because I was naked; and I hid myself.' "

32. See, for example, *Pirke de Rabbi Eliezer* 14:

> He said to him (Adam): Why didst thou flee—before Me? He answered Him: I heard Thy voice and my bones trembled, as it is said, "I heard thy voice in the garden, and I was afraid, because I was naked: and I hid myself" (Gen 3:10). What was the dress of the first man? A skin of nail, and a cloud of glory covered him. When he ate of the fruits of the tree, the nail-skin was stripped off him, and the cloud of glory departed from him, and he saw himself naked, as it is said, "And he said. Who told thee that thou wast naked? Hast thou eaten of the tree, whereof I commanded thee?"

Friedlander, *Pirke de Rabbi Eliezer*, 98.

33. Later rabbinic materials reaffirm the tradition of the first humans' glorious garments. The targumic traditions, both Palestinian and Babylonian, render "garments of skin" in Gen 3:21 as "garments of glory." This targumic interpretation is supported by an array of midrashic sources, including *Gen. Rab.* 20:12 and *Pirke de Rabbi Eliezer* 14.

34. On the temporal and spatial symmetry in the Jewish apocalyptic literature, see J. M. Scott, *On Earth as in Heaven: The Restoration of Sacred Time and Sacred Space in the Book of Jubilees* (JSJSS, 91; Leiden: Brill, 2005), 212–219.

35. Such an idea appears to be hinted already in Exod 20:20, when Moses tells the Israelites that fear prevents sin: "Do not be afraid; for God has come only to test you and to put the fear of him upon you so that you do not sin."

36. Andersen, "2 Enoch," 1.171.

37. Such proleptic glorifications that anticipate the future glorious transformation of the seer can be found in some Jewish and Christian accounts, including the metamorphosis of Stephen in Acts 6:15.

38. Andersen, "2 Enoch," 1.108.

39. In this respect it is noteworthy that in both accounts the glorious visage of the seer is put in correspondence with the glorious faces of angelic and divine subjects. Thus, *2 Enoch* 1:5 makes a specific reference to the glorious faces of Enoch's angelic visitors, which are compared with the sun: "Their faces were like the shining sun." Andersen, "2 Enoch," 1.106.

Bibliography

Texts and Translations

Adler, William. "Palaea Historica." In *Old Testament Pseudepigrapha: More Noncanonical Scriptures*, edited by R. Bauckham et al., 585–672. Grand Rapids, MI: Eerdmans, 2013.

Alexander, Philip. "3 (Hebrew Apocalypse of) Enoch." In *The Old Testament Pseudepigrapha*, edited by J. H. Charlesworth, 1.223–315. 2 vols. New York: Doubleday, 1983–1985.

Allison, Dale. *Matthew: A Shorter Commentary*. London and New York: T&T Clark, 2004.

Andersen, Francis. "2 (Slavonic Apocalypse of) Enoch." In *The Old Testament Pseudepigrapha*, edited by J. H. Charlesworth, 1.91–221. 2 vols. New York: Doubleday, 1983–1985.

Anderson, Gary. "The Exaltation of Adam and the Fall of Satan." In *Literature on Adam and Eve: Collected Essays*, edited by G. Anderson, M. E. Stone, and J. Tromp, 83–110. SVTP 15. Leiden: Brill, 2000.

Anderson, Gary, and Michael Stone. *A Synopsis of the Books of Adam and Eve. Second Revised Edition*. EJL 17. Atlanta: Scholars, 1999.

Aune, David. *Revelation 1–5*. WBC 52A. Dallas: Word Books, 1997.

———. *Revelation 6–16*. WBC 52B. Nashville: Nelson, 1998.

———. *Revelation 17–22*. WBC 52C. Nashville: Nelson, 1998.

Barrier, Jeremy. *The Acts of Paul and Thecla: A Critical Introduction and Commentary*. WUNT 2.270. Tübingen: Mohr Siebeck, 2009.

Bauckham, Richard. *Jude, 2 Peter*. WBC 50. Waco, TX: Word Books, 1983.

Beattie, Derek, and J. Stanley Mclvor. *Targums of Ruth and Chronicles*. ArBib 19. Collegeville, MN: Liturgical Press, 1994.

Beentjes, Pancratius. *The Book of Ben Sira in Hebrew*. VetTSup 58. Leiden: Brill, 1997.

Blanc, Cécile. *Origène, Commentaire sur Saint Jean. Tome I (Livres I–V)*. SC 120. Paris: Cerf, 1966.

Bonwetsch, Gottlieb Nathanael. *Die Apokalypse Abrahams. Das Testament der vierzig Märtyrer*. SGTK 1.1. Leipzig: J. C. Hinrichs, 1897.

Böttrich, Christfried. *Das slavische Henochbuch*. JSHRZ 5. Gütersloh: Gütersloher Verlaghaus, 1995.

Box, George Herbert, and Joseph Landsman. *The Apocalypse of Abraham. Edited, with a Translation from the Slavonic Text and Notes*. TED 1.10. London: The Macmillan Company, 1918.

Braude, William. *The Midrash on Psalms*. 2 vols. YJS 13. New Haven, CT: Yale University Press, 1959.

———. *Pesikta Rabbati*. 2 vols. YJS 18. New Haven, CT: Yale University Press, 1968.

Braude, William, and Israel Kapstein. *Pesikta de-Rab Kahana. R. Kahana's Compilation of Discourses for Sabbaths and Festal Days*. Philadelphia: Jewish Publication Society of America, 1975.

———. *Tanna Debe Eliyyahu: The Lore of the School of Elijah*. Philadelphia: Jewish Publication Society of America, 1981.

Brock, Sebastian. *St. Ephrem the Syrian, Hymns on Paradise*. Crestwood, NY: St. Vladimir's Seminary Press, 1990.

Budge, Ernest. *The Book of the Cave of Treasures*. London: The Religious Tract Society, 1927.

Chadwick, Henry. *Origen, Contra Celsum*. Cambridge: Cambridge University Press, 1953.

Charles, Robert Henry. *A Critical and Exegetical Commentary on the Revelation of St. John*. 2 vols. ICC. Edinburgh: T&T Clark, 1920.

———. *The Testaments of the Twelve Patriarchs: Translated from Editor's Greek Text and Edited, with Introduction, Notes, and Indices*. London: Adam and Charles Black, 1908.

Charles, Robert Henry, and Nevill Forbes. "The Book of the Secrets of Enoch." In *The Apocrypha and Pseudepigrapha of the Old Testament*, edited by R. H. Charles, 2.425–269. 2 vols. Oxford: Clarendon Press, 1913.

Charles, Robert Henry, and William Richard Morfill. *The Book of the Secrets of Enoch*. Oxford: Clarendon Press, 1896.

Collins, John. *Daniel: A Commentary on the Book of Daniel*. Hermeneia. Minneapolis: Fortress, 1993.

Colson, Francis Henry, and George Herbert Whitaker. *Philo*. 10 vols. LCL. Cambridge, MA: Harvard University Press, 1929–1964.

Cranfield, Charles. *The Gospel According to St. Mark*. Cambridge: Cambridge University Press, 1983.

Danby, Herbert. *The Mishnah*. Oxford: Oxford University Press, 1992.

Davies, William David, and Dale Allison, Jr. *A Critical and Exegetical Commentary on the Gospel According to Saint Matthew*. 3 vols. ICC. Edinburgh: T&T Clark, 1991.

Davila, James. *Hekhalot Literature in Translation: Major Texts of Merkavah Mysticism*. SJJTP 20. Leiden: Brill, 2013.

De Jonge, Marinus, in cooperation with Harm Hollander, Henk de Jonge, and Theodore Korteweg. *The Testaments of the Twelve Patriarchs: A Critical Edition of the Greek Text*. PVTG 12. Leiden: Brill, 1978.

Denis, Albert-Marie. *Fragmenta pseudepigraphorum quae supersunt Graeca*. PVTG 3. Leiden: Brill, 1970.

Epstein, Isidore. *The Babylonian Talmud*. London: Soncino, 1935–1952.

Ford, Josephine Massyngberde. *Revelation*. AB 38. Garden City, New York: Doubleday, 1975.

Freedman, Harry, and Maurice Simon. *Midrash Rabbah.* 10 vols. London: Soncino, 1961.

Friedlander, Gerald. *Pirke de Rabbi Eliezer.* London: Bloch, 1916.

García Martínez, Florentino, and Eibert Tigchelaar. *The Dead Sea Scrolls Study Edition.* 2 vols. Leiden: Brill, 1997.

Gaster, Moses. *The Asatir: The Samaritan Book of the "Secrets of Moses" Together with the Pitron or Samaritan Commentary and the Samaritan story of the Death of Moses.* OTF 26. London: The Royal Asiatic Society, 1927.

———. *The Chronicles of Jerahmeel.* OTF 4. London: Royal Asiatic Society, 1899.

Gaylord, Harry. "3 (Greek Apocalypse of) Baruch." In *The Old Testament Pseudepigrapha,* edited by J. H. Charlesworth, 1.653–79. 2 vols. New York: Doubleday, 1983–1985.

Gifford, Edwin Hamilton. *Eusebius, Praeparatio Evangelica (Preparation for the Gospel).* 2 vols. Grand Rapids, MI: Baker, 1981.

Gnilka, Joachim. *Das Evangelium nach Markus.* 2 vols. EKKNT 2.1–2. Zürich: Benziger; Neukirchen-Vluyn: Neukirchener Verlag, 1978–79.

Goldin, Judah. *The Fathers According to Rabbi Nathan.* YJS 10. New Haven, CT: Yale University Press, 1955.

Greer, Rowan. *Origen: An Exhortation to Martyrdom, Prayer, and Selected Works.* New York: Paulist Press, 1979.

Grossfeld, Bernard. *The Two Targums of Esther.* ArBib 18. Edinburgh: T&T Clark, 1991.

Guelich, Robert A. *Mark 1–8:26.* WBC 34A. Dallas: Word, 1989.

Guggenheimer, Heinrich. *The Jerusalem Talmud. Second Order: Mo'ed. Tractates Pesahim and Yoma. Edition, Translation and Commentary.* SJ 74. Berlin: Walter de Gruyter, 2013.

Gundry, Robert. *Matthew: A Commentary on His Handbook for a Mixed Church under Persecution.* Grand Rapids, MI: Eerdmans, 1994.

Haleem, Muhammad Abdel. *Qur'an.* Oxford: Oxford University Press, 2004.

Hayward, Richard. *Saint Jerome's Hebrew Questions on Genesis.* Oxford Early Christian Studies. Oxford: Clarendon, 1995.

Hennecke, Edgar, and Wilhelm Schneemelcher. *New Testament Apocrypha.* 2 vols. Louisville, KY: Westminster John Knox, 2003.

Holladay, Carl. *Fragments from Hellenistic Jewish Authors.* 4 vols. Chico, CA: Scholars, 1983–96.

Hollander, Harm, and Marinus De Jonge. *The Testaments of the Twelve Patriarchs. A Commentary.* SVTP 8. Leiden: Brill, 1985.

Jacobson, Howard. *A Commentary on Pseudo-Philo's Liber Antiquitatum Biblicarum, with Latin Text and English Translation.* 2 vols. AGAJU 31. Leiden: Brill, 1996.

———. *The Exagoge of Ezekiel.* Cambridge: Cambridge University Press, 1983.

Kee, Howard. "Testaments of the Twelve Patriarchs." In *The Old Testament Pseudepigrapha,* edited by J. H. Charlesworth, 1.775–828. 2 vols. New York: Doubleday, 1983–1985.

Klijn, Albertus Frederik Johannes. *The Acts of Thomas: Introduction, Text, and Commentary.* 2nd ed. NovTSup 108. Leiden: Brill, 2003.

Knibb, Michael. *The Ethiopic Book of Enoch: A New Edition in the Light of the Aramaic Dead Sea Fragments.* 2 vols. Oxford: Clarendon Press, 1978.

Koester, Craig. *Revelation: A New Translation with Introduction and Commentary.* AYB 38A. New Haven, CT: Yale University Press, 2014.

Kulik, Alexander. *Retroverting Slavonic Pseudepigrapha: Toward the Original of the Apocalypse of Abraham.* TCS 3. Atlanta: Scholars, 2004.

Kulik, Alexander, and Sergey Minov. *Biblical Pseudepigrapha in Slavonic Tradition.* Oxford: Oxford University Press, 2016.

Lohmeyer, Ernst. *Die Offenbarung des Johannes.* HNT 16. Tübingen: Mohr, 1970.

Lunt, Horace. "Ladder of Jacob." In *The Old Testament Pseudepigrapha,* edited by J. H. Charlesworth, 2.401–411. 2 vols. New York: Doubleday, 1983–1985.

Luz, Ulrich. *Matthew 8–20.* Hermeneia. Minneapolis: Fortress, 2001.

Macaskill, Grant. *The Slavonic Texts of 2 Enoch.* SJS 6. Leiden: Brill, 2013.

Maher, Michael. *Targum Pseudo-Jonathan: Genesis.* ArBib 1B. Collegeville, MN: Liturgical Press, 1992.

Marcus, Joel. *Mark 1–8: A New Translation with Introduction and Commentary.* AB 27. New York: Doubleday, 2000.

Marcus, Ralph. *Philo, Questions and Answers on Exodus.* LCL. Cambridge, MA: Harvard University Press/London: Heinemann, 1949.

McNamara, Martin. *Targum Neofiti 1: Genesis.* ArBib 1A. Collegeville, MN: Liturgical Press, 1992.

McNamara, Martin, Robert Hayward, and Michael Maher. *Targum Neofiti 1 and Pseudo-Jonathan: Exodus.* ArBib 2. Collegeville, MN: Liturgical Press, 1994.

McNamara, Martin, Robert Hayward, and Michael Maher. *Targum Neofiti 1, Leviticus; Targum Pseudo-Jonathan, Leviticus.* ArBib 3. Collegeville, MN: Liturgical Press, 1994.

Milgrom, Jacob. *Leviticus. A Book of Ritual and Ethics. A Continental Commentary.* Minneapolis: Fortress, 2004.

Milik, Józef Tadeusz. *The Books of Enoch: Aramaic Fragments of Qumrân Cave 4.* Oxford: Clarendon Press, 1976.

Mras, Karl. *Eusebius, Praeparatio Evangelica.* 2 vols. GCS 43.1–2. Leipzig: J. C. Hinrichs, 1954–56.

Musurillo, Herbert. *The Acts of the Christian Martyrs. Introduction, Texts, and Translations.* Oxford: Oxford University Press, 1972.

Nickelsburg, George. *1 Enoch 1: A Commentary on the Book of 1 Enoch: Chapters 1–36; 81–108.* Hermeneia. Minneapolis: Fortress, 2001.

Nickelsburg, George, and James VanderKam. *1 Enoch 2: A Commentary on the Book of 1 Enoch: Chapters 37–82.* Hermeneia. Minneapolis: Fortress, 2012.

Olson, Daniel. *Enoch: A New Translation: The Ethiopic Book of Enoch, or 1 Enoch.* North Richland Hills, TX: Bibal Press, 2004.

Philonenko-Sayar, Belkis, and Marc Philonenko. *L'Apocalypse d'Abraham. Introduction, texte slave, traduction et notes.* Semitica 31. Paris: Librairie Adrien-Maisonneuve, 1981.

———. *Die Apokalypse Abrahams.* JSHRZ 5.5. Gütersloh: Mohn, 1982.

Pietersma, Albert, and Benjamin G. Wright III. *New English Translation of the Septuagint.* New York and Oxford: Oxford University Press, 2007.

Porteous, Norman. *Daniel: A Commentary*. OTL. Philadelphia: Westminster Press, 1965.
Resch, Alfred. *Agrapha: Aussercanonische Schriftfragmente*. Leipzig: J. C. Hinrichs, 1906.
Robinson, Joseph Armitage. *Origen, Philocalia*. Cambridge: Cambridge University Press, 1893.
Rubinkiewicz, Ryszard. *L'Apocalypse d'Abraham en vieux slave. Introduction, texte critique, traduction et commentaire*. ŹM 129. Lublin: Towarzystwo Naukowe Katolickiego Uniwersytetu Lubelskiego, 1987.
Rubinkiewicz, Ryszard, and Horace Lunt. "Apocalypse of Abraham." In *The Old Testament Pseudepigrapha*, edited by J. H. Charlesworth, 1.681–705. 2 vols. New York: Doubleday, 1983–1985.
Schäfer, Peter, Margaret Schlüter, and Hans George von Mutius. *Synopse zur Hekhalot-Literatur*. TSAJ 2. Tübingen: Mohr Siebeck, 1981.
Schmidt, Carl, and Violet MacDermot. *Pistis Sophia*. NHS 9. Leiden: Brill, 1978.
Schoedel, William. *Athenagoras: Legatio and De resurrectione*. Oxford: Clarendon Press, 1972.
Seow, Choon Leong. *Daniel*. Westminster Bible Companion. Louisville, KY: Westminster John Knox, 2003.
Shutt, Robert. "Letter of Aristeas." In *The Old Testament Pseudepigrapha*, edited by J. H. Charlesworth, 2.7–34. 2 vols. New York: Doubleday, 1983–1985.
Smith, Jonathan. "Prayer of Joseph." In *The Old Testament Pseudepigrapha*, edited by J. H. Charlesworth. 2.699–714. 2 vols. New York: Doubleday, 1983–1985.
Snell, Bruno. *Tragicorum Graecorum Fragmenta I*. Göttingen: Vandenhoeck & Ruprecht, 1971.
Sperling, Harry, and Maurice Simon. *The Zohar*. 5 vols. London: Soncino, 1933.
Stefanovic, Ranko. *Revelation of Jesus Christ: Commentary on the Book of Revelation*. Berrien Springs, MI: Andrews University Press, 2002.
Stuckenbruck, Loren. *The Book of Giants from Qumran. Texts, Translation, and Commentary*. TSAJ 63. Tübingen: Mohr Siebeck, 1997.
Thackeray, Henry, and Ralph Marcus. *Josephus*. 10 vols. LCL. Cambridge, MA: Harvard University Press, 1926–65.
Van der Horst, Pieter and Judith Newman. *Early Jewish Prayers in Greek*. CEJL. Berlin: Walter de Gruyter, 2008.
VanderKam, James. *The Book of Jubilees*. 2 vols. CSCO 510–11. Scriptores Aethiopici 87–88. Louvain: Peeters, 1989.
Walton, John. *Genesis*. NIVAC. Grand Rapids, MI: Zondervan, 2001.

Secondary Literature

Aaron, David. "Shedding Light on God's Body in Rabbinic Midrashim: Reflections on the Theory of a Luminous Adam." *HTR* 90 (1997): 299–314.
Adler, William. "Abraham and the Burning of the Temple of Idols." *JQR* 77 (1986–1987): 95–117.

Alexander, Elizabeth Shanks. "Art, Argument, and Ambiguity in the Talmud: Conflicting Conceptions of the Evil Impulse in b. Sukkah 51b–52a." *HUCA* 73 (2002): 97–132.

Alexander, Philip. "Demonology of the Dead Sea Scrolls." In *The Dead Sea Scrolls after Fifty Years*, edited by P. W. Flint and J. C. VanderKam, 2.331–53. 2 vols. Leiden: Brill, 1999.

———. "Wrestling Against Wickedness in High Places: Magic in the Worldview of the Qumran Community." In *The Scrolls and Scriptures Qumran Fifty Years After*, edited by S. E. Porter and C. A. Evans, 318–37. JSPSS 26. Sheffield: Sheffield Academic Press, 1997.

Allison, Dale, Jr. "Behind the Temptations of Jesus: Q 4:1–13 and Mark 1:12–13." In *Authenticating the Activities of Jesus*, edited by B. D. Chilton and C. Evans, 195–213. NTTS 28/2. Leiden: Brill, 2002.

———. "The Magi's Angel (Matt. 2:2, 9–10)." In *Studies in Matthew: Interpretation Past and Present*, edited by D. C. Allison, 17–41. Grand Rapids, MI: Baker Academic, 2005.

———. "What Was the Star That Guided the Magi?" *BR* 9 (1993): 20–24.

Altmann, Alexander. "The Gnostic Background of the Rabbinic Adam Legends." *JQR* 35 (1945): 371–391.

Anderson, Gary. "The Exaltation of Adam and the Fall of Satan." In *Literature on Adam and Eve: Collected Essays*, edited by G. Anderson, M. Stone, and J. Tromp, 83–110. SVTP 15. Leiden: Brill, 2000.

Angel, Andrew. *Chaos and the Son of Man: The Hebrew Chaoskampf Tradition in the Period 515 BCE to 200 CE*. LSTS 60. London: T&T Clark, 2006.

Aster, Shawn Zelig. "The Phenomenon of Divine and Human Radiance in the Hebrew Bible and in Northwest Semitic and Mesopotamian Literature: A Philological and Comparative Study." PhD diss., University of Pennsylvania, 2006.

———. *The Unbeatable Light: Melammu and Its Biblical Parallels*. AOAT 384. Münster: Ugarit-Verlag, 2012.

Bakhos, Carol. *The Family of Abraham: Jewish, Christian, and Muslim Interpretations*. Cambridge, MA: Harvard University Press, 2014.

Balentine, Samuel. *The Torah's Vision of Worship*. Minneapolis: Fortress, 1999.

Ballentine, Debra Scoggins. *The Conflict Myth and the Biblical Tradition*. Oxford: Oxford University Press, 2015.

Bamberger, Bernard. "Fear and Love of God in the Old Testament." *HUCA* 6 (1929): 39–53.

Barc, Bernard. "La taille cosmique d'Adam dans la littérature juive rabbinique des trois premiers siècles apres J.-C." *RSR* 49 (1975): 173–85.

Barker, Margaret. *The Gate of Heaven: The History and Symbolism of the Temple in Jerusalem*. London: SPCK, 1991.

———. *The Revelation of Jesus Christ: Which God Gave to Him to Show to his Servants What Must Soon Take Place (Revelation 1.1)*. Edinburgh: T&T Clark, 2000.

Bauckham, Richard. "Jesus and the Wild Animals (Mark 1:13): A Christological Image for an Ecological Age." In *Jesus of Nazareth: Lord and Christ: Essays on the Historical Jesus and New Testament Christology*, edited by J. B. Green and M. Turner, 3–21. Grand Rapids, MI: Eerdmans, 1994.

Bautch, Kelley Coblentz. "The Fall and Fate of Renegade Angels: The Intersection of Watchers Traditions and the Book of Revelation." In *The Fallen Angels Traditions*, edited by A. Kim Harkins et al., 69–93. CBQMS 53. Washington, DC: The Catholic Biblical Association of America, 2014.

Beale, Gregory. *The Temple and the Church's Mission*. NSBT 15. Downers Grove, IL: InterVarsity Press, 2004.

Becker, Joachim. *Gottesfurcht im Alten Testament*. Analecta Biblica 25. Rome: St. Martin's Press, 1965.

Belleville, Linda. *Reflections of Glory: Paul's Polemical Use of the Moses-Doxa Tradition in 2 Corinthians 3.1–18*. JSNTSS 52. Sheffield: Sheffield Academic Press, 1991.

Ben-Daniel, John, and Gloria Ben-Daniel. *The Apocalypse in the Light of the Temple: A New Approach to the Book of Revelation*. Jerusalem: Beit Yochanan, 2003.

Blenkinsopp, Joseph. "The Structure of P." *CBQ* 38 (1976): 283–86.

Bloch-Smith, Elizabeth. " 'Who is the King of Glory?' Solomon's Temple and Its Symbolism." In *Scripture and Other Artifacts. Essays on the Bible and Archeology in Honor of Philip J. King*, edited by M. Coogan et al., 19–31. Louisville, KY: Westminster, 1994.

Bohak, Gideon. *Joseph and Aseneth and the Jewish Temple in Heliopolis*. EJL 10. Atlanta: Scholars, 1996.

Boustan, Ra'anan. *From Martyr to Mystic: Rabbinic Martyrology and the Making of Merkavah Mysticism*. TSAJ 112. Tübingen: Mohr Siebeck, 2005.

———. "The Study of Heikhalot Literature: Between Mystical Experience and Textual Artifact." *CBR* 6.1 (2007): 130–160.

Brakke, David. *Demons and the Making of the Monk: Spiritual Combat in Early Christianity*. Cambridge, MA: Harvard University Press, 2006.

Brand, Miryam. *Evil Within and Without: The Source of Sin and Its Nature as Portrayed in Second Temple Literature*. JAJS 9. Göttingen: Vandenhoeck & Ruprecht, 2013.

Bremmer, Jan. "The Five Major Apocryphal Acts: Authors, Place, Time and Readership." In *The Apocryphal Acts of Thomas*, edited by J. Bremmer, 149–70. Leuven: Peeters, 2001.

———. "Magic, Martyrdom and Women's Liberation in the Acts of Paul and Thecla." In *The Apocryphal Acts of Paul and Thecla*, edited by J. N. Bremmer, 36–59. Kampen: Kok Pharos, 2000.

Brock, Sebastian. "Clothing Metaphors as a Means of Theological Expression in Syriac Tradition." In *Typus, Symbol, Allegorie bei den östlichen Vätern und ihren Parallelen im Mittelalter*, edited by M. Schmidt, 11–40. EB 4. Regensburg: Friedrich Pustet, 1982.

Buchholz, Dennis. *Your Eyes Will Be Opened: A Study of the Greek (Ethiopic) Apocalypse of Peter*. SBLDS 97. Atlanta: Scholars, 1988.

Bucur, Bogdan. *Angelomorphic Pneumatology: Clement of Alexandria and Other Early Christian Witnesses*. SVC 95. Leiden: Brill, 2009.

———. "Christophanic Exegesis and the Problem of Symbolization: Daniel 3 (The Fiery Furnace) as a Test Case." *JTI* 10 (2016): 227–44.

———. *Scripture Re-envisioned: Christophanic Exegesis and the Making of a Christian Bible*. The Bible in Ancient Christianity, 13. Leiden: Brill, 2019.

Bunta, Silviu. "The Likeness of the Image: Adamic Motifs and *Tselem* Anthropology in Rabbinic Traditions about Jacob's Image Enthroned in Heaven." *JSJ* 37.1 (2006): 55–84.

———. "Moses, Adam and the Glory of the Lord in Ezekiel the Tragedian: On the Roots of a Merkabah Text." PhD diss., Marquette University, 2005.

Carey, George. "The Lamb of God and Atonement Theories." *Tyndale Bulletin* 32 (1981): 97–122.

Carrington, Philip. *The Meaning of Revelation.* London: SPCK, 1931.

Cassin, Elena. *La splendeur divine: Introduction à l'étude de la mentalité mésopotamienne.* Civilisations et Sociétés 8. Paris and La Haye: Mouton, 1968.

Castelli, Elizabeth. *Martyrdom and Memory: Early Christian Culture Making.* New York: Columbia University Press, 2004.

Chilton, Bruce. *Abraham's Curse: Child Sacrifice in the Legacies of the West.* New York: Doubleday, 2008.

Chilton, David. *Paradise Restored: A Biblical Theology of Dominion.* Ft. Worth: Dominion Press, 1985.

Cohen Stuart, Geert Hendrik. *The Struggle in Man between Good and Evil. An Inquiry into the Origin of the Rabbinic Concept of Yeṣer Hara.* Kampen: Kok, 1984.

Cohn, Norman. *Cosmos, Chaos, and the World to Come.* New Haven, CT: Yale University Press, 1993.

Collins, Adela Yarbro. *The Combat Myth in the Book of Revelation.* HDR 9. Missoula, MT: Scholars Press, 1976.

———. *Crisis and Catharsis: The Power of the Apocalypse.* Philadelphia: Westminster Press, 1984.

Collins, John. *The Apocalyptic Imagination: An Introduction to Jewish Apocalyptic Literature.* Grand Rapids, MI: Eerdmans, 1998.

———. *Apocalypticism in the Dead Sea Scrolls.* London: Routledge, 2002.

———. "The Mythology of Holy War in Daniel and the Qumran War Scroll: A Point of Transition in Jewish Apocalyptic." *VT* 25 (1975): 596–612.

———. *Seers, Sybils and Sages in Hellenistic-Roman Judaism.* JSJSS 54. Leiden: Brill, 1997.

Cross, Frank Moore. *Canaanite Myth and Hebrew Epic: Essays in the History of the Religion of Israel.* Cambridge, MA: Harvard University Press, 2009.

Dahl, Nils Alstrup, and David Hellholm. "Garment-Metaphors: The Old and the New Human Being." In *Antiquity and Humanity: Essays on Ancient Religion and Philosophy. Presented to Hans Dieter Betz on his 70th Birthday,* edited by A. Yarbro Collins and M. M. Mitchell, 139–158. Tübingen: Mohr Siebeck, 2001.

Davila, James. "The Hodayot Hymnist and the Four Who Entered Paradise." *RevQ* 17/65–68 (1996): 457–78.

Davis, Dean. *The Heavenly Court Judgment of Revelation 4–5.* Lanham, MD: University Press of America, 1992.

Davis, Stephen. *The Cult of Saint Thecla: A Tradition of Women's Piety in Late Antiquity.* Oxford: Oxford University Press, 2001.

Day, John. *God's Conflict with the Dragon and the Sea.* OP 35. Cambridge: Cambridge University Press, 1985.

De Silva, Aldina. "A Comparison Between the Three-Levelled World of the Old Testament Temple Building Narratives and the Three-Levelled World of the House Building Motif in the Ugaritic Texts KTU 1.3 and 1.4." In *Ugarit and the Bible*, edited by G. J. Brooke, A. H. W. Curites and J. F. Healy, 11–23. Münster: Ugarit-Verlag, 1994.

De Villiers, Pieter. "Prime Evil and Its Many Faces in the Book of Revelation." *Neotestamentica* 34 (2000): 57–85.

DeConick, April. "Traumatic Mysteries: Pathways of Mysticism among the Early Christians." In *Jewish Roots of Eastern Christian Mysticism: Studies in Honor of Alexander Golitzin*, edited by A. A. Orlov, 11–51. Leiden: Brill, 2020.

DeConick, April and Jarl Fossum. "Stripped before God: A New Interpretation of Logion 37 in the Gospel of Thomas." *VC* 45 (1991): 123–50.

Deutsch, Nathaniel. *The Gnostic Imagination: Gnosticism, Mandaeism, and Merkabah Mysticism*. Leiden: Brill, 1995.

Dimant, Devorah. " 'The Fallen Angels' in the Dead Sea Scrolls and in the Apocryphal and Pseudepigraphic Books Related to Them." PhD diss., Hebrew University of Jerusalem, 1974. [Hebrew]

Dods, Marcus. "St. Augustine's City of God." In *A Select Library of the Nicene and Post-Nicene Fathers of the Christian Church. First Series. Vol. 2*, edited by P. Schaff, 1–511. New York: Christian Literature Company, 1887.

Dorman, Anke. " 'Commit Injustice and Shed Innocent Blood': Motives behind the Institution of the Day of Atonement in the Book of Jubilees." In *The Day of Atonement: Its Interpretation in Early Jewish and Christian Traditions*, edited by T. Hieke and T. Nicklas, 49–61. TBN 15. Leiden: Brill, 2012.

Dulaey, Martine. "Les trois hébreux dans la fournaise (Dn 3) dans l'interprétation symbolique de l'église ancienne." *RSR* 71 (1997): 33–59.

Dupont, Jacques. "L'arrière-fond biblique du récit des tentations de Jésus." *NTS* 3 (1957): 287–304.

Ellis, Nicholas. *The Hermeneutics of Divine Testing*. WUNT 2.296. Tübingen: Mohr Siebeck, 2015.

Emerton, John. "Binding and Loosing—Forgiving and Retaining." *JTS* 13 (1962): 325–31.

Eshel, Esther. "Demonology in Palestine during the Second Temple Period." PhD diss., Hebrew University of Jerusalem, 1999. [Hebrew]

Evans, Craig. "Abraham in the Dead Sea Scrolls: A Man of Faith and Failure." In *The Bible at Qumran: Text, Shape, and Interpretation*, edited by P. W. Flint, 149–58. Grand Rapids, MI: Eerdmans, 2001.

Farrer, Austin. *A Rebirth of Images. The Making of St. John's Apocalypse*. Gloucester, MA: Peter Smith, 1970.

Feuillet, André. "L'épisode de la tentation d'après l'évangile selon saint Marc (I,12–13)." *EstBib* 19 (1960): 49–73.

Fishbane, Michael. *Text and Texture*. New York: Schocken, 1979.

Fletcher-Louis, Crispin. "Alexander the Great's Worship of the High Priest." In *Early Jewish and Christian Monotheism*, edited by L. T. Stuckenbruck and W. E. S. North, 71–102. London: T&T Clark, 2004.

———. *All the Glory of Adam. Liturgical Anthropology in the Dead Sea Scrolls*. STDJ 42. Leiden: Brill, 2002.

———. "The High Priest as Divine Mediator in the Hebrew Bible: Dan 7:13 as a Test Case." *SBLSP* 36 (1997): 161–93.

———. *Jesus Monotheism, vol. 1, Christological Origins: The Emerging Consensus and Beyond*. Eugene, OR: Cascade Books, 2015.

———. *Luke-Acts: Angels, Christology and Soteriology*. WUNT 2.94. Tübingen: Mohr Siebeck, 1997.

———. "Priests and Priesthood." In *Dictionary of Jesus and the Gospels*, edited by J. B. Green, J. K. Brown, and N. Perrin, 696–705. Downers Grove, IL: IVP Academic, 2013.

———."The Revelation of the Sacral Son of Man." In *Auferstehung-Resurrection. The Fourth Durham-Tübingen Symposium: Resurrection, Transformation and Exaltation in Old Testament, Ancient Judaism and Early Christianity*, edited by F. Avemarie and H. Lichtenberger, 247–298. WUNT 1.135. Tübingen: Mohr Siebeck, 2001.

———. "The Worship of Divine Humanity as God's Image and the Worship of Jesus." In *The Jewish Roots of Christological Monotheism. Papers from the St. Andrews Conference on the Historical Origins of the Worship of Jesus*, edited by C. Newman et al., 112–128. JSJSS 63. Leiden: Brill, 1999.

Fossum, Jarl. "The Adorable Adam of the Mystics and the Rebuttals of the Rabbis." In *Geschichte-Tradition-Reflexion. Festschrift für Martin Hengel zum 70. Geburtstag*, edited by H. Cancik, H. Lichtenberger and P. Schäfer, 1.529–39. 2 vols. Tübingen: Mohr Siebeck, 1996.

———. *The Image of the Invisible God: Essays on the Influence of Jewish Mysticism on Early Christology*. NTOA 30. Fribourg: Universitätsverlag Freiburg Schweiz. Göttingen: Vanderhoeck & Ruprecht, 1995.

———.*The Name of God and the Angel of the Lord. Samaritan and Jewish Concepts of Intermediation and the Origin of Gnosticism*. WUNT 36. Tübingen: Mohr Siebeck, 1985.

García Martínez, Florentino. "Man and Woman: Halakhah Based upon Eden in the Dead Sea Scrolls." In *Paradise Interpreted: Representations of Biblical Paradise in Judaism and Christianity*, edited by G. Luttikhuizen, 95–115. TBN 2. Leiden: Brill, 1999.

Geiger, Abraham. "Einige Worte über das Buch Henoch." *JZWL* 3 (1864): 196–204.

Gibson, Jeffrey. *Temptations of Jesus in Early Christianity*. JSNTSS 112. Sheffield: Sheffield Academic Press, 1995.

Ginzberg, Louis. *The Legends of the Jews*. 7 vols. Philadelphia: Jewish Publication Society, 1909–38.

Giulea, Dragoş. "The Watchers' Whispers: Athenagoras's Legatio 25,1–3 and the Book of the Watchers." *VC* 61 (2007): 258–281.

Goshen-Gottstein, Alon. "The Body as Image of God in Rabbinic Literature." *HTR* 87 (1994): 171–95.

Grabbe, Lester. "The Scapegoat Tradition: A Study in Early Jewish Interpretation." *JSJ* 18 (1987): 165–79.

Green, Alberto. *The Storm-God in the Ancient Near East*. BJSUC 8. Winona Lake, IN: Eisenbrauns, 2003.

Greenberg, Arik. *"My Share of God's Reward": Exploring the Roles and Formulations of the Afterlife in Early Christian Martyrdom*. SBL 121. New York: Peter Lang, 2009.

Gross, Abraham. *Spirituality and Law: Courting Martyrdom in Christianity and Judaism*. Lanham, MD: University Press of America, 2005.

Gunkel, Hermann. *Creation and Chaos in the Primeval Era and the Eschaton*. Translated by K. W. Whitney. Grand Rapids, MI: Eerdmans, 2006.

———. *Schöpfung und Chaos in Urzeit und Endzeit: Eine religionsgeschichtliche Untersuchung über Gen. 1 und Ap. Joh. 12*. Göttingen: Vandenhoeck & Ruprecht, 1895.

Gutmann, Joseph. "Abraham in the Fire of the Chaldeans: A Jewish Legend in Jewish, Christian and Islamic Art." *FS* 7 (1973): 342–52.

Harl, Marguerite. "La 'ligature' d'Isaac (Gen. 22, 9) dans la Septante et chez les Pères grecs." In *Hellenica et Judaica: Hommage à Valentin Nikiprowetzky*, edited by A. Caquot, M. Hadas-Lebel, and J. Riaud, 457–472. Leuven-Paris: Peeters, 1986.

Hayward, Richard. *Interpretations of the Name Israel in Ancient Judaism and Some Early Christian Writings*. Oxford: Oxford University Press, 2005.

———. *The Jewish Temple: A Non-Biblical Sourcebook*. London and New York: Routledge, 1996.

Herring, Stephen. *Divine Substitution: Humanity as the Manifestation of Deity in the Hebrew Bible and the Ancient Near East*. FRLANT 247. Göttingen: Vandenhoeck & Ruprecht, 2013.

Hiers, Richard. " 'Binding and Loosing': The Matthean Authorizations." *JBL* 104 (1985): 233–250.

Himmelfarb, Martha. *The Apocalypse: A Brief History*. Blackwell Brief Histories of Religion. Malden, MA: Wiley-Blackwell, 2010.

———. *Ascent to Heaven in Jewish and Christian Apocalypses*. New York: Oxford University Press, 1993.

Huizenga, Leroy. *The New Isaac: Tradition and Intertextuality in the Gospel of Matthew*. NovTSup 131. Leiden: Brill, 2009.

Hurowitz, Victor. *I Have Built You an Exalted House: Temple Building in the Bible in Light of Mesopotamian and North-West Semitic Writings*. Sheffield: JSOT Press, 1992.

———. "Inside Solomon's Temple." *BR* 10:2 (1994): 24–36.

———. "The Priestly Account of Building the Tabernacle." *JAOS* 105 (1985): 21–30.

Hurtado, Larry. *At the Origins of Christian Worship: The Context and Character of Earliest Christian Devotion*. Grand Rapids, MI: Eerdmans, 2000.

———. *One God, One Lord: Early Christian Devotion and Ancient Jewish Monotheism*. London: SCM, 1988.

Idel, Moshe. "The Changing Faces of God and Human Dignity in Judaism." In *Moshe Idel: Representing God*, edited by H. Tirosh-Samuelson and A. W. Hughes, 103–122. LCJP 8. Leiden: Brill, 2014.

Jacobs, Irving. *The Midrashic Process: Tradition and Interpretation in Rabbinic Judaism*. Cambridge: Cambridge University Press, 1995.

Janowski, Bernd. "Der Tempel als Kosmos—Zur kosmologischen Bedeutung des Tempels in der Umwelt Israels." In *Egypt—Temple of the Whole World / Ägypten—Tempel der Gesamten Welt. Studies in Honour of Jan Assmann*, edited by S. Meyer, 163–186. Leiden: Brill, 2003.

Jeremias, Joachim. "Adam." In *Theological Dictionary of the New Testament*, edited by G. Kittel, 1.141–143. 10 vols. Grand Rapids, MI: Eerdmans, 1964.

———. "Nachwort zum Artikel von H.-G. Leder." *ZNW* 54 (1963): 278–79.

———. *New Testament Theology*. London: SCM Press, 2012.

Jeremias, Jörg. *Theophanie: Die Geschichte einer alttestamentlichen Gattung*. WMANT 10. Neukirchen-Vluyn: Neukirchener Verlag, 1965.

Jervell, Jacob. *Imago Dei. Gen 1, 26f. im Spätjudentum, in der Gnosis und in den paulinischen Briefen*. FRLANT 76. Göttingen: Vandenhoeck & Ruprecht, 1960.

Kearney, Peter. "Creation and Liturgy: The P Redaction of Ex 25–40." *ZAW* 89.3 (1977): 375–387.

Kiel, Yishai. *Sexuality in the Babylonian Talmud: Christian and Sasanian Contexts in Late Antiquity*. Cambridge: Cambridge University Press, 2016.

Kister, Menahem. "Demons, Theology and Abraham's Covenant (CD 16:4–6 and Related Texts)." In *The Dead Sea Scrolls at Fifty: Proceedings of the 1997 Society of Biblical Literature Qumran Section Meetings*, edited by R. A. Kugler and E. M. Schuller, 167–84. EJL 15. Atlanta: Scholars, 1999.

———. "Observations on Aspects of Exegesis, Tradition, and Theology in Midrash, Pseudepigrapha, and Other Jewish Writings." In *Tracing the Threads: Studies in the Vitality of Jewish Pseudepigrapha*, edited by J. C. Reeves, 1–34. EJL 6. Atlanta: Scholars, 1994.

———. "The *Yetzer* of Man's Heart." In *Meghillot: Studies in the Dead Sea Scrolls VIII–IX*, edited by M. Bar-Asher and D. Dimant, 243–284. Jerusalem: Bialik Institute and Haifa University Press, 2010. [Hebrew]

Klingbeil, Martin. *Yahweh Fighting from Heaven: God as Warrior and as God of Heaven in the Hebrew Psalter and Ancient Near Eastern Iconography*. OBO 169. Göttingen: Vandenhoeck & Ruprecht, 1999.

Kloos, Carola. *Yhwh's Combat with the Sea: A Canaanite Tradition in the Religion of Ancient Israel*. Leiden: Brill, 1986.

Koester, Craig. *The Dwelling of God: The Tabernacle in the Old Testament, Intertestamental Jewish Literature, and the New Testament*. CBQMS 22. Washington, DC: Catholic Biblical Association, 1989.

Köhler, Ludwig. "Die Grundstelle der Imago Dei Lehre, Genesis i, 26." *ThZ* 4 (1948): 16–22.

Kozlowski, Jan. "Pionius Polycarpi Imitator: References to Martyrium Polycarpi in Martyrium Pionii." *Science et Esprit* 67 (2015): 417–434.

Kugel, James. *The Bible as It Was*. Cambridge, MA: Harvard University Press, 1997.

———. *In Potiphar's House: The Interpretive Life of Biblical Texts*. San Francisco: Harper Collins, 1990.

———. "The Ladder of Jacob." *HTR* 88 (1995): 209–27.

———. *Traditions of the Bible: A Guide to the Bible as It Was at the Start of the Common Era*. Cambridge, MA: Harvard University Press, 1998.

Kulik, Alexander. "The Mysteries of Behemoth and Leviathan and the Celestial Bestiary of 3 Baruch." *Le Muséon* 122 (2009): 291–329.

Lambden, Stephen. "From Fig Leaves to Fingernails: Some Notes on the Garments of Adam and Eve in the Hebrew Bible and Select Early Postbiblical Jewish Writings." In *A Walk in the Garden: Biblical, Iconographical and Literary Images of Eden*, edited by P. Morris and D. Sawyer, 74–90. JSOTSS 136. Sheffield: Sheffield Academic Press, 1992.

Lane Fox, Robin. *Pagans and Christians: In the Mediterranean World from the Second Century AD to the Conversion of Constantine*. London: Penguin, 2006.

Lehtipuu, Outi. *Debates Over the Resurrection of the Dead: Constructing Early Christian Identity*. Oxford: Oxford University Press, 2015.

Levenson, Jon. *Creation and the Persistence of Evil: The Jewish Drama of Divine Omnipotence*. San Francisco: Harper & Row, 1988.

———. "The Jerusalem Temple in Devotional and Visionary Experience." In *Jewish Spirituality. Vol. I: From the Bible through the Middle Ages*, edited by A. Green, 32–61. New York: Crossroad, 1987.

———. *Sinai and Zion: An Entry into the Jewish Bible*. Minneapolis: Winston, 1985.

———."The Temple and the World." *JR* 65 (1984): 283–298.

Loader, William. *Enoch, Levi, and Jubilees on Sexuality: Attitudes Towards Sexuality in Early Enoch Literature, the Aramaic Levi Document, and the Book of Jubilees*. Grand Rapids, MI: Eerdmans, 2007.

———. *The Pseudepigrapha on Sexuality: Attitudes towards Sexuality in Apocalypses, Testaments, Legends, Wisdom, and Related Literature*. Grand Rapids, MI: Eerdmans, 2011.

Lowin, Shari. *The Making of a Forefather: Abraham in Islamic and Jewish Exegetical Narratives*. IHC 65. Leiden: Brill, 2006.

Lupieri, Edmondo. "Apocalisse, sacerdozio e Yom Kippur." *ASE* 19/1 (2002): 11–21.

Machinist, Peter. Foreword to *Creation and Chaos in the Primeval Era and the Eschaton*, edited by H. Gunkel, ix–xx. Grand Rapids, MI: Eerdmans, 2006.

MacRae, George. "Some Elements of Jewish Apocalyptic and Mystical Tradition and Their Relation to Gnostic Literature." 2 vols. PhD diss., University of Cambridge, 1966.

Magliano-Tromp, Johannes. "Adamic Traditions in 2 Enoch and in the Books of Adam and Eve." In *New Perspectives on 2 Enoch: No Longer Slavonic Only*, edited by A. A. Orlov, G. Boccaccini, and J. Zurawski, 283–304. SJS 3. Leiden: Brill, 2012.

Mann, Thomas. *Divine Presence and Guidance in Israelite Traditions: The Typology of Exaltation*. Johns Hopkins Near Eastern Studies. Baltimore: Johns Hopkins University Press, 1977.

Martin, Dale. "When Did Angels Become Demons?" *JBL* 129 (2010): 657–77.

Meeks, Wayne. "Moses as God and King." In *Religions in Antiquity: Essays in Memory of Erwin Ramsdell Goodenough*, edited by J. Neusner, 354–371. SHR 14. Leiden: Brill, 1968.

———. *The Prophet-King. Moses Traditions and the Johannine Christology*. NovTSup 14. Leiden: Brill, 1967.

Meyers, Carol. "Sea, Molten." In *Anchor Bible Dictionary*, edited by D. N. Freedman, 5.1061–62. 6 vols. New York: Doubleday, 1992.

Middleton, Paul. *Radical Martyrdom and Cosmic Conflict in Early Christianity*. LNTS 307. London: T&T Clark, 2006.

Miller, Patrick. *The Divine Warrior in Early Israel*. HSM 5. Leiden: Brill, 1973.

Moore, George Foot. *Judaism in the First Centuries of the Christian Era: The Age of the Tanaaim*. 3 vols. Cambridge, MA: Harvard University Press, 1924.

Moss, Candida. *Ancient Christian Martyrdom: Diverse Practices, Theologies, and Traditions*. The Anchor Yale Bible Reference Library. New Haven, CT: Yale University Press, 2012.

———. *The Other Christs: Imitating Jesus in Ancient Christian Ideologies of Martyrdom*. Oxford: Oxford University Press, 2010.

Munoa, Philip. "Jesus, the Merkavah, and Martyrdom in Early Christian Tradition." *JBL* 121 (2002): 303–25.

Murmelstein, Benjamin. "Adam, ein Beitrag zur Messiaslehre." *WZKM* 35 (1928): 242–75.

Murphy, Frederick. "Retelling the Bible: Idolatry in Pseudo-Philo." *JBL* 107 (1988): 275–87.

Neis, Rachel. "Embracing Icons: The Face of Jacob on the Throne of God." *Images: A Journal of Jewish Art and Visual Culture* 1 (2007): 36–54.

Neufeld, Thomas R. Yoder. *"Put on the Armour of God": The Divine Warrior from Isaiah to Ephesians*. JSNTSS 140. Sheffield: Sheffield Academic Press, 1997.

Niehaus, Jeffrey Jay. *God at Sinai: Covenant and Theophany in the Bible and Ancient Near East*. SOTBT. Grand Rapids, MI: Zondervan, 1995.

Nihan, Christophe. *From Priestly Torah to Pentateuch: A Study in the Composition of the Book of Leviticus*. FAT 25. Tübingen: Mohr Siebeck, 2007.

Niles, Daniel. *As Seeing the Invisible*. New York: Harper and Brothers, 1961.

Noort, Ed. "Gan-Eden in the Context of the Mythology of the Hebrew Bible." In *Paradise Interpreted: Representations of Biblical Paradise in Judaism and Christianity*, edited by G. Luttikhuizen, 21–36. TBN 2. Leiden: Brill, 1999.

Oppenheim, Leo. "Akkadian pul(u)h(t)u and melammu." *JAOS* 63 (1943): 31–34.

Orlov, Andrei Aleksandrovich. *The Atoning Dyad: The Two Goats of Yom Kippur in the Apocalypse of Abraham*. SJS 8. Leiden: Leiden, 2016.

———. "The Cosmological Temple in the Apocalypse of Abraham." In *Divine Scapegoats: Demonic Mimesis in Early Jewish Mysticism*, edited by A. A. Orlov, 37–54. Albany: State University of New York Press, 2015.

———. *Dark Mirrors: Azazel and Satanael in Early Jewish Demonology*. Albany: State University of New York Press, 2011.

———. *Divine Scapegoats: Demonic Mimesis in Early Jewish Mysticism*. Albany: State University of New York Press, 2015.

———. *The Enoch-Metatron Tradition*. TSAJ 107. Tübingen: Mohr Siebeck, 2005.

———. "The Face as the Heavenly Counterpart of the Visionary in the Slavonic Ladder of Jacob." In *Of Scribes and Sages: Early Jewish Interpretation and Transmission of Scripture*, edited by C. A. Evans, 2.59–76. 2 vols. SSEJC 9. London: T&T Clark, 2004.

———. *The Glory of the Invisible God: Two Powers in Heaven Traditions and Early Christology*. JCTCRS 31. London: Bloomsbury, 2019.

———. *The Greatest Mirror: Heavenly Counterparts in the Jewish Pseudepigrapha*. Albany: State University of New York Press, 2017.

———. *Heavenly Priesthood in the Apocalypse of Abraham*. Cambridge: Cambridge University Press, 2013.

———. " 'The Likeness of Heaven': The *Kavod* of Azazel in the Apocalypse of Abraham." In *Dark Mirrors: Azazel and Satanael in Early Jewish Demonology*, edited by A. Orlov, 11–26. Albany: State University of New York Press, 2011.

———. "The Sacerdotal Traditions of 2 Enoch and the Date of the Text." In *New Perspectives on 2 Enoch: No Longer Slavonic Only*, edited by A. A. Orlov, G. Boccaccini and J. Zurawski, 103–116. SJS 4. Leiden: Brill, 2012.

———. "The Veneration Motif in the Temptation Narrative of the Gospel of Matthew: Lessons from the Enochic Tradition." In *Divine Scapegoats: Demonic Mimesis in Early Jewish Mysticism*, edited by A. A. Orlov, 153–166. Albany: State University of New York Press, 2015.

———. "Vested with Adam's Glory: Moses as the Luminous Counterpart of Adam in the Dead Sea Scrolls and the Macarian Homilies." *Christian Orient* 4.10 (2006): 498–513.

Ortlund, Erik Nels. *Theophany and Chaoskampf: The Interpretation of Theophanic Imagery in the Baal Epic, Isaiah, and the Twelve*. GUS 5. Piscataway, NJ: Gorgias Press, 2010.

Owen, Paul. "Aramaic and Greek Representations of the 'Son of Man' and the Importance of the Parables of Enoch." In *Parables of Enoch: A Paradigm Shift*, edited by D. L. Bock and J. H. Charlesworth, 114–123. JCTCRS 11. London: Bloomsbury, 2013.

Parry, Donald. "Garden of Eden: Prototype Sanctuary." In *Temples of the Ancient World: Ritual and Symbolism*, edited by D. W. Parry, 126–151. Provo, UT: Deseret, 1994.

Patai, Raphael. *Man and Temple in Ancient Jewish Myth and Ritual*. 2nd ed. New York: KTAV, 1967.

Patton, Corrine. "Adam as the Image of God." *SBLSP* 33 (1994): 294–300.

Paulien, Jon. "The Role of the Hebrew Cultus, Sanctuary, and Temple in the Plot and Structure of the Book of Revelation." *AUSS* 33 (1995): 245–64.

Pierce, Chad. *Spirits and the Proclamation of Christ: 1 Peter 3:18–22 in Light of Sin and Punishment Traditions in Early Jewish and Christian Literature*. WUNT 2.305. Tübingen: Mohr Siebeck, 2011.

Pokorný, Petr. "The Temptation Stories and Their Intention." *NTS* 20 (1973–74): 115–27.

Porter, Frank Chamberlin. "The Yeçer Hara: A Study in the Jewish Doctrine of Sin." In *Biblical and Semitic Studies. Yale Historical and Critical Contributions to Biblical Science*, 93–156. New York: Charles Scribner's Sons, 1901.

Putthoff, Tyson. *Ontological Aspects of Early Jewish Anthropology: The Malleable Self and the Presence of God*. BRLJ 53. Leiden: Brill, 2016.

Quinn, Esther Casier. *The Quest of Seth for the Oil of Life*. Chicago: University of Chicago Press, 1962.

Quispel, Gilles. "Der gnostische Anthropos und die jüdische Tradition." *ErJb* 22 (1953): 195–234.

———. "Ezekiel 1:26 in Jewish Mysticism and Gnosis." *VC* 34 (1980): 1–13.

Reed, Annette Yoshiko. "Enochic and Mosaic Traditions in Jubilees: The Evidence of Angelology and Demonology." In *Enoch and the Mosaic Torah: The Evidence of Jubilees*, edited by G. Boccaccini and G. Ibba, 353–68. Grand Rapids, MI: Eerdmans, 2009.

———. *Fallen Angels and the History of Judaism and Christianity: The Reception of Enochic Literature*. Cambridge: Cambridge University Press, 2005.

Reynolds, Bennie. “Understanding the Demonologies of the Dead Sea Scrolls: Accomplishments and Directions for the Future.” *Religion Compass* 7 (2013): 103–14.

Robert, Louis. *Le Martyre de Pionios Prêtre de Smyrne*. Washington DC: Dumbarton Oaks, 1994.

Rosen-Zvi, Ishay. *Demonic Desires: Yetzer Hara and the Problem of Evil in Late Antiquity*. Philadelphia: University of Pennsylvania Press, 2011.

Rowland, Christopher. “John 1:51, Jewish Apocalyptic and Targumic Tradition.” *NTS* 30 (1984): 498–507.

Rubin, Nissan, and Admiel Kosman. “The Clothing of the Primordial Adam as a Symbol of Apocalyptic Time in the Midrashic Sources.” *HTR* 90 (1997): 155–74.

Schäfer, Peter. *The Hidden and Manifest God: Some Major Themes in Early Jewish Mysticism*. Albany: State University of New York Press, 1992.

———. *Rivalität zwischen Engeln und Menschen: Untersuchungen zur rabbinischen Engelvorstellung*. SJ 8. Berlin: Walter de Gruyter, 1975.

Schofer, Jonathan. “The Redaction of Desire: Structure and Editing of Rabbinic Teachings Concerning ‘Yeṣer’ (‘Inclination’).” *JJS* 12 (2003): 19–53.

Schultze, Wilhelm. “Der Heilige und die wilden Tiere. Zur Exegese von Mc 1 13b.” *ZNW* 46 (1955): 280–83.

Schwartz, Howard. *Tree of Souls: The Mythology of Judaism*. Oxford: Oxford University Press, 2004.

Scott, James. *On Earth as in Heaven: The Restoration of Sacred Time and Sacred Space in the Book of Jubilees*. JSJSS 91. Leiden: Brill, 2005.

Scurlock, JoAnn. Introduction to *Creation and Chaos: A Reconsideration of Hermann Gunkel's Chaoskampf Hypothesis*, edited by J. Scurlock and R. H. Beal, ix–xiv. Winona Lake, IN: Eisenbrauns, 2013.

Segal, Alan. *Two Powers in Heaven: Early Rabbinic Reports about Christianity and Gnosticism*. SJLA 25. Leiden: Brill, 1977.

Segal, Michael. *The Book of Jubilees: Rewritten Bible, Redaction, Ideology and Theology*. JSJSS 117. Leiden: Brill, 2007.

Smith, Jonathan. “The Garments of Shame.” *HR* 5 (1965/1966): 217–38.

———. “The Prayer of Joseph.” In *Religions in Antiquity: Essays in Memory of Erwin Ramsdell Goodenough*, edited by J. Neusner, 253–93. SHR 14. Leiden: Brill, 1968.

Smith, Morton. “The Image of God: Notes on the Hellenization of Judaism, with Especial Reference to Goodenough's Work on Jewish Symbols.” *BJRL* 40 (1958): 473–512.

Snyder, Barbara. “Combat Myth in the Apocalypse: The Liturgy of the Day of the Lord and the Dedication of the Heavenly Temple.” PhD diss., Graduate Theological Union, 1991.

Spicehandler, Ezra. “Shāhin's Influence on Bābāi ben Lotf: The Abraham-Nimrod Legend.” In *Irano-Judaica II*, edited by S. Shaked and A. Netzer, 158–65. Jerusalem: Ben Zvi Institute, 1990.

Stadelman, Luis. *The Hebrew Conception of the World—A Philological and Literary Study*. Analecta Biblica 39. Rome: Biblical Institute, 1970.

Stager, Lawrence. “Jerusalem and the Garden of Eden.” *Eretz Israel* 26 (1999): 183–94.

———. “Jerusalem as Eden.” *BAR* 26 (2000): 36–47.

Steenburg, David. "The Worship of Adam and Christ as the Image of God." *JSNT* 39 (1990): 95–109.

Stökl Ben Ezra, Daniel. *The Impact of Yom Kippur on Early Christianity: The Day of Atonement from Second Temple Judaism to the Fifth Century*. WUNT 1.163. Tübingen: Mohr Siebeck, 2003.

Stone, Michael. "The Angelic Prediction in the Primary Adam Books." In *Literature on Adam and Eve. Collected Essays*, edited by G. Anderson, M. Stone, and J. Tromp, 111–131. SVTP 15. Brill: Leiden, 2000.

———. "The Fall of Satan and Adam's Penance: Three Notes on The Books of Adam and Eve." *JTS* 44 (1993): 153–56.

———. "The Fall of Satan and Adam's Penance: Three Notes on the Books of Adam and Eve." In *Literature on Adam and Eve. Collected Essays*, edited by G. Anderson, M. Stone, and J. Tromp, 43–56. SVTP 15. Brill: Leiden, 2000.

Strand, Kenneth. "An Overlooked Old Testament Background to Rev 11:1." *AUSS* 22 (1984): 317–325.

Stuckenbruck, Loren. *Angel Veneration and Christology: A Study in Early Judaism and in the Christology of the Apocalypse of John*. WUNT 2.70. Tübingen: Mohr Siebeck, 1995.

———. "Demonic Beings and the Dead Sea Scrolls." In *Explaining Evil. Vol. 1. Definitions and Development*, edited by H. J. Ellens, 1.121–44. 3 vols. Santa Barbara, CA: Praegers, 2011.

———. "Jesus' Apocalyptic Worldview and His Exorcistic Ministry." In *Pseudepigrapha and Christian Origins: Essays from the Studiorum Novi Testamenti Societas*, edited by G. S. Oegema and J. H. Charlesworth, 68–84. JCTCRS 4. London: T&T Clark International, 2008.

———. *The Myth of Rebellious Angels: Studies in Second Temple Judaism and New Testament Texts*. WUNT 1.335. Tübingen: Mohr Siebeck, 2014.

———. "The Origins of Evil in Jewish Apocalyptic Tradition: Interpretation of Genesis 6:1–4 in the Second and Third Centuries BCE." In *The Fall of the Angels*, edited by Ch. Auffarth and L. T. Stuckenbruck, 87–118. TBN 6. Leiden: Brill, 2004.

———. "Prayers of Deliverance from the Demonic in the Dead Sea Scrolls and Related Early Jewish Literature." In *The Changing Face of Judaism, Christianity, and Other Greco-Roman Religions in Antiquity*, edited by I. H. Henderson and G. S. Oegema, 146–165. JSHRZ 2. Gütersloh: Gütersloher Verlagshaus, 2006.

Stuckenbruck, Loren, and Mark Mathews. "The Apocalypse of John, 1 Enoch, and the Question of Influence." In *Die Johannesapokalypse. Kontexte—Konzepte—Rezeption*, edited by J. Frey et al., 191–234. WUNT 1.287. Tübingen: Mohr Siebeck, 2012.

Sullivan, Kevin. "Spiritual Inhabitation in the Gospel of Mark: A Reconsideration of Mark 8:33." *Henoch* 32 (2010): 401–19.

———. "The Watchers Traditions in 1 Enoch 6–16: The Fall of Angels and the Rise of Demons." In *The Watchers in Jewish and Christian Traditions*, edited by A. Kim Harkins, K. Coblentz Bautch and J. C. Endres, 91–103. Minneapolis: Fortress, 2014.

Tigchelaar, Eibert. "The Evil Inclination in the Dead Sea Scrolls, with a Re-Edition of 4Q468i (4QSectarian Text?)." In *Empsychoi Logoi. Religious Innovations in Antiq-*

uity. Studies in Honour of Pieter Willem van der Horst*, edited by A. Houtman, A. de Jong, and M. Misset-van der Weg, 347–57. AJEC 73. Leiden: Brill, 2008.

Tiller, Patrick. *A Commentary on the Animal Apocalypse of 1 Enoch*. EJL 4. Atlanta: Scholars, 1993.

Treiyer, Alberto. *The Day of Atonement and the Heavenly Judgment*. Siloam Springs, AR: Creation Enterprises International, 1992.

Tucker, Dennis. "The Early Wirkungsgeschichte of Daniel 3: Representative Examples." *JTI* 6 (2012): 295–305.

Tvedtnes, John, Brian Hauglid, and John Gee. *Traditions about the Early Life of Abraham*. Provo, UT: FARMS, 2001.

Van Bekkum, Wout. "The Aqedah and Its Interpretations in Midrash and Piyyut." In *The Sacrifice of Isaac: The Aqedah (Genesis 22) and Its Interpretations*, edited by E. Noort and E. Tigchelaar, 86–95. TBN 4. Leiden: Brill, 2002.

Van der Horst, Pieter. "A Note on the Evil Inclination and Sexual Desire in Talmudic Literature." In *Jews and Christians in their Graeco-Roman Context: Selected Essays on Early Judaism, Samaritanism, Hellenism, and Christianity*, edited by P. van der Horst, 59–65. WUNT 1.196. Tübingen: Mohr Siebeck, 2006.

Van Henten, Jan Willem. "Daniel 3 and 6 in Early Christian Literature." In *The Book of Daniel: Composition and Reception I–II*, edited by J. J. Collins and P. W. Flint, 1.149–69. 2 vols. VetTSup 83. Leiden: Brill, 2001.

———. "Martyrs, Martyrdom, and Martyr Literature." In *Oxford Encyclopedia of Ancient Greece and Rome*, edited by M. Gagarin, 1.365. 7 vols. Oxford: Oxford University Press, 2010.

Van Henten, Jan Willem, and Friedrich Avemarie. *Martyrdom and Noble Death: Selected Texts from Graeco-Roman, Jewish, and Christian Antiquity*. New York: Routledge, 2002.

Van Ruiten, Jacques. *Abraham in the Book of Jubilees: The Rewriting of Genesis 11:26–25:10 in the Book of Jubilees 11:14–23:8*. JSJSS 161. Leiden: Brill, 2012.

———. "Abram's Prayer: The Coherence of the Pericopes in *Jubilees* 12:16–27." In *Enoch and the Mosaic Torah: The Evidence of Jubilees*, edited by G. Boccaccini and G. Ibba, 211–228. Grand Rapids, MI: Eerdmans, 2009.

———. "Eden and the Temple: The Rewriting of Genesis 2:4–3:24 in the Book of Jubilees." In *Paradise Interpreted: Representations of Biblical Paradise in Judaism and Christianity*, edited by G. P. Luttikhuizen, 63–94. TBN 2. Leiden: Brill, 1999.

———. "The Old Testament Quotations in the Apocalypse of Peter." In *The Apocalypse of Peter*, edited by J. N. Bremmer and I. Czachesz, 158–73. Leuven-Paris: Peeters, 2003.

———. "Visions of the Temple in the *Book of Jubilees*." In *Gemeinde ohne Tempel/Community without Temple: Zur Substituierung und Transformation des Jerusalemer Tempels und seines Kults im Alten Testament, antiken Judentum und frühen Christentum*, edited by B. Ego et al., 215–228. WUNT 1.118. Tübingen: Mohr Siebeck, 1999.

VanderKam, James. "The Demons in the Book of Jubilees." In *Die Dämonen: Die Dämonologie der israelitisch-jüdischen und frühchristlichen Literatur im Kontext ihrer Umwelt*, edited by A. Lange et al., 339–364. Tübingen: Mohr Siebeck, 1997.

———. *From Revelation to Canon: Studies in Hebrew Bible and Second Temple Literature.* Leiden: Brill, 2000.

VanderKam, James, and William Adler. *The Jewish Apocalyptic Heritage in Early Christianity.* CRINT 3.4. Assen: Van Gorcum/Minneapolis: Fortress, 1996.

Vargas-Machuca, Antonio. "La tentación de Jesús según Mc. 1, 12–13 ¿Hecho real o relato de tipo haggádico?" *EE* 48 (1973): 163–190.

Vermes, Geza. *Scripture and Tradition in Judaism. Haggadic Studies.* SPB 4. Leiden: Brill, 1973.

Von Heijne, Camilla Hélena. *The Messenger of the Lord in Early Jewish Interpretations of Genesis.* BZAW 42. Berlin: Walter de Gruyter, 2010.

Wadsworth, Michael. "Making and Interpreting Scripture." In *Ways of Reading the Bible,* edited by M. Wadsworth, 7–22. Sussex: Harvester Press, 1981.

Weimar, Peter. "Sinai und Schöpfung: Komposition und Theologie der priesterschriftlichen Sinaigeschichte." *RB* 95 (1988): 337–85.

Weinfeld, Moshe. *Deuteronomy and the Deuteronomic School.* Oxford: Clarendon Press, 1972.

———. " 'Rider of the Clouds' and 'Gatherer of the Clouds.' " *JANES* 5 (1973): 421–25.

———. "Sabbath, Temple and the Enthronement of the Lord: The Problem of the Sitz im Leben of Genesis 1:1–2:3." In *Mélanges bibliques et orientaux en l'honneur de M. Henri Cazelles,* edited by A. Caquot and M. Delcor, 501–12. AOAT 212. Neukirchen-Vluyn: Neukirchener Verlag, 1981.

Wenham, Gordon. "Sanctuary Symbolism in the Garden of Eden Story." In *Proceedings of the Ninth World Congress of Jewish Studies, Division A: The Period of the Bible,* 19–25. Jerusalem: World Union of Jewish Studies, 1986.

Whitney, William. *Two Strange Beasts: Leviathan and Behemoth in Second Temple and Early Rabbinic Judaism.* HSM 63. Winona Lake, IN: Eisenbrauns, 2006.

Willis, Amy C. Merrill. *Dissonance and the Drama of Divine Sovereignty in the Book of Daniel.* Library of Hebrew Bible/Old Testament Studies. London: T&T Clark, 2010.

Wilson, Ian. " 'Face to Face' with God: Another Look." *ResQ* 51 (2009): 107–114.

Windisch, Hans. "Die göttliche Weisheit der Juden und die paulinische Christologie." In *Neutestamentliche Studien für G. Heinrici,* edited by A. Deissmann and H. Windisch, 220–234. UNT 6. Leipzig: J. C. Heinrichs, 1914.

Winkle, Ross. " 'You Are What You Wear: The Dress and Identity of Jesus as High Priest in John's Apocalypse." In *Sacrifice, Cult, and Atonement in Early Judaism and Christianity: Constituents and Critique,* edited by H. L. Wiley and C. A. Eberhart, 327–46. Atlanta: SBL, 2017.

Wise, Michael. "4QFlorilegium and the Temple of Adam." *RevQ* 15/57–58 (1991): 103–132.

Wold, Benjamin. "Sin and Evil in the Letter of James in Light of Qumran Discoveries." *NTS* 65 (2019): 1–20.

Wolfson, Elliot. "The Image of Jacob Engraved upon the Throne." In *Along the Path: Studies in Kabbalistic Myth, Symbolism, and Hermeneutics,* edited by E. Wolfson, 1–62. Albany: State University of New York Press, 1995.

———. *Through a Speculum That Shines: Vision and Imagination in Medieval Jewish Mysticism.* Princeton, NJ: Princeton University Press, 1994.

Wright, Archie. *The Origin of Evil Spirits: The Reception of Genesis 6.1–4 in Early Jewish Literature*. WUNT 2.198. Tübingen: Mohr Siebeck, 2005.

Wright, Nicholas Thomas. *The Resurrection of the Son of God*. Minneapolis: Fortress, 2003.

Wyatt, Nicolas. "Arms and the King: The Earliest Allusions to the *Chaoskampf* Motif and their Implications for the Interpretation of the Ugaritic and Biblical Traditions." In *"Und Mose schrieb dieses Lied auf": Studien zum Alten Testament und zum Alten Orient. Festschrift für Oswald Loretz zur Vollendung seines 70*, 834–47. AOAT 250. Münster: Ugarit-Verlag, 1998.

———. *Space and Time in the Religious Life of the Near East*. BS 85. Sheffield: Sheffield Academic Press, 2001.

Yassif, Eli. *The Hebrew Folktale. History, Genre, Meaning*. Bloomington: Indiana University Press, 1999.

Young, Robin Darling. *In Procession Before the World. Martyrdom as Public Liturgy in Early Christianity*. The Père Marquette Lecture in Theology 2001. Milwaukee: Marquette University Press, 2001.

Index

www.ingramcontent.com/pod-product-compliance
Lightning Source LLC
Chambersburg PA
CBHW020643230426
43665CB00008B/293

* 9 7 8 1 4 3 8 4 8 0 8 8 6 *